WALK WITH THE DEVIL

WALK WITH THE DEVIL

MY ENDLESS STRUGGLE AGAINST
THE CUNNING AND TRAPS OF THE DEVIL

ZAKARIAH ALI

To order additional copies of this book, contact:
Xlibris Corporation
1-888-795-4274
www.Xlibris.com
Orders@Xlibris.com
92090

CONTENTS

My Life In Cycles Of Adversities And Euphoria

I have struggled through life and been buffeted by ill winds at every turn but somehow a force greater than me kept me afloat through all the adversities and traps I encountered along the way. My life has generally has gone in cycles alternating between periods of adversities and struggles followed by periods of peace and contentment, happiness with a feeling of triumph or victory. Every epoch of my life that started on a high note usually ended on a low and sour note and one that started on low note ended on a high and exciting note. I have experienced epochs of heartaches and unbounded joy during the course of my life. The adversities and misfortunes that I went through from time to time often reminded me that there is a divine power that came to my rescue and saved me when I was helpless and unable to help myself.

The turmoil's that have roiled me from the dawn of my life have been a constant reminder that there is more to this life than meets the eye. Time and again I have been forced by circumstances and events beyond my control to appreciate that there is a loving God who cares for me even if I do not know it. I might have ascribed some experiences of my early childhood to dreams and nightmares. I might have boasted that any success that came my way was due to my hard work or ability but I know that my innate abilities means nothing without God standing behind me. That I survived into adulthood was due to divine intervention considering that no offspring of my mother lived beyond infancy. My mother and her family line died at relatively young age. The path I have followed in life was either due to destiny or thrust upon me by powers beyond my control. My carefully laid out plans and aspirations came to naught, I held on to whatever came my way and that which was thrust upon me in hindsight was better than the path I had set before me. The choice was made in spite of me.

I endured a year of brawls and scuffles at Issah middle boarding school when I returned to my hometown in 1958. The boarding school was one place where, whether I liked it or not, I had to take a stand. I stood up against bullies and that led to brawls and scuffles. I brawled with boys who were bigger than me without fear. I picked up some boxing skills when I was at Tarkwa and those skills came in handy at the boarding school. I therefore fought the bullies with my boxing skills but I was no match for their size. I was often bundled and thrown down like a rag doll. I was no match for the big boys but their size were not enough to silence me or deter me from running my mouth. As much as they sought to keep me quiet by throwing me about like a rag doll they could not silence me. Each time I was wrestled to the ground I got up and attacked again and again and each brawl ended with the same result. Only the school bell summoning us to another activity ended the fight. By the third term of 1958 my uncompromising aggression and big mouth had succeeded in turning the bullies and adversaries into colleagues and friends.

The first cycle of my life as far as I can remember began on the day I witnessed innocently the poisoning of my mother and her eventual death at about age four. After her death my baby brother and I became wards of my grandmother until I left for my father about a year later while my brother with a different father was left behind. The cycle began earlier when at about six months of age my mother strapped me unto her back and walked out on my father. Although I was still virtually a baby my mother's suffering and death must have traumatized me to such an extent that I never forgot her last few months on earth and her suffering and death had a profound effect on my outlook and relations with my world. I was plucked from my grandmother to be reunited with the father I did not know I had about a year after my mother's death. The reunion with my father made it possible for me to go to school. Thus the epoch of my life that began with my mother dumping my father, a broken home and the untimely death of my mother ironically changed the trajectory of my life. The direction of my life changed from that of a potential illiterate subsistence farmer to the person I am today, living in a western country. Up to the day my stepmother came for me I did not know anything about the existence of schools let alone imagine myself as a school boy. The first cycle of my life had a happy ending.

The decade of the 1960's was the most productive years of my life. The decade ominously began with my opportunity to go to the teacher training college began slipping through my fingers for lack of school supplies and money to pay my fare to Navrongo. For more than one month after schools began my fate hung in the balance. Finally after one month I made it to the school and was accepted. I completed the course. I discovered my latent ability and pursued home study courses that culminated with my entry into college in October1967. It took me about seven years from the day I entered teacher training college in February 1960 to become a college freshman in September 1967. Between 1960 and 1967 I trained as a teacher and gained valuable teaching and life experience before I entered the University.

The teacher training course was thus the best thing that happened to me since the day I entered the first grade as an ignorant child from the backwoods of the northern territories of the Gold Coast. The teacher training course removed the financial burdens of education from my life; I earned an income while in training. The traumatic disappointments of the latter fifties ended triumphantly, I overcame the financial disappointments and took the competitive examination that paved the way for my entry into post middle school education at the beginning of the 1960. Although I bemoaned my failure to write competitive examinations for secondary schools, I wonder whether I could have paid my way through secondary school had I gained admission into one. The prospect, on hindsight, did not look promising; the wives of my father supported their children through schools. The difficulties I had in obtaining money for examinations makes me doubt whether I could have had financial support had I gained admission to secondary school.

The third cycle or epoch of my life began with my life in total disarray after I graduated from college. I went through four years of college work without any problem till the final year when my graduation was nearly derailed by typos in my final dissertation. The lecturer was intent on limiting the number of graduating seniors; the typos gave him an excuse to squeeze me to the extent that I was grateful when I graduated with barely a passing grade. I graduated the final year on a sour note. My college transcripts, that I obtained later, indicated that I was not as bad as my final grade indicated. It was of little comfort but the transcripts informed me that I was one of the best students in my class.

The adversities and misfortunes that marked the beginning of my third cycle ended with excitement and triumph when I won a scholarship to study in Australia. I was in Melbourne from February 1975 to September 1979. The scholarship ended the financial downfall or misery and the disappointments, misfortunes and hunger that marked my life during this period. I returned from Australia victorious over the devil at the end of four years with every material property that my little heart desired. The causes of my grief and misery were remedied and I returned to my country a new man, physically and spiritually. I came back with a sense of self and spiritual awareness. I renewed my acquaintance with spirit and found God in practical terms and came full circle with the spiritual experience of my infancy.

Life can be fragile and our earthly conditions comfortable or otherwise are unpredictable; our condition can change in a jiffy without warning. In the eighties I started feeling very secure in my financial conditions. I had a good job, a car and earned sizable income from professional practice on the side. And then I was hit by a spate of bad luck. I exhausted my savings, my professional practice dried up and suddenly I found myself facing starvation in which I could not afford the equivalent of a nickel, the price for a lousy doughnut for my child, I reached the nadir of my life. I did not know what hit me but I suspected the devil and satanic forces; my life was turned upside down within a period of three to four months since my family came to Accra and we began putting together our home business

I was flat broke on my back, no hope, no recourse; I turned to God to rescue me from the inexplicable events that confronted me. And with the help of one Prophet Ebenezer Tweneboah who taught me how to fast and pray, the redemptive and saving power of God was made manifest in my life once again. I regained my financial footing and by the grace of God triumphed over the traps and works of the devil. I learned that the Old Testament fasting rituals as written in the books of Esther and Daniel still produce miraculous results as of old. Fasting combined with prayers invokes the power of God to overcome the power of the devil. I experienced the power and influence of the devil from a front-row seat. My soul was touched by evil and only by fasting and prayer did I overcome the adversities that engulfed me at the beginning of the 1980s. And I know from my experience of my life that indeed the Bible is the living Word of God. That He still answers prayers and supplications as He did for the likes of Esther and Daniel of the Old Testament.

The 1980s had inauspicious beginning but before the decade ended I was a new migrant in the USA starting life anew from the scratch. The adversities and misfortunes that confounded me and reduced me to penury in the early eighties culminated in my founding a church together with a freelance pastor to glorify God and teach others the salvation I found in fasting and prayers. The name of the new church was the Three Holy Names Church. The church indirectly still exists in one guise or another in Ghana under the same pastor with whom I started the congregation. The name of the church was changed by my partner when I left Ghana for fear I might return to Ghana someday and seek to share in the profits of the church. During that cycle of my life I saw the human face of the devil or Satan and learned that Satan like God dwells among us and within us. By the grace of God I triumphed over the devil and the cycle ended unexpectedly when I emplaned for the USA on a visitor's visa and never went back. The day I landed in the USA was the beginning of another cycle of life that has followed the same yoyo pattern, up one period and down the next.

I came to America but that did not end the yoyo pattern of my existence or life. Before I came to the USA I had not tasted red meat of any kind in over a decade, but the exigencies of keeping body and soul together forced me to become omnivorous once again. I could not maintain the modest lifestyle of subsisting on fish and vegetables. I was compelled by circumstances beyond my control to eat poultry, less than three months after I landed in the USA to keep body and soul together. I had modest successes culminating in buying a home in 1994. At the beginning of 2000 I felt so secure in my part time job that I resigned my full time job in 2003 to become a full time real estate appraiser. But I found out soon enough that success was fleeting in the aftermath of open heart surgery to replace my aortic heart valve in 2006. While I was recuperating I was summoned before an administrative law judge to answer for the misuse of my digital signature by one of my appraiser trainees while I was on vacation. I was eager to get the case behind me so I could recover in peace and so I admitted liability. That was a big mistake. I was suspended for three months, my practice dried up after the suspension. And when my practice started picking up again then came the recession of 2008 that dried up the practice from which I never recovered. I was therefore forced into premature retirement. The changes that were instituted devalued the profession by incentivizing low fees. The low fees has demoralized me from pursuing assignments. Throughout my life, my misfortunes and struggles have sometimes served as a sort of spring board to a different and unexpected direction in my life. The new direction was either lying dormant or a new idea that had never crossed my mind or considered possible to pursue.

Retirement turned me into a stay-at-home dad practically babysitting my children instead of sending them to day care. Sitting idle at home with nothing to do provided me the incentive to write a memoir to detail my life's experience as a cautionary tale for my children. I did not know much about my own father and most of my children do not know much about me. I did not live with my father long enough to get to know him and most of my own children have not lived with me long enough to know me. I hope the memoir will fill in some of the gaps in their memory and perhaps help them to see me in a different light than hitherto.

In Remembrance of My Mother

The Death Of My Mother

Sipped Poisoned Flavored Water From A Calabash

I do not know my exact age. My age is estimated from the year I went to school in 1950 allegedly at age six. My father told me that I was sent to school at age six; I must therefore have been born in 1944. I was born to illiterate and uneducated Dagarti parents at Hiawa in the present day western region of Ghana. My father and mother come from nearby villages in the present day upper west region of Ghana. The date of birth in my passport and other official documents are guesstimates calculated from the year I went to school.

I know very little about my early childhood, from birth to about the age of four when my birth mother died. But I was informed that my mother walked out on my father when I was barely six months old. She subsequently remarried at Nyagli, a village in the Wala district. My earliest memories of my existence from childhood date from the day my mother was poisoned.

Conversations with my father and stepmother informed me that my mother was the junior or second wife of my father. She walked out on him and returned to the northern territories and remarried. My mother was said to have had children before and after I was born but they all died in infancy. When she died she left behind a three or four month old baby boy. The boy, Mwinyebo, was nurtured and raised by my grandmother till he became toddler and then like the rest of my mother's previous children he died of a snake bite. I am the only lucky surviving child of my mother.

My mother gave birth to her last child Mwinyebo and according to customary practices, nurtured him for about three months before she resumed her normal daily chores. She re-introduced herself to society through the brewing of *pito*. *Pito* is sorghum or maize based alcoholic beverage. She met her untimely death after she forgot to set aside a pot of pito as a present for an old woman that lived in the next compound house. My mother must have died at a young age perhaps in her late twenties, judging by the age at which Dagarti girls were married off. Most girls were betrothed during infancy and married off at puberty. Some of my own playmates living with men I considered as their father or grandfather turned out to be wives with husbands waiting for the maturity of the girls. I witnessed the fun that was made of the poor girls when their hymen was broken by the 'father' while she screamed and clawed the father figure husband during their first intimacy. My mother was similarly betrothed to my father and must therefore have been married at a very young age.

Posaa, my mother was poisoned on the day she sold out her first brew of *pito* after the birth of Mwinyebo before dusk. Her lucky day, in selling out all the pots of pito she produced, was also her worst day. It was her undoing. The pito or alcoholic beverage that my mother brewed that week was tantamount to her coming-out party, to let the world know that the she had overcome the ordeal of childbirth. But the good news was ruined by Balegee. That coming-out party was her last hurrah with the world.

On the day my mother was poisoned I was playing in the late afternoon shadow cast by the waning sun against the kitchen when an old woman from a neighboring compound house strolled into our house. As soon as my mother saw her entering the house she remembered that she had forgotten to reserve the usual free pot of pito for her. The pito was sold out and the fermentation and pito room was bare and as a gesture of goodwill and respect she invited Balegee, the old woman to quench her thirst with flavored sour water from the pot used for cooking in the kitchen. Balegee walked slowly into the kitchen, removed the lid from the pot peeped into it and replaced the lid. And without another word she strolled out the house. And that was all it took to poison the pot of water and mother. I was the only person who saw Balegee take off the lid from the pot but without taking a drop of water from the pot. I was too young to know that what she did was unusual and danger lurked behind the simple act of removing and replacing a cover or lid over a pot of water. And I have often wondered what if I was wise enough to have alerted my mother she might have lived a longer life. I could have said something that could have alerted her or raised suspicions in her mind about possible dangers behind the peeking into the pot of water without any water being fetched from the pot.

It takes three grueling days to brew and bring pito to the market. But the process begins long before the start of the actual brewing. The sorghum or maize used for the brew is soaked in water for a few days, then incubated in the dark in big baskets to sprout. The grain sprouts are then sundried and when dry pounded into semi powder form in a mortar with pestles. The three day brewing process then begins after the pounding of the grain sprouts into semi powder. It takes about one month to brew pito from start to finish. The day my mother sold her last *pito* marked the day I became aware of myself as a living breathing human being. I do not know or remember anything about my infancy before that fateful day.

The day marked the unfortunate events that came to define the experience of my early life. The day's events deprived me of the opportunity to have bonded with my mother and formed lasting and happy memories about her. All I have are the sad and unhappy memories of the last three or four months of her life. My memories of my mother are from the date she was poisoned through her suffering and death. Those three or four months were seared into my memory, the groaning and moaning day after day until the day she fell silent. The smell and stench of putrefied flesh before her death sank into my memory and resurfaced about ten years after her death. The last time I saw her she was seated high at the village square surrounded by mourners. The untimely death of my mother deprived me of the opportunity to learn about my early childhood from the woman who gave birth and nurtured me up to about age four, the missing years of my life. Neither my father nor my stepmother could fill that gap or void since neither of them saw her again after she walked off with me.

Balegee was an old and cantankerous woman who lived in the same village, Nyagli. She apparently was on very friendly terms with my mother, or so it appeared. But I do not know whether they were mere friends or extended family members. The old woman and my mother were on good terms enough for my mother to give her a free pot of *pito* as a gesture of good will whenever she brewed *pito*. But on this particular day my mother forgot to put aside or reserve a pot of pito for Balegee and paid for the forgetfulness with her life. Balegee waited all day expecting my mother to take the pot of *pito* to her but my mother did not fulfill her expectations . She therefore decided to pick up the expected gift of pito by herself from our house. She crossed the fields separating her compound house from our house expecting to be met at the gate with the pot of pito followed by a polite apology from mother for her inadvertence. And when that did not happen she was miffed even before she exchanged any pleasantries with my mother.

As soon as my mother saw Balegee at the entrance of the compound house, she slapped her forehead and exclaimed, "Oh gosh, I forgot." My mother apologized profusely for having forgotten to reserve a pot of *pito* for her; she told Balegee that she had been besieged by customers very early in the day and every pot of pito sold out before noon. That was when she invited Balegee to soothe her thirst with cool flavored water from the pot in the kitchen. Balegee said nothing to show her disappointment or displeasure or that she was offended by my mother's audacity to sell out all her pito without reserving a courtesy pot of the beverage for her gratification. The cool water was flavored with fermented sorghum or maize meal or tamarind seeds to give it a sour taste. Balegee walked into the kitchen as if to get water from the pot as mother had suggested and instead craftily slipped poison into the pot. Fortunately or unfortunately the poison was targeted to my mother only.

This must have been the Harmattan season when the villagers generally take time off from farming to make repairs to their mud houses and the youth go from one pito house to another to have some fun. It is also the season of courtship when young men roam around the villages in search of partners and those who have girl friends elope with them to their villages to begin marriage life. Elopement was the preferred method of marriage among the men of my community because traditional wedding was considered expensive. When a young man and woman are in love and ready for marriage they elope. The family of the girl is later informed after the elopement, the dowry follows and the marriage consummated without an expensive and elaborate traditional wedding ceremony.

I was playing around the kitchen under the long shadow cast by the waning sun in all my birthday glory. I saw a familiar old woman enter the kitchen lift the lid from my mother's pot of water and replaced the lid. Nobody thought much of Balegee going in and out of the kitchen so quickly though she emerged without a calabash of water in hand. But the seed of my mother's demise was sown when she walked in and out of the kitchen. My mother felt the effect of the poisoned water upon tasting for the flavor and sourness of the water just before the start of the day's meal. "*Mmm*," my mother mused after she sipped the flavored water. The sour water stuck in her throat. She thought nothing more of it and went on to prepare the meal with the same water. She dished out the meal to various members of her family. I was not old enough, according to Dagarti custom, to eat with the men as such I used to eat with my mother. When my mother swallowed the first morsel of food, she mused again and exclaimed that the morsel was stuck in her throat. For the second time that evening, she felt that a foreign object was stuck in her digestive canal. She explained to to my father the unusual condition, the sensation that food and water are stuck in her throat.

She was not choking or coughing but she felt the discomfort and sensation of a foreign object within her upper digestive tract. I ate with my mother and filled my belly without feeling the same discomfort or sensation from the food and so were my stepfather and other members of the family who were served the same meal. My stepfather tried to ease my mother's discomfort by slapping and patting her on the back reminiscent of a choking victim. The primitive Heimlich maneuver had no effect whatsoever in easing the discomfort. And that was the beginning and the end of my mother.

MARKED FOR DEATH

Balegee was the personification of evil. She had an uncanny knowledge of poisons and the ability to target the poison to her victims without affecting unintended targets to cause mass casualties and arousing suspicions about her role in the event of any casualty or havoc. My mother irked her ire when she forgot to set aside a pot of *pito* for her gratification. She had an oversize image of herself and in her warped mind my mother demeaned and disrespected her and for that she deserved to die. But she had no intention to poison other members of my mother's family; Posaa was her perceived enemy and so her wrath was directed at my mother and no one else. The poison that Balegee craftily put into the pot of water should have affected all who drank and ate the food, but that was not the case. My mother was the intended victim and she was the only person who was affected by the poison. The other members of the household ate the same food without any adverse effect.

My mother felt the sensation of foreign objects in her upper digestive tract that she could not swallow or throw out. That sensation began to take a toll on her health. Balegee could have gotten away with her devious plan had the effects of the poison manifested after a few days or weeks. But my mother's discomfort was immediate and when oracles and seers pointed to poison as the cause of mother's illness it was not difficult to piece together the events of the day that pointed to Balegee as the most likely suspect or culprit. She was the only person who 'drank' the flavored water from the pot before my mother tasted the water for sourness when she was preparing to cook the evenings meal. Suspicious glances were already directed at her before the oracles and seers virtually confirmed those suspicions.

In our traditional society nothing happens in a vacuum, everything has a cause and effect. My stepfather swung into action to find the cause and remedy for the sudden discomfort and illness of his dear wife. He consulted oracles, seers, witch doctors and medicine men for answers and remedies. The oracles and seers pointed to poison as the cause of my mother's illness. The suspicion fell on Balegee and when she was confronted she confessed to it. Her confession and admission of guilt however did nothing that eased our anxieties or benefitted my mother. She confessed to knowledge of concocting poisons but had no knowledge of antidotes that could undo the effects of the poison. It is not for nothing that some people are suspected of witchcraft and labeled as witches. I do not know how else to describe Balegee, a woman with astute knowledge of poisons with the ability to home in on her victim without harming any innocent or unintended targets within a group of people such as a family. Directly or indirectly, Balegee passed an immutable death sentence on my mother. From that point onward any hope we still harbored dimmed, the end was only a matter of time.

My mother's condition deteriorated quite rapidly. She became weak and was confined to her room. My stepfather instead of throwing his arms into the air and waiting for the inevitable end, continued to roam the byways and back roads of every witch doctor and medicine man in the surrounding villages and hamlets hoping that one of them must know enough to undo the effect of the poison gnawing at his wife. His efforts in the end were all in vain. He urged mother to try all the herbal concoctions and potions he brought home from the various medicine men and witch doctors he consulted. But nothing was powerful or strong enough to undo the evil genius of Balegee, her condition only deteriorated. The poison gnawed at mother from the inside out and perhaps rotted her internal organs before she finally died. She moaned in agony by day and by night and the room I shared with mother smelled like death or rotten flesh. The smell of death or rotten flesh seeped into my subconscious mind and emerged with a ring of familiarity when I stepped into the mortuary at Wa hospital where I was on admission in 1959, about a decade after my mother's death. The smell of the morgue was eerily familiar though that was the first time I ever peeked or set foot into a mortuary.

My stepfather made animal or blood sacrifices to pacify the gods and the spirits of our ancestors with the hope that the spirits of the departed could intervene. My stepfather continued on his quixotic quest for cure or remedy till the night my mother took her last breath. No potion or sacrifice was strong enough to undo the effects of the poison.

Throughout the time that my mother was confined to her room in agony and pain, I slept with her in the same room. I slept with my mother throughout her illness as she groaned and moaned. I did not realize that the room had an awful smell of rotten or putrefied flesh until more than a decade after her death when the experience of familiarity surfaced and the latent memory became lucid. My mother coughed and sputtered blood and mucus throughout her illness up to the last night she passed away. Of course, I did not know that the smell was of rotten flesh until in 1959, years after she passed away when the poor condition of the Wa morgue triggered the latent and hidden memory of the stench of our room before my mother passed away.

BANISHED FROM THE VILLAGE

The life and light went out of our home the day Balegee confessed or accepted responsibility for poisoning my mother but said she did not have knowledge of antidotes that could undo the effects of the poison. The inevitable was only a matter of time. My stepfather and other family members hustled together speaking in hushed tones, impotent and helpless, unable to provide even palliative care to ease the agony and pain of the poison that was gnawing at my mother's internal organs.

In the meantime, the traditional justice system of the Dagarti people was set in motion after the confession. Balegee became the object of contempt and scorn by the villagers. She was ostracized by the rest of the village, as we waited for the decision on her punishment by the village elders. Her confession must have set every member of the community on edge. If she could target deadly poison at marked individuals then nobody could be immune from her wrath. No one in the village felt secure as long as she was around, her malice had no bounds if kindness could unleash her wrath. How many people had she poisoned in the past? Nobody will ever know, but it set tongues wagging that she must have been responsible for the deaths of her husband and children. Her cunning and wily nature and expertise in poisons that could be used to eliminate any member of society with whom she had a grudge made everybody in the small village nervous.

The chief and elders deliberated for some time and decided that banishment and expulsion was the appropriate punishment short of killing her by our own hands. That was the severest punishment or retribution that could be imposed upon her. Balegee as a result of her devious and nefarious deeds had forfeited her right to live in the community. She was not a native of the village, she became a member by virtue of marriage in accordance to Dagarti custom. And she would have lived all her days and buried in the village but for her dastardly deed. She was widowed, her husband and her children died long ago. She was in retrospect blamed for those deaths. What had long been rumored was now said in the open because of recent events. With no child or husband, her ties to the village were tenuous at best. Banishment and temporary staking like crucifixion were the severest punishment that traditional jurisprudence could impose for any improper or unlawful conduct. Balegee was notified of the decision of the chief and elders of the village to expel her from the village. At this time nobody cared where she went as long as she left the village and never came back. The village elders were eager to rid the society of the cancer and the menace in their midst.

On the day the banishment was enforced, the villagers gathered together in the square to bear witness to her expulsion. She was escorted out of her home clutching her belongings in a basket while crocodile tears streamed down her face. She was ordered to leave the village and never come back. She had a lot of company, the villagers who were eager to see her go away. The men, women, and children of the village followed her every step of the way as she gradually made her way out of the village. We hollered and hooted at her while the girls and women swept the ground on which she treaded as she walked out of the village as a sign of erasing or severing her connection with the village. She was reminded that she was a pariah and never expected to come back to Nyagli under any circumstances.

The expulsion assuaged our collective anger and fears with a measure of satisfaction that the person responsible for the inevitable end of my mother had been found and punished. But that was little comfort to my family as my mother still lay dying slowly from the effects of the poison. She did not even have the energy and satisfaction to witness the expulsion of Balegee from Nyagli. She was too weak to see the punishment of the person responsible for her miserable condition. We followed her noisily like a celebration or festival of sort hurling insults and invectives at her. If the expression of our collective anger and fears had any curative power, my mother would have been healed of the poison that was gnawing at her. After the expulsion, we held our collective breaths and waited for the inevitable end. In a way, it was a great relief when the final day arrived. Mother passed away during the night, the wait was over.

BEAUTIFUL AND PEACEFUL IN DEATH

As Mother wasted away, she became weaker by the day while she breast-fed Mwinyebo, my baby brother. My baby brother clung to her breast throughout her ordeal till the night she took her last breath when the baby was taken away from the corpse. When the end came, I did not know that indeed the end had come except the eerie silence in the room and around the house, the somber faces of the grown-ups as they went in and out of our room. I was kept away from the room I had shared with my mother. The visitors whispered in hushed tones as if trying to conceal something from me or sharing some secrets among themselves while they trooped in and out of my mother's room. I was sent outside to play with other kids as the house slowly filled with people.

Her death was broadcast to the surrounding villages and hamlets by the beating of tumpani or timpani drums in specific tones that conveyed to the neighboring communities that there was a death in the direction of the drums; our house was soon filled with long and somber strange faces before sundown. I do not know how my mother's remains were prepared for viewing and burial. But when I was ushered out to play I was not allowed back into our room and did not see my mother again until the last day I saw her seated high on a pedestal for public viewing at the village square. She was dressed in the finest clothes I ever saw her wear and adorned with trinkets, she appeared to be asleep. I had never seen her that pretty before. She sat on a high seat placed on a platform shaded from the hot sun while men and women cried and wailed. The women beat their flabby breasts and the men hopped helter-skelter around the surrounding fields. My mother sat quietly under the shade like a chief surveying her subjects at a durbar or festival.

My mother was the picture of perfect peace as she sat under the shade while familiar and strange people cried and wailed. The picture of peace I saw on my mother's still countenance was a transformation after her death. It was the first time since she fell ill that I saw her quiet and peaceful without contortions of agony and pain etched on her face. The facial wrinkles of agony and pain were smoothed over. She sat there quietly, not groaning, grimacing or moaning in pain.

Among the Dagarti people, the dead are seated on a high chair or pedestal for viewing. As she sat in the square there was a cacophony of drums, conch bells, singing, wailing and dancing around the square. The atmosphere in retrospect appeared more festive than somber and sorrowful, a small market of cooked meat sellers and women frying kose sprang up at the square within view of my mother's corpse. If so, it was well and good as mother's life was cut short better to celebrate the peace she had in death than be mournful and sorrowful. I was curios about the events I saw around my mother

23

as she sat motionless at the village square. I wondered what the tears and wailings was all about; mother appeared to be at peace with herself. She did not grimace in pain. Her countenance was not etched with pain. What then could be so wrong for people to be crying and wailing? Death is beautiful, death is peace. That impression of death left an indelible mark on my young mind. Death released my mother from an agonizing, miserable and painful existence and what is there not to like about the peace that ends all suffering.

The sight of her sitting quietly at the village square was a thing of beauty to behold! Then towards sundown, she was taken down and that was the last time I saw my mother. I was innocent and ignorant of death and perhaps I expected to see her again. Somehow I felt that some extraordinary thing had happened to my mother, but I did not know what it was. I did not see where she was buried. Our people are buried in family crypts or in graves in the courtyard or in surrounding fields near the homes. I have never been back at Nyagli since the day I was carried out of the village with my grandmother and uncle Samini.

The last three or four months of my mother's life must have been in 1948. It is said that there is a silver lining behind every dark cloud. My mother's untimely death was the catalyst that reunited me with my birth father. I did not know that the man I called my father was my stepfather. It is most likely that but for her untimely death I might not have been united with my father when I came of school age. Her untimely death opened the path for me to go to school. Her untimely death made it possible for me to reunite with my father just when I was of school going age. It is noteworthy that with the exception of one older sister, Cecilia, none of my older brothers and sisters from his first wife went to school. Perhaps Cecilia's desire to go to school must have paved the way for my father to consider educating me. About one year after my mother's death, my stepmother came to take me away from my grandmother. The baby brother my mother left behind clung to life thanks to nurturing and care by my grandmother who assumed the role of mother and breast-fed Mwinyebo though she was long past her menopause.

My mother died during the night. When I woke up in the morning, she lay still on her bed; that was the first time in a long time I did not hear her groan or moan. She appeared to be relaxed. I took in the new reality without actually comprehending what had happened and I was soon led out of the room. I was not allowed back into the room until the day I saw her again at the village square. I heard the beating of *tumpani* drums in soulful dirges that announced the passing of my mother. Soon after the drums ceased than streams of visitors began going in and out of our house. The drums were preceded by emissaries sent out to inform family and relatives scattered about in surrounding towns and villages.

The morning after Posaa was taken away from the village square; I woke up and, for the first time, felt very lonely and forlorn. Our house teemed with strange faces; but I felt all alone lost in my own house. None of the hordes of people in the house took any notice of me then suddenly, I was overcome with grief. I burst into tears and cried my heart out. My cries drew the attention of the strangers in the house. They consoled me but I was inconsolable, later some of them suggested that I must be hungry. They went to surrounding houses to scrounge for some leftovers to feed me. After I was fed I quieted down and did not cry again. I did not cry or shed a tear since my mother fell silent until that moment. How true the saying that it is a mother who knows the needs of her children. I would not have felt the pangs of hunger if Mother was still around even when she was bedridden I still had my meals regularly and on time. I guess the hunger triggered my sense of loss and grief. Among the strange faces I later learned were my mother's close family members including my aunt, grandmother, uncle and others I did not know. A day or two later I was packed along with my baby brother on my first and final journey out of Nyagli.

NEW HOME WITH GRANDMOTHER

My grandmother bundled Mwinyebo, my baby brother unto her back while I was hoisted onto the shoulders of uncle Samini, and we left for Duohi along bush paths. Duohi was my grandmother's home and became my new home for about another one year. I lived with my grandmother for the better part of a year until about the latter part of 1949 when I was taken to the Gold Coast colony to my father at Bogoso. My baby brother was nursed by my grandmother who fed him with her own breast milk. She massaged or treated her breasts until they yielded breast milk for the baby. I do not remember a lot of things about my younger brother. But I do remember the sleepless nights we all endured when he cried and wailed from hunger. She massaged her flabby breasts daily with shea butter until the breasts produced enough milk to satisfy the hunger of my brother and after that we had peace of mind at night. While the effort went on my baby brother tucked on the dry breasts and was force fed bland and peanut flavored porridge. Grandmother finally succeeded in lactating after what seemed like an eternity and breast fed Mwinyebo till he became a toddler.

Fate thrust on my grandmother the role of a new mother to Mwinyebo and me. She was forced to adopt her grandchildren following the untimely death of her younger daughter. Supplemental baby formulae were not known in the northern territories of the Gold Coast in the late 1940's. Children from all social backgrounds were breast fed till old enough to take solids beginning with porridge. Mwinyebo survived the death of our mother on grandmother's breast milk only to die prematurely from snake bite. I left him behind in 1949 when I was taken to my father but I did not forget him. I considered him the only real brother I had and childishly refused to accord Adjoa, my stepmother's baby, the same status. In my mind Mwinyebo was the only sibling that mattered until after death cruelly took him away. He forever remained on my mind as the only real brother I ever had however briefly. The untimely death of Mwinyebo helped to draw me closer to Adjoa and my father's other children. I was forced by circumstances to accept them as brothers and sisters and did so overtime without any reservations.

I was obligated when I grew up as the only surviving child of my mother, to keep her memory and seed alive. I was attracted to life in the ministry as a catholic priest, but my desire to have a family in memory of my mother was stronger than the priesthood. I became a Catholic by accident of education; had I been educated in the school of a protestant church I could have followed my heart into the ministry or the pulpit and still had a family. I might have ended up a convert to the church that educated me just as I converted to Catholicism because of education.

I found the life of priesthood very attractive but I could not make myself into an eunuch for the word of God. The pull of family life was stronger than priesthood. The vow of celibacy of the Catholic priest would have deprived me from fulfilling the solemn promise I made to myself to keep the memory of my mother alive. I hoped that someday God would find a way to call me to his service after I fulfilled my obligation to my mother and call me to his service as a family man.

When I left Nyagli with my grandmother, I also left behind the only "home" that I ever knew. The haunting memory of my mother has not diminished with age or time. I have never felt the urge to go back to the village where my mother cruelly lost her life. I did not have any longing or fondness for Nyagli to prompt or compel me to visit the village. When I returned to northern Ghana in 1957 I was not yet mature enough to have thought of visiting the grave site of my mother. Had I the common sense I would have gone back to Nyagli less than ten years since her passing, and most likely I would have met familiar faces who could have shown me the burial ground of my mother.

I made several visits to my grandmother at Duohi but it never occurred to me to visit Nyagli. I visited my aunt at Charia but uncle Samini was long dead. My surviving aunt too died in the early 1960's. I saw her alive shortly before she suddenly passed away most probably of heart attack. My grandmother had the misfortune of burying all her children before her own death. She was a vital financial lifeline for me at a time when I needed it most to pay for a competitive examination for teacher training colleges in 1959. Her help made it possible for me to get a foot hold onto the ladder of high education.

I have been insulated by fate from witnessing the death of another close family member or loved one. Most of my older brothers and sisters usually converted to the Islamic faith of my father in their old age. Thus when they died they were buried quickly in accordance with Islamic religious requirements. By the time I became aware of the death of a brother or sister the one might have been buried. I have been spared the helplessness one feels in witnessing the agony and pain endured by a loved one in sickness during the last days of life. Distance has either been my friend or the foe that has worked to shield me from being present at the funeral of any of my brothers or sisters. My younger sister, Adjoa Vida, died while I was in Accra; but by the time I had information about her death, she was long buried in her husband's village in accordance with Dagarti customary practice.

My sister Adjoa, died from a botched routine surgical procedure called dilation and curettage (D&C.) that was used both as a fertility treatment and abortion by doctors and nurses. Vida underwent the procedure for fertility treatment in her attempt to have another child. She never woke up from the operating table. The doctor who performed the procedure allegedly severed an internal organ. After the botched procedure she was transported over rough road from Wa to Bolgatanga, she died shortly after arriving at Bolgatanga. The doctor, as far as I am concerned, got away with murder for medical malpractice.

Apart from the loss of a premature baby I have not seen the face of any dead relative since I saw my mother at the village square at age four. I have seen the faces of school mates, colleagues and friends lying in state but never a loved one or very close relative. In all cases, the experience was unsettling, the picture of a corpse in repose is usually etched on my mind long after the funeral and burial are over. I think I have an overactive imagination and long after viewing a body at a funeral I tend to see visions of the body in repose at random intervals for about the next six months or more. The mental pictures tend to haunt me at random intervals and at unexpected circumstances or places. But what I dreaded most was seeing the image of the corpse in the dead of the night when I woke up or went to the bathroom or opened my eyes during sleep.

During the primary school days the pupils were marched to view the body and later to the cemetery to bury dead school mates. The images of my school mates lying in repose, the lowering of the casket into the grave, the pebbles we threw into the grave and the songs we sang played like a video over and over for months and years in my mind. I have thus become rather very reluctant to view corpses in repose, when I go to a funeral home I avoid viewing the body though invariably curiosity pushes me to see the body in the casket or bed. In Ghana I preferred going for the burial to viewing the corpse lying in state.

THE YEAR WITH GRANDMA

My grandmother was widowed at the time she took us in after the death of our mother. She lived with my uncle Samini, he was the man of the house that did the farm work and maintained the livestock while grandmother roamed the market circuits buying and selling. My grandmother was popularly known by her favorite word or exclamation, Elwelee.

The untimely death of her daughter bequeathed to her two boys, a four year old and three or four-month-old baby boy. She was long past her productive years but she had to breast feed her three month old grandson or watch helplessly as the baby wasted and withered away from lack of nutrition. About two or three times a day, grandma massaged her flabby breasts with shea butter; after which, she encouraged the baby to suck on the dry breast. A few weeks later the breasts became productive enough to satisfy the hunger of the baby. Meanwhile he was force-fed porridge either unsweetened or flavored with peanut butter or tamarind fruit. The urgency and the struggle to provide nutrition for my baby brother in the immediate aftermath of mother's death consumed all the attention and energy of grandma until she lactated again to provide enough breast milk to feed the baby. It was only after Mwinyebo started getting enough milk that we all had the peace of mind to sleep at night without being woken up by a crying hungry baby.

The significance of the events surrounding my mother's death had not yet sunk into my conscious and subconscious mind. I was oblivious about the death of my mother, but my playmates at Duohi often reminded me of the death of my mother. They taunted me about her death in retrospect I doubt whether they knew what they were about. They must have over heard discussions and conversations in hushed tones among the adults about the misfortunes of Elwelee; the death of her daughter that left her with two young grandsons. But the taunts were their way of telling me that I was a stranger in their midst. I lost the innocence of my mother's death thanks to the cruel jokes and pranks of my playmates. I was taunted or mocked as if I was responsible for my mother's death. The pranks and taunts lasted for only a few weeks before the attention of my playmates were diverted to the latest rumor and whispers in the village.

I guess I was a mommy's boy until she passed away. Though I do not remember much but I guess that she must have dotted on me as her only surviving child until Mwinyebo came along to share her love with me. I was the wiry and resilient child that survived and thrived in spite of the tropical diseases that claimed the lives of the children who were born before me. Mwinyebo, for instance, died of a snake bite, but I roamed the same fields and never once saw a snake. I was therefore an only child who was perhaps cherished and sheltered from any possible mishap before Mwinyebo was born. She must have cuddled me to such an extent that I was not familiar with horsing around with other kids of my age until after her death. At the time of day that Balegee came into our courtyard children of my age would usually have been playing outside under shady trees but I was playing under the shadow of a building in the house. But at Duohi, I was thrown into the wolf pack; I had to start learning things I should have known at my age. For instance I did know the rudiments of wrestling and was therefore the door mat of children younger than me to the chagrin of my uncle. I got into my first tussle at Duohi and learned how to set traps for mice and rats. And Duohi was the only place I ever attempted to kill lizard for food, when I went to Bogoso the boys chased them around for sport and nothing else. I was late learning the tradition and practices of my society and that irked my uncle Samini.

HOW I LOST MY FRONT TEETH

I learned to wrestle by fighting with kids of my age group. With no pervious experience in conflicts, my first wrestling brawl was a disaster. I was the doormat that other boys picked on, I was clumsy and ineptitude in the art of wrestling. Wrestling was the means of conflict resolution in our tribe. Fist fights were not common and in a brawl the first person to put the other on the ground was the victor. The victor thumped his chest and walked with his head high while the vanquished walked meekly away with his tail between his legs.

It was unusual for the vanquished to get off the ground and initiate another brawl, we were genteel in our brawls. I had never fought or brawled before I went to Duohi. My uncle Samini had no patience with my ineptitude and perceived weakness or lack of aggression. His disgust and impatience with my lack of wrestling skills irked him until he could not endure to see me humiliated, he thus lost his composure and kicked me down after I lost the latest brawl with a younger adversary.

I was picked on that afternoon for no obvious reason than that I was a punching bag. My uncle Samini sat nearby and saw the ensuing brawl and when I was beaten he lost his patience. This was his proverbial straw that broke the camel's back, my uncle lost his temper and composure and in his rage shoved and kicked me from behind. I lost my balance and fell facedown on a boulder. I busted my lips and broke my front teeth. To add insult to injury, he walked away without attending to my injury. My busted mouth and broken teeth became bacteria infected leading to a mouth ulcer. By the time the ulcer was healed part of my upper gum was eaten away along with the roots of my permanent upper front teeth. I lost the gum and roots of my upper teeth and never got permanent upper front teeth.

I never forgave my uncle for the loss of my upper front teeth before I ever went to school and I never forgave him for making me the laughingstock of my school and classmates. The taunts and mockery of my schoolmates was so relentless I could never take my mind off my 'empty mouth', the missing front teeth. The loss of the teeth remained forever fresh in my mind and the older I grew the more I hated my uncle for turning me into a laughingstock of children. I loathed him so much so that when he died about three years after I left him for Bogoso I only shrugged my shoulders as if to say 'who cares'. At the time I did not care whether he lived or died. This was the one sore memory I have of my year with grandma.

My uncle never lost any opportunity to reproach me for being a weakling. He often cursed and barked at me as if that would impart some skills into me, but no amount of shouts or threats could give me any feats of strength and skills to stand on equal footing with kids my age. He did not know that I lived a sheltered life with my mother and therefore I was not ready for the rough and tumble life of the playgrounds of Duohi. His anger boiled over, and that anger disfigured me for life. The missing upper teeth became my identifying characteristic from about age five to about age eighteen. The big gap earned me several nicknames throughout elementary school. One such nickname that I can still recall after all these years was "chuckle hole." I did not know the meaning or significance of chuckle hole, but I knew it was an insult and that was enough to start a fight. My uncle would have been proud of me if he had been around to see how aggressive I had become after he disfigured me.

I hated my uncle for turning me into the butt of jokes from the day I stepped into the four walls of a classroom in 1950 until in 1962 when I was convinced to buy dentures. The constant taunts and mockery for the large tooth gap was a constant reminder of the role my uncle played in my disfigurement. I cursed him as I cried and fought constantly over the taunts. He was my mother's younger brother, but I became mentally estranged from him for the emotional turmoil he had unwittingly inflicted on me. I did not have it in my heart to empathize or sympathize with him when he passed away. He must have meant well, but his good intentions went beyond the pale of traditional teachings, he turned me into the laughingstock of my schoolmates.

After years of torment, taunts, and mockery, I finally accepted the reality that the gap in my upper front teeth was an indelible part of me. From about form I or seventh grade I was able to look at myself in the mirror and laugh at me. I came to terms and accepted the large tooth gap as a part of me and that began the process of coping and healing with the mockery and taunts that I was subjected to. The ability to laugh at myself took the sting and the pain out of the mockery and taunts. Over the years I had developed self defense methods in which I laughed without opening my mouth to reveal the large gap in my teeth. I learned to laugh and smile without showing or revealing my teeth but when I could smile and laugh at myself I made no further attempts to conceal the gap in my teeth. I became less conscious of the lost teeth and over time it ceased to bother me.

I became so comfortable walking about with the gap in my teeth it took two days of convincing by technicians of a mobile dental team of Ghana army at Tamale to persuade me to allow them to make dentures for me at reduced price. I met some members of the mobile team in a drinking bar. The team considered that I was the source of pocket money to pad their pockets. I rebuffed them on the first day by telling them I was comfortable with my looks. I met them at the same bar the following day and they offered to make the dentures for me at half price, despite the offer of half price they still had to convince me to accept a denture and have one made for me. I had lived with the gap for so long I could not imagine how I would look without it. In the end they succeeded to persuade me to have dentures. When I made the dentures I used to take it off when I went to bed at night. Initially I used to go out without my dentures and often rushed back when I remembered that I left my teeth behind. I chewed a part of the dentures and it shook when I spoke but I continued to wear the shaky dentures till the nineties. The dentures became a part of me and now I cannot imagine life without it.

Habits die hard. Despite my attempt and determination to live with the tooth gap and became less conscious of it, the gap nevertheless robbed me of smiles. I smirked when I laughed and although I have had dentures since 1962 I have not learned to smile or laugh with joyous abandon. The smirk did not change after the gap was filled with dentures; I could not overcome the habit of my formative years to start showing my new artificial teeth. When a photographer says 'cheese', I clamp up with a smirk or sneer. On festive and happy occasions, my smiles caught in photos are smirks; I could not even smile to show my teeth on my wedding day.

My grandmother was popularly known as Elwelee, it is the only name by which I knew her. My grandma was a trader in local food produce. She went from one market town to another about three or four times a week to buy and sell. Considering that there are six market days in traditional Dagarti week, she was practically on the road about three or four days a week going from one market town to another. She carried on her head baskets of produce from town to town or village to village. It is no wonder that she outlived all her children largely because she led a very active life walking from one market town to another about three or four times a week. Her active lifestyle must have contributed to her longevity. She was blessed with long life but also cursed by having the misfortune of practically burying her husband and all her children.

It was at Duohi that I started to learn the hardscrabble life of the average northern farmer in the villages. I learned to live the tenuous circle of life from one season to another. Every season comes around with different problems and appropriate activities that keep the circle of life going around. During the dry season, the savanna grasses are tinder dry and with the aid of fire become fertile hunting grounds for small and big animals. The grasslands are set on fire to ferret out the animals hiding in the grasses. The dry season is also the season of renewal when we make repairs to our homes and new homes are built for those who have come of age. Hunting skills are honed and imparted during the dry season, boys learn how to string bows, burnish and put tranquilizers or poisons on arrows. I did not live long enough with grandma and uncle Samini to learn how to string bow and sharpen arrows for hunting. I followed the youths to hunt for game and honey during the one dry season I spent at Duohi. It appeared that everything I should have learned at Nyagli was crammed into one or two seasons at Duohi before I left for Bogoso.

Hunting skills for my age groups was a year round affair, Most of us hung around the village when the grown ups went to till and sow seeds in the farming season. The young boys hunted lizards, mice and rats all year round. Our weapons for hunting lizards were slings, catapults, stones and traps in the dark houses for mice and house rats. Whatever we killed or snared we roasted over open flames and tore it up among ourselves.

Our rooms were typically poorly lit and dark all year round. The houses are built and roofed with mud with small round holes in the walls for light and ventilation. Our mothers stored all their valuables and worldly possessions in large earthenware pots stacked from floor to ceiling at the back of the dimly lit rooms. They stored food stuffs, dry fish and meats, cloths and yarns and cotton for ginning and every conceivable item in the pots. The rooms were thus fertile grounds for mice and rats and we set traps to snare them.

My grandmother's room was lined from wall to wall and floor to ceiling with these large pots. They held everything from grains, cotton, dried meats, smoked fowl, fish, clothes and her trading merchandise. Beans and grains were stored in the pots in wood ashes that served both as insecticides and preservatives. My grandmother's room was heavily infested with mice and rats and the space between the pots was my first hunting grounds. We set traps between the pots at the back of the rooms and waited patiently to hear the click of the trap that a mouse or rat was caught.

One quiet afternoon, when the grown ups were on their farms, we the children set up traps in my grandmother's room. One of the traps snared a large rat. No sooner had we removed the rat from the trap than we roasted it and tore it among ourselves. The roasted rat meat whetted our appetite for more. And as we smacked our lips we set up the trap again at the same spot hoping to snare another rat or mouse. I was the hero that afternoon because the trap was set up in my grandmother's room. We could not wait to hear the click of the trap, so I kept watch on the trap. I could not see the trap in the dimly lit room so whenever I went to check on the trap I groped around to feel for the prize. As I groped and poked around for the umpteenth time, finally the trap snared my thumb. I yelled out in pain and rushed out from the dark room with the trap dangling on my left thumb. Commotion and pandemonium followed at the sight of the trap dangling on my thumb instead of a rat or mouse.

I wailed at the top of my lungs from fear and pain. None of my friends could free my thumb from the trap. Try as hard as they could none was strong enough to open the trap with his hands. Freeing a dead mouse or rat from the trap was easier because we stood on it and our weight opened the jaws of the trap to retrieve any mouse or rat but that could not be done with the trap dangling on my thumb. I cried until I lost my voice and unable to cry anymore. I was left on my own to cry and wail. I sat at a vantage point leading into the village with the trap on my thumb and waited for help from any adult that came home from the bush to free me from my agony. I sat there waiting while crying and weeping. After what seemed like an eternity an adult came home from the farm and freed my thumb from the trap. The serrated teeth of the trap lacerated my thumb but otherwise no bone was broken. I learned not to grope and poke around in the dark checking up on traps for a catch.

FARMING AND HERDING

The accident with the trap set me up for another activity of the hardscrabble subsistence farming life from season to season. After that week my uncle decided to take me to the farm with him instead of leaving me to loiter around with kids. I therefore entered into another phase of the learning curve of a boy growing up in the Dagarti community. My uncle involved me in two distinct but an integral part of subsistence life. I went cattle herding with bigger boys or to the farm with my him. I did not do anything on the farms; I collected wood and twigs to help with cooking on the farm. And I foraged for wild fruits to occupy my time while my uncle was busy on the farm. I spent most of my time in the bushes around the farms foraging and searching for wild fruits.

Grandma and uncle owned a few cows that were housed in a kraal around the village. On days that I did not accompany my uncle to the farm, I went cattle herding with the big boys who herded the cows from the village for feed and water. Herding livestock was arduous than going to the farm. The cows were driven long distances from the village in search of good feeding grounds and watering holes. The hard part of herding was the walking distances covered in a day searching for good grass and water. The first day I started herding I was assisted to ride on the back of docile cows that helped me to cover the long distance relatively painless. The herders knew the docile and tamed cows that could be ridden. Riding on the back of cows to the bushes for feed and water eased the discomfort of our young legs. The smaller children are gradually broken into herding cows by the older boys teaching them how to care and corral the animals to prevent them from going astray. The older boys followed behind the animals and ran in all directions corralling the animals to keep them in the pack ensuring that none strayed far from the herd.

After a few weeks of herding with the boys of the village I was asked to note and keep an eye specifically for the animals of my grandmother and uncle. I was indirectly on my way to herding in my own right. Although the boys from the village herded the cows together each boy kept an eye on the animals of his family. And at the end of the day, if any animal strayed from the pack, the responsible boy searched and brought the stray into the pack. My grandmother was held in high esteem for her trading activities and perceived wealth. A man's measure of wealth was the number of cows he owned. She was perhaps the only woman of means in the village. She owned some cattle in her own right and not by virtue of marriage. After all she was a widow. I was taken away to Bogoso just when I was becoming familiar with herding.

Herding cattle and foraging for food in the wild went hand in hand. Foraging for wild fruits was an integral part of roaming the wild bushes with cows. When we left for the bush in the morning we took along smoldering wood fire and some tubers of yams or sweet potatoes. As soon as we reached the feeding ground or watering hole we made fire and kept the fire alive until we roasted the yams for lunch. In addition to foraging for wild fruits, we hunted for rodents and small animals as we went about with our cows. And once in a while we might come across a bee hive in the wild. Harvesting honey was done at night during the dry season. The harvest was literally done by the whole village with straw torches and fires used to drive out the bees from the beehive.

During this period of my life none of us wore any clothing. We went about our daily chores on the farm or in the bushes oblivious that we were stark naked. The first item of any covering worn by boys and girls when they reached puberty were pleated leaves to cover up their frontal nudity. Nothing else was left to the imagination particularly the young girls. The grown men wore loin cloths while the women wore skirts or wrap around cloths around their midriffs or waistlines. Generally we were only concerned with covering up frontal unity and nothing else. The succulent breasts of young women were in full display ogled with no hindrance. The moral norms of our society protected our young women from harassment or groping except at *pito* bars or houses where dirty old men tend to grope the young in jest. The first day I wore a short and shirt was the day I left Duohi on the long journey to my father at Bogoso.

Each household or family enjoyed the fruits of their hard work. The grains and other produce harvested at the end of the season were strictly for the use of that household. During the farming season new farm land might be broken with the help of neighbors from near and far but the produce is not communally owned. Farmers help one another to break new ground and expand old farmlands. The farmer who receives help from his neighbors to break or expand his farm provided them with food and entertainment. It is not uncommon for the farmer's household to brew pito and prepare big meal for this occasion. The communities thus help one another to break ground for new farms, sow seeds, transplant saplings and harvest produce. The favor is returned at a later time when asked by other neighbors.

ATTACK OF MALICIOUS SPIRITS

One day I was at the farm with my uncle and while he was busy I roamed around the surrounding bushes in search of wild fruits. I did not go very far before I spotted a heavy-laden *sisigre* fruit tree. The *sisigre* fruit even when ripe is greenish and the fruit is similar in size to Champaign grapes except that the fruit is almost all seed with very little pulp. I climbed onto the tree and settled comfortably on a branch and began filling my belly with the fruits by sucking and swallowing up the seeds. I discarded the rinds as I sucked the fruity seeds into my mouth.

I do not know how long I sat on the tree gobbling the fruits before I was brought to my senses by sounds of music that sounded so close I was taken aback. The music sounded closer than the village and indicated some sort of festivity but that was atypical of the season and time of day. But the music sounded so close that I cast my eyes around trying to locate the direction of the music. And to my amazement I saw a group of little people drumming and dancing happily beneath the tree on which I sat high up on one of its branches.

The little people materialized from nowhere, they were not present when I climbed up the tree. I did not hear them approach, I only saw and heard them drumming and dancing under the fruit tree. I did not know who they were or where they came from and how they came to be under the tree without my detecting them approach. The rhythms and songs they sang were not familiar to me. They sang *njonjo njo* sprinted about and bumped butts similar to our women bumping butts during dancing. Suddenly I felt apprehensive and fearful and decided to bide my time on the tree until they went whence they came from. Meanwhile I could not resist eating the fruits and continued to gobble up the fruits despite my trepidation. I was afraid to discard the rinds under the tree and held the rinds in the palm of my left hand. My palm soon filled up and some of the rinds fell in their midst. The rinds therefore betrayed my presence to the dwarfs. They looked up to see where the rinds came from and as they looked up our eyes met and locked together. I guess they were as surprised to find me sitting above them as I was when I found them below me.

My presence caused some consternation among them. They pulled me down from my perch on the branch. I do not know how they reached up to where I sat despite their diminutive size. I took to my heels as soon as my feet touched the ground, running as fast as I could for dear life. They gave chase. I ran as fast as I could towards the village, it never occurred to me to seek refuge from my uncle at the farm. I could not outrun or shake them off from my trail. At some point they appeared to be gaining on me, my heart beat wildly with fear and just when it seemed I was within their grasp the ground opened up like some magic. The ground miraculously opened up and literally swallowed me to protect me from my adversaries. But the spirits followed me into the bowels of the earth. We run below the ground towards Duohi, running below ground slowed their advance and kept a distance between us. Then all of a sudden I found myself running on the surface of the earth again and closer to the village. As soon as I entered the unmarked boundary of the village, the dwarfs disappeared just as suddenly as they had appeared under the tree. I guess that they went back into the bush as mysteriously as they had materialized under the tree.

I was innocent and naïve, I did not know the nature of what I saw in the bush. I did not know that the dwarfs or entities were not human. That was the first time I saw dwarfs or people that were that little. The little people after they pulled me down from the tree never touched me again but the close encounter was enough to put me on the sickbed. I became seriously ill and was bedridden for weeks and on the verge of death. The traditional Dagarti custom of consulting oracles and seers uncovered that the cause of my illness was due to a brush with malicious dwarf spirits. I was asked for what I had seen or done and I narrated the story of the confrontation as above. A sacrifice of a lamb and fowls was made to pacify the spirits after which I recovered from whatever ailed me. But the spirits left a physical mark on me that lasted into adulthood before it disappeared. The encounter with the entities, but for the physical mark that was left on my body, would have been consigned to the realm of an overactive imagination, a dream or fairy tale.

The dwarfs were the spirits of idols created for protection of the farms of our family members. The spirits are the guardians and protectors of our farms against spiritual theft or sorcery against farm produce. It is widely believed that a sorcerer or evil person could rob the farmer of the fruits of his labor without physically setting foot on the farm. But at harvest the crops yield very little seed. The spirits represented by the idols prevent such events as when the crops appear buoyant and healthy but yield very little seed at harvest. A number of clay models were installed around the perimeter of every family farm to guard against demonic spirits and sorcerers. When the spirits apprehend an evil eye or one with demonic and wicked intentions they allegedly deformed that individual by transforming him into a hunchback. It was no wonder that hunchbacks were considered wizards and witches and did not elicit much sympathy about their deformities. I was not spiritually apprehended for theft, but the encounter triggered the process of transforming me into a hunchback. The sacrifice pacified them and cured me of the illness that followed, but a small bone spur stuck out in my sternum throughout my infancy and into adulthood that reminded me of the encounter. The bone was a constant reminder of the confrontation with the sprits. The bone was peculiar to me; I never saw any boy or girl with a bone spur sticking out of his/her chest like mine. And that was the only physical reminder of the experience. As much as I wished that the whole experience was a bad dream or nightmare, the bone spur constituted a constant reminder of the beliefs of my tribe and the effects the belief system had on me.

My family and tribesmen believe in the power of sorcery and spiritual theft of produce and take action to prevent sorcery and the results of such sorcery or spiritual thefts. When we experience crop failure under good weather and rainfall condition, the failure was often blamed on sorcery or people with demonic powers that intruded on the farm. The results of such phenomenon become apparent at harvest. One might obtain poor crop yield despite good rainfall and perhaps on land newly broken. So despite fertile soils, good rainfall and robust growth the crop yield might be very disappointing. Under this scenario the corn cobs are empty, sorghum and millet threshes are without seed. The spirits of the idols placed around the perimeter of the farm offer protection against unnatural crop failures that are blamed on sorcery and evil spirits. While growing up I heard stories of such unnatural crop yields that caused famine in one farm while the adjoining farm next door yields a bumper crop. I was an innocent and ignorant and do not know why the spirits took umbrage against me, perhaps it was because I saw them in their element.

The second and third commandments of the bible give credence to the existence of evil spirits and man made spirits, Deuteronomy 5: 7-8 "*You shall have no other gods before me. You shall not make for yourself a carved image-any likeness of anything that is in heaven above or in the earth beneath—*". And Ephesians 6:12 "*For we do not wrestle against flesh and blood, but against principalities, against powers, against the rulers of the darkness of this age, against spiritual hosts of wickedness in the heavenly places*".

If idols and images were just like toys or play things God would not be jealous of such toys. The spirits of the idols were real, the fears that gave rise to them were real. The bible confirms the existence of evil spirits and the struggles of man against such evil spirits and entities. The idols created by man assume spirit forms otherwise God would not be Jealous because both are spirits and we worship them in spirit. My family created idols that assumed the spirit form we imbued with them, that is why man is held to be the image and likeness of God. The idols and their spirits were part of my family's religious practices and thus relatively easier to pacify.

I tried to live down the encounter with the spirits as some kind of bad dream or nightmare, but despite my education and new found religious beliefs I could not eradicate the experience from my memory or explain it away logically. My direct experience of the supernatural was not compatible with logic or religious values. Had I seen bone cartilage sticking out of the chest or sternum of any of my class or playmates I would have concluded that the experience was but a dream and that it never happened. I was curious throughout the primary school to find out whether any of my playmates also had similar bone spurs sticking out of their chest when at play or doing physical training exercises. But despite my observations I never saw a similar bone spur or cartilage sticking out of the chest of any boy or playmate. I have continued to live with an illogical experience I could not explain or understand. The brush with the spirits sunk into my subconscious mind in much the same way that the last days of my birth mother sank into my subconscious mind. The possibility that only one individual of all the people in the household who ate and drank from the same source of poisoned water, was affected by the effects of the poison defies logic but that is part of my life's experience. I have been in awe and amazement of the circumstances surrounding my mother's death, running below ground with spirits fast behind me and never stopped wondering how they happened. Over the years the events dimmed from my active memory from time to time but never forgotten.

In 1958, I returned to the village of my grandmother, the village where I had the brush with the spirits. My uncle Samini was long dead, but that did not prevent me from going to farm with other relatives to enjoy once more the meals cooked at the farm. I walked around the perimeter of the farm and found the familiar clay figurines placed at vantage points around the farm. I looked at the idols and wondered whether the clay idols could come to life and affect me with the same fear and terror as they did about a decade earlier? I was tempted to kick them down from their positions but despite my pompous feeling of superior intellect born of education I could not bring myself to kick down the idols. I could not overcome the fear that behind the clay idols lurked spirits. I also roamed the bushes and ate fruits from the same *sisigre* tree where the spirits ambushed me. By the time I went back on this visit I had only two eyes, I could not see the spirits of a decade earlier even if they were standing by me. Had we not seen one another there would have been no confrontation.

When I came back to Duohi ten years later, I was blinded to spirits. The clay figurines and idols I saw around the perimeter of the farm were just that, figurines. They still held some mystery for me, and though I had only two mortal eyes, I knew from previous experience that behind the idols lurked unseen entities. To complete my return visit to the north, my stepmother and I visited the shrine of our family deity located under a large shady tree at Charia. My mother made a sacrificial offering of thanksgiving with a white sheep to our family deity or ancestral spirits for our safe return from the South of Ghana. During the blood sacrifices I saw and heard one constant phrase or word that never varied; every sacrifice began with paying obeisance or recognition of the almighty God before the ancestral gods or spirits. This practice was very similar to the practice of my western religious practices. But no matter what was said or done during the sacrifice I was more interested in the meat produced by the sacrifice than as a believing participant in traditional worship of ancestral gods and spirits.

TRADIDITIONAL CURES FOR SOME DISEASES

During the one year that I lived with grandma, the seeds of diseases that were probably incubating within me from poor drinking water at Nyagli burst out into the open and wrecked havoc on my health before and after I went school. These diseases and illnesses added to the burden my grandma endured as she struggled to nurse and nurture me and my baby brother. The diseases that affected me most at this time were guinea worm parasites and asthma known as *pewpew* in my dialect. The name is an apt description of the disease by reference to rapid heart beat and breathlessness that characterized my asthma attacks. The asthma and guinea worm infestations became markedly noticeable while I was with grandma.

I did not know the source of our drinking water at Nyagli or Duohi. But at Duohi we drank from the same ponds and watering holes as the cows we herded. The guinea worm spores incubated for about a year after ingestion and broke through the skin when mature. The mature worms formed painful boils and cysts with pus and came out when the boil or carbuncle broke open. The worms while painful and hobbling were not considered a serious handicap but a minor inconvenience. After repeated attacks I learned to handle the worms by delicately pulling out any worm gradually without breaking it to retreat into the body only to fester and reemerge at a later date. Initially I used to tug at it hastily pulling out the worm as soon as I could pinch hold it with the result that it retreated into the skin only to fester again. Overtime I developed expertise handling the worms, some were easily pulled out in one piece and others were pulled out over a number of days, one inch or less at a time. The worm being pulled from my body was wound around a twig gradually until the whole worm came out. When I went to Bogoso I substituted match sticks for twigs.

Every guinea worm attack began with an abscess, boil or cyst and in a few cases carbuncles. The guinea worm attacks began towards the tail end of my life with grandma and continued for about another two years after I went to Bogoso. From about the second grade the guinea worm attacks ceased most probably due to my having access to good clean drinking water at Bogoso. The spores of the parasites purged out of my system by the end of the second grade and I have been free of guinea worms ever since. I guess that the sharing of drinking water with cows at Duohi must have contributed to the infestation of the guinea worm parasite.

On about two or three occasions the worms formed painful carbuncles that did not break open without 'medical' intervention. The carbuncle was cut open with a hot knife to relieve me of the painful pus and worm. The blade of a knife was partially wrapped with sisal twines and heated red hot in a blacksmith furnace. The red hot knife was then used to cut open the swollen tissue. I was treated in this manner on about two occassions, once on my right hand and the second time on my left groin. The fresh wounds were dressed with herbs and shea butter to keep the wound moist to help drain the fluids and pus from the swelling and when drained dressed with herbs until the wound was healed. I was scourged by guinea worms and asthma during infancy. But by second grade I was freed of the twin scourge of asthma and guinea worm. I still have the scars from the cuts on my body, a reminder of local expertise in the treatment of asthma which even modern medicine cannot improve upon or replicate. When I went to Bogoso and had a carbuncle on my foot it was cut open with a hot knife heated in a coal pot instead of a blacksmith furnace. The wounds that

WALK WITH THE DEVIL

resulted from the 'surgeries' were never infected, the heated knife killed all bacteria and germs.

I began having periodic asthma attacks known locally as *pewpew*. During flare ups I gasped for breaths but what triggered the flare ups were not known. The frequency of the flare ups increased overtime and during one severe attack I was rushed to the home of the local witch doctor. And that was the best thing that ever happened to me. The witch doctor ground some burnt herbs into powder. I was held firmly by my uncle and another man in front of the entrance to the house. I guess the entrance to the house was part of the ritual. The witch doctor used a sharp knife to make about four to six incisions on the left side of my chest above the heart. The powder was then massaged into the fresh bleeding incisions. The ritual of massaging the black powder into the fresh wounds cured me of the *pewpew* or asthma. And I have never had another asthma or *pewpew* attack ever since that week.

By the time I went to Bogoso the condition was cured so I never had the opportunity for proper medical diagnosis or evaluation to confirm that *pewpew* was indeed asthma. The treatment despite the mystery that surrounded it was so effective that I never had another attack. But if the condition was asthma then it is most likely that I passed the condition to some of my offspring. Some of my children from two different marriages have been afflicted by asthma in their infancy and by grade one or two the attacks cease. I have passed on the dormant asthma to some of my children. Fortunately the attacks never lasted beyond grade one or two.

RE-UNITED WITH MY FATHER

About one year after Mwinyebo and I went to Duohi, a well-dressed woman showed up at the village one afternoon. As soon as she arrived she cried and wailed and ran helter-skelter around the bushes and fields surrounding the compound houses. She was soon joined in crying and wailing by women of the village. After about half an hour she was consoled, comforted and taken indoors to grandmother's home. The new arrival was my father's first wife and the cries and wails were her belated grieving and mourning for my mother. Among the Dagarti, relatives not at home at the death and funeral of a family member or relative grieve and mourn openly whenever they come back home from their travels. That was exactly what my stepmother did at the home of my grandmother when she arrived from her travels to the south.

After the traditional custom of offering cold water to strangers and visitors, she and grandmother exchanged greetings and pleasantries. They talked about the recent events and the changes in their lives. My grandmother must have informed my stepmother of the causes of mother's death. When the formal exchanges were completed, my stepmother had a private audience with my grandma and uncle alone in the room. At this private meeting she informed grandmother and uncle that she came to take me to my father. My grand mother later broke the good news to me, that was the first time I heard I had another father. And for the next two days until I left Duohi I was the envy of my playmates. It was as if I was going to some place out of this world. Anyway going to the south in the late forties was a big deal in the northern territories just as going overseas to England or America was a big deal in the south. My stepmother, unlike the women of the village, was fully clothed when she came for me, she wore a blouse and wrap around cloth.

FIRST BRUSH WITH CIVILIZATION

Two days later I was given a thorough bath and for the first time in my life, dressed up in a pair of shorts and shirt. We then set out on the first phase of the long journey to Wa through Charia. We walked for about six to eight miles to my stepmother's hometown, Charia where we stayed overnight at my stepmother's family home. The next day, we continued our journey from Charia to Wa, the district capital.

At Wa we transited in the house of my stepmother's older sister, Damnaniho, and her husband, Nasaamu an ex-serviceman. They lived in a large rectangular mud brick compound house adjacent to the market and Lorry Park. In 1949 both the market and Lorry Park were at the same location. My aunt's home was the first house I saw with bright shimmering corrugated iron roofing sheets. The day after our arrival was Wa market day. I strolled into the market to take in the sights of the big market. I smacked my lips and salivated at the delicacies and foods for sale at the market. Nothing else in the market mattered; my attention was focused exclusively on the edible foods and delicacies on display or being prepared. I mingled with the men and women at the market, gawking, salivating and hoping that a vendor or buyer would give me some leftover scraps or *kose*. Without a penny or a cowrie shell on me I could only look but not touch any food at the market. Cowrie shells in the late 1940s circulated side by side with coins or the currency of the country. The only money I was familiar with at this age was the cowrie shell; I was not familiar with currency notes and coins. The cowrie shell has remained as a means of exchange for certain traditional transactions such as dowry or bride price. The traditional requirement that a bride price be returned after divorce or break up has perpetuated the use of cowrie shell as a medium of exchange to date. It is the money that can be stored or saved without a great deal of temptations to spend it and when necessary return it to the groom in the event of dissolution of the marriage.

Among the Dagarti the dowry or bride price may be returned in the event of a divorce and the bride remarries. The circulation of the cowry shell is limited though it is still accepted for payment of some small items and foods at village markets. The limited use of the cowrie shell as money serves as an insurance policy against the use or spending of the pride price. It operates like a savings account over an indefinite period of time. In these modern times the bride's family tends to accept modern currency for greetings and other payments but the cowrie shell remains the preferred currency for payment of the bride price.

Meanwhile, I was so busy feasting my eyes on the delicacies and foods I was oblivious of my surroundings and other activities at the market. The market women and other traders raised their voices to warn me of danger but I took no notice of the cacophony and crescendo of the raised voices around me. Apparently I was in the path of a truck going in the reverse direction. But all my attention was on the edible foods. And when I finally raised my eyes, I froze up! I was petrified at the sight of a smoke belching 'monster' coming towards me. I was overcome with awe and fear; I could not move or run. I was unnerved by the sight of the 'monster' moving toward me I shook with fear like a leaf in the breeze. And as the truck moved closer and closer, the market women yelled louder, hurling insults and invectives at me but I was transfixed to the spot unable to move.

I was shocked at the sight of what appeared to be a big monster with smoke coming out of its nose or mouth. My heart pounded furiously and wildly with fear as I stared at the ferocious beast but I could not run away from it. I had never seen such a massive beast or object. Then suddenly somebody yanked me off my feet and put me aside out of the path of the monster while insulting me as a filthy and ignorant villager. He wracked his knuckles on my head for my stupidity. I watched in horror as the 'monster' slowly passed by. My mouth dried up, I turned around and ran home. I had no idea about what I saw at the market. I did not venture out of the house to the market again until the day we left Wa for Kumasi. I came to terms with my fears. The smoke belching monster was the vehicle that took me to my father. The monster was the first time I ever set eyes on any kind of automobile and I did not know what it was.

THE ROAD TO MY FATHER

Little did I know when I was gripped with fear at the market that one week later I would sit inside the belly of one of those "beasts or monsters" on the road to my father.

The belly of the beast that conveyed me was filled with bags of produce notably maize, sorghum or guinea corn, millet and groundnuts. I sat on bags of guinea corn, maize and peanuts all the way from Wa to Kumasi. The sacks of grains served as my sleeping place for the duration of the journey from Wa to Kumasi. I had very little bladder control, I wetted myself several times a day during the course of the journey. I ate, peed and slept on the bags of produce for as long as the journey lasted. And the journey took like forever. The truck rattled along the rough road until we reached the Black Volta River at Bamboi. The truck arrived at Bamboi after sunset when the pontoon had closed for the day. All the passengers got off the truck and spent the night in the open. My stepmother bought food from food vendors at the riverbank and after the meal I was returned into the truck for the night to continue peeing on the produce that served as my bed.

Throughout the long journey, my baby sister Adjoa was either strapped on my mother's back or seated on her laps. And while I smacked my lips from the fufu and light soup provided for me at the ferry she was literally glued to her mother's breasts. The next morning, the truck drove slowly onto the deck of the pontoon or ferry boat. The adults walked onto the deck of the ferry while I remained in the truck. The immense size of the Black Volta held me spellbound. I had never seen such large body of water in my life, the water appeared to have no end in sight from my position in the truck. I was filled with awe and wonder, as the water seemed to merge with the skies.

We continued our southward journey after we crossed the Black Volta. I did not see much of the road or countryside. Once the truck was in motion I could hardly keep my eyes open. I slept throughout most of the journey except for brief stops for meals at Tachiman. At Tachiman my stepmother again bought some more food for us. We headed for Kumasi none stop from Tachiman. In pre-independence Ghana, the Gold Coast was divided into three administrative regions: the Gold Coast Colony, Ashanti, and Northern Territories. The Black Volta was the boundary between the northern territories and Ashanti region.

We arrived at Kumasi after sunset. I was once again overwhelmed by wonders of the modern world. I could not take my eyes off electric street lamps and the ceiling lamp in the room I slept that night. Within the span of about two weeks, I went from riding on the back of cows or donkey at best to riding in an automobile, from cotton soaked shea butter oil lamps to lights shining like the sun in the sky and in the room. I was blown away by the wonders. I could not take my eyes off the street lights and the ceiling lamp in the room. The transition was too fast for me to comprehend and process within such a short space of time. I was bewildered by the dusty gravel streets at Wa and amazed at the bitumen sealed roads at Kumasi. My jaw dropped when I saw bitumen paved roads with cars and trucks zipping along at high speeds in all directions. We spent one night at the home of a family member at Kumasi. I did not know whether I was dreaming or seeing those wonders for real.

The next day we boarded a smaller mummy truck for the final phase of our journey to Bogoso. The mummy trucks were the passenger carrying vehicles of the Gold Coast. The passenger truck cabins were made of wood and width length timber planks served as seats. The planks were not bolted to the frame of the trucks so the passengers were tossed up and down as the trucks bopped along the rough roads of the Gold Coast. Bedford trucks were the preferred passenger and cargo trucks in the south while large Comer trucks were the vehicles that conveyed goods and people to and from the north and within the northern territories of the Gold Coast. Whether the passengers were conveyed from the north or within the south, cargo was packed on the floors and tail boards of the trucks and the passengers sat on the planks above the cargo. There was very little leg room to stretch during travel because of the way the trucks were loaded. Passenger travel was therefore very uncomfortable in the Gold Coast to say the least.

MY PARENTS WENT TO KUMASI ON FOOT

My father and stepmother walked from Wa to Kumasi on their maiden journey together as a couple. They took over two weeks to make the trip walking night and day with minimal rest between Wa and Kumasi. They walked along the same road plied by the trucks but were too scared to ride on one. While they walked along the road they avoided making any contact with the trucks because they considered them as dangerous monstrous beasts.

At this period in the development of the Gold Coast and the northern territories in particular vehicular transportation was probably in its infancy and not widespread. Allegations and rumors abounded of the diabolic powers of the 'monsters' on the roads. These allegations and rumors therefore influenced my parents from venturing near any vehicle; they walked more than two hundred fifty miles instead of travelling comfortably in one of the new trappings of modern civilization. One of the unfounded allegations about the automobile was that the lamp could cause blindness. As such during the night when my parents saw the light beams of a truck from afar they ran and hid in the bush until the vehicle passed by. And as the roar of the trucks got closer they shut their eyes tight lest they see the light and go blind.

I guess they really thought that the vehicles were living breathing monsters. They avoided the vehicles by day and by night. During the day they hid behind trees and watched the trucks go by from afar. And when they smelled the exhaust fumes they held their noses exclaiming how awful the smell of the fart or flatulence of the beast was. I was petrified in the market when I saw a truck for the first time at age five or thereabout, my parents before me, thought that the trucks were living things capable of doing harm or capable of flatulence. They were filled with fear and trepidation of the automobile; I was filled with awe and wonder on my first journey.

MY FATHER'S TRADE

My father on his first solo trip to the South went to Obuasi, the gold mining town in the Ashanti region. He took a job as a mine laborer. But he worked at his new job for only one day and run away from the mines not bothering to collect his wages for the one day he worked. He was scared out of his wits when he was transported to the bowel of the earth to hew the rocks or whatever assignment he had for that day. When he came up at the end of the day he packed his bags and baggage and left Obuasi. He headed west towards the cocoa growing areas of the present day western region or Gold Coast Colony in the thirties and forties before independence. He settled at Hiawa as a farmhand or sharecropper on a cocoa farm. It was at Hiawa that he brought down his first wife, my stepmother and later my birth mother. I have no idea how long my mother lived with my father at Hiawa before I was born. My father relocated to Bogoso, a mining town located only about twenty miles west of Hiawa, after my mother left him. At Bogoso, my father finally found his calling as a trader in northern apparels and followed this profession for the rest of his life. He traded in northern attires and clothes. He bought woven cotton cloths and smocks from the north and sold them to northerners working in the mining towns and various population centers. He began his trading activities at Bogoso and gradually extended his reach to Tarkwa, Abosso, Prestea, Obuasi, Sekondi and Takoradi.

MOTHER ABANDONED FATHER

My birth mother walked out on my father when I was barely six months old. She gave hints of her intention to walk away from the marriage by bestowing on me a proverb for a new name. The name she gave me was *Apuru* loosely translated meant buds or flower buds. She openly called me by my new name but nobody got the hint or the meaning behind the new name and if my father did, he did not show it or considered it serious. It was her way of telling my father that while he had seen the buds he will not eat of the fruit again. I was given this new name long past the customary or traditional periods for bestowing names on new born children. The new name was a name only my mother could like and thus it did not stick. And I never knew I had another name until when I reunited with my father after her death. The meaning and significance of *Apuru* became apparent only after she departed, but by then, it was too late.

My mother's untimely death brought me back to my father. Until I met my father at Bogoso I did not know that the man I had known as my father was not my real father. The facts surrounding the divorce of my mother from my father are murky. Neither my father nor my stepmother was able to give me any definitive reason for the divorce, maybe there was none. They traded allegations against one another. My father blamed the 'insane jealousy' of my stepmother as the leading cause or instigator of the divorce. According to father my stepmother hounded my mother till she could take it no more and walked away. My stepmother on her part thought that the divorce was more or less due to the age difference between my father and my mother. She denied ever being envious or jealous of my mother. She told me that it was she, who after all betrothed my mother to my father as his second wife. She could not therefore have been envious or jealous of the woman she had personally courted for her husband. Or did she get a buyers remorse after my mother became my father's second wife. They were close family members, sisters according to our extended family relationships. She could not have been jealous or envious of her own sister. My mother simply became disenchanted with marriage to a man who was old enough to be her father. Some of her step children were as old as she was. If that was the case, it was rare in our tribe and my mother must have been years ahead of her time.

I was not able to pry from my father and stepmother how long my mother was married to my father. I do not know how many children my mother had with my father before I was born. And I do not know the number of children she had with my stepfather before Mwinyebo. For some unknown reason, my father and stepmother never said anything else about my mother beyond the cause of her walk out from them. They kept their opinions about my mother to themselves. They both stuck to their version of the cause of my mother leaving her matrimonial home. That is all I know about my birth mother beyond her sickness and death.

My father and stepmother did not like talking about my mother as such I never knew that she had another name other than Posaa. She was born on a rainy day and the name Posaa was a nickname based on the weather conditions on the day she was born. I learned about my mother's given name in 1968 when I met a distant relative from Nyagli at Takoradi. The relative was introduced to me by my father while I was on vacation during my first year at college. This relative was my sister by extended family relations informed me about my mother's given name of Banombo. She was also the only person I ever met from Nyagli since I was taken to Duohi. She was the first person apart from my parents, my uncle and aunt who knew my mother during her lifetime. I decided to honor the memory of my mother by naming my first baby girl after her if and when I had a girl. I fulfilled that promise seven years later; I named my first daughter, Banombo, after the given name of my late mother.

My father blamed the untimely death of my mother on his first wife. He exacted his revenge against my stepmother by repeating the mistake of my mother; he walked out on his first wife and children for his third young wife. My father did not have a bank or savings account, he kept his money in nooks and crannies of the room but his favorite hiding place was the straw mattress. While he was away from Bogoso for more than one year, mother found money hidden in the mattress and used some of that money to care for his own children. And for that he accused her of theft and threw her out of the room they shared together.

VISIONS OF A MOTHER

My stepmother loved me as much as any of her own children. She did all she could to bring me up to be an honorable and honest citizen and that I think she succeeded. She instilled in me the qualities of honesty and hard work from her own example. Over time the memory of my mother began to fade, replaced by the memories of my prevailing life with my step mother. But I saw a series of visions including a woman in skirt that brought back memories of my mother just when she began fading into the background. The vision of the woman in a skirt was so real I did not know she was not real. I was so naïve and ignorant that sometimes I could not distinguish between human beings from spirit beings. Some of these visions appeared lifelike I spoke to them unaware I was seeing things. I usually left them with a shrug as they never responded to any queries. One night when I woke up to urinate I saw a woman in skirt like my mother sitting pensively on a stool behind the door in our room. I stood before her and asked her why she was sitting down instead of being in bed. She said nothing so I went out and by the time I came back she was not there again. I was later informed by my stepmother that the entities were the spirits of our ancestors. The vision of the woman in skirt persisted in my memory years after I saw it, I came to the conclusion that perhaps the vision of the woman was the image of my mother when she was in good health. I naively called the 'woman' mother when I saw it. Thus the visions reinforced the memory of my mother. At the time I saw the series of visions I was still in my formative years and the visions did not strike a chord as visions of my mother till years later. The vision of a woman in skirt gave me another image of my mother different from the picture of her corpse in repose at the village square.

My stepmother worked hard to endear herself to me so as to ease the pain and trauma of loosing my mother at such an early age. She consoled me by telling me that I was as much her child just as I was my birth mother's child. She inferred that had my mother been alive she could have gotten custody of me from my mother by virtue of their relationship. My stepmother encouraged and insisted that I call her 'mother' instead of stepmother. Initially I resisted the pressure to call another woman as my mother, but over time I called her mother like the rest of my half siblings without more. Even though I resisted initially, eventually I followed my siblings and automatically called her my mother.

FIRST YEAR AT SCHOOL

A few months after my arrival at Bogoso, I started first year at the same Catholic school where Cecilia was a student. I went to class one in January 1950; I had only been at Bogoso for barely three or four months and therefore spoke only my native dialect. I did not speak Fanti, the language of instruction between class one and three, but I started learning the alphabets and the rudiments of writing like every pupil. Thus I learned both the Fanti and English alphabets at the same time with the native Fanti speakers. And by time I was in class four in the upper primary school, I spoke Fanti as fluently as any Fanti speaker without accent. By the fifth grade, I was good enough to help some of my classmates to read and write their own native dialect, Fanti. Thus if I had my own way bilingual education would be open to all pupils irrespective of language or dialect. I was afraid of going to school because of fear from the exaggerated tales of corporal punishments, but once I started I loved it. I liked school during the first year so much so that initially I was often dissuaded from going to school on Saturdays because I did not know the difference between weekdays and weekends.

At the time of my enrollment, I spoke only my dialect. Thus I was at a disadvantage when I started classes in the first grade but I spoke and understood Fanti before the year ended. Cecilia was happy to have a member of her family enrolled at the same school. Though I never saw or interacted with her on the campus. She was my fist teacher, she tutored me at home before and after I went to school. And on the day I entered the first grade, I already knew the alphabets and numbers. Thus even though I could not speak Fanti I was the top student in the first grade class.

I was scared before I went to school the first day a because of widespread stories about corporal punishments administered by sadistic teachers against pupils, but I was happy to put on my new khaki school uniform. I was provided a new pair of khaki shorts and shirt for my first day of school. I could not help admiring myself in my new school uniform as I was marched to school on the first day.

The school uniform was made by a local tailor from khaki fabric provided by my father. Custom tailoring was the way the general public got our clothes. Ready made clothes were generally worn by the rich while the rest of us depended on custom made clothes by the local tailor. We bought the fabrics and the local tailor or seamstress measured, cut and made the clothes to fit.

On arriving at school on the first day my father and I were taken to the head teacher's office. The head teacher took my height against a scale on the wall; next, he asked me to stretch my right hand over my head to touch my left ear. My right hand touched my ear and this was the indication that I was old enough to be in school. Stretching the hand to touch the opposite ear was the standard method of determining who was mature enough for admission to school. After these initial proceedings the head teacher then opened a large notebook and entered my particulars; my name, age, father and mother's name. The notebook was the admissions register into which every pupil's name and other particulars were entered for posterity. The formalities completed, I was introduced to my new class

I was the second child of my father to ever go to school and the first one who was voluntarily sent to school. None of my older brothers and sisters, with the exception of Cecilia, ever went to school. Cecilia grew up at Bogoso and the sight of her playmates going to school was the impetus that forced her to coerce her mother to send her to school when she was past puberty. When I first met Cecilia in 1949, she was already a teenager in the upper primary school class five or six. Cecilia must have paved the way for me to follow her into school.

NEW FAMILY AT BOGOSO

Bogoso was unlike any place I had ever known. The town had no electric lights or bitumen paved streets but it was heaven compared to Duohi or Nyagli. The paved streets and electric lights of Kumasi that jaded me for one night soon faded from memory. My family lived in one room typical of single room occupancies of most families throughout the Gold Coast. We lived in a large rectangular compound house containing about ten rooms and as such ten other families.

The paved concrete courtyard was the first play ground I ever played on that was not in the dust or gravel. The sturdy construction of the compound house and elaborate tongue and grooved timber ceiling of our room was the most beautiful I ever saw. There was nothing comparable to it from my home at Nyagli or Duohi. The mud ceiling of my grandmother's room consisted of twigs and mud while the ceiling of our room at Bogoso was polished tongue and groove hardwood. Compared to the mud houses in which I was raised, this house was beyond my imagination for its beauty and elegance. As I became accustomed to my new surroundings I saw how ordinary our house was, but it was definitely impressive when I saw it the first time. I was particularly impressed with a toilet in the house; I did not have to go to the bush to ease myself. The toilet was a bucket removable toilet but that was my introduction to domestic or house toilets. That was a novel and unknown concept to me considering my background from villages in the northern territories.

For the two years that my father was home, we were good companions. We used to walk to the banks of the giver Bogo to do our laundry together, a distance of about two miles from home. At the river we washed our clothes in the water atop a crop of boulders using sticks as mallets to assist in washing large and soiled clothes. We carried the wet clothes back to the house to dry. My father made some of the smocks and other clothes he sold by himself out of strips of woven cotton fabrics. He sewed the strips of cloth into the desired clothes with a needle and thread. When he made the clothes I held the edges of the cloths while he stitched them together. He manually made clothes for both men and women in this laborious manner. He was good with the needle and thread.

The cordial relationship between my father and I came to an end when he went on an extended business trip that lasted for more than one year and he disappeared only a few days after he returned. His departure left a hole in my heart that my mother could not fill despite all her efforts.

DEPRIVED OF 'SPIRIT SEEING' EYES

By the time I arrived at Bogoso with my stepmother, my father was already aware of my encounter with malicious spirits at Duohi. My father was apprehensive of the consequences of seeing beyond the veil of darkness people with demonic spirits, who practiced their nefarious deeds beyond the prying eyes of ordinary human beings. Such people with demonic and malevolent spirits will like to keep their secrets from their fellow men and would do everything within their powers to prevent exposure by an ignorant and innocent child with 'seeing eyes'. Another encounter with evil spirits like what happened at Duohi could kill me. His fears were that while I could 'see' I had no complementary esoteric powers to protect me from the powers of sorcerers and those with demonic and malevolent spirits. But for the intervention of the head of family and the fact that the spirits were connected with our family I might have been killed by the spirits at Duohi. My father therefore sought to exorcise the 'seeing eyes' from me to prevent any similar accidental encounters with other worldly entities or demonic and malicious individuals with malevolent spirits.

My father brought back from one of his frequent business trips some roots and herbs. He brewed the mixture of herbs and roots in his ablution kettle, cooled the brew overnight and gave me a cupful to drink first thing in the morning while I was seated on his prayer mat. As soon as I drank the bitter concoction, I threw up all the contents of my stomach. He repeated the ritual the next day; he sat me down on his prayer mat again and forced me to drink another cupful of the bitter brew. I threw up for the second time and the ritual was repeated the third day. And the third time was the charm; I did not throw up after drinking the concoction or potion on the third day. That was also the last time my father gave me the bitter brew to drink. And that was all it took for me to lose the spirit sight gradually over a number of years. I did not know at the time that the purpose of the brew or concoction was to close my "spirit seeing eyes" until years after the fact. The 'seeing eye' faded gradually over a number of years until I was left with nothing but the two regular mortal eyes like everybody else.

It was not immediately apparent but the 'seeing eye' began fading from the day I drank the bitter brew and did not throw up. The loss of the 'seeing eye' was a blessing in disguise; it freed me from fears of the dark and cowering from what I could see in the dark but which was not seen by others. The loss of the sight made me feel like any normal child of my age. I used to cower at night from the spirits or entities I saw in our room and in the courtyard. I was always terrified from the entities I saw around the house particularly during dark nights. I freaked out at night when I saw an entity take a step away from its usual place of sentry. But a few years after I drank the bitter concoction, the haunting and unpleasant experience of seeing spirit entities gradually came to an end.

I used to see spirit entities in two forms, shadow and dark ghostly figures and visions with such clarity they were indistinguishable from mortal physical beings. The most common forms were shadows or figures under cloak of darkness. But on a few occasions I saw entities that appeared as clear as mortal beings. These did not normally frighten me like the dark shadowy figures. On one or two occasions I spoke to the spirits unaware they were not human. On one particular occasion I woke up to pee at night and saw a woman sitting on a stool behind the door. I asked my 'mother' what she was doing behind the door. I went to bed thinking nothing more of it. During the day I asked my mother again what she was doing behind the door during the night and refused to speak to me when I talked to her. It was then that she told me that she was not the person I saw during the night because she did not get up until the time she woke up to start preparing her catering meals. I lost the 'seeing eye' completely when I was rather mature enough to discern the difference between human beings from spirit beings.

When I grew up I regretted the loss of the spirit-seeing eye, and wished my father had never deprived me of the 'eye'. But it never occurred to me to ask my father whether he could undo whatever he did to deprive me of the spirit-seeing eye during my infancy. I lived with an experience and knowledge of a past that I cannot authenticate. I pursued spiritual self awareness but my best spiritual moments never captured the magic of my infancy; the magic that used to scare me. But my experience in the spiritual realm as an adult gave me an appreciation of the fears of my father.

SIBLINGS FROM DIFFERENT MOTHERS

At Bogoso I soon discovered that Cecilia and Adjoa were not my only siblings, I had siblings who were older than Cecilia. Within a period of about two to three years I met all my other older siblings, a brother and two older married sisters. I was the second youngest child of my family at the time. Some of my older half brothers and sisters were as old as my mother and had children of my age group. None of my older brothers and sisters had ever seen the four corners of a classroom. And with the exception of Cecilia all my older brothers and sisters grew up at home in the northern territories. It appeared that most of them were born before my father began his adventures seeking greener pastures in Southern Ghana. Cecilia on the other hand grew up partially at Tachiman and Bogoso; she was the only sibling who was in school when I arrived.

Adjoa or Vida was the baby of the family. A few years after arriving at Bogoso my oldest sister, Mariama brought down her daughter, Bazoora, to live with us. Bazoora and I were of similar age but she was already betrothed to a man, this was typical of girls in northern territories. Bazoora used to be haunted by spirits at night and to protect her from haunting spirits she was brought to Bogoso. Her parents assumed that with a change of environment the haunting might end. But the haunting continued unabated at Bogoso. She was haunted at irregular or random intervals at night while we were all asleep. She was allegedly haunted by a pair of spirits, male and female. If the story we were told as children could be believed, the male spirit was perhaps a pedophile who loved Bazoora and that made his female companion jealous of Bazoora. The female companion thus took her ire and frustrations on Bazoora by poking her eyes with her fingers whether to make her blind or disfigure her we never knew. But the effect was that Bazoora's eyes on the nights she came under attack were red bloodshot. We often kept vigil with her while she writhed in pain from the spirit attacks. My mother used to look on helplessly while she was tormented; her only remedy was to burn incense. I do not know whether the incense was helpful because the torments usually ended around dawn or towards daybreak. As Bazoora grew older the haunting became fewer and far between and eventually came to an end. Bazoora was taken back to her betrothed husband in the north as a child bride at around the age of ten.

When I was in class three, my older brother Mumuni came down from the north. After a brief stay with the family, he left to work in one of the gold mines located around the Tarkwa urban area. Our house was like a rest house or transit stop for our close and distant family members' en-route to other towns in the then Gold Coast Colony. Their destinations were mostly the gold mining towns of Prestea, Tarkwa, Abosso, or twin port town of Sekondi-Takoradi. Our roomy house used to overflow with visiting family members that spilled into the courtyard on warm nights. We literally slept on top of one another on the hard cement floor and sometimes spilled into the concrete courtyard.

I had an attitude toward my new baby sister when I became part of the family. Although I traveled with her from Wa to Bogoso, I could not immediately accept her as my sister on the same footing as Mwinyebo, the brother I left behind. He had a special place in my heart and I did not want Adjoa to replace him in my heart. My older sister, Cecilia, had no such qualms or misgivings about me. So were the other older brothers and sisters when they met me; they accepted me with open arms as if they had known me all my life. They showed no partiality between me and the other siblings.

My stepmother was the person who brought me from the north. But when we reached Bogoso our relations was frosty and tense at the beginning. She was eager for me to get over the loss of my mother by asking me to refer to her as my mother instead of stepmother. But I was not quite ready to refer to another woman as my mother, I was old enough to know the difference between mother and stepmother. The request to refer to her as mother was therefore very difficult to accept initially. I could not transfer the affections of my mother to my step mother on short notice. I resented being forced or pressured to forget my mother. The death of my mother did give to my stepmother the right to erase her memory from my mind. I did not comply with the request. I loved my mother and the little brother I left behind and those were the memories I held dear to my heart. Our relations would have evolved naturally to mother child relationship without any animosity or resentment if my stepmother had not made any attempts to hasten the process of development.

She impressed upon me that she and my mother were sisters, but I wondered why she brought only me and not Mwinyebo who needed nurturing more than me. When I asked for an explanation for insisting I call her my mother, she explained that my mother was her baby sister. And had my mother not passed away she would have had the same parental rights over me as the children of her own womb. I was not convinced or satisfied with her explanation because I knew nothing about her until the day I saw her at Duohi. However, as time went by I fell in line with how my sisters called her and also referred to her as my mother instinctively without thinking or reflecting over how I called her.

In the same way, I found it difficult to accept my new baby sister, Adjoa. The baby brother I left behind with my grandmother was still in my heart. It was not easy to accommodate more than one sibling in my heart; I had space in my heart for only Mwinyebo, Adjoa was an usurper and I could not let that happen. I needed time to get used to my new surroundings and relationships instead of being rushed against my will. My stepmother was moving too fast for me to adjust to my new reality, my new family was now my only family. That rush bred some resentment towards my stepmother and sisters. But as time went on, my heart opened up to accept my new siblings in the same way that I loved Mwinyebo. And finally when I lost Mwinyebo through a sake bite at Duohi, they were all I had. My worldview changed from the day I received the message that my baby brother was dead, Adjoa became my only younger sibling. We bonded and lost all vestiges of being born by different mothers.

I guess it is natural for a mother to have some partiality towards their youngest child or what we know as the 'last born'. I did not like the partiality or pampering Adjoa received from her mother as the youngest child or last born. I resented Adjoa for the junk food we all craved but that was provided only to her. Cecilia and I ate the regular family meals while Adjoa subsisted on breast milk and watery tea and bread with some drops of evaporated milk. My older sister Cecilia and I looked on every night, salivating while our little bratty sister Adjoa was fed tea and bread. We scrambled for the crumbs and the leftovers when she was done. Little did I know that mother was not doing her any favors by feeding her sugary tea and bread.

Adjoa was so pampered that she could not be weaned from breast milk before age six. Indeed when she began grade one she used to come home at lunch time to suck breast milk. The tea and bread was about the only solid food she ate apart from breast milk. By the date she went to school her teeth were rotted and full of cavities from all the sweet teas she drank. I would have traded the rotted teeth for a bite of bread dipped in a cup of warm spicy tea. The tea was brewed in our saucepan as such the tea had a peppery and spicy taste. Similarly our cocoa drinks had the same peppery and spicy taste. The peppery and spicy taste in our beverages was of little consequence to us. We yearned to have the same privilege as our younger sister. So I was naturally jealous of her even if what she ate was not healthy. If looks could kill, Cecilia and I would have killed her with our envious looks.

MASTERING HOME TOILET

Having a toilet in a house was a new experience. The tenants were required to sit on the wooden box over the bucket of latrine so as to keep the box clean. Sitting on a toilet was a tall order for me, I was accustomed to squatting when I went to toilet in the bushes as such I could not keep up with the request. I knew of only one way to answer nature's call and that was to squat. I was impressed with a toilet in the house, but I could not sit and defecate when I went to toilet. The major problem I faced whenever I went to toilet was how to clean up after defecating. In my village I went to toilet in the bush I cleaned up with whatever came in handy such as leaves, twigs, corncobs or even a stone. At Bogoso I was required to clean up with paper. The most common source of paper used for toilet were newspapers and toilet rolls for the well heeled. My parents were illiterates who neither read newspapers nor bought toilet roll so I used whatever I could lay hands on before I stepped into the toilet.

Whenever I visited the toilet without a stick, twig, or corncob, I cleaned my butt on the doorjamb. The caretaker of the house frequently painted over the feces on the jamb but no sooner had he finished with the paint work than I defaced the freshly painted surface with fresh feces. The caretaker suspected that I was the culprit but he could not prove it. So he set a trap that caught me red handed. He painted the doorjamb with coal tar one afternoon and kept a secret vigil for the culprit. In no time at all he caught me with fresh tar on my butt and feces on the doorjamb. Though he caught me red-handed I refused to admit that I was the source of the fresh feces on the doorjamb. I was a resourceful liar, I told Mr. Acheampong, the caretaker that I got the fresh paint on my butt by leaning against the doorjamb unaware that it was freshly painted. I stuck to my story line, and never wavered from it.

CATERING FOR MINE WORKERS

My mother's main occupation was a caterer principally for mine workers of northern origin. She worked about six days a week and as time went by, I came to appreciate her hard work in caring for us. Typically her workday began at around two or three o'clock in the morning. She woke up at that hour to start preparing the meals she sold to the mine workers at daybreak. Her main fare was *konkonte* served with either peanut butter or palm nut soup mixed with fresh or dry okra. She preferred smoked and dry fish in her soups because they did not break up into bits during cooking as compared to fresh fish. Konkonte was a cassava paste prepared from dried cassava flour. When she was done we had our share while still piping hot before we carried the konkonte to the mine compound or campus for sale.

The whole family trooped behind her up to the top of the hill overlooking Bogoso where the gold mine was located. It was a family business and we all did our part to advance the business. Cecilia used to wake up with mommy to help her with the preparation and when done carried the hot soup while mother carried the konkonte and I used to carry the bowls and ladles. We normally left before daybreak and arrived at the mine when the night workers were preparing to leave and the day workers were arriving. The market was therefore the meeting grounds of the night and day shift workers in the morning before the start of their day respectively. The food under normal circumstances sold out before sunrise and we returned home to prepare for school on time.

Cecilia left for Kumasi a few years later to continue her education at a large urban center. It then fell on me to pick up her duties. I carried the soup and sold any leftovers later at the night market on the street in front of our house. After 1955 when the mine operations began to wound down, the mop up labor force that was wounding down the closure of the mine was no longer enough to buy all the food my mother prepared. I used to sell the leftovers at night and what I could not sell I gave away to some of my class and schoolmates who hung with me at the night market.

CRAVING FOR MEAT

After father left home meat became very rare in our meals. My mother was in the catering business so we never lacked food at home. On the contrary, we were bored to death eating the same food day in day out. We ate *konkonte* for breakfast and fufu for lunch and leftover *konkonte* again for dinner. If variety is the spice of life then we certainly lacked any variety or spice in our diet. We cheered on the rare occasions we had meat in our meal. Generally we ate cheap; my mother used inexpensive ingredients and condiments to prepare our soups.

When I arrived at Bogoso I did not have discriminating taste and ate whatever was set before me with relish. I had a big and insatiable appetite, I did not know when to say 'I've had enough'. I stopped eating only when the plate was empty. My stepmother speculated that I had an insatiable appetite because I was given some herbal potions to eat whatever was set before me without discrimination so as to ensure my survival after the death of my mother. The potions were allegedly given to me by my grandmother at Duohi. However by my fourth year at Bogoso the stimulant must have worn off and I began to have a discerning taste with preference for some particular foods.

I yearned for meats but since my mother could not satisfy my craving for meats I pilfered from the cooking pots of our neighbors with whom we shared a common kitchen. I stole the meats while they were on fire boiling hot. I slipped into the kitchen when nobody was in the courtyard to catch me in the act. I stared at the sauce or soup bubbling in the boiling pot and as soon as I saw a piece of meat boil up to the surface I dipped my fingers into the boiling pot, plucked up the meat and put it into my mouth while steaming hot if perchance I heard any outside noise; otherwise I ran with my prize to the backyard to do justice to it. And when done I would come back and repeat the process over and over again until I had my fill and the pot almost empty. My victim was caught in a bewildering dilemma, the pot was on fire boiling but almost empty of

57

the meats. They were usually stumped, unable to explain how the meats vanished from the boiling pots or saucepans.

I progressed from pilfering to cooking my own soups to satisfy my cravings. I scavenged for scraps of meats and bones from the floor of the butcher's shop at the market. Sometimes a kind hearted butcher on seeing me gathering bones and scraps of meat from the floor gave me a piece of meat to add to my collection. From the butchers shop I went next to the vegetable stalls to scavenge for peppers, tomatoes, garden eggs and other ingredients. On occasions I arrived at the vegetable stalls just when trucks from the fishing towns along the coast were arriving with cargo of fresh and smoked fish at the market for sale. I loitered around the trucks and at the least opportunity separated a piece of fish from the basket.

I was an enigma to the market women and traders. Ghanaians of the 1950's were very superstitious. We were a superstitious society who believed that sometimes the gods came among us disguised as filthy individuals. I was very filthy and smelled like a skunk, I rarely took a bath. But instead of being shunned or berated for being filthy they literally accepted and entertained me. The traders indulged me with good fish and vegetables for fear I was a god in disguise out to test their kindness and generosity or humanity. I mingled around the fish mongers while the baskets of fish were being unloaded and occasionally I succeeded to pull out a fish through the netting covering the baskets. I was never berated for thieving or poaching from the baskets.

I played cook with my younger sister at the backyard using the fish, meats and other ingredients and condiments I scavenged from the market. I prepared real sauces or what is popularly known as light soup in Ghana with discarded tins of canned foods on fires made with firewood. As time went on I progressed from using tins to actual cooking utensils but always made sure the cooking pots were cleaned and returned to their place before mother came home. I confined my cooking games to only light soups that satisfied my appetite for meat without the need for anything else. On one occasion my mother berated me for wasting good meat that was presented to me at the market by a butcher instead of contributing it towards the family meal.

I gained cooking skill that came in handy years later when I began life as a bachelor teacher at Tamale in the early 1960's. As a young bachelor I taught some of my bachelor friends to cook simple meals, skills they did not have. Boys of northern Ghana were not usually involved in housework as such most young bachelor's began life with very little cooking skills. I wrote recipes or the most basic directions to guide my friends to cook such simple meals like rice and stew. There were no books on cooking at Tamale in the 1960s.

THE EXTENDED FAMILY

The extended family system was like an insurance system of goodwill that the members drew in times of difficulties and need. Our house at Bogoso was like the home of the tribal head of family transplanted from the north to Bogoso, everybody was welcome as long as you spoke Dagare, no matter how close or distant the relations. Nobody was ever turned away from our door. Our home was the first 'port of call' where they received information about the location of other family members scattered around the various job centers. Our home was a magnet for our tribesmen visiting the south from the north because my father was one of the early pioneers who left the north in search of greener pastures in the south. Our tribesmen tended to congregate at centers with supporting tribal networks. The support network provided sustenance and guidance until the new arrival could stand on his own two feet. We took expectations of support from one another for granted.

I benefitted greatly from the support of other family members both as a child and as a young adult before I became financially independent. I imposed myself upon any person who was said to be a relative as a matter of course whether I knew them personally or not. All I had to do was find the location and name of the relative no matter how distant to make that person's home my home. I introduced myself as the son of Gornah Ali and expected to be accepted without more. My father was widely known and invoking his name brought unquestioned acceptance and hospitality. I took the hospitality from our family and tribesmen for granted and I was never disappointed.

During the two to three years I was at Tarkwa as a student I was sustained by the generosity and kindness of the extended family members from all walks of life against the intransigence of my father in parting with money because of his propensity for stinginess. I depended on my disparate family members for pocket money and sustenance during weekends and on holidays. The pocket money I got from various family members combined with monies from odd jobs helped me to pay for my school fees at certain crucial times during the school year. I politely solicited for money from relatives without irking them and combined what I was given with savings from my 'piggy bank' to pay my school fees when sent away from school for not paying the fees.

BURNED IN HOT ASHES

The vibrant life at Bogoso began to fray when the gold mines, the lifeblood of the town, began to wind down until it finally closed in 1955. Our tenement or roomy house was a microcosm of the downturn in the fortunes of Bogoso. The neighbors I met when I came to Bogoso in the latter part of 1949 had left. The original co-tenants left town long before the mines officially closed down. The exodus began as soon as it became apparent that the gold mines planned to shut down within a few years. My family was the last of the original tenants to leave Bogoso in 1957, two years after the mines closed down officially. The tenants I met when I came to Bogoso in 1949 gave way to new set of tenants who did not depend on the mines for their livelihood. They were self-employed or gainfully employed in other occupations. Among the new batch of tenants were Kwame Atta and Mamma Ewule. Kwame Atta was a self-employed taxi driver and Mamma Ewule was a farmer who later became a pastor of a spiritual church called Nakaba. The church proliferated in the south west among mostly the Nzemah people. The constant stream of family members and tribesmen passing through our home to other job centers dwindled to a trickle.

During the boom times, one of our next-door neighbors sun dried his soft beautiful blankets in the courtyard. He accidently discarded money that was saved or stored under the blankets. I found a bundle of beautiful colorful papers in the courtyard. I picked and showed the colorful papers to my mother not knowing what it was and she asked me to put it in the room. After putting it down I went back into the courtyard looking for more colorful papers, I found another beautiful paper and added it to the bundle in the room. I was less than two years removed from my village and I did not know that the colorful papers were money. I was not yet familiar currency notes, I knew money only as coins or cowrie shells. My mother later told me that the bundle was money worth more than £10.00 (ten pounds) and warned me to keep my mouth shut. A short time later I saw the tenant searching frantically around the courtyard for the bundle. The tenant literally turned the courtyard upside down in his effort to find the bundle of money he had lost. Every tenant in the house, including my mother, denied seeing any money in the courtyard. Ten pounds sterling (£10.00) was a lot of money in the Gold Coast of the early 1950's this tenant must have lost a fortune and he did not take it lying down.

My superstitious mother was apprehensive and ambivalent about the find, she was in a dilemma whether to return or keep it. She decided to consult the oracles or ancestral spirits for advise. She turned over the money to one of our relatives, Bomboden, to consult oracles and seers for advice on the appropriate course of action to take. Bomboden was a good for nothing relative and when he left home with the money he did not come back for another three or four months. And when he came back he was empty handed. The money was gone; mother kicked herself but there was very little she could do about it. It was then she told me unflattering stories about Bomboden, he was a notorious thief back home in the north. That at one time the village elders bound him to a stake for robbery. Mother thought that he had turned over a new leaf in the south but she knew better after the incident. My mother consulted a seer and performed the recommended sacrifice to ward off the effects of any curse by the victim.

A few weeks after I found the money, I was sent to the milling station across from the lorry park with a basin of desiccated dry cassava to mill into konkonte flour, the main ingredient for *konkonte*. The milling station served the whole of Bogoso Township. It was the place where the residents ground corn into flour and milled rice after harvest. The husks of milled rice was discarded around the mill houses and incinerated from time to time.

When the kids met there we tended to horse around before departing with our head loads of flour. When I finished grinding the *konkonte* flour, I put down my head load of flour on the ground in front of the mill house and joined a group of boys playing kick ball. After a few minutes of playing kickball, we became bored and sought for more excitement. One of the boys threw down a challenge daring anybody who could jump over a small mound of ashes beside the mill house. The mound of ashes appeared small and harmless. There was nothing to indicate that it was warm or hot beneath the calm surface. I accepted the challenge with confidence, I was certain I could jump over the mound in one leap. Although I have never tried to do any long jump but I was sure I could jump over the mound of ashes in one leap. I sized up the heap, took a few steps backward, and sprinted towards the mound at full speed like a long jumper and when I got to my target I jumped as hard and high as I could but I landed only about three or four from the edge of the mound of ashes.

As soon as I landed I noticed that the harmless mound was very hot. But instead of jumping back out I foolishly continued and plowed through the ashes to the end. While I leapt up and down in the hot ashes I cried and wailed and did not stop crying or wailing until I got to the house. My legs and feet were singed or "cooked" by the time I came to the end of the heap. I was all alone when I went back for my head load of flour, my playmates were no where to be found, they scattered away from the mill house in panic.

I picked up my load of cassava flour and made my way towards home wailing at the top of my lungs. I cried so loud and plaintively that my family overheard my cries while I was more than two blocks from the house. Mother and Cecilia rushed out of the house to meet me sensing that something must be wrong. My mother relieved me of the load on my head and my sister carried me on her back to the house. Blisters were already forming on my legs by the time I reached home. Confusion and pandemonium broke out in the house, nobody had any clear idea about how to treat the extensive burns on my legs. They were bewildered and confused so they followed every reasonable suggestion made to them. Among the suggested remedies was salve the blisters with ink, palm kernel oil or castor oil. For a start my sister emptied her small bottle of ink onto my 'cooked' legs and rushed to Lagos town to buy a bottle of palm kernel oil.

The blisters on my legs only got worse as the evening wore on, I cried until I lost my voice and could cry no more. The pain subsided by nightfall and I reveled in the sudden attention and sympathy from my mother and sister. They did everything in their power to ease my pain and make me comfortable. I was provided with a pillow, for the first time, to prop up my feet. My foolishness and stupidity had a bit of silver lining and for the first time in my life I slept on a blanket with my feet propped up on a pillow. My regular bed of straw mat had one layer of blanket added to it. I was pampered for several weeks and did not do any of the usual house chores. For the next several weeks I was relieved of all household duties, I did not draw water from the waterside, dispose of garbage, or run errands to buy any knick-knacks from the local Nigerian merchants at Lagos town. I loved the attention so much so that I wished my burns would not heal. I did not go to school for several weeks, my classmates and teacher paid me a surprise visit one afternoon, when they came I was hopping around the backyard; they prayed for me at the backyard. Not quite long after the visit I went back to school.

The blisters broke open gradually into open sores and wounds. And when the sores and wounds healed, my legs were scarred into variegated skin colors. The new skin colors provided a lot of fun for my playmates who called me by some fancy nicknames. My legs were scarred for life and the loss of skin color lasted for many years. The natural skin color of my legs were restored after a few years but in the interim the various hues and colors of my legs during the healing process earned me several matching colorful nicknames.

The jump into the hot ashes was later explained as the result of a curse by the victim whose money I found in the courtyard. No sane person in his right mind would have behaved the way I did. My mother sought for the underlying cause of my foolishness by consulting oracles and seers. Her worse fears were confirmed. She was told that the burns were the result of a curse or retribution by one of our neighbors who lost valuables in the house. But why me, I asked. I did not get any benefit from the find. I was the victim of the curse because I was the person who allegedly found and held the bundle before Bomboden. I suffered the spiritual and physical consequences for innocently stealing from our neighbor. My mother further informed me that it could have been worse but for sacrifice she was advised to make to pacify the gods. Bomboden who benefited from the loot went unscathed from the curse but I have the scars to show for not returning the money to the rightful owner.

ADVENTURES IN SCHOOL

We lived in a large rectangular compound house of about ten single rooms with three or four storefronts. The Residents shared common bath, toilet and kitchen. My family practically lived in the courtyard because apart from a bed with a straw mattress we did not have any other item of furniture in the room. On the other hand there were concrete bunk seats in the courtyard that provided space for relaxation in the afternoon and evening.

The tenants came from all parts of the country; but the store fronts were operated by Kwahu traders, the reputed merchant class of the country. The Kwahu are generally the merchants of Ghana, who have commercial operations throughout the country. When it became apparent that the gold mine planned to close down the tenants began their exodus long before the Marlu Gold Mine was formally shuttered. The white collar tenants in the house were the first to leave and the storefronts gradually shut their doors one after the other.

Akan was generally the dominant language spoken in the house, but the tenants spoke different dialects of Akan. There were Asante Twi, Akuapim Twi, Fanti, Wassaw, and Nzima speakers all in the same house. The Akan I learned to speak was greatly influenced by the different Akan dialects spoken at home and school. The Akan I spoke and still speak is a mishmash of the various dialects I heard spoken during the period I was learning the language both at home and school. I read and wrote Fanti perfectly at school but my spoken Akan was a mixture of the various dialects. I read and wrote Fanti better than I spoke it.

On the first day I was being sent to school I cried and entreated my father to enroll me at the *makranta* or *madras* school at the end of the street. My pleas fell on deaf ears as we walked pass the madras on the way to St. Michaels Roman Catholic School at Bogoso. My father was a Muslim but he was not interested to give me an Islamic religious education. The only reason I chose the madras was my bias towards my father's religion. The madras at Bogoso was a one room school; the pupils chanted the Quran lessons or passages together. The teacher sat in front of the pupils and watched them chant their passages. I never saw the teacher use a cane on any child while I passed by by the school and so naturally I thought that the madras was free of corporal punishments.

I also guess I must have been attracted by the appearance of the cultural similarities between the students and I. Islamists or Muslims were considered as northerners. The students of the madras and I were ethnically considered as northerners, we were all *pepe*. The pupils of the madras wore no formal school uniforms like khaki shorts and shirt; they wore loose gowns similar to my father's. I therefore appeared to identify with the ethnicity of the madras students than with the students of regular schools. I did not know or have any interaction with any pupil of the madras school. The people of northern origin did the dirty jobs in the cities and towns around the Gold Coast, the "hewers of wood and the drawers of water" but we were not respected for our contribution to the country. Northerners were the butt of jokes and scorn by our fellow countrymen.

My father was an illiterate Islamic follower. I never saw him read a page of Quran or write a word of Arabic, I doubt that he was literate in Arabic. He however realized the importance of education in the Gold Coast and did not want to deprive me of the benefits of education as my older siblings. I did not appreciate the wisdom of my father at the time until years later. In 1966 I lived in the house of Islamic scholars at Tamale. My landlord and his brothers wrote and spoke fluent Arabic but to all intents and purposes were illiterates in Ghana. The brothers communicated in Arabic whenever they desired to conceal something from me. They were products of madras schools. They could not read, write or speak English, the lingua franca of Ghana for government and official business. That was the first time I appreciated the wisdom of my father for giving me formal education. While my landlord and his brothers spoke and wrote Arabic fluently, they could not participate fully in the civic life of Ghana. English is the glue that binds all the disparate tribes and ethnic groups of Ghana together.

I started school with a toothless mouth and a name that was considered funny by my schoolmates. My name on the day I went to school was Gyakaria Wala. Generally the Dagarti people tend to have one name, so to make up a second name as required by British protocol we adopted our ethnicity or tribe as our second or surname. Thus most of us had the same last name either Dagarti or Wala. My surname at school was Wala. The name Gyakaria provided rich fodder for jokes, mockery and taunting. My name was the first source of sorrow and misery caused by bullies and schoolmates. My schoolmates caricatured my name by combining English and Fanti to mock and taunt me. I was called fire carrier as "*gyakaria*." *Gya* is fire in Fanti, the Fanti word was added to the English word carrier to create an eponym of my name. That name used to drive me mad.

The eponym was not the only source of my grief, I had a large tooth gap in my front upper teeth but one would not have known that from the invectives and insults that were directed at me about the missing teeth. A stranger would have gotten the impression that I was toothless. My life was miserable at school but there was very little I could do to remedy the taunts and mockery. I was left with no other option than fight for my honor and in order to silence my adversaries. I fought and quarreled constantly during my first five years at school until I gradually accepted the lost front upper teeth as part of my persona in the fifth grade. I became tired of the unending fights and hostility towards my schoolmates which had hitherto been the bane of my school life. I gradually came to the realization that there was very little I could do to change the appearance of my mouth or smile. I was ignorant of artificial teeth and even if I knew of the existence of dentures or artificial teeth nobody would have bought them for me. But I would have been consoled with the knowledge that when I grew up I could have dentures to replace the missing teeth.

I became tired of quarreling and fighting over name-calling and meekly accepted the offensive names associated with the missing front upper teeth and literally made fun of myself as I grew older. I learned to live down the offensive names and the acceptance of the reality considerably reduced the hurt and sting of the insults and nick names. When I was in the fifth grade or class five I transferred from the Catholic school to Methodist school. And during the transfer I changed the spelling of my name from Gyakaria to Zakariah. The change in spelling took away the ammunition from my adversaries at school. But my last name did not change for another four years. I lived with the peculiar last name until 1958 when I went back to my home town. My form III teacher replaced my second name with that of my father.

TRUANCY AT HOME AND SCHOOL

The lack of a father figure at home in no small measure contributed to turn me into a truant and vagabond for about two to three years. As a stepchild, I had the impression that my stepmother did not love me quite as much as she loved her own children. I was not used to parental discipline. Apart from uncle Samini who booted me down for being a weakling neither my mother nor my grandmother ever lifted a finger against me. And my father never lifted a finger against me up to the day he disappeared from my life.

I therefore resented harsh discipline from my stepmother and the fear of corporal punishment often caused me to run away from home when threatened. My stepmother on the other hand belted me whenever I misbehaved. And the fear of being belted sent me away from home most often for days at a time until my mother and sister searched and brought me home at night.

I subsisted on the generosity of friends and strangers alike when I ran away from home. I did not have the common sense to know when to go come back home until my mother's motherly instincts sent her out to search for me from my hiding places. I used to spend the nights with night watchmen, sleeping in cardboard boxes like a homeless person. And during the day I had facilitators of like minded friends. My best friend was *Kwabenaka*, who like me did not like school. We hung out together during the day and parted company at night. We did everything in common except sleep together at night. The home of *Kwabenaka* was vacant and quiet during the day so he had the house all to himself during the day. He shared his meals with me or we cooked *ampesi*, plantain with *kako*, salted cod fish. I went my own way at night, hung around with night watchmen who allowed me to keep watch with them by sleeping on or in cardboard boxes.

Whenever I run away from home my mother and sister often sought for me from store fronts where I used to keep company with security guards known as watchmen. I was often found chatting either with the watchmen or soundly asleep in a cardboard box. I was often found playing with the watchmen in the early hours of the night otherwise I had to be awoken while leeping soundly in a cardboard box late in the night. But one day they went and sought for me late at night. I was fast asleep in a cardboard box when they found me and roused me to go home. My mother ordered me to go home, I replied in a sleepy voice that 'if I went home my mother would spank me'. And then came the foreboding voice, 'this is your mother' and at once I became wide awake afraid of what lay ahead of me. I followed her home meekly without a whimper. I was spared the cane that night and from that night I never ran away overnight from home.

The first-grade was my best year during my first eight years at school. I was home tutored by my older sister Cecilia before I started school. As such, I was the top student in my class in 1950. I would have continued doing well at school for much longer if I had endured the whacks she gave me on my head when she tutored me. I disliked being beaten by her when she tutored me. I fought and quarreled with her whenever she beat me; our relations became so cantankerous that my mother intervened to stop the tutoring and the beatings. When she stopped teaching me at home, I sank into mediocrity. In the 1950s, testing at school began from the first grade and continued throughout the ten years of elementary school. But by the time of independence testing in elementary school was administered from the fourth grade upwards. Every school child had to attain a minimum level of school attendance and proficiency to earn promotion to the next class at the end of the year. There were no automatic or social promotions during the colonial era.

I was punctual and regular during the first two years at school. I began to slack in the third grade for fear of corporal punishments in the class. Our class three teacher, Mr. Quarshie, was a graduate of the Catholic middle school. His younger sister, Victoria was my class three classmate. Victoria was the object of his vengeance whenever they had a quarrel or disagreement at home. Mr. Quarshie made his sister's life very miserable and by extension the rest of the class. Mathematics and spelling drills went hand in hand with canning for wrong answers. We were all flogged or caned for wrong answers but Victoria was beaten with a ferocity that set her apart. To avoid corporal punishments I started arriving late in class after the early morning mathematics drill was over. That was how I became a truant at school for the next two years. Initially I stayed away from class for one or two lesson periods and gradually progressed to staying out of school the whole day.

During the fourth grade, the mathematics and spelling drills accompanied by canning continued unabated. During the drill exercise, the teacher walked around the class going from row to row and randomly barked out questions on multiplication tables expecting answers instantly. Woe to any student who gave a wrong answer or failed to answer promptly. I was very slow with the multiplication tables, I knew most of the tables in sequence but I did not know them out of sequence without starting from the beginning. Therefore I always ended up at the receiving end of the teacher's cane. I began avoiding early morning sessions again, and as time went on, the avoidance of early morning drills developed into full scale truancy.

My mother was very particular about school attendance. When she found me at home when I should have been at school she sent me off to school despite my protestations. I could not persuade her that I hated school because the teacher wielded canes; corporal punishment was taken for granted it was considered an indispensable part of school life. Our parents and teachers made that clear to us through such aphorisms as 'spare the cane and spoil the child'. When I resisted going to school I faced the conundrum of punishment at home or at school. My mother used to threaten to spank me by shaking a cane or stick at me, the fear of the cane sent me scurrying out of the house for school but sometimes I vanished between home and school. I used to hide in the bushes halfway to school and remained in the bush until I saw my school mates on the way home from school. I then emerged from the bush in my uniform and went home as if I had been at school. My mother did everything she could to get me to go to school including throwing stones at me if that was what it took for me to leave for school.

I used to outsmart her by hiding in the bush and not making it to school. Although I often ran away from school but I always satisfied the minimum attendance required and with a little bit of luck scrapped through examinations and earned promotion. I never missed the term-ending lesson revision and examinations to qualify for promotion. I succeeded in keeping my mother in the dark about my habitual truancy. I had a good memory for cramming and I used to cram enough at the end of the term to pass the examinations.

I Longed For My Absentee Father

By the fifth grade I was mature enough to endure the regular punishments at school without running away. However after the end of the first term I got fed up with my old school and sought for a new school environment. I went on the lam again after the first term this time as protest for my desire to transfer from the Catholic school to the Methodist school. My wish was granted; I obtained a transfer certificate that took me to the Methodist school at Bogoso.

I was very restless in the fifth grade and the transfer from the Catholic School to the Methodist School did nothing to ease the restlessness. Suddenly I longed for my absentee father. I had not seen him for over three years since the day I ran away from home to prevent him from taking me back to the north. I became aware that my father had settled at Tarkwa on return from the north. So after another term at Methodist primary school I asked my mother for permission to transfer to my father at Tarkwa. My mother would not let me go so I blackmailed her by threatening to drop out of school unless I went to Tarkwa. My mother finally relented and granted me my wish to go to my father.

I transferred to Tarkwa during the third term of 1954 or during the last four months of the calendar year. At Tarkwa my father once again enrolled me at the local St. Mathews Catholic School. I completed the third term and earned promotion to the sixth grade.

My father lived at Tamso, a village about three miles from Tarkwa. I therefore commuted about six miles a day to and from school. There was a municipal bus service route between Tarkwa and Tamso, but all the school children from Tamso walked to Tarkwa. We walked to school either because the buses were not affordable or we were expected to walk to school as a matter of course. It was not considered onerous for children to walk three to six miles to school and back. We went to school in groups through a shorter bush path. When we emerged from the bush path at Tarkwa we had only about a quarter more mile to get to our school. It took us about thirty to forty minutes to walk through the bush path to Tarkwa.

We banded together in gangs on the journey to and from school because of fear of head hunters and child kidnappers. Stories of kidnappings and missing children were endemic in the villages. When we had scores to settle we did so on the way from school. Although we walked to school through the same bush path we were nevertheless in gangs or groups. A fight or quarrel with a group member was tantamount to a quarrel with the group. We did not engage in group violence, the group members ensured that brawls were fair and devoid of weapons or ambush. I was one of three boys in my group consisting of Tawia, Quayson and I. I was the smallest in the group but the most senior at school. My two friends were bigger and stronger than me and they protected me from the village bullies.

My fear of corporal punishment had diminished considerably by the time I was in the sixth grade. I was beginning to come to terms with myself and as we used to express it, I took action 'in my own capacity'. I coped quite well with my class work without falling behind. I dreaded arriving at school late particularly while the students were still assembled on the parade ground in the morning. Students who arrived late were flogged on the assembly ground as an example for the whole school on the consequences of tardiness at school. That was a spectacle I could not imagine going through and I avoided tardiness as much as possible. When late I hid at vantage point from where I could observe the parade and when they marched into the class rooms I followed into my class. I could take caning before my classmates but not in front of the whole school.

The primary and middle schools at Tarkwa and Bogoso were located on the same campus. But each section was operated under a different principal or head teacher. The Tarkwa school complex was in two buildings while the Bogoso complex was in three buildings. The head teacher of the middle school at Tarkwa loved corporal punishment and never minced words when he warned the school to be of good behavior. He delighted lashing pupils during the morning school assembly and was very proud and boasted about that. We detested him so much so that we gave him a nickname that was based on a scar below his jaw line. We called him Africa without Madagascar. During the third term of 1956, the head teacher served notice on my class. He threatened that in order to prevent us from becoming rascals he would light fire under our butts in the New Year, 1957. That warning was more than I could stand and I began planning to leave the school at the end of the year and go back to Bogoso. The threat prompted me to go back to Bogoso in January 1957.

Campaign For Independence At Bogoso

I returned to Bogoso during the frenetic phase of the political campaign for independence. My experience of the campaign for political independence was limited to the communities where I lived during the struggle at, Bogoso and Tarkwa. The one headache that hobbled me throughout most of my school life was lifted from my head after independence, abolition of school fees. The monthly school fees of four shillings remained the same from the year I went to class one in 1950 until they were abolished by the new government of Ghana. My fee problem was solved after independence in 1957 with the introduction of fee free education. I went through the rest of the elementary school without ever being sent home for school fees.

The introduction of fee free education was the immediate benefit of independence as far as I was concerned. The government assumed responsibility for school fees for parochial and public schools. The parochial schools were expected to admit all applicants irrespective of their religious affiliation but they were free to continue to proselytize to all within their schools.

The Convention Peoples Party, C.P.P was the dominant political party at Bogoso and Tarkwa. Tarkwa was a larger urban area than Bogoso and must have had some of the minor tribal and regional parties but I did not experience these at Bogoso. From Bogoso it appeared there was only one party that was fighting for independence and that was the Convention Peoples Party led by Dr. Kwame Nkrumah. The CPP colors and symbols were everywhere at Bogoso and Tarkwa. Peugeot 204 were the preferred vehicles of the CPP and they were the only party vehicles that cruised the streets of Bogoso with their megaphones blaring. The picture at Tarkwa was a bit different but the CPP was still the dominant political party in town.

As an elementary school kid my sources of information basically came from rumors, party slogans and jingles and of course our teachers. Although I did not know it but the political opinions or news we heard from our teachers reflected their political points of view. My form II teacher was a CPP supporter and my Form IV teacher was an opposition supporter. My political inclination followed the political views of my teachers. What I learned from my teachers therefore must have been biased. Subscription service for wired loud speakers known as radios brought into our homes programs of BBC and later Ghana Broadcasting System. Hard news was delivered in English, Ewe, Twi, Ga and Fanti. Rumors are not broadcast else they cease to be rumors. Those who were better off had shortwave radios which were known as wireless because they were unwired. At Tarkwa there were radios at vantage public places. The problem I had in the primary and middle school was that I could not, with the exception of Twi and Fanti, understand spoken English on the radio. I had similar problems with movies; I could not understand the dialogues and therefore loved action and adventure movies. Westerns and action movies were thus more popular with the general population than non action movies. A movie that had no action was boring and dull. I therefore depended on rumors, slogans and jingles for information than on the popular media.

Political campaigns at Bogoso and Tarkwa were largely peaceful, but there were widespread rumors of political violence at Kumasi the headquarters of those against independence known as *yentie* in Asante or those who objected to the self government now of the CPP. The opposition parties at Bogoso were identified by insulting jingles and slogans tied to their leaders, Dombo and Barfour. Dombo and Barfour were the face of opposition political parties against the dominance of the Convention Peoples Party. Mr. S.D. Dombo was the head of the Northern Peoples Party; it was the largest opposition group in the national assembly hence his name was synonymous with opposition. But from my vantage point at Bogoso I did not know who Dombo was. I knew Dombo because of the jingles and slogans against Dombo and Baffour. I sang the Dombo jingles some of which were insulting without any awareness that Dombo was my kinsman. Dombo and Baffour were linked together in opposition though before independence the NLM of Baffour and NPP of Dombo were different regional political parties.

The party of the Ashanti's was National Liberation Movement NLM. From our perspective at Bogoso, the CPP campaigned for immediate self government while the NLM was against self government. If I had a vote in 1957 I would have voted for the Convention Peoples Party of Dr. Kwame Nkrumah. The Convention Peoples Party or CPP as far as I was concerned was the only party in town. The NPP and NLM did not appear to have any influence beyond their regions in the period before independence; they were not present at Tarkwa and Bogoso. We knew of them through rumors, slogans and jingles of the CPP. We followed the political party vans whenever they were in town for entertainment by the jingles and slogans we parroted but with very little appreciation.

'Self government now' was the rallying cry of the CPP whose motto was "forward ever, backward never'. My teacher in Form II who was a CPP sympathizer persuaded us as his pupils to sympathize and support the CPP and independence. Some of the benefits of independence was the possible availability of goods from the wider world instead of just from Gt. Britain. Goods from other countries according to my teacher were not allowed entry into the country thus depriving the country of the benefits of cheap goods from other countries. If trade was one of the justifications for independence then that goal was realized shortly after independence. Japanese made motor cycles supplanted British made motor cycles with the introduction of Honda and Kawasaki motor cycles. The British made cycles were kick started while Japanese made motor cycles were started like cars. An uncle who once owned a British motor cycle rued the disappearance of the heavy British machines.

The other practical evidence of international trade was the introduction of the first Panasonic transistor radios in Ghana during the early sixties. The small red rectangular boxes were the boom boxes of the era. For the first time, radios or shortwave radios were really unwired clutched under armpits and blaring from street corners. I saw these mini boom boxes when I was a teacher at Tamale in the early sixties. These mini boom boxes replaced such iconic radios as the Grundig which were operated from large battery packs or electricity.

My Form IV teacher, I. Pont, was a staunch opposition supporter, so I went from a CPP sympathizer to an UP sympathizer due to the indoctrination of my class teacher. By 1959 all the disparate political parties opposed to the CPP in parliament merged into one opposition party, the United Party. The NPP and the NLM led the merger of the other smaller parties into the United Party which became the official opposition party. Had the NPP merged with the CPP the fortunes of the north in particular the North West section of Ghana might have been different. The allocation of development and infrastructure projects was based on political influence and affiliation. The constituencies of the opposition parties were generally bypassed in allocation of development projects. It was worse in the North West section because the NPP was the party of the North West with the exception of Tumu that was represented by Imoru Egala in the CPP. It was easy to bypass the North West because of the homogeneity of its politics. Egala did not bring any significant developments to the North West but his family was influential and one of his progeny, Liman became president of the country during the third republic. Wa lagged behind the rest of the North in economic development during the first republic.

At independence, Tamale and Wa were the two most populated centers in the north. However Wa was bypassed as the administrative capital of the newly created upper region in favor of Bolgatanga, which was then a small village. This was seen as payback for Dombo and the other NPP members for their opposition to the CPP government.

FORGING A NEW NATION

The greatest legacy that Nkrumah bequeathed to Ghana was his ability to unite the various ethnic groups and tribes in the country into a coherent whole despite our differences. Our ethnic and tribal differences boiled down to bad mouthing of one another without violence or strife. It was alleged shortly after independence by a member of the opposition party, B. K. Adama from Wa constituency that the government of CPP was drawing up plans to turn the people of the north into the servants of the people of the south or as he succinctly put it to make northerners the drawers of water and hewers of wood for the people of the south. The allegation was strenuously denied by the government. In the wake of the allegations, the CPP government worked hard to meld the various ethnic groups and tribes of the country into a cohesive unit without intertribal violence. Any Ghanaian can live in any part of the country without fear of violence or retribution.

The opposition party which was an amalgamation of regional and parochial parties sought to enshrine our differences through a federal form of government. At independence, Ghana consisted of three administrative regions: the Gold Coast Colony, which was the communities along the coast from east to west, Ashanti, and Northern Territories. The tribes of the Gold Coast colony considered themselves more civilized than all the other tribes of the country because the first adventurous European traders landed on the coast they came into contact with the native peoples along the coast. And the Ashanti's were proud of their prowess in wars and battles with victories over the coastal tribes in numerous wars and battles. The northerners had nothing to crow about, we became a protectorate of the Crown for protection from slave raiders of the Sahel region of Africa. Had the opposition succeeded in carving up the country into tribal fiefdoms the peace that Ghana has enjoyed since independence might not have been possible. It was the foresight of the first prime minister and president of Ghana that the country did not splinter into tribal kingdoms fighting one another for scarce resources.

The northern territories were a protectorate of the British colonial administration. The British colonial administration protected the north from Samori and Babatu, slave raiders from the Sahel region. Samori and Babatu were scourges on the north; they were reputed to be ruthless slave raiders who plundered the north until the British colonial administration intervened. The Ashanti dominated the interior of the country, but their domination stopped at the edge of the Black Volta River. The legendary tales of Samori and Babatu the slave raiders were widespread when I was a child. But the peculiar thing about the North West was that most households owned slaves. However, the slaves were treated as indentured servants who were treated humanely. They were absorbed into the fabric of the family they served as equals, the men and women married into the family and today they are our fathers and mothers, brothers and sisters without distinction.

Some of my family members are descendants of slaves who are an integral part of the family. Their father, a slave was betrothed to one of my sister's. They are an integral part of the family. And when education was introduced into the north slaves and their descendants were the first beneficiaries. The slaves and their descendants were considered expendable so when the colonial administration asked households to contribute children to populate the new schools the expendables were the people who were sent to the new schools that were being introduced. It is ironic that the expendables became the lords of their communities when they became civil servants under the colonial administration.

EDGE OF PUBERTY

I made a complete turn around in my personal hygiene by the time I began school in the New Year at Bogoso in 1957. I was approaching puberty and was suddenly aware of my personal cleanliness and hygiene. Before 1957 I was generally dirty and scruffy, I loathed bathing or showering with the results that I was filthy and smelly for most of the prior seven years of school life. I was twice infected with itch scabies before 1957. Before then when I cleaned up I washed mostly only my face and feet and dabbed on shea butter or Vaseline in the morning before going to school. I scarcely ever took a full bath before going to school. The tropical heat and humidity did its part to make me smell like a skunk.

I was said to be at loggerheads with water when I was on vacations, I neither washed my face nor feet from the first day of vacation to the last day. And I wore the same draw string pair of shorts night and day until my mother or sister removed it off me to save their nostrils. I was oblivious to the fact that I was filthy and smelly. My mother and older sister often tried gentle persuasion to take a bath voluntarily and when persuasion failed they coerced me by either splashing water on me hoping that when wet I would wash myself or one held me firmly while the other washed me thoroughly with sponge soap and water. They did for me what I would not do voluntarily for myself. It usually felt good after a forced bath and I slept soundly that night without scratching myself like a hound.

However, when I returned to Bogoso in 1957 I suddenly found religion regarding personal cleanliness and hygiene. The sight of girls made my heart aflutter. The mere glance or smile of a girl was enough to set my heart agog. I took baths and ironed my khaki uniform to the shine before going to school every morning or at least every Monday morning. I prepared fastidiously for the Monday morning inspections. Our school teachers inspected us from hair to toe for personal cleanliness every Monday morning including uniform, hair and nails. I washed and ironed my khaki uniform voluntarily without coercion to impress girls and by so doing passed the inspections with flying colors. I trimmed my finger and toe nails and cleaned my teeth every morning with a chewing stick. The chewing stick was the poor man's toothpaste. The stick was chewed soft and used to scrub the teeth. Until I got to form II or the eighth grade I cleaned my teeth infrequently but I made a U-turn and polished my teeth at weekends with pulverized stem of plantain and charcoal. I worked at preserving the remainder of my teeth.

I showboated quietly in the eighth grade, I was not boisterous and I did no sports to put me in front of my schoolmates but I loved to attract attention to myself particularly from girls. And the only way I figured doing that was with my uniform. One of my friends showed me the way. The uniform of Pius appeared fresh and shiny from Monday to Friday. Pius taught me the secret of shiny khaki uniform. The secret was in the method of washing and drying the uniform, the khaki was brushed with soap and water on a table or any level surface and drip dried without wringing. A mixture of starch and kerosene was then brushed over the dried uniform before it was ironed with a hot box iron filled with embers. The mixture of starch and kerosene gave the uniform a shine and my uniform looked like that of a policeman who wore stiff shiny khaki uniforms.

Imperceptibly I was changing; I was beginning to take notice of girls even if I was too shy to talk to them, I was content and happy when girls looked my way or smiled at me. I could not think of a better way to grab the attention of girls than to wear shiny khaki short and shirt to school. By making my uniform as stiff and shiny as a policeman I hoped to grab attention. The attention I hankered for was only in my mind with no basis in realty because throughout the time I tortured myself I never ever exchanged a word with a female schoolmate outside of normal classroom interaction with my classmates.

EDUCATION AS MEANS TO AN END

Initially my heart was not in education, I went to school more or less to please my mother. I never saw the rational for school. As far as I was concerned school was pure torture; my mother and father got bye without education. I could also get bye without education instead of being bothered and tortured in school day after day. I therefore rationalized that I could make a living as they had done without going to school. And none of them could give any cogent reason why I should continue to be tortured in school. But I continued anyway half heartedly. By the fifth grade I gave up the quixotic attempts to drop out of school but my academic performance was still mediocre though I began to show some promise by being counted among the best ten in my class for the first time since first grade. I did not study consistently; I used to cram towards the end of every term to prepare for examinations. In form II or eighth grade I paid close attention to my school work and actively participated in all class lessons. And I was regular at school as such my schoolwork improved remarkably.

I participated in class activities voluntarily. I made vital contributions during class debates, the debates taught me something about myself that I was not aware of, I was a skilful debater and quite fluent in the spoken English. It was the first class where all lessons, except the local vernacular, were taught in English. I became a sought after debate partner during class debates because I had the knack of leading any group of which I was a member to victory in debates. My weakness in class was mathematics and that weakness has dogged me all my life. I studied hard for mathematics examination but I never excelled, I was content with a passing grade. My eighth grade class teacher, Mr. Essel, was the first teacher who genuinely disliked corporal punishment and was the first teacher who made me aware of my strengths and weaknesses. He allowed me to flourish and progress at my own pace without coercion.

I attempted to take competitive examination for admission to secondary school in Form II with the encouragement of Mr. Essel, my class teacher. Admissions to secondary schools were open to form II and III students through competitive examinations. I decided to take part in the examination for secondary schools that year, 1957. Accordingly all my school mates bought and completed the requisite application forms and returned them to the head teacher or principal, Mr. Acqanda for transmission to the West African Examination Council. The completed forms were sent late to the Examinations Council and thus we were denied the opportunity to take part in the examination. I missed my first window of opportunity and thus pinned all my hopes on the following year when I would be in Form III or ninth year in school.

At the end of 1957, I went back to my hometown with my mother and younger sister Adjoa. I was entering Form III in the New Year starting in January 1958. I was admitted at Issah middle boarding school located over thirty miles from Wa. When it came time to complete the application for the competitive examination all students who wanted to take part in the examination were permitted to go home for the registration fee required for the examination. My school was far from home and I did not have the fare to pay for transport to go home for the examination fee so I asked one of my school teachers who was on a shopping trip to Wa to collect the required money from my mother for me. I was certain that once my mother saw a teacher she would oblige me with the fee out of respect for the messenger, school teacher. There was nothing I could get from my mother that the teacher could not get twice over.

My optimism was misplaced; It appeared that secondary school or higher education was not part of my destiny. My mother informed the teacher that she could not afford the £1.00 registration fee at that particular time. If my teacher could not pry £1.00 from my mother I could not have pried it from her either. I was disappointed but at least I did not have to walk over thirty miles only to be disappointed. I missed the last window of opportunity open to me to compete for a place in secondary school. Any possibility I had for high education was derailed. I resigned myself to complete middle school and enter the civil or local council service.

TEACHER TRAINING PROGRAM

The government of independent Ghana introduced fee free compulsory education throughout the country. The new education program required competent and trained teachers for its success. To obtain enough qualified trained teachers to cope with the expected increase in school enrollment, the existing four-year teacher training program was broken up into two stages. The first stage was a two year training program that led to the award of a Cert-B teaching certificate. And after two years of teaching experience the Cert-B teachers were trained for another two years to qualify as Cert-A teachers. The Cert-B teachers were trained for primary schools while the Cert-A teachers were trained for both primary and middle schools. The teacher training program which thus far had been limited to untrained teachers already in the system was opened up to middle school Form IV students. The first class of middle school participants in the new program was the class of 1959. Entry into the Cert-B teacher training colleges was also by competitive examination conducted by the West African Examination Council. The new teacher training program thus opened another window of opportunity for me to have a post middle school education.

I walked for more than thirty miles, in the company of other students, to Wa to obtain money for the examination. We walked for about two to three hours through bush paths to Wa through Naro and Tibani. I arrived at Wa exhausted only to find that my mother had traveled out of town. However in her absence my aunt, Damwaniho, gave me the requisite fee of £1.00. But she did not give me any extra money for transport back to school. I walked to Wa with a group of students but I was scared to return by the same long bush path alone. I therefore went to my grandmother at Duohi for extra money to cover the transport fare back to Issah. My grandmother also gave me £1.00; that potentially gave me £2.00 which was more than enough money to pay for the examination. I started dreaming of what to do with the extra sixteen shillings. Before I left for Duohi my aunt gave the money she gave me for safekeeping with a neighbor with instructions that it be given to me when I was ready to go back to school.

I was full of anxiety and excitement while on my way from Duohi to Wa. I kept pinching my pocket after every few yards for assurance that the £1.00 was safely ensconced in my pocket until I got to my final destination at Wa. I slept in the courtyard at bedtime because of heat and humidity at that time of year. At bedtime I folded my shorts with the £1.00 neatly tucked in my pocket and used it as my pillow for the night. When I woke up in the morning the shorts was no where to be found. Somebody stealthily removed the shorts from under my head took out the money and threw away the shorts. I searched every corner, nook and cranny of the courtyard for the shorts while I sobbed uncontrollably. While crying and searching around the courtyard like a crazy person, my aunt's husband returning from his morning walk came home with the shorts in his hands. I smiled when I saw him with the pair of short in his hands but the smiles soon faded when I realized that the pockets were turned inside out. I was distraught; my registration for the examination was in jeopardy. When I went back to school I had only sixteen shillings, four shillings short of the required registration fee. It appeared fate had dealt me another fatal blow; I was in danger of losing the opportunity to compete for a place in the burgeoning teacher training program.

I used four shillings of the one pound my aunt left for me to pay for my fare back to school. But for my aunt's foresight, I would have lost that amount too. But this time lady luck smiled on me, my classmate and best friend in the school, Kundigu, made up the difference and I duly registered for the examination. Kundigu was given more than £2 by his father to pay the registration fee. He was generous enough to make up the difference of four shillings for my registration. We were both successful in the subsequent examination. My success in the examination saved my life. The admissions process required medical examination, the medical examination led to the discovery of a severe jaundice infection that I was not aware I had. The examination prevented me from becoming the seventh victim of a jaundice outbreak in the school that year.

Kundigu went to the college at Bawku while I went to the college at Navrongo. The teacher training program was the poor man's path for any higher education after middle school. It was the only education program that paid the students regular monthly allowance or stipends while in training. Thus students who could not afford secondary school education for financial reasons were blessed with admission to teacher training colleges. The payment of regular monthly allowance to trainee's relieved our families from any further financial burden or responsibility.

ANCESTRAL WORSHIP

I retained glimpses of the 'seeing eye' for about four to five years after my father purged my 'seeing eye' through herbal potions. I continued to see spirits while the eyes gradually faded though they were not as sharp as before. What remained of the fading eye sight turned me into the family oracle. Since I did not have any spiritual insights beyond the vision my mother used to follow up my stories and queries by consulting oracles and seers for the significance of the visions. The advice of the oracles and seers gave her some spiritual guidance or road map of her life and traditional religious practice.

For instance when I asked my mother what she was doing sitting pensively behind the door one night; she did not say anything more after her denial. She went on to consult her favorite seer or oracle and was told that the entity I saw was the spirit of some of our ancestors. The seer informed her that the spirit visitor was disappointed when she found no food in the house. Mother was therefore advised that we should maintain our connection with the spirits of our ancestors by leaving bits of food in the utensils for them at the end of the day. And that our bowls or plates should never be completely clean without any scraps of leftovers in a bowl or plate as an offer for the spirits of the ancestors. And from that day mother ensured that some scrap of leftover food was always left overnight. The ancestral spirits are said to be around us at all times and are a part of our everyday life. We acknowledge and pay our respects to them everyday through pouring of libation with drink or water and deliberately leaving scraps of leftover foods around the house at all times. I grew up cognizant of my ancestors and have continued with the practice of my mother in my own household albeit unconsciously.

Once or twice a year my mother prepared meals as an offering to our ancestral spirits. It was one time in the year when the food was prepared specifically with common condiments and ingredients including spices of the North in preparing these meals. The meal was usually made of millet or sorghum paste or *sawo* in dagare, served with soup or gravy. When mother finished preparing the food she went out with it while still piping hot and offered it to beggars in the streets. I used to look forward to the yearly offerings because the meals were different from our usual bland daily fares. Since the meal was prepared for offering on behalf of our ancestral spirits all ingredients and condiments would have been known or used by them during their

WALK WITH THE DEVIL

lifetime. My mother worshipped our ancestral spirits and never took any step without asking for their blessings. She converted to Islam in the last years of her life. I wonder how she reconciled her ancestral beliefs with her new Islamic faith.

I wake up once or twice every night to pee or pass water ever since infancy. On another occasion when I woke up at night and stepped into the courtyard I saw my 'mother and sisters' sitting in our part of the communal kitchen busily preparing the catering meals that would be taken to the gold mines at dawn. I had no idea what the time was but after I finished peeing I went into the kitchen to join them. But as soon as I entered the kitchen 'my family' froze up and sat stiffly like statues. They sat stiffly behind the pots on fire but no one glanced or looked in my direction as I stood behind them trying to attract their attention. After a minute or two in which nobody spoke to me I went back to sleep. When I woke up the second time that night I saw my mother and sister still cooking. I went to them again and this time they acknowledged my presence and spoke to me. I realized that they were still at the same stage I saw an hour or two ago and they impressed upon me that they had not been up for long. I was left confused and perplexed but otherwise said nothing.

HAUNTED BY SPIRITS

While I could see spirits and visions I lived in fear of dark nights; my life at night was a nightmare whenever I woke up to pee because of what I used to see in the darkness; ghostly and shadowy figures lurked in the room or the courtyard. I got used to the dark figure standing sentry at particular spots in our room and courtyard every night. The figures were not menacing but I was often petrified with fear whenever I woke up at night to urinate. To prevent myself from seeing the shadowy figures I used to feel my way to the courtyard or urinal with my eyes closed though I could not help stealing glances at its usual standing place. Sometimes I felt my way to the courtyard and back without actually opening my eyes.

I was often so scared at night I never ventured beyond the immediate bounds of our doorway. Our room was opposite the room of one Bukari, a *Farafara or frafra* from the Bolgatanga area of the north. He was a sanitation laborer. A shadowy or dark figure stood in front of his door at the same spot every night. I was afraid to look but could not help peeking at it as I peed through a crack in the door. I used to be so scared of the ghostly shadow standing opposite our room I never ventured near the center of the courtyard when I went out at night to urinate. The dark shadow more than anything else was the reason our entrance doorway often reeked of urine.

The dark and ghostly figure was so constant at night that I stared wondering whether the ghostly figure was a figment of my imagination. To find out whether the ghost was a creature of my imagination or not I decided one night to go beyond my comfort zone towards the center of the courtyard. .I started harboring doubts after observing that I saw the ghost only during dark moonless nights and never on full moon. I summoned courage and took my first tentative step beyond the immediate bounds of our doorway towards the bath area across from where the ghostly shadow stood sentry at the opposite doorway. I held my breath, my eyes fixed on the shadow as I attempted to move towards the urinary area. And as soon as I went beyond our side of the courtyard the dark figure also moved from its place at the opposite end towards me. I freaked out and rushed back into our room and banged the door behind me. But I still had to urinate and so I cracked open the door enough to peek and push my penis through the opening. I saw the dark tall figure through the crack gesture as if amused by my fright. He went back to his spot in front of the door.

When the exodus from Bogoso began, Bukari was one of the early workers who left town. He did not work in the mines so I do not know whether he was let go by the town or local council. But he left town long before Marlu Gold mines ceased operations. When he left the spirit that stood constantly in front of his doorway also disappeared. I do not know whether I stopped seeing the spirit because of the effect of the bitter potion my father gave me shortly after I arrived at Bogoso or that the spirit left town with its master. I was greatly relieved I could go beyond his doorway at night without being petrified by fear.

MY FAMILY WAS SCARED OF ME

I became aware within a short time after arrival at Bogoso that my sister Cecilia and to a lesser extent my mother were scared of me. They were afraid because of a misconception that I had some spiritual powers. I took full advantage of Cecilia and stoked her fears when it was advantageous for me to engender her fears. I cowed in the night before spirits and shadow figures while my older sister and stepmother were scared of me in their hearts. During my first year at Bogoso Cecilia would not be found dead with me alone in a room without a third party. I was an innocent kid who knew nothing but Cecilia was petrified of me. Despite their fears they could not help asking me to narrate the story of my encounter with the malicious spirits at Duohi time and again for their amusement. They kept the encounter fresh in my mind because I narrated it about once or twice a week in my first year at Bogoso. And I never tired of narrating the tale for the umpteenth time. The narrative helped freshen the story line constantly. If they asked me to narrate the story with a view of poking holes at the story for inconsistencies to debunk the tale they never found any. Cecilia in particular used to huddle with my mother while I narrated my experience to them and would not come near me for hours after I finished.

Cecilia was afraid to be with me alone without the presence of a third party but there were certain chores we did together without a third party. She would not sleep or sit in a room with me without my father or mother. But when we went to the bush to harvest firewood I was with her alone harvesting firewood from the tropical forest. I was not comfortable in the bush. The sight of thick forests used to spook me, I came from the open savanna and was not used to forests. I used to be in a hurry to leave the forest when we went to harvest firewood than she realized. If I wanted to hasten our departure from the bush or forest all I had to do was point to none existing spirits lurking behind trees or on top of trees and we would hurriedly flee from the forest. She accepted my exaggerations as a matter of course. The exaggeration of spirits sitting on trees or peeking at us from behind forest trees always ensured that my sister did my share of the harvesting of the wood so as to hasten our departure from the bush.

My stepmother while she never showed any fears nevertheless harbored some fears of me in her heat. For instance one day I spanked my baby sister, Adjoa and my mother spanked me in return. I did not like the reprisal because I felt I was justified to beat her. So after my mother spanked me I told her that, "You will see," without more. Whether my words carried some power behind them I did not know, but a day or two later her middle finger became swollen and tender. She applied the usual remedies to no avail. She applied hot fomentation and liniment to the finger but it only got worse.

She concluded that I must have jinxed her when I told her 'you will see'. She was spooked by my words though I did nothing beyond uttering 'you will see'. I did nothing, not even brooding afterwards to affect the hand that was used to spank me. I thought nothing more about the utterance after I uttered them. Finally she sat me down and spoke to me. She literally asked me to forgive her. She reasoned with me that if I did not let the hand heal we would all go hungry as she was the breadwinner of the family. If she could not work she could not feed us. I smiled innocently after this exchange, said Ok! I went about playing with my playmates without giving any further consideration to what she said to me. But miraculously, the swellings and tenderness in her finger was healed by the next morning. As far as I know I had nothing to do with the healing. But she believed that I had something to do with it. I guess she was spooked by her own fears but not because of any evil spells or powers I possessed.

FATHER ABSCONDS FROM HOME

The first time I met my father he looked elegant in his flowing Islamic gown or cassock that he wore with a matching hat. During my first two years at Bogoso I was often by his side when he was not away on business. Ironically I was his second son; he had four girls and a boy with my stepmother, his first wife. My father used to take me with him whenever he went to the butcher's shop at the market to buy meat. The meat was my father's daily contribution for the family meals. Father was a notorious miser, very stingy with money. When he went out of town on business, the burden of feeding the family fell solely on my mother.

When I was in the second grade, father went on an extended business trip to our hometown ostensibly to replenish his stock of cloths and smocks. He did not come back for more than one year. He was away when I jumped into hot ashes and suffered severe burns on my legs. My mother was the sole breadwinner and the one who took care of my burns not counting other childhood infections and diseases that afflicted Adjoa and me while he was away on business.

He returned after more than one year with a devious agenda that he proceeded to implement as soon as he entered the house. Thus instead of showing gratitude to mother for keeping his home and children safe and sound, he accused her of stealing his money hidden in the mattress. He then threw out my stepmother and her children together with their belongings like worn out dolls into the center of the courtyard.

It appears my father never had a bank or the popular post office savings bank account common during the colonial period. The mattress was his piggy bank where he used to stash his money. Before he left he stashed some money into the mattress. And while he was away mother found the money and used some of that money to supplement her income and bought medicines and generally took care of the family. He invited me to remain with him at his side while my mother and sisters huddled together in a vacant room in the house. I guess he took me by his side because I had no mother.

He remained for less than one week before he informed me that was going back to the north on another business trip and planned to take me along with him. I disclosed his intentions to my mother and sisters. I could not bear to go away from them so we planned to sabotage his plan. We conspired against his travel plans and on the day of his departure I left home very early in the morning and did not come back till late in the afternoon. And by the time I came back he had grown weary of waiting and left without me. We moved back into our room after he departed. I did not see him again for another three years until I sought for him by transferring to Tarkwa.

It is said that one never knows the value of a thing until the thing is no more. While father was with us, we scoffed and sneered at him for the measly six pence worth of beef he made towards feeding his family for a day. After he deserted the family, beef became a rarity in our meals. And it was this lack of meat in our diet that led me to pilfering from the cooking pots of our neighbors. Come to think of it sixpence was a lot of money in the Gold Coast of the early 1950's. It took about that much to feed the whole family for a day. Some of us longed for the days when father contributed only sixpence worth of beef for the family meal. In his absence we could not afford even an occasional six pence to add beef to our meals. Our soups were prepared with cheap smoked fish and an ample supply of vegetables such as *kontombire*, i.e., cocoyam leaves, bean leaves and okra etc. The meals were healthy but we longed for the taste of meat. The absence of my father was greatly felt when either Adjoa or I fell sick. The burden of caring for sick children while trying to provide for them was an extra burden that fell solely on the shoulders of my stepmother. When one of us fell sick, mother was torn between the exigencies of income or staying home to care for the sick child. But by the grace of God Adjoa and I thrived and grew up relatively healthy and well adjusted individuals was as a testament to the hard work and parenting skills of our mother.

My father never forgave my stepmother for the estrangement and untimely death of my mother. My father never had anything good or complementary to say about my stepmother.

I would never know the truth about the cordiality of the relations that existed between my mother and stepmother while they were married to the same man. While my mother was alive I never knew that the man I called father was not my real father. After her death I never lived or stayed more than a few hours with any of her close relatives to have learned from them what I did not know about my mother during her lifetime. During the one year that I lived with my grandmother she was more concerned keeping us alive than telling me about my mother's history. She never broached that I had another father somewhere until the day my stepmother arrived at Duohi to take me to my father. It appears my grandmother closed the chapter on my mother's life and concentrated on raising the two boys bequeathed to her care as best as she could. My grandmother and her children took the secrets about my mother with them to the grave before I became mature enough to ask them.

We were all happy to welcome our father back home after more than one year away. But our joy was short lived when he started throwing away the few worldly possessions of my mother and sisters into the center of the courtyard. Fortunately there was a vacant room in the house that provided shelter for my stepmother and sisters for the one week duration that my father remained before vanishing from Bogoso for good. My father split apart his family that day. My whole family, father, mother and sisters lived in different rooms of the same house for about a week until my father completed his devious plan to dump his wife and children.

My older sister never forgave my father for the way he threw them out like old rag dolls. She never really reconciled with him until the sunset years of his life.

About a year after father left home on his second journey we heard rumors that he was back and residing at Tamso, a village near Tarkwa with a new wife. Tarkwa is only about twenty-four miles west of Bogoso but our father never came to Bogoso to see how we were faring and we also pretended that we did not care about him. The thoughts of my father receded into the back of my mind till the fifth grade when I became restless at Bogoso and sought a change of environment or scenery. My sister left Bogoso for Kumasi before I was in the fifth grade. Our household then consisted of my mother, Adjoa my baby sister and me.

I Learn To Work For Money

When I came to Bogoso I was a backward villager who had not experienced or been touched by modern civilization. When I landed at Bogoso I did not know any any form of money beyond the cowrie shell which was the virtual currency of the north-west. But at Bogoso the cowrie shell had no value beyond serving as decorations on some traditional crafts or jewelry. But within three to four years of arrival I knew enough and learned to work for money by selling water to weary travelers at the lorry park. The change came slowly and imperceptibly almost without any warning. As soon as I was strong enough to carry a five gallon tin of water on my head then women started paying me to fetch water for them. The women in my home paid me to fill their barrels with water from the waterside. And that taught me that I could make money from water. I thus gladly filled their barrels at the expense of my own family. The street in front of our home used to serve as the venue for market at night and in the morning we rushed out combing through the dust and gravels for lost pennies. On some occasions I found a penny buried in the dust but my biggest find was a sixpence.

Bogoso had two main sources of water in the 1950's, a mechanical water pump and a spring located about one to two miles from town. The mechanical water pump known as bore hole was located on the grounds of the local council. The long lines at the bore hole made it a challenge to fetch water from it as such water from the pump was reserved for only drinking in my house. It reduced the necessity to visit the pump to fetch water regularly. We used the water from the riverside or spring for cooking and other household chores. Fetching water from the spring was less of a hassle than from the pump. And although we used to claw and struggle to get into line it was still more convenient. However before long, the council built a concrete dwarf wall around the perimeter of the spring. And overnight any sign of water shortage or service problem at Bogoso was solved.

The mechanical pump became redundant after the spring was walled, it became a white elephant or a monument to the foresight of the local council. The perimeter wall created a mini reservoir with an inexhaustible source of water supply. The concrete wall and boulders making up the spring reservoir were scrubbed at least once or twice a month to remove unsightly algae from the walls and boulders caused by stagnation of water in the reservoir.

The distance of the spring from town coupled with the plentiful supply of water and its proximity to the lorry park was what inspired some of us to begin peddling bottles of water at the lorry park to travelers. I used to collect empty beer bottles from bars, rinsed them and filled them with water for sale at the lorry park during weekends, vacations and when I played hooky from school. I peddled the water at a penny per bottle. Before I peddled water at the lorry park I sold water in five gallon containers to our neighbors and neighboring households at three pence per container. Once I tasted money from the sale of water I became reluctant to fill our drum with free water for my household use. It was financially more rewarding to fetch water for strangers than my own family.

My reluctance to fetch water for my family often put me into direct conflict with Cecilia who resented shouldering all the burden of fetching water for our domestic use while I busied myself fetching water for sale. And I was the worse for the friction, she expressed her frustration by beating me when we crossed paths either to or from the waterside. She used to beat and spill the water that was on my head when we crossed paths. I cried and went back to the waterside to fulfill my obligation to the woman who hired me to fetch water for her. Beating the heck out of me did not change my course or goal for the day. One afternoon I drank a cup of water from our drinking pot that annoyed Cecilia. She beat me up and asked me to replace the water because I did not take part in fetching the water for the house. I walked up to the grounds of the town council, a distance of more than a quarter of a mile, and returned with a cup of water to replace the water I drank from our container. Nobody in the house believed that I went all the way to the water pump for a cup of water. Selling water taught me the first lesson that money comes from hard work. It also taught me the genesis of responsibility when I helped to pay my own school fees with the proceeds. The first time I bought snack at school I did so with money I made from selling water.

Later on I diversified my activities to include hawking bottles of kerosene around town. I got the seed money for peddling kerosene from the sale of water. I peddled the kerosene around town and nearby villages in the evening after school. A bottle of kerosene used to sell for about three pence. I carried the bottles of kerosene in a small basin that held up to six or seven bottles. My favorite place or location apart from Bogoso township for selling my kerosene was Green Compound. Green Compound which was located along Bogoso-Prestea road was the residential housing for the workers of the gold mine. It derived its name from the predominant color of the roof coverings of the houses in the complex.

I saved my money in a piggy bank that I devised from empty cans or tins. And when I needed money I cut it up took out what I needed and started another tin bank. I progressed gradually with savings in tins to my first savings passbook from the Post Office Savings Bank. Peddling bottles of water and kerosene taught me the value of savings and thrift. My parents usually replaced or supplied my school uniform when worn out and nothing else. I bought the first pair of shorts that was not a khaki school uniform from my own savings. I did not like school and played hooky, but I disliked expulsion from school for not paying school fees on time. The other thing that could have subjected me to ridicule was tattered and worn school uniform. Fortunately I was spared that agony, I never wore worn out school uniform but apart from drawstring shorts I never had any other clothes at home. I did not like to portray myself as being so poor I could not pay my school fees and had to be expelled. Thus when I discovered that I could make money from peddling water and kerosene I helped to pay my school fees whenever possible. If I had the four shillings, enough to pay the fees, saved in a piggy I emptied it and paid the fees. And after paying the fees I pretended that it was still outstanding so that I could recoup it from my father when he was ready. I preferred running away from school on my own terms to being expelled for not paying the school fees.

Until the eighth grade or form II I was generally very filthy. Although I peddled water for cash I did not make hygienic use of water myself, indeed I wonder why any traveler would have bought a bottle of water from me. Most often I was wacked at school on Mondays for being filthy and unkempt. I applied shea butter oil or palm kernel oil on my arms and legs to create the façade of cleanliness particularly when going to school on Monday mornings. It was the one day in the week that we were thoroughly inspected from hair to toe.

CURSED FOR THEFT OF CASSAVA

As I grew older I turned over a new leaf and became sympathetic about the plight of my mother as a single parent. After Cecilia left Bogoso for Kumasi I literally became the man of the house; I was alone with my mother and younger sister, Adjoa. My school attendance was still spotty at best, though by this time I had stopped running away from home. I appreciated and sympathized the personal sacrifices our mother made for our welfare. Our means of support and livelihood continued to be the catering for mine workers. But as the fortunes of the mines diminished the customer base of my mother's catering business dwindled and that in turn affected her income. She worked as hard as before but made less from her efforts.

The labor force at the mines began declining from about 1953 until the mine operations officially ended in 1955. After 1955 only a residual labor force that engaged in mopping and safety operations remained. But the residual labor force was not enough to keep my mother fully employed in the only job that she knew, catering for the mine workers. Old habits die hard; my mother could not adjust to the new reality of a smaller customer base, she continued to prepare the same quantity of food day in day out for sale to fewer and fewer customers. I sympathized with her struggles to feed, clothe, and provide for our needs. As such I did not make unreasonable demands on her but helped in whatever way I could by doing odd jobs for other people for cash. However, by this time I had stopped hawking or peddling kerosene and water around town and at the lorry park. Bogoso was in decline.

I was also mature enough to participate in the social life of Bogoso. I used to steal into entertainment shows such as comedy and magic at the local 'concert hall' near our house. I did whatever I could do to earn or make money to go to a show but when all else failed I joined other kids to use unconventional means to gain access into the hall. We used to climb through the windows of the baths and toilets to gain access to the premises. After security bars were put into the windows we switched to the openings from which the bucket latrines were removed. We used to push the bucket of latrine aside and crawled through the opening into the toilet. We then emerged into the concert hall smelling of urine and carbolic, but the smell was of little consequence to us. When I reflect over how we used to crawl through toilet openings my skin crawls with the very thought of it. But at the time the only thing that mattered was gaining free access into the entertainment venue.

I ran errands and did odd jobs for some of my neighbors for payment in kind or money. For instance one day one of our new neighbors, Mamma Ewule, asked me to help her to carry some items to her farm with a promise to give me some cassava in return for my efforts. The farm was located over three miles out of town but I jumped at the offer happy to get some cassava for my mother. However when we reached the farm, she suddenly realized that the cassava plants were immature; she therefore promised to pay me after harvest at a later date. I felt betrayed and disappointed because she must have known that her crops were not mature enough for harvesting before she made the offer to me. But there was little I could do but go back home empty handed. I went back home along the same path or route to the farm, through farms located along the path. When I got to one cassava farm it was still quiet so I took advantage of the farmer's absence and uprooted a cassava plant. When I found that the plant was mature, I harvested a few more cassava plants. I harvested enough cassava to suffice for meals for two or three days for my family of three. I gave the stolen tubers of cassava to my mother telling her it was a gift from our neighbor, Mama Ewule. When Mama Ewule came home that evening my mother thanked her for her kind gesture. Mama Ewule perhaps out of guilt for her broken promise to me did not tell my mother the truth about where the cassava came from.

The next day when Mama Ewule returned from her farm she gave me bad news about the stolen cassava from the previous day. She called me aside and whispered into my ear that the farmer had either cast a spell or curse for the cassava that was stolen from his farm. She said that on her way back she noticed that the sticks of cassava had been gathered into a heap and sprinkled with blood and chicken feathers, a sign of a curse or spell against whoever uprooted the plants. She advised me to ask my mother to find the farmer, confess my crime and compensate or pacify him. She told me that it would take money to pacify the farmer, pay for the cassava so as to prevent or undo the effects of the curse or spell. I thought over her advice and decided that I could not ask my mother to spend money I knew she did not have. A day after I received the bad news, I went to the scene of my crime to see for myself what Mama Ewule had told me. And sure enough I saw the sticks of cassava gathered into a heap and sprinkled with chicken feathers and what looked like blood.

Although I decided against telling my mother about the curse or spell, I tried to find out what it would take to prevent or undo the curse or spell. I was informed that it would take a bottle of gin or schnapps, sheep or chicken and some money to compensate the farmer to undo his curse or spell. I had no idea how much the items would cost but I decided that I could not impose that kind of financial burden on my poor mother. Besides, I could not look into her eyes and make a confession that would require the expenditure of money I knew she did not have. I preferred to keep quiet and bear the consequences of my indiscretion rather than face ignominy. I was scared but I kept my fears stoically to myself even if that meant death. I preferred death to disgrace and ignominy.

At the back of my mind I feared the possibility of death, but in the meantime I confessed my sins before God and turned over a new leaf. I was prepared to meet my maker but I prayed fervently for God to forgive and save me from the curse. I started a regime of regular prayers by day and by night while looking for signs that death was sneaking up on me. As the days and weeks passed with not even a minor illness I became confident in the saving power of God. At the beginning of my regular prayers I set myself a deadline for the devil to do its worse with the assumption, that if the deadline came and went and nothing happened to me, then I could only conclude that the power of God had prevailed over the devil. Meanwhile I kept steadfastly to regular morning and evening prayers everyday. And after the two to three months deadline I had set for myself came and went and nothing happened to me, I declared victory. I never had even a headache during the three months deadline I set for myself. I proclaimed that the power of God had triumphed over the devil. I never mentioned the stolen cassava, the curse or spell to my mother throughout my ordeal.

I did not panic over the curse or spell while I prayed; I counted the days, weeks and waited for the wrath of the devil. At the end I concluded that the God that I serve is mightier and stronger than the god of the evil curse or spell. God accepted my repentant heart and made me victorious over the evil curse. Mamma Ewule never broached the subject of the curse or spell to my mother while I struggled with it. She also did not make good the promise to give me some cassava after harvest. The experience taught me a valuable and lasting lesson on the power of prayer. I learned at first hand that God answers the prayer of a repentant heart. I turned over a new leaf; I stopped pilfering and thieving even from my mother for good. I was taught a practical lesson in honesty that I never forgot.

Seduced By Girl Next Door

I was in class two when I was seduced by Akuah Serwah, the daughter of our next door neighbor to have sex with her. I am averse to calling the experience rape because I do not equate being coaxed by a woman to have sex with her to rape because I cannot have an erection when I am frightened. But girls on the other hand, can be forced to have sex with a man whether willing or not. I cannot have erection or with a shotgun to my head, do or die.

I was still an ignorant and innocent child when I was coaxed by the much older girl to have sex with her. Akuah Serwah was as old as Cecilia, my older sister. She was a budding entrepreneur, who like my mother, used to prepare food for sale to workers at the gold mine. She used to wake up about the same time that my mother woke up to prepare her food for sale early in the morning at the gold mine. She therefore aligned herself with my mother and slept with us at night. We used to go up together to the mines to sell the foods and came back together as a group. We used to sleep together on straw mats spread across the hard cement floor.

Akuah in effect became part of our family and the arrangement worked well until she started seducing me to have sex with her while my mother and sister were busy in the kitchen. When she had her food on fire she came back into the room ostensibly to nap for a few minutes. And it was when she came to have a nap that she tickled my penis until I had an erection and then she sat on the erected penis. While sitting on my penis she would ask me to piss into her but I could never piss while she had my penis in her. I guess that despite her age and maturity she perhaps did not know that ejaculation and urination are not the same; otherwise she would not have asked me to pee into her. Perhaps she did not know that I was not yet old enough to ejaculate like a man. I attempted on several occasions to piss into her when she asked me to but could not do so.

Our relations began to unravel when I became okra mouthed and started boasting or telling my playmates about having sex with Akuah. Word soon reached the older brothers of my playmates who sought me out to hear the story from me. I told them all the lurid details of how Akuah used to tickle my penis to have sex with her. I was happy that other boys were interested in my story and I told the same story over and over again. Eventually Akuah herself also heard the story floating around town about having sex with me. She rushed to my mother in tears complaining that I was spreading false rumors and stories about having sex with her. I was playing in the backyard when my mother called for me in a loud and stern voice. I knew I was in trouble when I heard her stern voice though I did not know what I had done to earn her reproach. Akuah was beside herself, tears streaming down her face. She confronted me as soon as she saw me and my mother turned to me for an explanation. I began to narrate the nightly encounters with Akuah while they were busy in the kitchen. I was in the middle of my story when my mother shut me up with a slap across my cheeks. I rushed out of the house in tears crying and wailing. I did not know why she slapped me for telling her the truth.

The lurid tales of sex with Akuah ended her catering service. Her parents became so embarrassed that she was sent to live with relatives in another part of town. The events must have precipitated the early departure of Akuah and her parents from Bogoso. They left Bogoso less than one year later.

The world is indeed a small place. I never dreamt of ever crossing paths again with Akuah after she and her parents left for their hometown sometime in 1953 or thereabouts. My family followed in 1957, about four years after Akuah and her parents left Bogoso. But in 1968-69 I came across Akuah at Sunyani while I was on a short vacation from the University of Science and Technology, Kumasi.

I visited Cecilia who was then stationed as a nurse at Sunyani in 1968-69. Akuah was also then a housewife at Sunyani with her husband. Akuah and my sister apparently renewed old friendships; it was my sister who informed me that Akuah was resident at Sunyani. I was anxious to meet her when I heard that she was in town. I was taken to her house one afternoon, but it was a great let down when we came face to face for the first time in over a decade and half. The meeting was cold and lacked any sense of acquaintance or familiarity. I guess we could not let go the unfortunate events of our childhood, we were still haunted by our past experience and behaved like complete strangers. We did not have much to say to one another beside obligatory customary greetings. She could hardly look into my eyes, she looked away from me during the period we were in her house. It was a great relief when the visit was cut short because of the uncomfortable feeling between us. And that was the last time I saw Akuah.

Our lives as adults were a far cry from our lives as children at Bogoso. She came from an educated family that appeared to be financially better off than we were. They were everything we were not, her father read newspaper, went to toilet with toilet roll holding it aloft in his hands for all to see, and they brushed their teeth with pepsodent or chlorophyll toothpaste while we were content with chewing sticks or sponges. I was envious of their modern lifestyle; the Town Hall arm chairs and gadgets like gramophone and shortwave radios were things I could only ogle at but not touch. We lived in the same compound house but in different worlds. But it appeared she did not live up to the standard of the life they lived at Bogoso. And for the first time I felt sorry for her, I wondered whether my childhood blabbing that she had sex with me had adversely affected her life after they left Bogoso. The gulf between our lives was still apparent but this time the roles appeared to have been reversed, my sister and I appeared to enjoy modern lifestyles, their style that I used to envy, while she had the appearance of an uneducated farmer who had never seen the four walls of a classroom.

Abstinence From Adolescent Sex

I went to my father at Tarkwa during the last four months of 1954. Within a short time after arrival I became part of the rowdy scene of the local boys and girls in the village. There were certain immutable facts of life that I came to accept as inevitable. And these included the derogatory and demeaning attitudes of the people of the south towards the people of the north. The brawls and fights with schoolmates were not isolated incidents but part of a general pattern. The people of northern Ghana were the butt of scornful jokes and invectives by the people of the south particularly the Akan speaking group. The adults of northern origin in the south endured the scorn and derision the same way that I endured mockery and taunting through most of my primary school life and tried to silence my tormentors by brawling and fighting them to no avail. I was fluent in the Akan language but that did not make me immune from scornful ethnic jokes.

The immediate impression I formed when I went to Tarkwa was the teeming number of northerners of all stripes in the mining villages dotted around Tarkwa. The residential compounds of the mines at Tamso, Amantrem, and Abosso were full of northerners. I think most of the underground unskilled workers were northerners. Despite our numbers we were still subjected to mockery and derision based on nothing but our origin. I thought that the presence of a great number of northerners in the Tarkwa area would inoculate us against demeaning and scornful ethnic jokes did not offer us such protection. I mingled with the children of the village and did everything in common with them but I was ever conscious of my minority status. When I arrived at Tamso I was relatively ahead of most of my playmates in school and that won me some grudging respect. My first adversary, Quayson with whom I was egged to fight at Tamso became my first friend.

My friendship with Quayson was mutually beneficial to both of us as members of minority tribes. His parents were migrant laborers from the Ivory Coast and to that extent we were all in the same boat. Quayson was mature and stronger than I was and protected me from some of the village bullies. And we remained tight friends until he left for the Ivory Coast with his parents at the end of 1955 for good. Quayson re-introduced me to the hardscrabble life of farming life in the Gold Coast which I had forgotten since I came to Bogoso. Quayson taught me village life, a life I would never have known or experienced. We tried our hands at farming, fishing and hunting. We failed miserably at both farming and hunting but were moderately successful on fishing as a pastime. We succeeded in catching enough fish that we ate at home. I learned about the hard life of the subsistence farmer from Quayson when we failed at farming and hunting. We made our own fishing tackles from hooks and bamboo saplings with pieces of calabash as floats. And for bait we used worms that we dug up ourselves. My next sexual experience after Akuah was in the company of Quayson when as part of a gang of boys and girls sex became part of the games we played on weekends.

During weekends our principal games or activities were soccer matches or kick balls around the village or fishing at Nsuta or Effuenta. and at night we engaged in telling ananse and fairy tales among ourselves. We used to gather in clusters and groups telling *ananse* stories and fairy tales at night on weekends for hours at a time. We used to gather in the open on full moons but on moonless nights we used to gather on verandahs of the homes of some of our friends but our most favorite place on these nights was an eatery or *'chop bar'* that belonged to the mother of one of our female companions. The eatery or *chop bar* was our favorite gathering place because it offered us some security. We used kerosene powered hurricane lamps to see our way in the dark room.

The *chop bar* or restaurant was a ramshackle of a bamboo shed covered with rusty corrugated iron sheets and furnished with only long wooden benches and tables. We took turns sharing ananse stories or fairy tales and sing songs as the story or tale demanded. We were all primary school students but a few of us, like Quayson, were quite mature and were very influential in what happened during the gathering of the group. Whether by design or coincidence, the first time I found myself in the group there were an equal number of boys and girls pressed together in the dimly lit shed.

The first night I found myself in the chop bar I was excited when the story time turned to games of groping and actual sex. I do not know exactly how innocent stories among friends became sex games in which everybody in the group was involved. Though I was in the group for the first time the leader of the group made sure that there was no odd man or girl, we were all paired and I had a 'girl friend' the very first day I was in the group. By the end of the night we not only told several *ananse* stories but we also enjoyed sex with our partners. At our next gathering I realized that the experience of the previous week was not a one time affair or happenstance, it was carefully choreographed to happen. Sex was the finale to the story time on each moonless night.

For no apparent reason I felt guilty after the night was over. And the guilt led me to resolve that I would not have anything to do with the sex orgies if there was a repeat performance. At age eleven or so I was as smooth as a bottle and despite the initial excitement and euphoria of the first day I did not find copulation as exciting as the anticipation and groping. The groping and the expectation were more exciting and satisfying than the actual sex act in which I did not know what I was doing. Maybe it was because I did not know how to penetrate or perhaps my my partner and I did not enough about sex so I did get any pleasure from sex that night. But I was happy when the finale came and we all trooped to our hovels. The *ananse* stories and sex plays continued on several moonless weekend nights until Quayson left Tamso at the end of 1955. The group then fell apart.

During our next gathering I discovered that it was easier to make a resolution while cooped up alone in my hovel and day dreaming about how to keep my resolution against sex. Making the resolution was the easier part, keeping the resolution while staring at copulation was entirely different. The latter required some extra willpower to keep the resolution. I took an active part in the story telling until the moment the hurricane lamp was blown off, the room went dark and the groping began. I was tempted and excited like all the others inwardly I struggled to maintain the resolution I had made to myself against having sex. I vacillated, my body was stiff and willing but I stuck to my resolution to abstain from taking part in the sex activity the next time and this was it. Sometimes it takes very little effort to overcome a temptation or abide by a resolution, my friends made keeping my resolution easy on me. When I expressed doubt and unwillingness to participate in group sex that night; my friends quickly reorganized their routine into a round robin of sex. We were five boys and girls and each of my four male companions had sex with each of the five girls that night while I sat and watched squirming and suppressing my arousal and erection. I stuck it out even as my penis was stiff and I squirmed in my seat I still managed to stay clean of sex that weekend in the dark chop bar. My refusal to cooperate that night was but a minor inconvenience. I guess the boys who were sexually active like Quayson took advantage of the surplus girl to have sex to their heart content that night. Thinking of it now they must have had stamina or perhaps most of them did not know what they were doing on those moonless nights. When I saw the boys hopping from girl to girl with so much abandon I was greatly tempted to break myself imposed resolution, but I endured the erection and squirmed till the night was over and we dispersed to our homes. I found that watching my friends having sex was more fun and exciting than having sex myself. My colleagues tolerated my quirks without reproach or resentment and I never stopped being present during the ananse stories and watched my friends copulating every weekend that we gathered at the ramshackle chop bar. The activities of the group came to an end after Quayson left Tamso at the end of 1955. If any crime was committed during the orgies then I guess I was a full and willing participant and an accessory to the crime and as such as guilty as those who committed the crime.

I built up strong will power from the experience. It was not easy to watch my friends having sex without taking part myself. I squirmed with excitement while they were at it but I kept the promise I made to myself though none of my friends was aware of my promise. I learned how to be a member of a group and yet avoid being swept up by the excitement of the moment. I chose to have an independent mind instead of following group mentality. I valued my friendship; while I never broke with my friends I did not slavishly follow them in every group activity. My group members accepted my individuality just as I accepted them without rancor.

ABSTINENCE FROM SEX VINDICATED

My best friend Quayson left Tarkwa-Tamso at the end of the school year in 1955 and I returned to Bogoso at the end of 1956. I continued my elementary school education for the next three years at Bogoso and Issah in northern Ghana. After I left Tamso at the end of 1956 I lost contact with my friends and playmates at Tamso. I returned to Tarkwa on a short visit in 1960 when I was in my first year at St. John Bosco's Teacher Training College, Navrongo. On return to Tamso after more than four years I found that the lives between my old friends and I had diverged in ways big and small. Most of them had dropped out of school; some our female companions were teen moms and some of the boys were also teen fathers.

Most of the premature fathers and mothers used to be members of my group. The children of the village fell into two broad categories according to the socio economic status of our parents. The boys and girls within my group were mostly the children of illiterate and uneducated low income mine laborers or farmers as such we were considered riff-raffs. The children of the educated and burgeoning middle class families of the village did not associate with the riff-raffs. The children of the high income families did not suffer the same fate as the riff-raffs. Most had completed middle school and gone on to certificate B teacher training colleges or secondary schools. I was the lone bright spot in my group who had achieved any measure of success. I had succeeded in completing middle school against the odds and gained admission into a Certificate B teacher training college at Navrongo.

I do not know which came first with my former companions and playmates, school drop out or premature parenthood. And I do not know whether poverty or the company they kept contributed to the sad state of affairs in their young lives. Before the introduction of fee free education in Ghana school fees were very influential in determining school attendance and enrollments. Though the standard fee was four shilling a month, that amount was a lot of money and was not easily affordable by most low income families.

I guess the slap by mother after I blabbed about having sex with Akuah Serwah must have had some positive influence on me at the subconscious level and saved me from frolicking in premature sex. I gained enough self-discipline from the prior encounter to exercise enough self restraint against sex at Tamso even as I squirmed while I watched my friends enjoying sex. The early sexual encounter with Akuah made me overtly shy to the extent that I found it very difficult to talk openly about sex; sex was almost a taboo subject for me to discuss in the open. Of my two friends, Quayson left Tarkwa before me and by the time I returned Tawia had dropped out of school though he was better off during the period we were together; his father was the chief driver of Tamso.

In 1961 I went back to Bogoso on a short visit. I discovered during the visit that, with the exception of two former classmates, most had also joined the bandwagon of the exodus from Bogoso. Only two of my classmates were still in town, Kwaku Nwona and Victoria Quarshie. They still lived in the same homes that were built by their fathers. My companion in truancy and 'magic lessons' Kwabenaka, had also dropped out of school. I assumed that going back to my hometown must have helped to stabilize my life and contributed to my good fortune. Fate was kind to me. I overcame the impulse of herd mentality and the need for acceptance by my peers and found some success in life that eluded most of my playmates.

Odds Against School Dropout

The gods must have been kind and generous to me and against all the odds made it possible for me to continue on the path of education to its logical conclusion against my better judgment. I never dreamed or yearned for any white collar job as a child. The blue collar jobs and craft trades were more attractive and appealing to me during my childhood. I was attracted and drawn to the crafts and tradesmen I saw at work when I went about my daily chores during infancy. I was first fascinated by the carpentry trade because there was a carpentry workshop located along the path to the garbage dump. I used to see them at work whenever I passed by the shop on my to dispose of garbage and often stopped by the workshop to admire their handiwork of cabinets, chairs and tables crafted by them. I practically passed through the workshop every morning on my way to and from the garbage dump and overtime became familiar with the carpenter and his apprentices. When I began running away from school from about the third grade I considered carpentry as alternative to school. Some of the carpenter's apprentices were not much older than I was so carpentry to me was as good as school. I used to stop briefly by the workshop and as time went on the stops became longer and I began lending a helping hand whenever I was asked to pick a tool or hold down any plank of wood that was being cut or planed. I was happy whenever I was asked to help with any trivial task at the workshop.

I thought I had rapport with the master carpenter and his apprentices and took it for granted that he would accept me as one of his students. So one morning after discarding my garbage I stopped by the shop and offered myself as an apprentice or student to the master of the shop with great expectation. To my great surprise he spurned my request though not explicitly. He told me he could not have me as an apprentice or student without my guardian or mother's consent. He then asked me to let my guardian or parent make a formal request to him and hand me over with the customary drinks and fees. I never expected such an outcome when I made the request; I was flustered and did not know what to do. I had expected that the master carpenter would have accepted me unconditionally to hang out together with his apprentices at the workshop. The request that I bring my guardian or parent ended my dream of carpentry as the alternative to formal schooling with its corporal punishments. I knew that my mother would never consent to allow me to drop out of school for any reason;

I never bothered to broach the subject to her. My stopovers from then on became infrequent until I found something else to absorb my interest.

I was soon attracted and drawn to driving when a driver, Kwame Atta became a co-tenant taking up the room formerly occupied by the family of Akuah Serwah. Kwame Atta was a professional driver who most likely owned his own car. The new man became the center of my attention and interest. I do not know whether it was because I was a filthy and scruffy child but I greatly admired the grease and oil spattered clothes worn by the mechanics during their working hours. The repairs and maintenance works were done on the concrete floor in the courtyard so I had every opportunity to observe them at work. I found the oil soaked and grease stained shorts and shirts they wore very beautiful. I hung around his apprentices, driver mates and other assistants eager to help in any capacity such as running errands if asked. But I was most often considered a nuisance who got in their way. Kwame Atta, his apprentices and hangers-on kept me at arms length despite my attempts to endear myself to them. However, once in a while Kwame allowed me to ride with him when he was hired at night.

I was miffed when I found that Kwame had adopted or at least had an errand boy that was only slightly older than I was. I was envious of this boy, he 'usurped' the position or relationship I hankered for with Kwame that had rather gone to somebody else. I tried so hard to get into the good graces of Kwame by hanging on his every word but to them I was a menace or nuisance that often interfered with their work. I saw a driver and fitters at work under my nose and that became the new dream profession and my aspiration. I aspired to be a driver or auto mechanic. The driver in my house would not let me get close to them but that did not stop me from seeking the position at the lorry park where there were a lot of drivers, driver mates and mechanics.

My impression that driving was an alternative to schooling was reinforced when our landlord sent his son from Kumasi to learn how to drive from Kwame Atta. The son, Kwaku Antwi, was in middle school form III when he came down from Kumasi. He took driving lessons from Kwame during weekends. He was a privileged student because of the landlord tenant relationship he had with Kwame Atta. Kwaku was a proficient driver by his final year in the middle school. He was scheduled for a driving test before his final examination. The schedule unfortunately coincided with his final middle school examination. He skipped the final middle school examination in favor of the driving test; the driving license was as good as the middle school graduation certificate. He passed the driving test and his father bought a Bedford passenger truck for him that he used to ply the Kumasi-Bogoso route.

I would have done anything for the privilege to learn driving or auto repairs. The driving profession was held in high esteem in the Gold Coast. It was such an esteemed and honorable profession that a popular high-life song was composed that praised drivers to high heaven. The song extolled the virtues of drivers and the solidarity that existed between them. It was one profession the members could not go hungry for lack of work. Drivers helped one another or doubled up as driver mates and earned a living helping fellow drivers at the lorry parks loading passengers and their luggage into trucks or helping with maintenance and repairs.

I could not convince or ingratiate myself to Kwame to accept me into his fold and allow me or give me the opportunity to get a whiff of my dream. I could have combined formal schooling with informal apprenticeship and auto repairs on weekends and after school. But Kwame would not have anything to do with me. My friend Kwabenaka knew some driver mates and suggested that we follow some of those friends to find our own masters for apprentice positions. We consulted some of those driver mate friends at the Lorry Park. They pointed out their masters to us and we then approached the masters of the mates in search of apprentice or driver mate positions. A driver mate was the assistant to the driver in the operation of a passenger truck. The mates canvassed for passengers, ushered the passengers and loaded their luggage into the vehicles. The mate collected the fares from the passengers for the driver; he was in effect the right hand man of the driver. The driver mate earned his keep from the master who gave him allowance or *chop money*; the mate was the ward of the driver. The prospect of collecting fares and earning allowance excited us even before we spoke to any driver. The mate graduated when he became a driver in his own right under the tutelage of the master after years of apprenticeship as a mate. The masters of our friends turned us down out of hand, one driver even threatened to report us to our headmaster or parents for being bad boys. And the one who was charitable enough asked for our parents or guardians. Parental consent was the death knell of any attempt I made to seek an alternative to school as an apprentice in a craft or trade. I did not have the courage to tell my mother that I wanted to learn a trade instead of going to school. And once again the ethics of the tradesmen or craftsman prevented me from dropping out of school to pursue a trade or craft.

I unwittingly had my revenge against Kwame Atta through his wife Esi. I guess that Esi was a bored housewife who eased her boredom by cheating on her husband. While Kwame was at work, Esi prepared sumptuous meals for her lover. For instance she used to prepare meat balls from Exeter corned beef for him. The price of a can of corned beef was two shillings and sixpence. Most of us looked on longingly for a can of corned beef but it was out of the means of most regular working class families of the Gold Coast. I was her errand boy. Apart from giving me a taste of the food she was also a good tipper who gave me generous tips. She was so generous with her tips I could never say no to her. She used to give me a tip of about six pence to one shilling for every errand. I unknowingly facilitated her cheating with a local police sergeant. I carried the dinners to him at the police quarters in the afternoons when Kwame was at work.

The tips made me a lot of friends at school because it enabled me to splurge on snacks at school. And for once I had money to snack and to spare. Kwame Atta eventually got wind that his wife was cheating on him with a policeman. Things came to a head when I was called to confirm the errands I ran for her. I answered every question truthfully and Esi was sent packing from the house. Shortly after this incident

Kwame Atta himself relocated to Tarkwa. I used to cross paths with Kwame Atta at the lorry park or railway station when I also relocated a few years later after my transfer from Bogoso to Tarkwa. My older brother, Mumuni, hired Kwame to teach him how to drive and eventually became a driver with the Land Survey Department.

I could not drop out of school to learn a trade as a driver or mechanic but I did not give up my dream or aspiration to be an auto mechanic or driver when I grew up. I considered technical education as the means of achieving my dream. I was encouraged by observation of students of the Tarkwa Technical school when I passed by the school. I planned to go to Tarkwa Technical School to study auto mechanics but I never got the opportunity after I left Bogoso for my hometown at the end of 1957. I did not get the opportunity to go to a secondary or technical school. Thus my ambitions of auto repair or professional driving were stillborn. My dreams of a career in auto repairs died when I left the environment that created my interest in the profession or trade.

My dreams and ambitions were still born because of the ethical integrity and standards of the craftsmen and tradesmen of the Gold Coast. The craftsmen and tradesmen of the Gold Coast were honest with high ethical standards. Their honesty, integrity and personal ethics thwarted every attempt I made to drop out of school in favor of an apprentice in a trade or craft. They refused to entertain our request without any formal request from our guardians. Our requests were very often dismissed out of hand by our contacts, those who were charitable enough asked us to bring our parents or guardians. But for the integrity of the Gold Coast tradesman I would have dropped out of school and vanished into a nether world out of the reach of my mother's influence. The honesty and integrity of the Gold Coast master tradesman made it possible for me to continue in school even though I feared and hated school. The only tradesman or master who did not ask for our parents blessing turned out to be a homosexual fraud.

Fraudulent Magician

No sooner had our quests for driver apprentice been derailed than my partner in truancy Kwabenaka came up with another cockamamie idea, magic. He informed me that he found a magician who was willing to teach him magic. And the good part was that the magician did not require any parental consent for his students. He told me he was already taking lessons from the magician in his house. The magician, Mr. Enchill, asked him to invite interested friends along with him. This was too good to be true; I could not wait to be introduced to the magician. This was one opportunity where I could learn the magician's trade without letting my mother into my secret. By the time my mother became aware I would be a magician.

Accordingly I went to the home of the magician with Kwabenaka one Friday evening. Mr. Enchill the magician welcomed and entertained us with what any kid of our age craved, Ovaltine cocoa beverage drink and bread. After we finished with our drink he then gave us a demonstration of how to conjure money from a paper with mysterious diagrams and drawings. He folded the paper over a two shilling case coin and when he unfolded the paper 2-two shilling case coins or four shillings dropped on the floor. He then turned over the mysterious paper to us and asked us to make copies for our own use. He promised to bless or consecrate our copies when we were done so that we could also conjure coins. He gave us plain sheets of paper to start making our copies after the demonstration. We labored at it doodling the signs and diagrams on the paper for about an hour before he ushered us into bed to start one of the rituals of the training for magic; empowering us with juice. I had no idea of the juice power but I was excited with the prospect of conjuring coins at will when I finished making a copy of the magic paper. I imagined the myriad ways I will spend my conjured money.

Mr. Enchill told us the preparation and training would enable us to become courageous and bold during future magic rituals at the cemetery. The source of our magical powers would be provided by spirits after rituals at the cemetery. We were warned that it was a taboo to fear or panic at the cemetery during the ritual initiation and any show of fear or panic would cause madness or craziness. And that it was for that reason we were required to sleep in his house so that he could teach us and empower us with juice that would embolden us to stand firm at the cemetery in the face of anything that might show up. The juice would strengthen our spine and make us bold and fearless at the cemetery.

I did not know or understand the nature of the juice Mr. Enchill intended to give us but now I know that it had nothing to do with magic. Mr. Enchill, was a closeted homosexual who preyed on the innocence and ignorance of little children and sexually abused and molested them. Kwabenaka and I slept in the same bed with our magic teacher. The juice he gave us was nothing but abusing us to ejaculate his semen. We played and fondled with his penis and he robbed his erected penis against us until he ejaculated; he gave us juice. We played with his prick until we fell asleep. When we woke up in the morning our tummies were slimy with his juice. Mr. Enchill cleaned off the semen, feasted us on more Ovaltine cocoa drink and bread and sent us home. We were expected to return later that night to continue the sexual molestation in the guise of completing the copies of the magic paper we started making the night before.

The quest for training in magic ended just as quickly as it had started, unceremoniously. Mr. Enchill did not coach me on what to tell my mother when I went home. I guess it never occurred to him to prepare us for the ruse because Kwabenaka slept in his home for a few nights without any consequences before I was brought along to his house. When I went home in the morning, my mother confronted me about where I had been the previous night. I told my mother proudly that I went to the house of Mr. Enchill to study magic. My mother was enraged and shouted at the top of her voice for all to hear while threatening to report Mr. Enchill to the police. My mother's threats ended my brief flirtation and association with Mr. Enchill, the homosexual child molester. I did not have the courage to defy mother to go back and never did. I saw Enchill once in a while on the streets of Bogoso and on some local festivals.

At the time of this incident in the early 1950's I knew nothing about homosexuality, not even the terminology or the word. I became aware of homosexuality years later and realized that I had been sexually molested by a phony magician. I felt sorry for my molester. He gave me the taste of the good life; I slept on a soft mattress instead of the hard cement floor I was accustomed. I sympathized with him for sleeping with two filthy smelly boys in the same bed. I could not imagine myself in his shoes. I would not have slept with me at that age. Mr. Enchill by all appearances and standards of the 1950's Gold Coast, was an educated middle class member of society. He appeared to live well. I do not know how Kwabenaka came across him but I am sure we were not the last boys he 'taught magic'.

MAGICIAN IN MY HOUSE

Not long after the incident with Enchill a new tenant moved into the room opposite our room. The new resident had a teenage son in the middle school by name Aglawo. He dabbled in magic or what was known as "dealings" with one of his friends by name Aggrey. They were both students at the local Catholic Middle School. Their ritual practices concentrated on conjuring spirits of saints to divine or prophesy the results of pending soccer matches between local schools in which our school was involved. The conjured spirit was asked to intervene if a negative result was divined or prophesied.

The Sixth and Seventh Book of Moses was the most popular book of magic favored by student 'dealers'. The magic or conjuring ritual consisted of placing a glass of scented water on a pentagram or other such diagram drawn on the floor. They then recited some incantations from the *sixth and seventh book of Moses*. My duty was to stare into the glass of water for any apparition. That was what brought me into contact with the two friends. I was invited to assist them to look for spirit entity or apparition that might appear in the glass of water to answer their inquiries. They believed that I was innocent in the sense that I was a virgin and more likely to see saintly spirits when they were summoned by magic rituals. Stare as hard as I could I never saw any entity or apparition in the glass of water. Eventually Aggrey, who was a sexually active adult, took over that responsibility from me. He stared while Aglawo read or recited the incantations.

They dispensed with my service though they allowed me to watch their dealings.

Aglawo progressed from conjuring spirits to money through the glass of lavender scented water. This time I did not stare into the water but after chanting till he was literally hoarse I was asked to dip my fingers into the glass to ascertain if there was anything in the water. Was Aglawo training to be a magician? I do not know. Was he playing tricks on me and for what reason, I may never know. But sometimes I fetched about four shillings from the glass of water and turned it over to Aglawo. Once in a while he rewarded me with a tip of about three to six pence for my effort. I have no idea where or how the coins ended up in the glass.

GOLF AND TENNIS BALL BOY

Through some friends at school I learned about per diem jobs for ball boys at the local gold mine golf course. Thus for about one year or so I used to rush to the golf course by four o'clock to earn a spot as a ball boy. The ball boys were selected on a first come first served basis. Thus all I needed to do was to be at the course before the White players made it to the golf course themselves. I earned about sixpence for each day that I made the cut and was selected. And at the end of a day of retrieving golf balls from the surrounding bushes I received my pay. In other words for each day that I was selected as a ball boy I earned six pence on the spot, enough money to feed my family for a day. But I did not give my earnings to my mother. To make it to the golf links by four o'clock meant I had to skip some classes or run away altogether so that I could make it to the golf course on time. I therefore kept any money I earned from the course for myself to avoid betraying myself to my mother. I saved my money as usual in an empty milk tin that served as my piggy bank. A few years later when I went to Tarkwa I found work as a ball boy at the local tennis court. Whenever I made the selection at the local tennis court I earned sixpence on the spot.

I was exposed to golf and tennis during my infancy but I never felt that the sports were for me. The impression I had was that golf and tennis were sports for 'kings', the elite or the rich and the powerful. The spotless white uniforms worn by tennis players was beyond me. Thus far, the only items of clothing I wore regularly were my khaki school uniforms. The allowance I earned or made for each day of work was enough to feed my family for a day. And if I managed to work continuously for ten days I made more than enough to pay my school fees for one month. I never imagined or saw myself playing golf or tennis. The cost and expense of golf or tennis was beyond my comprehension. I could not imagine how much I had to earn to afford the game of golf or tennis or be in the same league with the players.

First Meeting With A Whiteman.

I was more confused than enlightened when I began religious studies at school. I was a convert at heart to Catholicism. As such I fought for baptism for about ten years before I was finally baptized. Religious studies were part of the normal academic curriculum and as such compulsory but catechism lessons for baptism were voluntary. Catechism lessons were conducted or taught outside of the normal classroom instructions. Religion was not a condition or requirement for admission at St. Michael's Catholic school else I would have been denied admission. On the first day that my father took me to school he was dressed in the long flowing gown and hat typical apparel of Muslims. Catechism instruction was one of the few lessons or classes that the cane or corporal punishment played no part during instruction and teaching of catechism lessons.

Church attendance was mandatory for all students. Church attendance was not however limited to the Catholic Church but to all religious institutions. If I could show that I went to the mosque on Friday or to the Seventh Day Adventist Church on Saturday I was off the hook for not going to the Church on Sunday. Student church attendance on Sundays were monitored and recorded for Monday morning inspection. And at the Monday morning assembly students who did not go to any church were caned or punished on the assembly grounds before classes. Woe unto students who were also scruffy on Monday, cleanliness is next to godliness, so those of us who had matted hair, overgrown toe and finger nails faced retribution for slovenliness. I dreaded Monday mornings because of the personal inspections. I was often clean shaven but my nails were unkempt and I was not particularly fond of church attendance because I did not have suitable clothing to wear to church other than school uniform. As such I was often caned on Monday mornings for scruffiness and church attendance.

When I was in class three I took catechism lessons for baptism. I was an eager and diligent student of the catechism class and for about three to four months I faithfully attended the classes which were held after normal classes and on weekends. The Catholic Church at Bogoso had no resident priest; therefore the tests for baptism were given when a visiting priest came into town. The catechism class was scheduled for baptism after test on a Saturday before the visiting priest. We were called one by one to go before the priest and our teacher to take an oral test to determine whether we were ready for baptism. I was well prepared academically for the test; I memorized most of the standard catechism questions and answers. The students who were selected for the test were those considered most likely to pass the test. The quizzes were held at the middle middle school of the school complex which also served as the church on Sundays. The Form I to Form III classrooms were separated by partitions. On Sundays the partitions were opened to create a large open hall for church services.

I was called to appear before the priest when it was my turn. I was scared out of my wits when I sat face to face before the white man for the first time in my life. It was like an inquisition before a bogey man or monster I had only seen from afar and never at close range. I sat within three feet of the priest and could see the green colors of his eye balls. I became tongue tied before the White-father. I was so shaken at the sight of a white man in a white cassock, the uniform of the order of the White-Father, I could not open my mouth to answer any question. Sitting before that priest was the closest I ever came near a white person and it was the first person I ever came close enough to see his green eye balls. Thus when I found myself sitting so close that I could see look into his green eye balls I was so petrified I froze up from pure fear. I could not take my eyes away from his green eyes even as I looked around for an escape route should the "monster" attempt to 'eat me alive'.

The proximity to the White Father, was more than I bargained for. I held my breath and would have taken to my heels but for the presence of my catechism teacher sitting next to me. I could not take my eyes off his green eyes and long narrow nose, my lips quivered, my eyes opened wide. I was so scared of the white man that I could not open my mouth to respond to any of the questions that were asked though I knew the answers to all of them. In the end I failed the catechism test because I was scared sitting face-to-face from a white man first time in life. I was glad when the inquisition was over and I was let out of the inquisition hall and out of the sight of the green eyed "monster".

After my knee-jerk reaction at the sight of a white man, I never took part in another catechism class for baptism. And I never came any closer to another white person until I went to Teacher Training College at Navrongo in 1960. Some of my tutors were White Fathers but I never went close to any of them beyond normal class interaction. I was baptized finally at Tamale in 1962, about ten years after I failed the first catechism test.

Prior to the test for baptism the closest I ever came to a white person was from the opposite side of the street while they shopped at the local CFAO store or passed by in a car. While they were in the store I stood with other kids at the opposite side across the street begging for money from them by shouting at then 'Kwesi Broni kyem penne' i.e. white-man favor me with a penny. We dared not cross the street or step onto the verandah of the store to gawk at them within close range in the store. We had the impression that every white person was rich but we were scared to venture close to them. We would have freaked or scurried away had any of them ever attempted to breach the width of the street by getting closer to us. We would have increased the distance between us if they had come any closer.

FAITH AND FAMILY

I have never had faith as defined in catechism lessons at school, my faith has always been tinged with doubt: "faith is a supernatural gift of God which enables us to believe without doubting whatever God has revealed". The lessons on faith I was taught at school was not compatible with the faith and beliefs in my home and my personal experience of spirit. The faith I acquired through education was therefore wobbly at best. My father was a Muslim and my mother was an ancestral worshiper. I failed my first test for baptism in the third grade, perhaps it was good that I failed the baptismal test. In the ten years it took before I was baptized I matured into my understanding of faith though the failure delayed my baptism into the ranks of the Catholic faithful. My faith as a Catholic was waning at about the time that I was finally baptized, ten years after I flunked the catechism test. I did not know where I stood on matters of faith. I questioned the doctrines on which I was raised and took for granted as a Catholic school student.

My faith was in conflict with the faiths or religion of my parents. I was conflicted with the connotation that only the followers of Christ are destined for heaven as in John 14:6, *"I am the way, the truth and the life. No one comes to the Father except through me."* I wondered whether my parents were bound for hell because they were not followers of Christ. I became a Christian by accident of education, and had my mother lived I wonder whether I would have been educated. Did I become eligible for heaven while my dead mother was bound for eternal damnation because she was not that lucky to have been educated and converted into a follower of Christ? The doctrine that only the followers of Christ would go to heaven therefore did not appear to make sense about an omniscient, omnipotent and loving God of all creation. To accept the doctrine was tantamount to the acceptance that faith had become a wedge between my family and me instead of bringing us together.

I sought for an understanding of scriptures as a source of conciliation with the different faiths of my household that ought to bring us together instead of dividing us from one another. I read the bible and prayed for an understanding, an understanding of the oneness of God. I found inspiration and consolation from some passages of the bible that appeared to be at odds with the passage that condemned my mother to hell. Matthew 22:37-40.—*'You shall love the Lord your God with all your heart, with all your soul, and with all your mind. This is the first and great commandment. And the second is like it: You shall love your neighbor as yourself. On these two commandments hang all the Law and Prophets'.*

This was finally the conciliatory scripture that I had been searching for most of my life as a Catholic school student and each time I read this passage I broke into a big smile. My faith was tied up with the fate of my parents. I refused to be separated from my parents in this life by faith. If man's salvation was dependent on the name of Christ to the exclusion of everything that Jesus stood for then it made a farce of the parable of the Good Samaritan; Luke 10:30-37. This is not incompatible with Christ's message of love and redemption in Luke 10: 30-37 and Matthew 22: 37-40. I am bound to my parents by love not by faith. By faith I am apart from them. The parable of the Good Samaritan is a story of unconditional love and the followers of Christ do not have monopoly on love though Christ, by his life and death demonstrated the ultimate unconditional love. Faith separates or keeps us apart but love transcends faith and binds all disparate faiths together into a coherent whole.

The conciliatory passages in the synoptic gospels that love transcends faith is further expounded upon by by the epistles of St. Paul in 1Corinthians 13: 1-13 that last verse reads thus *In a word there are three things that last forever, love, faith and hope but the greatest of these is love*. That love transcends all and is the only gift of God that unites us while faith separates and drives wedge between us. Faith can drive a wedge between families and by extension nations. I could not accept a wedge between my family and me because of the different faiths we followed. I came to the conclusion that whether my parents were bound for eternal damnation or heaven depended on what was in their hearts and not merely by what they believed.

The burden that had been on my heart about the fate of my mothers' soul was lifted. My mother and stepmother could go to heaven by their deeds as defined by love. *"Love is patient and kind. Love envies no one, is never boastful, never conceited, never rude; love is never selfish, never quick to take offence. Love keeps no score of wrongs, takes no pleasure in the sins of others, but delights in the truth. There is nothing love cannot face; there is no limit to its faith, its hope, its endurance"* 1Corinthians 13; 4-7 Revised English Bible.

In a way I solved the dilemma or confusion surrounding the spiritual fates of my family but my faith was not the same as when I was introduced to the Catholic faith in the primary school. I accepted whatever I was taught in the primary school without any doubt or skepticism until I was old enough to discern the truths for myself. For most of my adult life my faith has vacillated from unwavering faith to doubtful faith. I went to church more as social event where I met friends and lovers and renewed acquaintances than for matters of faith or salvation. The childlike quality of faith that I had was replaced by doubt and skepticism. I questioned the very existence of God and finally came to the conclusion that if God was real then it was possible to experience Him. I do not see the air but I experience the air when I breathe. It is therefore possible to experience and feel God in my daily life though I might never see Him standing in front of me.

My faith was renewed, a renewal that was based on experience than on the words of my pastors and preachers. For this I had my grounding in the Bible. I characterize myself as believer in the mold of Thomas the Apostle. In other words my faith is not based on an abstract idea but on what I have seen, felt or experienced similar to the Apostle Thomas who doubted the resurrection of Christ until he was convinced otherwise by Jesus. His faith became stronger when Jesus revealed himself to Thomas. And although Jesus said bless are those who have not seen and yet believe. No where was Thomas condemned for doubting the resurrection of Christ. Doubt is therefore part and parcel of the development of my faith or belief. I believe what I have experienced or seen. I believe in spirits because I have both seen and experienced the work of spirits. I believe that evil spirits exist because I have seen and experienced the works of evil.

After I was baptized in 1962 I questioned myself whether I was baptized in body or in spirit. I sought for baptism for more than ten years and when I was finally baptized it was a great let down. I did not feel any differently before and after I was baptized. I was under the impression that baptism would put me right with God but I felt no spiritual illumination, ecstasy, inspiration, or any of the myriad gifts of spirit promised to believers. Was I really baptized? I doubted whether the baptism was real or make belief. Within a year after my baptism, I began to drift from the Catholic Church. I was getting hungry for spiritual experience that I could not obtain or experience from the only church I have ever known. I declared myself a free thinker with no church affiliation and went from one church to another in search for that something that I could not really identify. But I was confident that I would know it when I came across it.

SPIRITUAL ECSTASY

I experienced brief periods of spiritual ecstasy as I child but I did not know or understand it. I used to feel strange and unusual sensations during infancy whenever I passed by an Apostolic church while they prayed together 'in tongues'. I used to shiver from hair to toe and tears welled up in my eyes. To prevent shedding tears while observing them from outside I ran away at that stage over the involuntary tears. I did not know the name of the church but it was one of the new breed of spiritual churches that started in the early fifties. The new breed of spiritual churches that sprung up at Bogoso in the 1950's were known as Apostolic Churches. I did not know or understand the cause of the gentle shivers and the tears that welled up in my eyes but they were enough to send me running away from what I did not know or understand. I never felt similar sensations at my Catholic Church. I even had a condescending attitude towards them because I was a member of the one true church. I did not know what to make of the new churches that played musical instruments, sang and danced during worship. The church where I experienced the ecstatic sensations was one of the new crop of Apostolic Churches that worshipped in a storefront at the outskirts of town. When I drifted from the Catholic church I began worshiping at some of these spiritual churches. And whenever I worshipped at one of these churches, I experienced these ecstatic moments that often filled me with inexplicable tears. But I scarcely got similar sensations in the conventional and genteel churches.

I have some faith but based mainly on what I have seen or experienced. I wrestled with God like Jacob Gen 32: 24-26 until I got a revelation or understanding of some subtle truths. I have been skeptical and sometimes contemptuous at the rabble-rousers of modern day preachers who drive wedges between people of different beliefs and faiths. I believe that these rabble rousers have ulterior motives for driving wedges between us, they do so for financial gain. When they stoke violence and we claw at one another they laugh all the way to the bank. We empty our pockets and give them the little that we have. They become fabulously rich while we become fabulously poor. These leaders, for their own financial gain have turned the great commandment of love and redemption into a foot note in the message of Christ. Money is the god that we worship cloaked with the bible. We have ceased being 'our brother's keeper' and have instead become our brother's executioner.

Christianity, distilled to its most basic element, is profoundly simple: love and redemption. But this simple message has been turned on its head with emphasis on the branches of the tree at the expense of the tree itself. Faith makes it easier to cloak our prejudice and bigotry thus avoiding personal responsibility for our bigotry and prejudice in the name of faith. The instigators of hatred and divisions fish the bible for the minutia of quotations to bamboozle, confuse and divide us instead of uniting us in the love of Christ.

By faith we are divided and see our neighbor as 'other' instead of seeing our neighbor as part of the quilt of the fabric of our common humanity.

I had peace in my heart when I came to the realization that love is the greatest commandment of God that reconciled me with my family of different faiths and united us by his love. Love transcends faith and one who has love naturally has an abiding faith born of love. When we love we become like children we trust completely without doubt. The unquestioning faith in God comes from love. I see myself as a child of God and demand the rights of a child without any doubt or reservation. Mankind commits horrible atrocities against one another in the name of faith. That which cannot stand or justified by Love is acceptable and justified by faith. We kill and maim in the name of faith, but we do not kill and maim those we love. The Christianity I embraced in spite of my skepticism is based on love and its attributes as lucidly written by St. Paul in 1 Corinthians 13: 1-14

I consider myself a Christian, but a skeptic one. The foundation of my faith is based on doubt. Thomas the Apostle was not consigned to hell because he dared to doubt that Christ had indeed risen, he was rewarded with the revelation of the Lord himself. When I became a discerning student I fell in love with the doubting Thomas. John 20: 29 *'Jesus said to him, "Thomas, because you have seen Me, you have believed. Blessed are those who have not seen and yet have believed ".* Jesus lives and continues to reveal himself to the Thomas' who want to see to believe. I was taught that "Faith is a supernatural gift of God which enables us to believe without doubting whatever God has revealed." Mankind would be far better off if love was the basis of our faith. 'Love is a supernatural gift of God which enables to believe without doubting whatever God has revealed.'

I became interested in reading the bible because of my propensity for argument in the middle school. And I hated being brow beaten each time I held bible discussions with a member of the Jehovah Witness. I started holding bible discussions with the Jehovah Witnesses when I was in the eighth grade or form II. I found to my chagrin that the regular religious lessons I was taught at school was not enough to help me to hold my own against members of the Jehovah Witnesses during discussions of bible. So I became interested in reading the bible so as to cope with them during discussions. I read the bible from cover to cover at least twice during the eighth grade. I did not become a good bible scholar but it gave me the understanding to tell alternate bible stories even if I could not provide direct quotations of chapter and verse.

I was forced to read the bible from cover to cover again as a teacher when I had a room mate who as a member of the Seventh Day Adventist Church used to floor or expose my ignorance whenever we held discussions on the bible. I did not like the way my ignorance was always exposed so I took it upon myself to read the bible. I read the bible from the background of the Catholic Church. Again I was not as good as my Seventh Day Adventist friend but that was the beginning of my search for wisdom from the bible as an adult.

RELIGIOUS TOLERANCE

My father did not foist his Islamic faith on any of his children, not even when I implored him to enroll me at an Islamic school did he deviate from his character. My father did not require his children or wives to follow in his footsteps and live by his Islamic faith. But most of his children followed his faith voluntarily as adults. And those of us who did not convert to Islam or before we converted nevertheless followed the practices and traditions of our father's faith. Irrespective of our individual religion or faith we followed the Islamic tradition of giving names to our new-born by slaughtering sheep or ram on the seventh day. As a child I loved the Islamic naming ritual because of the abundant supply of food and meat made available as a result of the ritual. I saw this ritual performed several times during the first half of the 1950's at Bogoso for the babies of my brothers and sisters when they came to Mommy to have their babies.

At Tamso, my father lived in a small Islamic community. Two branches of Islam lived together, prayed together and broke bread together during the fasting season of Ramadan. I knew then that there were two branches of Islam though I never heard the name Shia or Sunni. The two branches of Islam lived together in peace and harmony without tearing one another apart. We had no mosque but during the Ramadan they prayed on the paved ground my father made for prayers. Shia and Sunni lived and prayed together, of course it did not hurt that we spoke the same dialect and were from the same tribe. The only difference between the two was the way they stood during prayers; one with arms by the side and the other with arms folded on the chest. The significant thing was that they lived together in harmony in the same community of three multi occupied compound houses.

SECOND REUNION WITH MY FATHER

Just as my father blamed my stepmother for my mother breaking up with him, I blamed my father's third wife for his dumping my stepmother and her children. I was in class five when I met my father's new wife and I did not like her. I kept respectable distance from her and I think the dislike was mutual. She did not coddle me as such though she fed me during the two to three years I lived with my father at Tarkwa-Tamso. But as far as her children were concerned I did not see any difference between us, we were brothers and sisters period.

In retrospect, I had no reason to dislike her. She did not treat me any differently from her own children. The whole family ate from the same pot without any partiality. She did not show any open partiality towards her own children at my expense. I am an only child among my father's children from two other women but I had cordial relations with all my half brothers and sisters. When I became an adult, I accorded her the respect and obedience she deserved as my stepmother without any ill feeling or rancor. After my father passed away, she came to my office and reminded me of my obligations towards my brothers and sisters, as the oldest surviving son of my father.

The Dagarti are a patrilineal society. Succession goes to the eldest male child. Under our customary law of succession I was the oldest surviving son of my father and thus his heir. I have older sisters but women under our customs take on the lineage or become a part of the husband's family. It is for this reason that my sister Vida and my other older sisters were buried in their husband's hometown and my birth mother was buried at Nyagli, her husband's home village. I accepted that responsibility that was thrust and tried as much as possible to be a good bother to my younger brothers and sisters while I was in Ghana. I benefited from the extended family system and I remained faithful to it. I overcame the blame game and did not hold her responsible anymore for the sins of my father during my infancy.

I lived with my father for less than three years before I went back to Bogoso. My stepmother never married again for the rest of her life. We encouraged her to enter into a new relationship but she said a man would serve no purpose in her life because she was past her child bearing age. She maintained that if she could not bear another child then it was a waste of time to remarry. In my mother's eyes the main purpose of marriage was procreation, and since she was past child bearing age there was no reason to marry again. My father and mother was to all intents and purposes a divorced couple but in the eyes of our traditional law they were a married couple. My father never took the necessary steps to legitimize the separation. They lived separate lives for over thirty years. But when my died my mother was treated like a legitimate widow in accordance with traditional practices, her head was shaved clean as a sign of a widow mourning her husband.

It would appear that my father imparted some of his characteristics and habits to his male children. My older brother, Mumuni, dumped his first wife after he married a second wife. He lived with the second wife at the expense his first wife. The only difference between my father and my brother was that my brother kept his wife with our mother and maintained her through regular remittances. But the abandonment caused his wife to have illicit affairs that resulted in the birth of children for my brother.

I was not disappointed when I arrived at Tarkwa in the third term of 1954. Tarkwa was a large urban community with two movie houses and other forms of entertainment particularly boxing that were not available at Bogoso. But above all, unlike Bogoso, Tarkwa had electricity. My father lived at Tamso village where there were no streets, potable water or electricity. The village was endowed with one public toilet and dug out wells for water supply. The village township and the residential compound for mine workers was less half a mile but they could not have been more different or far apart in amenities. The compound was supplied with street lights and potable water at public stand pipes.

A few weeks after my arrival at Tarkwa my father sent me to live with Samai an extended family member at the residential compound for mine workers. I slept in a room lighted by electricity and not by a kerosene lamp. It was novel to flip a switch on the wall and presto there was light. What dazzled me for one night while on my way from the north became a routine part of daily life. At Bogoso I was far removed from electricity, I saw lights shining against the dark skies on the hilltop where the mine properties and bungalows were located. But Bogoso Township was a dark town, kerosene lamps lit up the night like fire flies. I considered it a privilege living at the mines residential community where there were modern amenities such as running water and electricity. I had supper in the village with my father after school before proceeding to the compound for the night. I drank potted water and walked under the safety of street lights at night.

I had a buyer's remorse only a few months after arrival at Tarkwa. The father I met was different from the father I knew before he disappeared from home. He was remote and reticent. He was not the same man who was my companion a few years earlier, we used to go to places together such as the butcher's shop and the riverside to do our laundry. The camaraderie and friendship that we had were missing. I was more of an outsider and not an integral part of my father's new family. It was therefore a great relief when I was sent over to live part of the time with uncle Samai. As time went on I spent more time with Samai and my friends than with my father. I went for days at a time without stopping at my father's house for meals.

I had chilly and frosty relations with my new stepmother, Salamatu. She did right by me as was required of her, she showed no partiality or hostility towards me. Unlike some stepmother's, I ate the same food with the rest of the family. But there was no warmth between us and we had very little to say to one another. Perhaps it was because at the back of my mind I held her responsible for my father's vanishing act from my stepmother and siblings. I found Salamatu so fair and beautiful I thought my father was too old for her. I was infatuated with her beauty and had an Oedipus complex toward her. I asked my father why at his age he would take such a young woman as a wife. My father accused me of selfishness asking me where I would be "if I had not married your mother?" I think my father's wife and I mutually disliked one another. She fulfilled all her obligations towards me as a stepmother but without any love or warmth. I sensed that perhaps she did not love or care much about me.

The passage of time culminating with the death of my father finally broke the ice and brought us close together as mother and son. When my father passed away, I was the oldest surviving son and as such the heir of my father and indirectly the head of the Ali family. She came to me at the office unexpectedly in Accra after my father passed away. She affirmed my role and obligations for my younger brothers and sisters in the aftermath of my father's death. When I was in Ghana, I assisted with the education and care of my younger brothers and sister until the day I left.

I was introduced to other members of our extended family within the various mining communities around Tarkwa. My worldview widened as I became acquainted with more of my relatives scattered around Tarkwa urban area. Most of them were low wage laborers but their social status was not a factor in my relations with them, they were my heroes. One of my relatives for instance was a housekeeper or cook to a white expatriate mine official. It was from his work in the bungalow that I got a peek into the life of the white man in colonial Ghana. I was as happy as a lark whenever I hanged around the bungalow while he was at work. I could not do that with those who worked below surface or underground. I appreciated every little gesture of kindness from my relatives and I was very proud of them.

The generosity and warmth of my relatives made the three years I lived at Tarkwa worthwhile. Their kindness eased the burden of living with a father who was a notorious miser. My father was so stingy that he habitually pinched his pocket particularly when he came across familiar people, to muffle or prevent sounds of coins jingling in his pocket. He paid my school fees late mostly after I was expelled from school. And he never gave me any pocket money for school or extra money for any purpose beyond what was absolutely necessary, he had no margin of errors when it came to spending any money on a child. Samai used to give me pocket money for school and did so throughout the three years I was at Tarkwa. I was so frugal I used to save a greater proportion of my pocket money in a tin piggy bank. I scarcely bought lunch or snack at school, I snooped around students during lunch and snack breaks for handouts from my mates rather than buying anything myself.

My school fees were often paid late and I was sometimes forced by circumstances to make up the difference from my own resources. Despite the generosity of Samai he drew the line in the sand when it came to school fees; he refused to shoulder any responsibility for my school fees.

I was more mature by the time I went to Tarkwa and was more regular at school. The only period I was absent from school was either due to sickness or expulsion for late payment of school fees. I disliked the ignominy from the monthly expulsion and disruption arising from the forced absence from school. I did extra odd jobs for extra money in addition to my pocket money. I used to carry the luggage of weary rail passengers who arrived around noontime from Sekondi-Takoradi for a fee. We used to rush to the railway station during the lunch break to help weary rail passengers' transport their baggage to their homes or final destination for fees.

My father invariably paid the school fees but at his own pace and time. This vicious cycle of expulsion from school was repeated month after month right from the day I went to class one in 1950. It only ended when the government of independent Ghana abolished school fees for primary and middle school in 1957. I was not charged any more school fees during the last three years of my elementary school education whether in the public or parochial schools.

WALKING TO TAMSO AT NIGHT

Tarkwa was everything that Bogoso was not. There were two movie houses at Tarkwa in the 1950's, Hippodrome on the west of town and another one on the east side. Hippodrome was a modern movie house with terraced seats and balcony. But I lived three miles from Tarkwa so I could not satisfy my curiosity for movies. I liked movies but I was afraid to walk the road to Tarkwa for movies at night except during daylight hours when we walked to and from school.

The village strong man, a boxer by name Napoleon, persuaded some us to walk with him to see the Three Musketeers starring Gene Kelly one night in 1955 or 1956. We went to Tarkwa by bus and came back on foot along the road. The Three Musketeers was the first movie I saw in an actual movie theater. After seeing that movie I braved the hazards of the night and my own fears to see other movies from time to time. I usually left Tamso around seven o'clock for Tarkwa and returned after the movies ended at about ten thirty or thereabout. Public transport used to shut down for the day by the ten o'clock at night. Commuter transport of any kind whether public or private was not usually available after ten o'clock at night.

I was very familiar with the twists and turns of the road from Tarkwa to Tamso. But walking the road alone at night was different from walking the same road during day time. Rumors of child kidnappings or head hunters were widespread though no body ever saw a headless body or knew any family whose child was kidnapped, but the rumors persisted. My fears were spooked by the section of the road that passed through the cemetery at *Effuanta*. I was often frightened of meeting malevolent spirits, ghosts or goblins whenever I left Hippodrome and made my way towards Tamso than kidnappers and headhunters. Half of the distance was lit up by street lamps but the remaining distance was pitch black on a moonless night.

The fear of the unknown or the invisible was more powerful than the fear of kidnappers and head hunters while walking at night beside the cemetery along the road. Head hunters and kidnappers could be seen with the naked eye but ghosts and spirits struck more fear into my heart though I never saw anything on the road but I was often petrified with fear as I made my way along the dark road. I used to slow down and reserved my strength as I approached the forest and as soon as I entered the cemetery zone within the bamboo forest I took to my heels running as fast as I could while looking behind me for any furtive figure until I was clear of the cemetery area. And then I slowed down to catch my breath while walking briskly. *Effuanta* was the last village before Tamso, so once I saw the roofing sheets of the village looming ahead I breathed a sigh of relief. Despite my fears and apprehension I went the same route time and time again until I left Tarkwa at the end of 1956. I used to run through the dark portions of the road as fast as my legs could carry me, slowed down to exhale after going through the dark and unlit sections of the road.

In spite of all my fears and anxieties I never saw or heard any rat or nocturnal creature rustle through bushes. I used to be so scared walking the road at night that had any nocturnal creature such as a hedgehog or rat rustled through the forest I would have passed out from fear. By the time I returned to Bogoso at the end of 1956 I could run the three miles from Tarkwa to Tamso non-stop as such I considered myself a cross country runner though I ran from fear of ghosts, goblins and zombies. In 1964 I tried to compete in cross country races when I was a student at Peki. My attempts failed, I found I had the breath or heart to run a cross country race but my legs could not carry me over the distance. By this time of my life I did not see the other worldly creatures or entities before my father purged the 'seeing eyes.'

INFESTATION OF VERMIN IN THE RESIDENTIAL COMPLEX

The residential compound for mine workers where I lived with my uncle Samai was heavily infested with vermin, particularly mice and roaches. Our room for instance was heavily infested with bedbugs, mice and roaches. Bedbugs were not a vermin that evoked any sense of dread or unease in me. They were a minor irritant or inconvenience in the context of everyday life. It appears the straw mattress was a natural breeding ground for bedbugs; they hid in the folds of the mattress. Once in a while I sprinkled or sprayed kerosene on the mattress to kill the bedbugs or I fished and squashed them between my thumb nails when idle. But since I slept mostly on the floor I did not contend with bedbugs at night.

Mice and roaches scurried about the room at night particularly after the lights were switched off. Most often I heard the mice scurrying about but rarely saw or felt them in the dark room; the roaches on the other hand shared my straw mat with me at night. I battled the roaches as I slept on the floor every night. The room was so heavily infested with the roaches that they practically crawled over me while I slept. I was used to the roach menace and squashed them even in my sleep without butting an eyelid. The roach menace would not have left any lasting memories had not one entered my ear canal while I was soundly asleep one night. I woke up from my slumber with the roach in my ear. Instinctively I tried to pull or yank it out and as I did so it crawled deeper into the ear canal braking off its limbs as I tugged and yanked at them. I switched on the light and sat on my mat scared with the roach in my ear while my uncle was fast asleep. I had no idea how to get it out. Then suddenly it hit me, water! I fetched a cup of water and flushed or drenched my ear with water. As I poured the cup of water into my ear I felt it crawling backwards and I waited patiently for the roach to come out. As soon as it hit the floor I jumped on it and smashed it into smithereens under my foot. Then I switched off the light and went back to bed for the rest of the night greatly relieved.

HELPING ADULTS TO READ

Many of my fellow tribesmen worked at the various gold mines located in the small towns and villages around Tarkwa. Some of them worked hard for self improvements to earn promotions at work. The gateway for promotion to senior or supervisory positions in the mine hierarchy was a blasting license. The blasting license was the first rung of the ladder in the hierarchy of senior positions. One could also not advance to a Blast-man without some fluency in English. The ambitious ones among them attended adult education classes and schools at night for English reading lessons. This was when the little English I knew as a primary school student was utilized by them. My kinsmen saw me as a convenient alternative to formal adult education programs because I lived among them in the same community. I was often hired to teach them the rudiments of reading and speaking English.

The standard textbook for adult education in the mid 1950's was the Royal Primer. The Royal Primer was in two volumes or books, Book I was similar to present day kindergarten curriculum. It dealt with the basic alphabets and two letter word formations, such as no, go, to, so etc. and the second volume went a stage further to include three and four letter words.

I taught reading and writing English to about one or two adults per night and for my effort I was paid about two shillings per month. My uncle Samai was one individual who never went beyond the the first book or primer and as such never went beyond a machine operator at the mines until his career was cut short by lung disease contracted at the mines. He was paid a lump sum on his retirement but he fritted away the money within two years when he attempted to follow my father's footsteps as a trader. One or two of my students passed the blasting license and went on to earn promotions to senior positions.

FATHER FOUND ME A WIFE

On my second vacation with my father at Tamso as a student of St. John Bosco's College, I found a beautiful young woman residing with him; she was not there during my first visit from Navrongo. I assumed that the young woman was one of the many relatives who passed through my father's house from time to time. But unbeknown to me my father was already arranging a traditional marriage for me by having my future wife waiting for me. She was about my age group and we soon became playmates and horsed around the bushes and surroundings of the village.

The girl was very attractive and we had lots of fun together but I assumed that she was one of the many distant family members that are as good as family. Maybe the girl was aware of my father's intentions but I was not as such I made no attempt to hit on her. My father in effect betrothed the girl as my future bride. He hoped that if I met the woman he had chosen as my future wife we might get along. Indeed we did get along but not romantically as was expected by my father. I did not hit on her but based on his observation of the two of us romping together he made his intentions known to me. He disclosed his intentions just before my vacation came to an end. I liked her or perhaps even loved her, but it was platonic kind of love with no romantic feelings. It never crossed my mind to take advantage of romping around with her into a romantic affair. I informed my father that I was yet too young and green to contemplate marriage. He offered to take care of 'my wife' until I was ready or started working. I refused the offer and to his credit he did not insist or pressure me to marry the girl he had chosen for me. I was about sixteen or seventeen years old at the time, marriage seemed a weird institution at that age.

MARRIAGE OF CONVENIENCE

About ten years later I fell in love with Frances, a high school student from the same village as my stepmother, *Salamatu*. I was ready to jump into the marriage institution and accordingly informed my father about my romantic involvement with Frances. As a conscientious Dagarti father, eager to see me settled down with a woman before he passed away, he went ahead and performed the preliminary customary or traditional greetings similar to engagement. He paid obeisance to the girl's family with the appropriate traditional gifts to inform them that their daughter and his son were an item. However the love affair with Frances fizzled after about two years.

About five years after Frances and I broke up the marriage bug bit me and I decided to get married. The woman I chose as my eventual bride was not chosen because of love but on my perception of a moral character and desire to be seen as having good and moral character. When I was contemplating marriage I was already a father of two with two different women. I did not like the image of myself as a philanderer and womanizer who had fathered two children with two different women and I was not married. I also considered limiting my family size to a maximum of three children. Since I was already a father of two children without a wife it made any family plan of three children appear quixotic if not impossible to realize after marriage. I did not think I could persuade another woman to abandon her own desires for say three children in favor of only one child while raising three children. I concluded that my family plan would only be possible if I made the mother of one of my children my wife. I therefore followed my head instead of my heart in my choice of a bride.

My choice of a marriage partner was therefore constrained by considerations of my ideal family size. I did not know the whereabouts of Dora, the mother of my first child. The choice for a bride was thus limited to Obenewa, the mother of my second child. I convinced myself that if the mother of my second child was good enough to to have a a fling that resulted in the birth of a baby, she should be good enough to have another child as a wife. That was how I ended up marrying the mother of my second child who went on to bear four more children within eight years The understanding we had before marriage went out of the window the moment we became man and wife. She followed the counsel of her sister who encouraged her to bear as many children as she could without regard to our understanding before marriage. She abandoned our family plans without giving me any hint about her change of heart.

I jilted the woman I loved and had intended to marry in favor of Obenewa, the mother of Akuah, my second child. The decision backfired and my family plan was blown out of the water shortly after we became man and wife in accordance with custom and tradition. I knew from the beginning that the marriage was doomed to failure since it was not based on love It was more or less a marriage of convenience though I really intended to make it work despite my misgivings. As a product of the Catholic Church I worked hard to sustain the marriage, but in the end I could not undo the weakness that had been built into the marriage from the beginning. It broke down under the weight of the financial burdens I had sought to avoid. And I ran away from home when we had five children between us. When I walked out from home I never imagined that I would remarry and have more children, but it is often said that man proposes and God disposes, I could not avoid following my path of destiny. I remarried a few years after I left home and and I had three more children with my new wife. In effect I had my ideal family size the second time around but that made me a father many times over.

Return To Mother At Bogoso

When I left my mother for Tarkwa in 1954 I did not see her again until about the middle of 1956 when I paid an emergency visit to her at Bogoso. I had a sort of premonition that alarmed me and prompted me to see her as a matter of urgency. So the following morning when I left for school I took two shillings, enough money, to cover my return fare from Tarkwa to Bogoso. The full adult fare was two shillings and children were charged half fare or one shilling.

After school I hopped onto a passenger truck for Bogoso and arrived shortly after sunset. I expected the worse but I was happy to find my mother going about her normal daily chores. She appeared to be in robust health; I breathed a sigh of relief when I realized that my fears were unfounded. I snuggled up to her and Adjoa to enjoy her motherly warmth and affection. My heart had grown tender for my mother and sister during the two years or more that I had been away from Bogoso.

When she finished with her work for the day she sat on a stool in front of the door and rolled up her cover cloth up to her knees. She then took out a bottle of Sloan's liniment and proceeded to apply and massage her swollen and knobby knees with the liniment. She massaged her knees thoroughly with the liniment and when that was done she took a tablespoon and readied herself to take the liniment by mouth. She cleared her throat and poured out spoonful of the liniment all the while soliloquizing about the unpleasant taste and the burning sensations that followed every spoonful of the liniment taken by mouth. On hearing her soliloquy I asked for the bottle and after reading the directions on the bottle I informed her that the liniment was recommended for external use only. She breathed a big sigh of relief and massaged her arms and chest with the spoonful of the liniment she had intended to take by mouth with a great sense of relief. "Uh huh this must be why my chest is on fire when I take it by mouth".

Apparently she had been taking the liniment by mouth for a few nights since she bought it from a petty drug peddler. The peddler informed her that the liniment was meant for both internal and external uses; he took advantage of my mother's illiteracy and misled her. I relieved my mother from the misleading advice of a petty drug peddler. I do not know whether taking liniment by mouth has any lasting adverse effect. But I was glad that the hunch to see my mother led me to prevent her from following the misleading advice of a petty drug peddler.

I went back to Tarkwa after the weekend. The short visit rekindled my interest once more in Bogoso. I began planning how to outwit my father and obtain a transfer certificate and go back to Bogoso without his knowledge. My father would not have allowed me to return to my mother at Bogoso. In the Gold Coast transfer certificates were required to move from one school to another. During the last week of the third term in 1956 I informed the head teacher that my family planned to go back to the North at the end of the year and so I required a transfer certificate. At the end of the year the head-teacher gave me the transfer certificate with no questions asked. I went back to Bogoso and re enrolled at my old school, St. Michael's Roman Catholic School in January 1957. My return to Bogoso was perhaps instrumental in my successful completion of middle school and subsequently gained admission to a certificate B teacher training college which formed the foundation of my path for future higher education. Most of the friends and playmates I left behind did not fare quite as well, they did not complete middle school.

At the end of 1957, I went back to my hometown to complete my middle school education. I completed middle school and obtained the middle school leaving certificate, the minimum education qualification required for jobs in the civil service or teaching career in the Gold Coast and Ghana in the late fifties and sixties. I was taken to the South in 1949 as a backward and ignorant kid who had never seen the automobile. The country was called the Gold Coast, by the time I came back at the end of 1957, the country was a newly minted independent nation with a new name of Ghana. I was not the same ignorant and backward kid that left the northern territories almost a decade earlier. I was more worldly and accustomed to a lot of technological developments of which I was ignorant when I left my village for the South a decade earlier.

Jeers, Mockery And Bullies

When I arrived at Bogoso I spoke only my native dialect. The language barrier was the first cause of friction between my school mates and me. I had to overcome the language barrier after I enrolled in school in January 1950. The inability to speak Akan made me the target of ridicule and mockery both at home and school. And that in turn made me overtly aggressive towards those I perceived as laughing and mocking me. The aggression started at home where I constantly brawled and fought Kwabena Kitewa or Kwabena Jr., a playmate and my first Akan language teacher. I was often at the receiving end of the aggression but I never gave up attacking him for mocking or laughing at me.

Kwabena was both a friend and foe at home. He was the son of our next door neighbor and we were about the same age group. We were playmates that used to make our own toys from scrap metals, bottle tops and packing cases. But the miscommunication and misunderstanding often led to brawls. I was not any skillful at fighting than I was at Duohi. I had limited wrestling skills and none of fisticuffs. Kwabena often out boxed me when we had a fight but I never stopped attacking him for perceived jeers, mockery and taunting or goading me to fights. A word spoken with a mocking tone followed by laughter was enough to rouse my ire as being ridiculed or made fun of. And before anybody could intervene between two boys shouting at one another in different tongues we would be enjoined in a brawl. I could not outbox him in any fisticuffs or exchange of blows but I could not tolerate what I perceived as insults or mockery. We were at one another's throats so frequently that the adults stopped taking notice when we went at one another.

Kwabena was both an indispensable friend and an implacable foe who made my life miserable at home. As long as Kwabena out boxed or bested me, his parents did not care about our brawls. My mother and sister ached for me, but they could not intervene in fights between two boys of similar age. They urged me secretly to fight back which I always did but I just was not good enough at fisticuffs. I was no match for Kwabena in any fisticuffs when I rushed at him with my head down trying to bowl him down.

The constant brawls with Kwabena usually ended harmlessly, no blood was ever spilled. But that characterization changed dramatically one Saturday morning when I accidentally spilled the blood of Kwabena during a brawl. We used to make our own cartoon movies. We cut stick figures from cardboards, and with a hollowed out old bucket covered with calico and a candle or lamp we showed our own cartoon character movies with our own running commentary. The cardboard characters we created were held aloft with broom sticks from the spine of palm leaves. The hollowed out old bucket covered with a piece of white cloth or calico served as our movie screen. We also made string puppets from cardboards and while playing with the puppets or exhibiting our cardboard characters we made noises and grunts imitating what we had seen at the public cinemas. I never saw a commercially made toy as an infant; our play things were all made from scrap materials we could lay hands on.

One Saturday morning we were making toy cars from wood when a misunderstanding arose between us and we started shouting at one another in our dialects. Within a short time we were at one another's throats in front of his parents' room and as usual nobody bothered to intervene because I always came out worse off in any scuffles. But this time the outcome of the fight was very different. I rushed at Kwabena who unleashed a barrage of blows against me and for once he lost his balance when I rushed at him. He fell down head first and hit his forehead against the sharp edge of the handle of a galvanized iron bucket that was nearby. A cut opened above one of his eye brows and blood gushed out of the cut. The sight of blood spurting out of the wound alarmed his mother and sister, they both wailed as if he was on his deathbed. His mother threatened amidst her tears to report me to the police but the cool head of his father prevailed. His father was more reasonable, the wound was an accident caused by frequent brawls between two children of similar ages. He stemmed the blood flow and dressed the wound. And for once I was the victor in a brawl with bloody consequences.

I won my freedom from Kwabena from that day. My mother and sister quietly cheered and congratulated me on the outcome of the latest brawl. I guess my instincts that Kwabena insulted and ridiculed me had some veracity because the incidence of quarrels, brawls and scuffles between us suddenly came to an end, he stopped making faces at me. The cause of peace was not hurt when I started speaking the Akan dialect haltingly at first but quite fluently by the end of the year thanks in no small measure to Kwabena.

A large tooth gap in my upper front teeth was fodder for jeers mockery, taunting and laughter throughout most of the elementary school. The first five to six years of my elementary school were unhappy years because of the bullying, mockery and laughter that I endured. I had several derogatory nicknames bestowed on me by school mates based on where I came from and of course the large tooth gap. I got into brawls over abusive nicknames, mockery and laughter. Discipline at school prevented open hostilities on school campus, most of the fighting and brawls took place on the road to and from school. I was reminded time and time again in mocking tones that I was a northerner or *pepe nyi,* the derogatory term for people of northern origin and Northern Ghana in particular.

My schoolmates were so cruel they lost no opportunity to tell me directly or by inference that I was inferior to them. I was considered inferior because most of the menial jobs in the town were done by people of northern origin. The dusty streets and open gutters or drains were cleaned by people of northern origin, the bucket toilets and garbage were cleared and removed by people of northern origin. The nicknames that were bestowed on me reflected the menial jobs they saw done predominantly by northerners. Some of my peers who appeared friendly and sympathetic were rather condescending towards me instead of providing comfort. I had to fight for acceptance and respect, I could not stand the sneers, the name calling; *pepe, koko latrine boy and other derogatory epithets*. It was not an easy life being about the only northerner in the school.

The constant onslaught and abuses made me ashamed to be identified with my people during the first four to five years at school among the Akans. It did not matter that the northern territories was a vast area of various ethnic groups. The jeers, mockery, taunting and incessant discrimination was to make all northerners feel under siege in the south. Any differences that existed between any groups of people in the north were set aside in the south. We had to band together to survive in a hostile environment. Ethnic discrimination was a big part of the Gold Coast experience. I did not fare any better when I went to Tarkwa. My relatives who dated Akan women were called the same derogatory names behind their back. The funny thing was that when I became fluent in Akan language they flattered me by telling me that I was different from my own people. But I concluded that I was not any different and never accepted the flattery.

The offending epithets followed me until I became mature and developed a thick skin and rationalized the hostile environment. I rationalized the hostility towards me by convincing myself that the hostility and name calling was the symptom of ignorance and narrow mindedness. That the mockery and name-calling was due to ignorance, insecurity and that they had a very narrow worldview. I could do very little about another person's ignorance and feeling of insecurity. I accepted the maxim that 'hard words break no bones'. It was not beneficial fighting ignorant and insecure people. The ethnic majority felt insecure at the presence of the minority in their midst despite their superiority in numbers and the levers of power controlled by them by virtue of their numbers.

This is the crux of discrimination everywhere. The dominant ethnic group feel insecure at the sight of the minority that live among them and appear to be prosperous. Ethnic minority is relative. In my part of the country I am in the majority and the attitudes and name calling are reversed. I became quite a talkative over time and my mouth became my weapon of choice in confronting my antagonists. Those who are part of a dominant people at one location or country should remember that the world is now a small village. The dominant becomes the minority depending on where one's fortune might land him in this global village.

Those who mocked and laughed at me hid behind my ignorance of the Akan language. But once I became proficient in Akan they did not dare insult or say unkind things openly against me, they did so behind my back. And as they say, what you do not know does not hurt. I took no offence when I overheard what was being said in secret. The secrecy signaled to me that my adversary was cowardly hence he hid behind anonymity. This attitude made a world of difference as it reduced considerably the frequency of violent confrontations and quarrels with my tormentors or classmates and schoolmates. I found that I did not have to fight over every perceived contempt or disrespect; it was enough that I could run my big mouth and retort without a brawl. I became a fast talker who could out talk most of my adversaries and attackers.

Of the bullies that confronted me during my early years at Bogoso none was more tenacious than Sunday. I could not avoid Sunday no matter how hard I tried to do so. He was in my face both at school and in town. He was a Nigerian who lived in the quarter of town known as Lagos Town. Nigerians-Yoruba and Ibos were the dominant small scale retail traders from whom one could buy every conceivable item in small units or part of a penny. One could buy half a yard of cloth, a half penny salt or farthing of salt or putrefied fish. And they were very obliging to their customers. They served one willingly no matter the time of day or night. I could thus not avoid Sunday as long as my family and neighbors needed small items from Lagos Town. I was often sent on errands to buy salt, pepper, smoked and salted fish or *kako* and salt peter or *kawu*. I could not walk through Lagos town without looking over my shoulders for my nemesis. And it appeared Sunday had a nose to ferret me out when I was in his neighborhood.

My liberation from Sunday came suddenly and unexpectedly like my freedom from brawling with Kwabena. One weekend I was sent on an errand to Lagos Town by a neighbor. I came face-to-face with Sunday, and after exchanging a few words, the exchange turned hostile but instead of standing up to him I took to my heels and ran for dear life. I ran towards home hoping for deliverance from my older brother Mumuni and another relative who were on visit at the time. I expected the two strong young men to come out to save me from the hands of Sunday. So as I ran towards home I shouted at the top of my lungs imploring the young men to come to my aid.

And just as I expected, when they overheard me wailing they rushed out of the house in alarm only to find me running away from a boy who was hard on my heels. They ordered me to stop right there and face Sunday. "Face him or face us" they said. I was between a rock and a hard place; I could not go home for fear of my brothers and I was frightened to death of Sunday who was just behind me. I stood between them shivering like a leaf. I turned towards Sunday who slowed down at the sight of my brothers but on realizing that they meant him no harm came at me with all his might. But in a surprise move and with my heart pounding I met him with all the force I could muster to save myself from a bigger threat, my brothers. I was forceful enough to knock him off his feet and he fell flat on his back, and for once I prevailed over my nemesis in front of my brothers. As soon as he hit the ground I took off again running as fast as I could lest he should get up and wallop me. I was greatly relieved when my brothers allowed me to enter the house with smiles of approval.

My brothers did not come to my aid as I had anticipated but their presence and their threats gave me courage to make a surprise move against Sunday. In the eyes of my brothers, I was the victor as soon as Sunday hit the ground. And I did that without any help from them. But I doubted whether I could duplicate the feat without their presence behind me. I was left pondering whether I could prevail again the next time I met him without the presence of my brothers. As it happened, my fears were unfounded. I succeeded in instilling some fear in Sunday, he was not sure that he could beat me as he had done previously. He made threats but never followed through the threats. He let every one know that I beat him with the help of my brothers but never attempted to find out how I would fare against him without my brothers. We became mutually afraid of one another. I was freed from ever tussling with Sunday. Despite all his threats he never made another hostile move against me.

ECONOMIC DECLINE OF BOGOSO

About two or three years before Marlu Gold Mines at Bogoso ceased operations the elders of the town through the town crier warned of looming economic disaster. The gold mine was the mainstay of the economy of Bogoso and the surrounding towns and villages. I don't know how the elders got wind of the intentions of the company to shut down the mine long before it ceased operation as a viable going concern. The town crier was the main source of information for most residents of Bogoso who had no radios, 'wireless' or read any newspaper. The gong was the principal means of attracting our attention before any announcement was made through the streets of the town. I never saw a newspaper until I went to Tarkwa in 1954. In looking back, I have wondered how they were so well informed about the mundane and the serious. For instance the town crier warned of approaching storms, armed robbers and other undesirable characters such as head hunters and kidnappers including superstitious evil and ungodly characters on their way to town. In particular the townspeople were warned to keep their eyes on their youngsters when kidnappers and head hunters were said to be on their way to town, similarly they were enjoined to be kind and generous towards some unsavory and distasteful characters who may be gods masquerading as ill and obnoxious characters.

My mother's quick thinking following a warning about the arrival of kidnappers prevented me from being kidnapped by three men. The people of the towns were warned by the town crier about a week before this particular incident. The inhabitants were cautioned and warned about the imminent arrival of criminals in town and implored them to be vigilant and pay attention to vulnerable children against kidnapping. I was returning home from the night market one night when I saw three men with cloth hoods over their heads standing in triangular formation near the gate of our house. Just as I was about to jump into the house one of the men politely asked me where I was going to which I replied that I was going home to deliver an errand to my mother. One of them then asked whether I could run an errand for them for a reward after I finished with my mother. The reward was all I needed to hear. And as soon as I delivered my mother's chewing tobacco to her I turned around and darted for the gate. My mother stopped me in my tracks asking where I was going. When I told her of the three men outside the gate asked me to run an errand for them she retorted asking me whether I didn't hear the warning by the town crier. She then started shouting at the top of her voice blasting the men at the gate with her own threats. And when I followed her to the gate they had vanished.

At another time we were warned of the arrival of a deity, god or spirit entity masquerading as a filthy and obnoxious person. We were warned to be kind and generous towards him. I don't know whether there was some conspiracy between the town elders and some of these disgusting and obnoxious characters but a short time after the announcement a drooling beggar arrived in town. The beggar walked stiffly with unsteady steps, shaking or shivering and drooling over himself. I guess the beggar must have been suffering from Parkinson disease which was known as the *awoso-awoso* or shake, shake disease in the local dialect. The shaking and the dripping of saliva was disgusting but we were all cowed because of the warning by the town carrier. He was served with finest plates and cups when he asked for food or water. He hung around town for about two weeks and disappeared. He was treated like a king while he was in town. He made a fortune and disappeared before he overstayed his welcome.

Obviously the chief and elders of the town had their ears to the ground and were better informed than most inhabitants of the town. They warned of timely events before they occurred or happened. About two or three years before there was any inkling that The Marlu Gold Mines was in trouble, the town crier warned the inhabitants of the impending closure of the gold mines. They asked the residents to pray for divine intervention to avert the economic decline that would follow the closure. A few weeks after the initial announcement we were enjoined to join the chief and elders of the town to pray and offer sacrifices to the deity or gods on the banks of the river Bogo. Bogoso derived its name from the river or stream located at the outskirts of town along the Bogoso-Prestea road. We were asked to pray and appease the gods who were said to be dissatisfied with the mine operations and had therefore sabotaged the operations by hoarding the gold ore against profitable exploitation. The action by the gods was said to be responsible for the unprofitable operations which led to the planned abandonment of the mine. We were therefore advised to pray to the gods and offer sacrifices to pacify them.

Bogoso was a vibrant and prosperous town during the first half of the 1950s. The prosperity of the town depended on the gold mine, which was the main source of employment of the town and surrounding communities. In about 1952 or thereabout, the town crier gave the first hint of profound adverse economic changes on the horizon of the town. The inhabitants were warned to watch and pray together for divine intervention against the pending economic decline. That first warning perhaps more than anything else began the gradual decline and exodus from Bogoso. But the traditional authorities appeared to believe that the problems besetting the mines were caused by the guardian spirits or gods of the town. A series of ritual prayers, libations and blood sacrifices were planned to appease the gods and guardian spirits of the town.

A date was set at which all able bodied residents of the town were asked to meet on the banks of the Bogo river, to pray, pour libation and offer sacrifice to the god of the river which was said to be the guardian spirit of Bogoso to intervene against the plan to close down the mine and maintain the growth and prosperity of the town. On the appointed day, a Saturday morning, a cross section of the town assembled on the banks of the river. I was among many children who followed the adults to the banks to satisfy our curiosity and gawk at the ritual ceremonies but with very little understanding or appreciation of the seriousness of purpose of the hullabaloo on the river bank.

The chief and his elders together with a retinue of fetish priests and priestesses all dressed in white cloths and their bodies painted or smeared with white clay. The atmosphere was more festive than somber. There was traditional drumming and dancing similar to a durbar, the fetish priests and priestesses pranced about and swooned in ecstasy as if possessed. The drumming was followed by prayers and pouring of libation. The ritual culminated with the sacrificial slaughter of two unblemished white sheep on the banks of the river.

The ritual was repeated after another four weeks with a twist. A thatched hut was erected on the far side of the river bank as a home for the gods. After the last sacrifice to the gods we waited for the gods to turn things around. The turn around came about thirty five years later when most of the original fetish priests and priestesses who prayed for the turn around were probably not around to see the revival for which they had prayed.

After all said and done life continued in the town as before. I passed by the banks of the river several times on my way to Green Compound to sell bottles of kerosene and witnessed the gradual disintegration of the hut which was a forerunner of the fortunes of the town that built the hut for gods. When I returned from Tarkwa after having been away for about three years Green Compound was in ruins, the roofing sheets were stripped from the buildings. The compound was symptomatic of how Bogoso had sunk economically during the years I was away.

Despite the prayers and ritual sacrifices of the people of Bogoso the mine officially ceased operations sometime in 1955 but it appears safety and mopping up operations continued for about another three or four years. My mother continued plying her trade at the mine grounds until we left Bogoso. Our house exemplified the decline and exodus from Bogoso. Within a year of the announcement some of the old tenants I met in 1949 left the town for greener pastures. But the town was still relatively buoyant and the rooms were quickly taken over by new tenants. By the time I came back from Tarkwa at end of 1956 there was no familiar tenant left in the house and the three or four store fronts were shuttered. There were four businesses in the storefronts dealing with everything from hardware to African fabrics and prints and an office. They were all gone by the time I returned from Tarkwa at the end of 1956.

I heard a telephone ring the first time and heard the disembodied voice coming from a telephone device in an empty storefront office of the house. My imagination was fired in all directions when I overheard a voice emanating from an empty office during one afternoon. I was awe struck when I heard 'hello hello' coming from an empty room. That was the closest I ever came to a telephone. I hung around the verandah of the office until the officer returned and I saw him later talk into a telephone receiver mounted on the wall. I was greatly exited by what I saw and it set my imagination agog. Thus far I knew of only radio or wireless but I remember imagining a device from which I could see people walking on the streets of Kumasi, the only other town I knew. I do not know whether television had been invented when my imagination went wild when I saw a man talk into a telephone receiver in the early fifties for the first time. Through modern technology most of the things I imagined have all become a reality. About the only thing that has not been realized the way I saw it in my mind's eye is the ability to see ordinary folks going about their chores in towns and cities. My sister had left Bogoso and I therefore imagined seeing her going about Kumasi. The nearest to that might be Skype. My curiosity about telephones were finally satisfied in about 1957 when an official of the local post office made it possible for me to speak by telephone to his counterpart at Tarkwa post office. It was a brief conversation but it was worth it.

When I came back from Tarkwa vacancies were commonplace in Bogoso. Most of the store fronts in the town were shuttered like the four in my house. The town was but a shadow of its former glory. The vibrant community that introduced me to the modern world was reeling from lack of alternative economic activity. There was no viable economy left after the mines closed their doors sometime in 1955.

The economic blight was conspicuous. The streets were littered with shuttered storefronts and vacant houses. CFAO the only expatriate owned store where we used to goggle white customers had closed its doors. Most of the Yoruba and Ibo small scale retail traders at Lagos Town had joined the exodus and left for more viable communities elsewhere in the country.

The exodus of Yoruba and Ibo traders epitomized the economic decline of Bogoso. The Nigerian small-scale trader was ubiquitous throughout the country. It was a popular maxim that any community without a Yoruba or Ibo trader was inhospitable to outsiders. The Nigerian petty trader was part and parcel of the landscape of the country. But in 1968, the government of the second Republic of Ghana under Dr. K. A. Busia expelled all aliens, the majority of whom were Nigerians, from the country in a program called Aliens Compliance Order. The Aliens Compliance Order was in effect a deportation of all Nigerian merchants and traders to make way for Ghanaians to capture the 'commanding heights' of the economy. The country has never been the same since the mass expulsion of the so called aliens from the country.

By 1957 the mine had officially been shuttered for about two years and rumors abounded about plans for alternative uses of the mine properties. But none of the many rumors we heard panned out. As students of the Catholic school we heard unconfirmed reports and rumors that a branch of the venerable St. Augustine Teacher Training College had been set up at Bogoso in some of the abandoned real estate of the mines. The rumor was widespread in the school so I took it upon myself to verify the truth by going up to the old grounds where my mother used to sell konkonte to mine workers. I came away satisfied that a college existed at Bogoso for the first time. I met and spoke to some of the students in their converted bungalow dormitories. The college was the silver lining in an otherwise bleak economic picture following the closure of the gold mine, but the economic impact of the college on the town was limited.

It appears there was a kernel of truth regarding the causes of the unprofitability of Marlu Gold Mines. And it also appears that the prayers and ritual sacrifices of the traditional authorities and people of Bogoso were answered about thirty years after the fact. I wonder whether there was some truth in the belief that the guardian spirits of the town were unhappy with the former owners and had spiritually put impediments in the profitable extractions of the gold ores. The Marlu Gold Mines caused a lot of environmental damage to the forests surrounding the mines. Poisonous sludge was discharged from their refinery into the surrounding forest lands. The trees died from the poisonous sludge discharged into the forests. It was rumored that the discharges were laden with cyanide and that it was the cyanide that caused the degradation of the forests.

The dead trees were harvested for firewood by the inhabitants. We, the youths of Bogoso, used to go to the forests on Saturdays en-mass to harvest the trees for fuel. The sludge had a pleasant smell and caused quick sands in parts of the forest that was saturated with the sludge. We did not know any better to protest the degradation of the environment; it was a resource for fuel. If the gods of Bogoso were displeased with the mine operators it must have been due to the harm that was being done to the environment. The degradation of the adjacent forest lands did perhaps upset the guardian spirits of the lands. While we the inhabitants did not know any better the gods must have known what we the inhabitants did not know. Thirty to forty years was enough time for the forests to perhaps recover and for the gods to smile on Bogoso again.

Mother Of The Clan

After a journey that took like forever I was finally united with the father I did not know existed. And in my 'new family' I was no longer the older of two but one of the youngest. My family lived in a room of a sturdy built house that was palatial compared to where I came from. The room had two pane large jalousie windows instead of a hole in the wall for light and ventilation. My lifestyle changed overnight, different from the life I was accustomed or knew.

My new family consisting of my father, mother and two sisters crowded together in a single room. The house though magnificent by the standards of the mud huts I left behind at Duohi and Nyagli had one flaw; there was no privacy between my mother and father. At Duohi grandmother had a separate room from my uncle and mother and I shared a room while my stepfather had his own room. My father and mother were widely known within our extended family and tribal clan. My father was also one of the earliest migrants from our clan to the south in search of greener pastures. As such new and seasonal migrants from out villages tended to stop over in our house before going to other job centers in the south. Our tenement room was therefore overcrowded with unexpected visitors from time to time particularly when the farming season was over during the dry season in the north.

Our room was sparsely furnished; the only item of furniture in the room was a double or full size bed with a straw mattress made from jute fabric. The straw mattresses were made on the side of the streets by people of northern origin from either Upper Volta or Mali or countries north of the Gold Coast. Before the advent of Styrofoam and foam materials breakable, delicate and fragile merchandise were packed with straw for exports. The imported beers, Heineken, and Beck beers wore straw sox in wooden crates. The straw used for packaging was recycled into straw mattresses. The straw mattress was the standard and most affordable common bedding in the Gold Coast. Kapok mattress was a luxury that most families like mine could not afford.

Straw mattress and bedbugs were inseparable. The folds of the straw mattress were fertile breeding ground for bedbugs; but apart from occasionally spraying the mattress with kerosene and other insecticides against mosquitoes; the bugs were considered a minor annoyance. We delighted in fishing them out of the folds of the mattress and killing them with our fingers. Despite our crowded room every visitor whether close or distant relative or merely a fellow tribesman was nevertheless welcome to stay as long as he desired. The inconvenience caused by visitors in an already crowded room never affected or influenced the welcoming hospitality of my mother despite the obvious problems.

My father had five surviving children with my stepmother before I became part of the family. They had five girls and a boy but one of the girls had already passed away and two were married before my arrival at Bogoso. My mother must have been a skilled traditional midwife, skilled enough for my married sisters and other family members to entrust their lives and that of their unborn babies into her hands. They came to Bogoso to give birth when they were due, and they had their babies in the overcrowded one room that was our home. I saw the birth of some of my nephews and nieces as a child during that period of our family life.

The sight of pregnant women used to excite me because I associated them with extravagant feasts that followed the birth and naming ceremonies for new born babies. They were always welcome despite my being banned from our room during the birthing process. I was often disappointed if a visiting pregnant woman left without giving birth. Special meals were always prepared for the new mother, and during the time she was provided with the special meals the whole family ate the same food as the new mom. The meals were usually rich in fish, meats and spices; meals that we did not have before the new mother and which was stopped after a few weeks. But the best part of a birth in our home was the Islamic naming rituals of new babies. Most often a sheep was slaughtered as part of the ceremony. The ceremony thus provided meat for the household for about two weeks following the naming rituals. My father was the only practicing Muslim in the family and he made no effort to convert any of us but all his children invariably followed his footsteps in naming their offspring according to Islamic traditions

The visitors passing through our home usually peaked between October and April when farming was suspended in the north till the rainy season. The youths used to migrate during the dry season to work in the south during the dry season. They returned home at the onset of the rainy season with the goodies they acquired with their wages. Their needs were very simple but their lives were enhanced when they went back home with bicycles and corrugated iron roofing sheets. The bicycle improved their mobility and the roofing sheets made them stand out in their communities. The bicycle and roofing sheets were status symbols of affluence or civilization in the forties to the sixties. The bicycle was of course much faster than travelling on the back of a donkey. The sight of a roofing sheet on a room in any compound house was the indication of our 'been to' to the south. The term 'been to' was used in the south as reference to people who had been to Europe or America. The bicycle and the roofing sheets were the external signs of one who had crossed the Volta river to the south for work to make money and acquire goodies of life. And a young man with a bicycle was the most eligible bachelor in his neck of the woods.

Bogoso, during most of the first half of the 1950s, was a magnet for job seekers in the gold mine. I liked the company of strangers or visitors; they were often generous to me. I delighted in pestering the visitors for pennies and most often they obliged. But I pestered them out of earshot of my mother. I knew no shame in soliciting for pennies and I asked almost every visitor for a penny just before I left for school. I never asked more than a penny because a penny in the early fifties could buy me a snack at school and perhaps with change. In the early fifties before my eyes were opened I did not know what to do with any coin that was more than a penny. I therefore used to turn anything more than a penny to my mother until I became a wise guy.

Not all visitors who came to us were congenial or friendly towards me. There was one particular woman who for no obvious reason did not like me. The woman like any of those who passed through the house was an extended family member. I knew her as Aunt Hawa and she used to come about twice a year for a few days at a time. As much as I would have liked to stay out of her way I could not because we all sprawled together on the floor on straw mats at night. And if perchance I rolled over onto her mat she pinched me hard enough to wake me or shove me violently from her mat that I used to wake up and cry. But my mother did nothing about the pinches and violence against me during the night.

At one time aunt Hawa and another male relative met in the house at about the same time. The man was an easy going playboy who used to travel with a gramophone and records. Thanks to that gentleman I got to touch, feel and operate a gramophone instead of merely gawking at one in the room of our next door neighbor. When Aunt Hawa and the man met in our home they became an item. If my mother went out and left me in their care they drove me out of the room and locked the door behind them.

I used to play havoc with the gramophone if I was left alone with it at home. I used to load small items onto the turntable, wound up the gramophone and toggled with the speed. I then watched in glee as the things flew off the turntable at high speed. But nothing was more fun than listening to the distorted sounds produced by a record with the wrong speed. The drawl and the high pitch when I toggled the speed from slow to high was exhilarating, almost intoxicating. That was the only pleasure I derived from the gramophone because I did not understand the words or lyrics of the records. Of all the records he brought with him I could only relate to one and that one was a laughter record with very few words.

I knew nothing about aunt Hawa other than seeing her once or twice a year. I knew her only as an aunt and nothing else. I came across her years later when I was in my mid twenties at Takoradi. I was on the long vacation as a student of the University of Science and Technology, Kumasi. I met her in the house of the only person I ever met who knew my mother while she was alive. This individual was introduced to me by my father as a sister. My sister was an established business woman at Takoradi; she brewed pito in addition to other trading activities. I stumbled into aunt Hawa accidentally at the home of this relative and discovered that she did not know me. Aunt Hawa at this time was a wrinkled older woman whom I knew from that day was a prostitute.

I narrated my experiences with her during my infancy at Bogoso to my sister. While I was able to recognize her she could not make me out because I was practically a baby when she used to come to Bogoso. My new sister and I decided to play a prank on her to avenge for her violent attitude towards me during my infancy at Bogoso. Since she did not know me I pretended to solicit her services as a prostitute. After she consented to be my date for the night I then tried to jog her memory about Bogoso so as to put her to shame. But she pretended she had never met me as a child though she had recollections of my mother. My prank was a let down because she said she could not recollect ever meeting me as a child. When it was over I felt rather sorry for aunt Hawa. I thought it was unfortunate that with her failing eyesight she still tried mightily to present herself as a young woman to potential clients some of whom might take advantage of her.

The hospitality my mother extended to our extended family and tribesmen gave me a sense of entitlement when I met our family members in any walk of life from my infancy up to a young adult. I enjoyed the hospitality and generosity of our extended family into my early adulthood. When I went back to Tarkwa as a young adult and a student at St. John Bosco's college, I still enjoyed the hospitality that they used to extend to me when I was in the primary school. My uncle Samai still gave me pocket money though he was retired. I still went to the house of any family member at anytime it suited me and expected to be entertained. The extended family members who helped me as a child continued to extend a helping hand to me as a young adult. I resolved to return the favor if and when I took my place in society as an adult particularly to my uncle Samai. Unfortunately uncle Samai passed away from the ravages of a lung disease before I could return his generosity in kind. The hospitality and generosity I enjoyed in a way prepared me to accept the responsibility of family when that was thrust upon me after the passing of my father without a second thought. While I was in Ghana my doors were open in the same way that the doors of my extended family members were open whenever I needed help. I maintained the bonds with my extended family until the day I left the shores of Ghana.

STRUGGLES AND TRUIMPHS IN LIFE

REVERSE DISCRIMINATION

I started productive life after middle school as a teacher in training at Navrongo. And as a trainee teacher I was paid monthly stipends or allowance and was provided with three square meals a day; life had never been so good. The St. John Bosco's Training College campus was a calm and progressive campus far removed from the rough and tumble life of Issah middle boarding school or the primary schools at Bogoso and Tarkwa. The days of brawls and scuffles, the hallmark of my first year at Issah middle school were behind me. I considered my conflicts of the past as part of growing pains that taught me some valuable lessons of life.

St. John Bosco's Training College at Navrongo was a multi ethnic campus with students from across the country. But the majority of students were from the north and in particular from the north east where the college is located. The students from the south were in the minority. The reversal of fortunes between northern and southern students from my perspective revealed to me that racism, tribalism or discrimination is perhaps universal. It was ironic to find some of the very pejorative and offensive epithets that were used against me in the south directed at the minority southern students on the campus. The pejorative terms were eerily similar to the pejorative terms I endured in the primary and middle school in the south. I was conflicted with reverse discrimination. Having been subjected to discrimination throughout most of my elementary school education in the south I was naturally predisposed to see them paid in their own coins. But I also had empathy with the southern students because my formative years were in the south.

The insecurity and self defense mechanism of superiority complex is not limited to one tribe, race, color or people. The factors that breed racism and tribalism appear to be universal. When white people throw pejorative epithets against blacks and slam doors in our faces, it is from a sense of insecurity even if they do not know it. What they do not know is that blacks are not cowed in our hearts but we yield to the reality of superior numbers. It is in the nature of man that the victim of discrimination and oppression believes and carries in his heart that he has some unique qualities that rouses the envy and ire of his persecutors and tormentors. It is that place within him that the victim retreats for comfort and consolation. When the victim loses that inner perspective he loses his humanity. Racial minorities have survived and thrived for eons among their adversaries in spite the cruelty, persecution and violence perpetrated against them over the years.

The white race is by nature aggressive because they were placed in a hostile natural environment by their maker. The need for survival in that hostile environment led to the many wars and atrocities among themselves long before they ever set sail in search of salubrious climes and resources. Our history lessons in schools conveyed the impression that the journeys of discovery into Africa was for altruistic or propagation of the gospel to a savage people. Colonial occupation followed the discoveries and the bible and by the time we became aware of their true intentions, our lands were gone. The white man brought us the bible and took our lands in its place.

The white race id generally imbued with a sense of insecurity that makes them uncomfortable with non conformist minorities within their midst. The non-conformists raises their hackles and unleashes all manner of oppressions to make the minority conform to them or deprive them of their humanity. It is in that oppressive atmosphere that they thrive. Cultural differences heightened their sense of insecurity and they lashed out at those with different beliefs and culture. Cultural and language nonconformity made the white man feel insecure in his own land. The atrocities and persecution of minorities in their midst has gone on from time immemorial and is heightened particularly during lean times. The intransigence of Ian Smith of Rhodesia and Apartheid South Africa were borne of the same strain of insecurity inherent in the white race. The sense of insecurity and the aggression and violent reactions were not limited to Europe but wherever they set foot in the so called new world. All white people appear the same to me and I do not see any difference between them just as the Whites do not see any differences between Blacks.

Segments of the white race in the world today still resent cultural differences of people or groups of people who live in their midst. Racial animosity is generally frowned upon today but the insecurity we feel towards racial minorities among us still persists in our hearts. We have found flowery languages of expressing the same animosity and encouraging intimidation and violence against the minority without saying so explicitly. The current atmosphere of racial tolerance is only skin deep, if history indeed does repeat itself, then it is only a matter of time before adverse conditions unleash bouts of violence against racial minorities.

It is a paradox that dominant ethnic groups of any society despite their overwhelming numbers and power nevertheless feel threatened by minorities living among them. And this fear and insecurity is exacerbated during times of economic dislocations. The minority become scapegoats blamed for the ills of the society and the economic problems that affects everybody but more proportionally against the minorities who have very little voice. It is that feeling of insecurity that is at the heart of tribal feuds, racism, bigotry, and prejudice. I realized as a victim that prejudice, name calling and hostility for no apparent reason are the result of insecurity. The dominant group lashes out at the minority to protect their privileges. And the protection of privileges is done in various guises some with high sounding altruistic names. The dominant majority protect their privileges through unfair laws and practices that enshrines their privileged positions. For instance I consider school zoning as tantamount to balkanization and inimical to the interests of the underprivileged. They are given substandard education during their formative and vulnerable years. Education is the great leveler but since they are denied good foundations in education in their formative years the underprivileged remain forever on the margins of society where the privileged have engineered for them. The poor in percentage terms subsidize the rich in the public realm but derive less from it than the rich and the privileged. Kids are bottled up into low performing schools by the powers that be based on their areas of residence and not on their preference. The convenience of the caregivers or parents in choosing schools for their wards is immaterial under school zoning. By the time the kids are of an age when they can utilize opportunities outside their residential areas, most are already in the rut. So we eventually end up at the margins of society because we could not make the most of our abilities during our formative years.

Thus in 1960-61, I saw the tables of disdain, disrespect and discrimination turned against southern students of St. John Bosco's College at Navrongo. The students from southern Ghana were subjected to the same cruel jokes and invectives that were directed at northerners in the South. I felt the cruelty when people become the butt of jokes or demeaned because of who they are; their ethnic or national origin. I could have reveled in the discomfiture of my past tormentors, a condition they had never known until they found themselves in the minority at Navrongo. But I could not take solace in their discomfiture. I empathized with them and realized that they must also be hurting in the same way that I was hurt when I was called pejorative names. The situation at Navrongo taught me that ethnic dominance is relative; one can be part of a dominant ethnic group in one location only to find oneself a tiny minority at another location. We would therefore reap the fruits of discord that we sowed when we were in dominant position when the roles are reversed. The sins of our fathers will be visited upon us when we cease to be the dominant group.

Discrimination is so insidious that it has adverse effects on the self esteem of those who are the victims of discrimination, mockery, taunting or name calling and the like. It took a great deal of will power for me to accept myself and maintain some semblance of self esteem. But some of my compatriots of similar age group growing up at Nsuta lost their self esteem to such an extent that they were ashamed of their parents and shied away from being associated with them in public. They lost their self esteem during their infancy through invectives, insults, mockery and taunting so to save face they avoided association with their kinsmen from the north. At the time I was at Tarkwa-Tamso two siblings at Nsuta were ashamed to associate with me lest they betray their ethnicity. I spoke fluent Fanti or Akan with no accent. But the two siblings did not have enough self esteem to acknowledge their ethnicity in public. This is what discrimination and prejudice do to children.

The invectives and name-calling that were directed at me helped me to find my identity and drew me closer to my kinsmen at Tarkwa. I became proud of my ethnicity and origin and made no attempt to conceal my origin or identity. At the height of the jeers and taunting I became ashamed of my name and sought to adopt another name, but the Christian names I adopted were spurned by my schoolmates. I was forced to face the reality of who I was, I saw myself in the mirror and decided that I liked what I saw in the mirror. I therefore decided to keep my given name without any embellishments. If I cannot become a Christian as me or go to heaven as me then I want nothing to do with that God. If God intended me to be a Jew or an Englishman I would have been born that way. I also considered dropping my Muslim name but decided against the change because the name could not be mistaken for any ethnic group but a northerner in my country of origin. I also shied away from being identified or called by the common Akan name corresponding to the day I was born such as Kwabena for a boy born on a Tuesday or Kofi for one born on a Friday. I broke up with one of my early relationships when I realized that my girl friend was ashamed of my ethnicity and tried to cover it up by calling me Kwabena in public. The name she called me was not one of endearment but to hide her shame of dating a northerner.

LIFE LESSONS FROM FRIENDS

Of all the activities my friends and I did during the three years I was at Tarkwa two practical lessons of life left a lasting impression on me. I have already recounted how we used to entertain ourselves with stories that used to degenerate into sexual proclivities. The ananse stories engaged us during the night. We did not have much to occupy us at weekends and on vacations. We occupied our weekends with fishing. Our fishing grounds were the streams that coursed through the manganese mining town of Nsuta Wassaw lying about three miles from Tamso. The streams were fertile fishing grounds for sardines. We made our own tackles from scratch using hooks, strings or twines, bamboo saplings or twigs and calabash as floats. And for baits we dug up earthworms which are abundant in the tropics. While we used to enjoy fishing it was not enough to occupy our time during school vacations. This boredom in 1955 led us to attempt hunting rodents and latter cultivating a cassava farm. We were always led in our farming, fishing and hunting activities by our trusted friend, Quayson. Quayson came from a farming family and as such was experienced in those practical activities than Tawia and me. Tawia and I knew next to nothing about farming and hunting, his father was a driver and my father was a trader. Our failed attempts at hunting and farming greatly influenced me to continue the path of education through to its conclusion which in 1955 was middle school Form IV. My expectation was to train for a trade such as auto repairs or driving after middle school Form IV. Of the three farming activities we attempted only fishing bore fruits. We failed miserably at hunting and cassava farming.

I still have fond memories of the fishing experience, I have never eaten any fish that was fresher than the fish I caught at Nsuta. I would have liked to pursue it as a past time with my children but I am scared of the consequences in case of an accident. I cannot float or swim if I fall into water. My children born in the USA learned to swim at YMCA but my children born in Ghana are stones when it comes to water.

Quayson was our chief farmer who led us in our efforts at farming and hunting in the fields and bushes on the hills overlooking the village. Theoretically I knew how to trap and hunt rabbits or rats in the wild from stories about trapping or hunting but I had never attempted trapping or hunting since I left my village. This was my first adventure in trapping or hunting of rats or rabbits in the tropical forest environment. In the north we burned the grasses during the dry season and chased the rodents and other animals as they fled from the fires.

We followed faithfully all the directions for trapping and hunting rats from their burrows. First we located the network of burrows that made up the lair of the rats. We stuffed all the exits located except two, we then lit fire and fanned smoke into the lair and kept watch at the remaining exit for the rat.

Two of us kept watch at one of the tunnels left open while one fanned smoke with palm leaves into the network of tunnels or burrows. We stood ready with a machete wielded by Quayson and I was armed with a club. The smoke drove out the rabbit from its lair and it rushed out through the entrance where we stood guard waiting for it. But it blew past us before any of us could even lift up his weapon let alone make a strike. It disappeared into underbrush and left us agape. It was a big disappointment after putting in so much work to smoke out the rat. The failure discouraged us from trying another hunt. If there was no rat in the burrows we might have continued with our quixotic quest for a rat or rabbit. But we struck out on our first attempt due to ineptitude. We never tried to hunt again. My take way from the adventure was that if three of us could not kill one lousy rat I could never make a living by hunting.

We failed at hunting but we still had to find something to do during school vacations. We decided to cultivate a cassava farm during one vacation. We chose the same hillside overlooking Tamso where our attempt at hunting foundered. Once again we were led in the cultivation of the cassava farm by Quayson. We cleared a small patch of brush land. After about two to three weeks we burned the cut bushes and saplings and gathered the charred remains in heaps around the farm land. We then prepared the land for planting with cassava sticks and when we were done planting we waited for the next phase.

The easiest part of farming was clearing the land and planting the cassava sticks. The hard part was maintaining the farm till maturity and harvest. In the tropics the prolific growth of weeds makes subsistence farming a daunting task. We cleared weeds from our farm on one or two occasions. And after that we were done. Our enthusiasm for the farm waned. We did not set foot on the farm again. We observed the farm from the roadside. We were happy to see the cassava plants growing from the valley below but we could not be bothered to step foot on the farm and clear weeds that were overtaking the plants. We watched from the roadside as the weeds gradually choked and swallowed the farm. We failed on two ventures that required labor and hard work. Fishing with our home made tackles was the only past time we were able to to do successfully. After the two fiascos the only way forward for me was to earn my middle school leaving certificate or go to a technical school to learn auto repairs. The cassava farm was the last time I ever made any attempt at cultivating or growing anything.

Although I never thought of it at the time, but our failures in farming and hunting demonstrated the wisdom of my father in sending me to school. Perhaps his own cowardly and scared experience as a laborer for one day in the mines influenced his decision to educate me and the children that came after me.

Our failure at farming and hunting affected my outlook from then on. Although my zeal for education did not change I saw the possibilities in education. My test preps improved from cramming in the last two weeks to a little longer. My illiterate kinsmen held me in high esteem, they thought I was a good student and encouraged me to continue working hard in school. The mere fact that I could teach them to read made them think the world of me. I was inspired by my form II teacher and started looking to education as the means by which I can attain my dream profession of an auto mechanic. The Tarkwa technical school students held me spell bound each time I passed by the school and saw the students doing practical auto repairs on the school campus. I was impressed with their practical studies I aspired to go to the school for studies in auto mechanics or repairs.

The seeds for home study courses that paved my way for college education were sown in Form II. Through the inspiration of my class teacher I read on my own volition without a stick. I was absent from school for about two weeks due to illness and during that time I memorized the introductory chapter of the Vicar of Wakefield which was one of our class text books and a long poem titled People Will Talk of You. When I went back to school I showboated with my rote memory, sitting at my desk and reciting the poem for all to hear. The teacher liked the poem and asked the whole class to memorize it. The foundation of my future general certificate of education courses were laid in form II. The subjects I liked and excelled in that class became the core subjects I pursued in the studies for the general certificate of education exams. I sleepwalked through most of the elementary school memorizing lesson notes, facts and figures without ever doing more than required to earn promotion. When I started doing well in middle school Form II I started to like school.

It was no accident that my favorite subjects in middle school form II of history, geography and hygiene or biology; were the subjects I read for the general certificate of education through correspondence courses. The discipline of independent work at home was laid in the eighth grade. Our illustrated geography text book kindled my interest in other cultures. *Man the World Over;* was virtually a pictorial book. I don't know whether it was a confusion borne of the pictorial illustration but I have been confused ever since then about the meaning and application of the term Semites to only Jews. I came across the term Semite in 1957 as an elementary school eighth grade of Form II student. The term, during that period, had the connoted of middle east culture with pictorial illustrations of Arabic in nature. Although I read the book more than half a century ago yet the impressions I formed have stuck with me. I have come to terms with the modern definition or equating Semites with Jewry without actually understanding why only Jews are Semites. The Arab and the Jew if biblical history is accepted as accurate are from the same heritage, they are descendants of the patriarch Abraham. The pictorial illustration of our geography text book portrayed Semites as Bedouins Arabs. Back then we did not know that Syrians and Lebanese, the dominant expatriate merchant class of the Gold Coast were also Arabs. Arabs were the Saudis and Jews lived only in the pages of the bible and Jerusalem was in heaven. Looking at Arabs and Jews with the eye of an African I see no difference between them except in what they wear. I could not pick an Arab from a Jew in a lineup unless they wore some distinguishing clothes that set them apart. Take away their robes and they are all the same. I do not understand why they have been at one another's throats for so long. Are they fighting over an almighty God who cannot fight his own battles or fighting for sand and stone?

Over the years I have not really added to the basic knowledge of history of the world and Atlantic or African Slave trade since the middle school. The Form II history textbook, *Africa in the Eighteenth Century* would still be as relevant today as it was in 1957.

Hygiene as a subject is not taught in school these days. In the fifties we studied hygiene instead of biology. And when I was introduced to biology in the sixties I did not see any difference between the two. I do not know whether the sands of time have altered the emphasis in content between biology and hygiene. Biology appears to have supplanted hygiene as a separate discipline in schools. Biology was the only science subject I could study at home without laboratory or experiments when I attempted to study some science subjects at home. Biology was easy to follow at least at the high school level. The illustrations were easier to visualize and follow; I could follow illustrations and dissect a frog by myself. I could not make a head and tail out of rudimentary physics and chemistry by myself.

The subjects that were interesting to me in the middle school Form II continued to guide me through teacher training colleges and culminated in successful completion of the general certificate of education that paved the way for me to gain entrance into college in the late 1960's.

"NEITHER A BORROWER NOR LENDER BE"

At the age when most children would be dreaming or spending their allowances on sweets I was forced by necessity to drop my pennies into a can piggy bank. There were certain things that my mother could not or would not buy for me as a child; any clothing that was not school uniform except a draw string short. I learned to buy any casual wear by myself. I bought my first shorts and later shoes through my own efforts. But they were so precious to me I never wore them even for one day, they were my treasures and I saved them until I practically overgrew them I also never had a blanket, except the few months when I was nursing burns on my legs and I never had a good cloth to cover myself during sleep. As such I was accustomed to sleeping without any cover cloth during infancy. By the time I grew up I was used to sleeping naked without a cover cloth. My mother used to buy raggedy cloths that were donated to beggars as alms or sacrifice, they were so worn out that they ripped into two the first time I covered myself with the cloth. I used to cover myself from head to toe when I had a cover cloth and if I stretched myself in the middle of the night the cloth tore into two infuriating my mother. She then braided me for being destructive, you just tore up a 'brand new cloth' the accusation went. So of necessity I formed a savings habit in infancy. But by the time I had been through St John Bosco's Training College at Navrongo where I started earning regular allowances or income the thrift habit had evaporated into thin air. I did not have the same compelling reasons to be thrifty. My monthly allowance and daily meals were assured. I continued with the same extravagant habit after I left Navrongo and began my teaching career at Tamale in 1961. By 1963 I was beginning to live within my means. But it was only in the sense that when I had a goal I scrimped to meet that goal and after that I was back to my extravagant best. When I went to Peki College in 1963 it was only with a loan from the Principal that I was able to enroll for correspondence course for the general certificate education. Between 1961 and 1963 I struggled to make it from one month to the next. Financially I stumbled through the first two years as a teacher until I went to Peki College between 1963 and 1965.

I learned the value of frugality and thrift again after I witnessed the discomfiture of two associates in 1965, the year I returned to Tamale after completing my teacher training course at Peki. In the first instance a co-tenant that I considered more affluent and better paid than me was unable to undertake or fulfill a family emergency for financial reasons. His experience caused me to assess my own financial condition; I could not have done any better if I were in his shoes. I learned the value of thrift once again. Prior to seeing the uncomfortable situation of the cotenant I could barely manage my pay from one month to the next. As a teacher I was trained to appreciate that my job was a sacrificial vocation in which the government or society could not compensate me enough for my sacrifices. Teachers therefore tended to have the mentality that other public servants, with comparable qualifications, were better paid than teachers. Society demanded from us demonstration of exemplary character as role models for the young minds we tutored but were not compensated enough for the dedication and sacrifices expected of us.

His discomfiture was not lost on me. I imagined that I would have been in exactly the same condition if I had received the same type of telegram announcing the passing of my family member. I would not have had the funds to be at the funeral or perhaps reply the telegram. As I wondered what I could have done in similar circumstances it occurred to me that I did not even have any savings account. The post office savings account I opened at Bogoso was moribund a long time ago. The lesson I took from this incident was to reorder my priorities and put aside a small portion of my monthly income for for any emergency situation no matter how meager the amount set aside. And from that month I started making regular savings from my monthly pay packet no matter how small the amount. It was about the only time when I used to prepare an actual monthly budget by itemizing my expenses instead of just going over them mentally as I do now. I never borrowed any money from my employer or friend to tide me over till the next payday again.

The second incident involved a close friend and fellow teacher by name Danso. We were so close that his younger sisters used to help with my cleaning and cooking chores from time to time. Then one day I saw Danso in a very somber mood. He had backed himself into a corner which could cost him his job and perhaps send him to jail unless he was able to extricate himself from the situation. Some of the teachers during the time I was a teacher were in the habit of sleeping with the primary and middle school girls under our tutelage. We called our little lovers "chicken soup". Danso had thus eaten one chicken soup too many and was facing the consequences of impregnating a school child. The chicken had come home to roost. His only recourse was an abortion. But he did not have the thirty cedis required to pay the doctor's fee. That was how I got to know the secrete which under normal circumstances I would never have known. He would not have discussed or disclosed his problem to me if he had the resources to pay for the abortion. I lent him thirty cedis (¢30) to cover the doctor's fee. He promised to repay me within a specified period starting from the next pay day.

The next pay day came and went and I did not hear or see Danso. His sisters ceased coming around to my house and I wondered what had come over them. So as any good friend would do, I followed up to the home of Danso to find out whether all was well with them. I discovered on arrival that Danso was deliberately avoiding me because he could not repay the loan as he had promised. I forgave the loan but learned my second lesson in life from the incident; "neither a borrower nor a lender be"

Money can make and estrange friends. I therefore resolved as much as possible not to let money come between me and my friends. I would not borrow or lend money to a friend unless I could spare that money. Our friendship was on the verge of breakup because of money that he borrowed and could not repay as promised. The experience from the incident taught me to keep money out of my friendships, better to be a scrooge than to lose a friend because of money I could not afford to give away. For instance; one time I foolishly lent my rent money to a colleague and when the landlord called for his rent I could not pay because the friend had not repaid the money as promised. That became my financial modus operandi with friends and I did not expect anything less of myself. I did not expect any friend to bail me out with monies he required for his immediate financial need when I had a financial need. The rent fiasco was a lesson I learned the hard way. Money can be the glue that binds friends together; it can also be the cause that rends friendships.

DO NOT FEAR THE INEVITABLE

I saw the pain and suffering of my mother before her death during my childhood. I also saw transformation that came over her after her death, the facial contortions and marks of pain that were etched on her face were gone the morning I saw her corpse seated high for funeral on a pedestal for public viewing. That transformation eased my trauma and the experience was forever imprinted into my memory and influenced my perception on death. When I saw my mother's corpse seated in state at the village square she looked beautiful and relaxed than any time during the last three or four months of her life. I therefore tend not to grieve for the dead but for those left behind and I grieve for the sick and suffering. Anybody who has watched helplessly as a loved one went through pain and suffering before death feels greatly relieved when the end finally comes; death ends the agony, pain and suffering of the individual for good. The image of my mother's last day on earth sitting peacefully without any marks of pain etched on her face left a lasting positive impression on my young mind that death is not a monster and taught me to accept the inevitable without dread or fear.

And throughout most of my life I have tried to keep faith with the sick and the dying but rarely grieve for the dead, the inevitable end of life. I gave whatever comfort and solace I could to the sick and suffering while they were alive but when death came there was not much that could be done again for the individual.

I grieve and weep for the sick and celebrate life when the destination of life's ultimate journey is reached. I have shed tears for the agony, pain and suffering of the living but I have found it difficult to shed tears for the dead per se. I wept and shed tears for my younger sister when the details of her death became known to me; I imagined the helplessness, the pain and suffering she endured before she passed away. She was transported along rough and bumpy road for a distance of over 190 miles from Wa to Bolgatanga after a botched D&C operation. What she went through before she finally passed away was what moved me to tears. She did not deserve to die that way, she walked into an operating theater strong and healthy for a routine procedure and came out a comatose, on the verge of death, was what moved me to tears.

ISSAH MIDDLE SCHOOL 1958-59

Our life at Bogoso came to an end in December 1957 when we joined the exodus from the town. I have no idea how long my mother had lived at Bogoso before I arrived in the latter part of 1949. My younger sister and I obtained transfer certificates from our respective schools before we left Bogoso for our hometown. Vida was a student at the Methodist primary school while I was a student at the Catholic school. My mother finally left Bogoso two years after the operations of the gold mine formally came to an end when she could no longer support her family on trade, catering for the mine laborers.

We boarded a mummy truck, wooden truck, on the first phase of our journey to Kumasi. We transited one night at Kumasi in the same house and room where we stayed overnight on our way from Wa in 1949. The next day we continued our journey in a larger wooden truck on our way to Bamboi along a bumpy and dusty road. The journey to Wa was exactly the mirror image of my first journey from Wa almost a decade earlier. We stopped at all the familiar places, Tachiman, Bamboi, Bole and finally Wa. We stayed overnight at Bamboi because the ferry had shut down for the day before we got there.

The first time I crossed the Black Volta on my journey to the south in 1949 I was an ignorant five year old child who was awestruck at the immense size of the Black Volta and the pontoon that ferried us across the mighty river. I was still awed at the size of the Black Volta on my return journey, it was still the largest body of water I had seen, but I was not as bewildered as the first time. I was mature on my return journey and was able to walk onto the deck of the ferry and watched the water churning under the motor of the ferry boat. As usual my mother bought some food from one of the many eateries along the riverbank for us. I kept watch over the arriving trucks and passengers during the night. I waited patiently with passengers on either side of the river bank to continue our journey at daybreak.

I stared at the shimmering waters of the river under the moonlight. I understood as I stared at the immense body of water why the nomenclature for the river and the ocean are the same in my dialect. The Volta River is the largest body of water most of us from the north saw for the first time on our journey to the south. And if we lived in the interior of the country and never went down to any costal town; the

Volta River at Bamboi or Yeji is the largest body of water we would ever see in our lifetime.

When we arrived at Wa I spent the next few days preparing for admission into the only middle school in town to continue with my elementary school education. At the beginning of the first term in January 1958, I was accompanied to Wa Middle Boarding School by my aunt's husband, Mr. Nasaamu, to seek admission into the school. We were ushered into the head teacher's office and after the two of them exchanged pleasantries he examined my transfer certificate. After examining the certificate of transfer he offered me a place in a class below my due class, the class I just completed. He told me that the Form III class I was due was full. But somehow I did not believe that he was telling me the truth, his demeanor said otherwise, he was not being completely honest with me. I refused the offer which in effect amounted to demotion for no obvious reason. The School was the only one within the district council area. If I refused the offer there was no other school anywhere, but I stuck to my guns. I decided that I would rather go back to my father at Tarkwa than accept demotion.

I was preparing to go back when one day Mr. Nasaamu brought news that the Wa District Council had established a new middle school at Issah, a village about thirty-three miles north east of Wa. He offered to take me to the new school on the next market day when transport would be available to the town. I put my plan to return to Tarkwa on hold pending the outcome of the trip to the new middle school. On arrival at the school I was offered admission to the Form III class. I did not return to Wa with Mr. Nasaamu, I went to Issah fully prepared to start classes. Issah middle boarding school was relatively new and was not widely known; the top class in the school was Form III.

My classmates and teachers had low expectations of me before I had taken any class test or written an essay. I was considered dunce and stupid and did not deserve to be in the top class of the school. My only saving grace was that I was quite fluent in English and that bewildered them. The students and teachers were prejudiced against students from the South. They regarded themselves as more proficient in the spoken English language than their counterparts from the South. The head teacher at Wa must have thought that I could not cope with the form III class work hence his offer to demote me to a lower class. I was mediocre student throughout most of the first two terms largely because of the hostile school environment. But once I overcame the hostility I blossomed and earned the grudging respect of my classmates and teacher.

Hunger was my number one enemy at the school. The pangs of hunger numbed my feelings and concentration. I could think of nothing but the hunger that gnawed at my tummy. And I had no pocket money to buy anything at Issah village market to supplement the meager meals we were served. The hunger gave me a voice. I was unashamed to talk about the hunger that gnawed at my tummy because of the meager food rations we were served. The constant bickering about meager food rations rankled some of the school prefects. Suddenly I found myself in the cross hairs of the prefects. I was at the receiving end of severe disciplinary actions for no apparent reason. When I complained about unfair disciplinary measures I was told 'do before you complain'. I was not trained that way. Who would listen to me after the edict was complied with; I could not get redress after the fact. This was the most unjust edict I had ever heard and I did everything possible to avoid compliance. That put me into conflict with the prefects who tried to force me to comply with punishments for indiscipline. The refusal to comply with doing manual labor as punishment often resulted in brawls and scuffles with the particular prefect who gave me the punishment. The prefects often attempted to beat and manhandle me to enforce compliance and silence my complaints and chatter about insufficient rations. But I refused to be silenced or compelled to comply with any punishment I considered unfair and unjust.

My mouth was both my asset and liability; I shouted aloud about the unfair ration sizes between the prefects and the rest of the student body. My mouth got me the sympathy of the little guys in the school while the big bullies tried to shut me up. Generally my complaints and resistance to comply with unfair punishments or meager rations went no where. No staff of the school ever intervened to halt or investigate the cause of the constant beatings that was meted out to me. I was considered a troublemaker and the school monitors did everything they could to stop me from stirring up trouble. The prefects were content with their privileged positions and did not want anything that would upset the status quo.

Things came to a head when in desperation after dinner one evening I announced to the whole school that I was going to lodge a complaint with the head teacher and set off on a one man demonstration to the head teacher's quarters. After walking a few yards I looked behind me and was surprised to find virtually the whole school following me. The head teacher was taken aback when he came out after I knocked at his door to find the whole school in front of his house. He met us and patiently listened to what I had to say, as the self appointed spokesman. He promised to look into our grievance and advised us to go back to our various chores. The following day we saw improvements in our rations and that continued for a few more weeks. The pangs of hunger that used to gnaw constantly in my tummy eased considerably after that evening.

But I paid a high price for daring to lead a student demonstration over the meager food we were served. There was a concerted effort to punish me for daring to lead the protest. I was however used to the bullies and their tactics and was unfazed by anything they dished out to me in the aftermath of the demonstration. I was consoled with the knowledge that a vast majority of the student body was behind me in my struggle with the prefects. The demonstration was the singular event that eventually freed me from bullies when their attempts to cow me proved futile. Some of them even became friendly with me, the dining hall prefect who shared the same dormitory with me became my friend. I won a grudging acceptance and respect from the bullies even if they were reluctant to admit it. The ration sizes in the immediate aftermath of the demonstration were increased but over time the rations were reduced but the reduced ration size was still better than before the demonstration, it was still enough to keep gnawing hunger away.

It was easier to get from under the weight of an unjust punishment by starting a fight than doing the task. I came out the worse after every brawl or scuffle but I preferred the brawl to doing the task even if that meant that I was beaten. I did not want to give the burly prefects any satisfaction that they had succeeded in silencing or subduing me. I scuffled with them by fisticuffs or boxing but my blows were ineffective against my much bigger opponents. They bundled me with all my blows and threw me on the ground like a doll. I nevertheless held my own and refused to yield ground or give them any satisfaction by crying or showing that I was hurt. I received as much as I gave though what I gave had no effect on the prefects who were much heavier than me and most often I was the worse for wear. It was amazing that other than a black eye I never sustained any serious injury despite the constant beatings and brawls I had with the prefects during the first two terms of 1958.

The first two terms of the school year were hellish both physically and mentally. The hunger at the school radicalized or turned me into a rebel. My rebellious streak became strident the more the prefects tried to silence me or make me submit. I have to add that I was not exactly a meek and humble student. I was strident and chose brawls and scuffles over compliance with unfair and unjust punishments. I was beaten by day and by night the only time I was not in a brawl or fight with a bully was during class hours. I was punished at the least provocation to do tasks that in my opinion far outweighed the offense. The common form of punishments favored by the prefects were clearing or weeding plots of land that ended up serving no purpose other than the demonstration of where power lay or sweeping the streets and pathways around the school or filling drums with water. During the dry season when our wells practically dry, any punishment for two buckets of water was cruel. I openly defied any prefect that punished me to fetch water in the dry season and my defiance was often met with physical altercations and beatings. Fortunately while I used my fists most of my opponents wrestled me and threw me on the ground. I never had any problem with the other students, I was in the cross hairs of the prefects and I gave them plenty of reasons to beat me.

I foraged for wild fruits in the bushes around the school at the height of my hunger. I ate whatever I could lay hands on not knowing whether it was edible or not. I just wanted to fill my tummy with whatever on the surface looked like a fruit or bulb and tasted good enough to curb hunger. I was so poor that during vacations I walked the thirty miles to Wa through bush paths with students whose villages were along the way. It was while walked home through bush paths that I came across Tibani, my father's birth place and home village. Issah was also the first time I was away from home and that exacerbated the hunger, starvation and poverty that affected me at the school.

Pissed in the Classroom

One of the immediate results of leading the student demonstration was the sudden change of attitude of my class teacher towards me. He forced me to urinate in the classroom perhaps as a payback for the demonstration. He never said so explicitly, but his exploitation of my bladder weakness to embarrass me was not an accident. I think it was premeditated. Our breakfast at the school consisted mainly of plain maize meal porridge. I was normally the first student from the class to go to the bathroom to empty my bladder after breakfast. I was never refused permission by my teacher, Mr. Lansagna, to go to the bathroom in the morning. But I was denied permission to leave for the bathroom the following Monday morning after the demonstration. My class teacher refused me permission on the grounds that my urination habit was disruptive of the class and I should therefore wait until the mid-morning break. But I could not hold on for that long so I run out anyway. The next morning when I attempted to leave he posted the big boys at the doors and windows with instructions to prevent and restrain me from leaving the classroom.

I surveyed the openings for any weak spot but found none, I could not run out of the classroom without being restrained. I sat down twisting in my seat from side to side until I could no longer hold on and let go. I urinated while sitting in my seat. As the urine dripped unto the floor, the class burst out in rapturous jeers and laughter but I did not butt an eye lid. When I finished urinating he ordered me to wash the floor. I left the classroom went into the bushes and did not come back till dinner time. I spent the rest of the day foraging for wild fruits in the bushes. I washed the floor during the night study period when my classmates were busy doing their homework. My class teacher indirectly punished me by disgracing me for leading a peaceful demonstration against meager food rations and I also deliberately disrupted the homework period to avenge my disgrace.

After this nightmare, I stopped eating plain cornmeal porridge in the mornings. I gave away my porridge to the students with whom I shared a table at breakfast. I restricted myself to two meals a day until the end of the year. When I came back in January 1959, I was assigned as a houseboy to Michael, one of two new teachers posted to the school. Michael replaced Mr. Lansagna, the Form III teacher who left for further studies. The other new teacher was assigned to the Form IV class. As a houseboy I was divorced from regular school activities other than classes. I stopped eating school meals up to the day I left for Wa to take the final middle school examinations and never came back.

Failed As A Class Monitor

The cream of the Form III students left for secondary school at the end of the year leaving the dregs behind. Of those left behind I was considered one of the best in the new Form IV class, tenth and final class of elementary school. I made a positive first impression on our new teacher, I. Pont. He appointed me the new class monitor. In my new position I was responsible for distributing class books, packing them in the cabinet and taking work books and the teacher's handbooks to his quarters. I was given a responsibility for the first time in school and reveled in my new status. As far as I was I had come a long way since the first term of 1958.

I discovered sooner than later that I lacked the patience and temperament to be a good monitor. I did not have the patience to do my tasks systematically without messing up. My impatience became apparent within the first two days into my new responsibilities. On my first day on the job I packed all the student workbooks, the teacher's handbooks together with a bottle of ink and attempted to carry all of them to the teacher's house. I did not like to go to the teacher's house twice and I did not ask any of my classmates for help. When I attempted to carry all the books on my head the bottle of ink fell off the pack on reaching my head, dropped and shattered on the concrete floor. The following I attempted to carry all the books together again and had the same results. The result of second mishap was worse than the first because the ink was spilled on the teacher's table. I. Pont liked me but this was too much for even the mild mannered teacher to tolerate, he appointed Kojo, one of my classmates as my assistant.

I took the hint and relinquished my duties to my assistant and from that day I remained a monitor in name only. Kojo, to his credit, never committed the same blunders that I did in my first week as a monitor. It appears I had a knack to make a good first impression on some of my classmates and teachers at meetings. Thus in 1963-64 I impressed my college mates and the agriculture tutor during the inaugural meeting of the agricultural society I was selected to be the secretary of the club. My duties among other things included feeding a batch of day old chicks and cleaning the hen coop. My prior experience was feeding my mother's free range chickens at Bogoso but not day old chicks. I overdosed the day old chicks with chemical additives to their water and over a third of the day old chicks died within the first two weeks. I was indirectly deposed and once again I was given an assistant. After that I remained a secretary that only took down minutes and nothing else while the care of the chickens was left to other students. Eventually I became a slacker and stopped attending the meetings of the club; I have no idea what became of the day old chicks.

After I was indirectly deposed as the class monitor I continued by duties as a housekeeper for Michael. He taught me how to prepare some of his favorite meals and I took the cooking skills I learned from him with me when I left Issah. I was very happy with my new life on the campus as a houseboy. I ate and slept in my own room at the teacher's quarters and thus did not have to deal with the general student body except classes. I interacted with my mates in the classroom and at the wells otherwise

I had little in common with them. My new life on the campus was a far cry from my first year at the school.

SEASONAL WATER SHORTAGE

Issah middle boarding school was supplied with water from two dug out wells located at the outskirt of the school. The wells supplied water all year round but during the dry season the water flow from the wells were reduced to a trickle that required a lot of patience to fill a bucket of water. In the rainy season the wells filled to the brim and we turned the well waters into swimming pools or diving ponds. We washed in the wells and drew the same water for cooking and drinking. I never for one moment considered the consequences of polluting our only source of drinking water. I could not swim but I was assured that one could not drown in a well and as such I used to dive and swim and pee in the well after which I filled my bucket with the same water for cooking and drinking at the school.

In the dry season when the wells were reduced to a trickle, we carried out buckets down to the bottom of the wells with a calabash in hand and patiently skimmed water with the calabash into the bucket until it was full. The bucket of water was then carried to the surface from the bottom of the well by balancing it from one hand to the other while using the other hand for support to climb up the spikes in the concrete lining of the well.

On hindsight I think we were our own worst enemies; we contaminated and polluted the only source of drinking water. It was only in recent years that I attributed my brush with death partly to the contaminated waters. The wells were naturally contaminated by oil from the ground. The waters had shimmering oily substance on the surface; we skimmed the shimmering oily substance from the water before filling our buckets. The shimmering oily substance led to speculation that the area was rich in such as iron ore and oil including my class teacher, I. Pont. Puddles of water in the surrounding bushes and valley also had oil sheen on their surfaces.

By the time the Form IV students left the campus for Wa to write our final examination it was widely known that three of our schoolmates died at home, but the student body was never told that some of our school mates died. They became sick on the campus, went home for treatment and never came back, they died at home. The deaths of the students were perhaps considered as random unrelated events and no one associated the deaths with the school or the possibility that the three students died of infections they picked up at the school. I never did until years after I left Issah. By the end of the year a total of six students had died from the same type of infection, jaundice. I would have been the seventh casualty, but thanks to the medical examination at the end of October 1959 my infection was caught in the nick of time and that saved my life.

JAUNDICE OUTBREAK ON CAMPUS

In October 1959, I left along with the rest of my class to take the final examination for the middle school leaving certificate; I never went back again. Fate intervened to prevent me from ever going back to the school. The results of the Certificate B Teacher Training College examinations were released on the same day that we completed the last paper of the final middle school leaving examination and were due to return to Issah the next day. The successful students were asked to remain behind for the required medical examination at the hospital before going back to campus. We finished the last examination paper on a Friday and began the medical examination early the following Monday morning. I was admitted as an inpatient at the Wa hospital shortly after I submitted my urine and stool sample to the hospital laboratory. It was discovered that I was infected with jaundice. The medical exam saved my life, without the medical examination the illness would have been caught when it would have been too late to be successfully treated. I did not know before the exam that I had a life threatening disease.

Before I left Issah for the final examinations I used to experience sporadic pains on the right side of my tummy that caused me to double up but after a minute or so the pain subsided. The bilirubin was already passing through my urine giving it a reddish yellow color but I thought it was normal. I went about with my life without any idea I was sick. It never occurred to me that the orange colored urine and occasional pain on the right side of my tummy had any connection. When I was directed to the in patient ward on the first day of the medical examination I protested that I wanted to complete the examination and go back to school to complete the year. The laboratory technician told me bluntly, "You will be dead by the time the medical examination is completed." I thought he was joking and romped about the hospital compound refusing to comply with the instruction to rest in bed or confine myself to the bland non-fat diet provided by the hospital.

I was admitted into a side ward with the window facing the courtyard that gave me a clear view of the compound including the hospital mortuary. The mortuary was directly in my line of vision whenever I looked out of the window. I used to see the wrapped corpses of dead patients on gurneys wheeled to the mortuary in the early hours of the morning before the arrival of the staff for the morning shift.

On my first day as an inpatient, the staff nurse advised me to rest in bed, but I was full of restless energy to be confined to bed. I hated the bland and tasteless diet that was supplied by the hospital. I therefore used to sneak to other patients for their leftovers. I broke every rule I was asked to observe during the first week of admission. During the second week, I was immobilized with 24-7 intravenous infusions. The intravenous drips curtailed my movements around the hospital and confined me in bed, but I was still eager to get about so I used to adjust the flow of the drips to speed up the delivery in the mistaken belief that when the bag of infusion was emptied I would be let loose to romp around the hospital. But my mischief was caught whenever the nurse came to my bedside to check on me. The demeanor and mood of the nurses began to darken when they came by my bedside around the middle of November but I was still as happy as a lark itching to be let loose on the hospital until later in the month. I took my care and treatment as a matter of course and the intravenous medication and the constant monitoring as nuisance. By the third week of November my belly was bloated to about double its normal size, despite the abnormal size of my belly resembling that of a full term pregnancy it never occurred to me that my life was on the brink. Perhaps it was well and good that I never perceived that my life was in danger, my mental attitude could have had an adverse effect on my recovery.

While I was tethered to the infusion pole, one of my schoolmates, Bakana, was admitted while unconscious into the same side ward with me. His condition was worse than me, my belly was bloated but otherwise I was still conscious and lucid. He never regained consciousness until he passed away on the third day. The side ward was big enough for one bed, so Bakana was placed on the floor at the foot of my bed. He died from the same type of infection that tied me up at the hospital. He was the fifth student from the same school, the sixth student also died in the same hospital. I heard about him but I was not in good shape to look for him, when he died I was in critical condition still bound to infusion pole.

I was paralyzed with fear the night my wardmate passed away. He died early in the night and I was forced to sleep with his corpse till dawn when the morning staff removed the body to the morgue. That was the closest I ever came near or saw a person take his last breath. I watched in silence as his life ebbed away, in his final minutes he shook like a leaf in the breeze without much struggle, the nurse was by his side when he took his last breath. Though he did not struggle or thrash about but during his final moments the nurse was by his side. He placed his hands on him as he shivered under the bed sheet until he became still. He then casually pulled the bed sheet over his head and left the dead body with me in the room. I was scared when I saw the death of Bakana. I feared that the same fate awaited me and could not wait for the dead body to be removed from the room. The corpse was removed around dawn but I was still paralyzed with fear. I was scared to look out of the window lest I see his body being sent to the morgue but my curiosity got the better of my fears. I looked out of the window but by then it was too late to see the corpse being wheeled into the mortuary.

I lay on my back tethered to the intravenous infusion and froze with fear. If fear could kill, I guess the death of Bakana would have killed me that day. The only thing that kept me in the side ward after the death of Bakana was my own frail condition and the intravenous medication hanging on my bed or pole; otherwise I would have moved to the main ward. The death made me very prayerful; I promised God that I will be a good boy if He spared my life. I recited every prayer I knew from my favorite prayer book, Prayer Book for Boy Scouts. I prayed unceasingly, recited prayer after prayer as if my life depended on the number of prayers I could recite by heart. For about two weeks after the death of Bakana, my life also hung in the balance.

By the fourth week of November 1959, my condition became critical. I hallucinated and drifted in and out of consciousness. The nurses monitored my condition constantly around the clock. As I drifted in and out of consciousness, I saw visions of my own death. I saw visions of my dead body being wrapped in white sheets thrown onto a gurney and wheeled towards the morgue. As I stared at visions of my lifeless body being sent to the morgue I wept quietly and the tears streamed down my face into my ears and onto the pillow. I prayed and shook my head from side to side in an attempt to shake off the vision or wake up from the dream. This vision haunted me for about two weeks. I saw the vision at dawn at about the same hour that the morning orderly went around the wards to collect corpses of patients that had passed away during the night. I saw these visions at about the same hour that Bakana's lifeless body was removed from the ward to the mortuary for about two weeks. I prayed for salvation and made a thousand and one promises to God as I watched virtual video of my still and lifeless body under white sheets being taken to the mortuary. Mercifully the vision always disappeared at the gates of the mortuary; I never saw my dead body go through the gates of the morgue.

After seeing this virtual video for about two weeks the visions stopped as suddenly as they began to my great relief. And from the day I stopped seeing the vision of my corpse I started to mend. My recovery progressed so rapidly after the visions stopped that I was discharged about two weeks later on Boxing Day, December 26th. I could have been discharged earlier but the staff wanted to give me a memorable Christmas send off.

The doctor and the staff of the hospital gave me a warm Christmas send off. They were happy for me none so more than Dr. Hoffman, the physician in charge of the hospital. During my admission whenever Dr. Hoffman went to any of the regional capitals for conferences or meetings such as Accra, Kumasi or Tamale, he brought back some new drug he found to help with my treatment. As already mentioned above, two students from my school died at the hospital while I was on admission at the hospital. The difference between the students and me was that I was lucky and admitted at the hospital in the nick of time for treatment.

BRIBERY AND CORRUPTION IN GHANA

Bribery and corruption was institutionalized in the early years of the new nation soon after independence by the new political elite and made it virtually part of our new culture. In the Gold Coast no law enforcement official was feared more than sanitation inspectors popularly known as sama-sama *or tangaase*. The sanitation inspectors wore khaki uniforms and helmets armed with nothing but a book and shiny stainless steel ladles. The sanitation inspectors enforced rules of hygiene. The sanitation inspectors or *sama-sama* were the equivalent in the community of our school teachers who ensured that students observed good personal hygiene by inspecting our uniforms, teeth, hair and nails at school. The only difference between our teachers and the *sama-sama* was that the teachers enforced hygiene at school and the sanitation officers enforced hygiene in the community. They were dreaded because they had behind them the power of summons that resulted in fines for slobs and litter bugs who caused or created environment hazards. Housekeepers rushed to tidy up when the *sama-sama* was spotted approaching a neighborhood or walking along nearby streets. The fear of the *sama-sama or tangaase* ensured that our backyards and courtyards were spotlessly clean and the water stored for domestic uses did not become cesspools and breeding grounds for mosquitoes and other bugs. The sanitation inspectors went about their work without expecting favors or rewards; bribery and corruption was still alien to our culture and had not yet been institutionalized or seeped into our collective consciousness to become part of our culture.

There were two different police organizations in the Gold Coast before independence. The central colonial administration controlled a police force that was known then as general police, GP. And the various local authorities had their own police services under their control. At Bogoso the local police service was located in the center of town while the general police or GP was located on the outskirts of town away from the population center. The two services were distinguished from one another by their uniforms. The police were generally unarmed though they were trained in firearms. The local police service patrolled the streets of the local jurisdiction armed with nothing but wooden baton and whistles at any time of day. The general police handled motor traffic and were only seen around lorry parks and along main roads. The two police services were merged into one police service shortly after independence. And the modern day police in Ghana began carrying firearms after the first military coup that deposed the Nkrumah government in 1966.

We loved to hate our local police officers; they were unbending in the enforcement of the law and their duties in general. Local toughies liked to take them on because they were armed with only batons and whistles. The police stood between us and common criminals and settled domestic squabbles. Whenever the town crier warned residents to exercise caution in anticipation of armed robbers, the local police bore the brunt of the bad men when they arrived in town. Armed robbers of the Gold Coast were armed mostly with machetes. The robbers tended to hack the police when they confronted or met the police in the commission of their criminal and nefarious nocturnal activities. But rarely did they hack the police to death. A policeman in trouble blew his whistle to summon help from colleagues; it was not uncommon to hear whistles across town during the night, a sign of police in action or in trouble. The heroism of one of our local policemen at Bogoso made him popular when he was attacked and hacked with machetes by robbers while he was patrolling the town at night. This was in spite of warnings that armed robbers were about to descend on the town by the town crier. The place where he was hacked became an unofficial shrine where passerby's stopped to look at the blood stains on ground where he was attacked by the armed robbers. The spot was along the path which I took to dispose of garbage. And I like many residents stopped to gawk at the blood stain on the grounds when I reached there. The stains were still visible about three days after the attack. He survived his wounds and went back on patrol duties with the scars to show for his bravery but still armed with only a baton and whistle.

The integrity of the local law enforcement officers, the local police and sanitation officers, of the Gold Coast were beyond reproach. I did not come into contact with the general police force apart from a visit to their barracks to hawk kerosene. And I do not think that they were as corrupt as present day MTU police officers. But I can say with confidence that if the present day MTU had half the integrity of their Gold Coast counterparts, Abban would not have attained the cult hero status he gained in the eighties. He refused to take bribes and directed the bribe giver to pay it to the government, hence the nick name Abban. A neighborhood of the Gold Coast virtually came to standstill when a sanitation officer was spotted on the way to the neighborhood. We scurried to clean up and put things in order before he entered the courtyard. I remember the women of my house tipped over barrels of water because of sediments at the bottom of the barrels. Standing water in barrels with sediments around the home was anathema to the *sama-sama*. Sanitation officers used to spray stagnant rain waters in the gutters, streets and bushes and they expected us to do the same in our homes. The incidents of malaria were not as rampant in the Gold Coast as it became after independence because the old rules were considered outmoded and 'institutionalized' bribery and corruption blunted law enforcement. The local authorities ensured that stagnant rain waters were sprayed to prevent them from becoming breeding grounds for mosquitoes. Barrels of water with sediments were considered similar to stagnant waters and the owners of such barrels of water were ticketed for causing environmental hazards. Homemakers rushed to put garbage into containers and clean around the home before the *sama-sama* got to the house usually on random visits. The sanitation officer was a figure of integrity that struck fear into the hearts of sloppy homemakers.

In retrospect, the local council or *tangaase* was efficient and responsive to the needs of the community. When we were squabbling over water from a small spring, they built a concrete perimeter dwarf wall around the spring that provided inexhaustible source of water supply and ended the squabbles. And they maintained the reservoir by cleaning the concrete walls and rocks at regular intervals. Our dusty streets and open drains were cleaned every morning. It was tempting to dispose of garbage into the open gutters but except in a downpour people did not generally empty garbage into the drains tempting as that might have been. But during downpours garbage was emptied into the swollen drains. The children used to swim in the swollen drains during downpours and ducked the garbage that floated by us as we swam in the open gutters. At the village of Tamso the bushes between houses were cut down about every three months to minimize the menace of bugs

If cleanliness is next to godliness the communities of my formative years were communities of godliness. Against the odds and poverty the authorities enforced good hygiene and sanitation habits. There was no potted water at Bogoso and most families and households stored water in steel drums for household chores. To prevent the stored waters from becoming dirty stagnant waters attracting mosquitoes and all sorts of bugs and insects the local sanitation authorities, *sama-sama*, conducted surprise inspections of the water storages at random intervals. The officers stirred the standing waters in the drums with ladles for evidence of dirt or sediments and thus kept the residents on their toes. The khaki uniform and the ladle carried a lot of authority. The integrity of the sanitation inspectors, *sama-sama*, was unimpeachable; that was the impression I carried with me when I left Bogoso at the end of 1957.

The influence and integrity of local law enforcement officials was felt in our daily lives at Bogoso. Bribery and corruption was not yet in our psyche and our dealing with the *sama-sama or tangaase* was transparent and above board. The sanitation officers could not be influenced with monetary incentives to overlook the obvious such as a barrel of dirty stagnant water. Their integrity could not be bought at any price. It was not uncommon to see local bullies and toughies entangle with these officers for their intransigence in enforcement of the local ordinances. Bribery and corruption came into vogue after independence. The demonstration effect of the conspicuous consumption habits of the new political class helped to institutionalize bribery and corruption and that has bedeviled the development of the country since independence.

By 1961, the lifestyle and consumption habits of the new political rulers had permeated all classes and levels of societies in the country. The lifestyle of the new political elite was not subtle, it was almost arrogant as if they were entitled, they flaunted their ill gotten wealth with pomp. The corrupt practices were so widespread that even those of us who were students in far away Navrongo were aware of the lavish lifestyles of our new rulers.

The life style of members of the government and party functionaries was the topic of conversations between those of us who did not belong to the political class. The nouveau riche introduced or popularized the concept of the single family home or self contained home or flat after independence. The affluent people of the Gold Coast rarely put up one family or self contained homes, when they did it was a flat within a large compound house of multi generational occupancy. The affluent within the family built to accommodate both their immediate family and the extended family. But within a few years after independence the self contained home or flat became the aspiration of every public servant no matter his hierarchy in the service from the first republic and thereafter. The concept of the single family home or self contained home or flat was partly the natural progression of our national development but the process was hastened by the example shown by the office holders of the new government and their party functionaries. Nobody raised an eyebrow when a party functionary with modest means suddenly became the owner of the latest mansion in town and drove the latest expensive model luxury car he could not buy on his legitimate income. And amidst the display of conspicuous consumption and extravagance they pleaded with the general public to sacrifice for the development of the country.

The integrity and trust between the people and their government began to fray only a few years after independence from colonial administration. The rulers and party functionaries of the new nation created a lifestyle infrastructure that encouraged bribery and corruption to keep up with the nouveau riche. The debasement of our character made the twin practice of bribery and corruption virtually respectable and acceptable way of life. Our national priorities were skewed towards conspicuous consumption and flaunting of wealth irrespective of how the wealth was attained, wealth became the new god we worshipped.

In this mad rush to prosperity some basic commonsense values were lost. There was a lack of accountability at all levels of government and that in effect institutionalized bribery and corruption.

The cancer of bribery and corruption in time engulfed every facet of the Ghanaian society from the lowest-paid office messenger to the top of the hierarchy. In a poor country with low incomes the effect of conspicuous consumption by our leaders led to the creation of hostile work environment, where bribery became the only way to obtain a service from our government or state enterprise.

When we were asked by our government to sacrifice present consumption for a better tomorrow, the exhortation was met with some skepticism. It was considered a cynical exploitation of our good and docile nature. The only people who appeared to receive the exhortation with any degree of enthusiasm were those who stood to gain from any government project, those who got the popular ten percent cut from contracts. Mistrust of the government was deep and endemic only three years after independence. A position in the new government was not based on merit or skill but on whom one knew or role in the governing political party. The first district commissioner of Wa for instance, was widely rumored to be an illiterate. It is said that he was appointed a district commissioner to get at the intelligentsia of the district who were overwhelming supporters of the opposition party. It was during the first republic that the term "square pegs in round holes" was coined to describe misfits in crucial positions of government by the opposition. The term was an apt description of the appointments of misfits to high government positions with responsibilities for vital governments departments and state corporations.

In 1960 or thereabout, the government launched a public relations campaign for the Volta River Project-VRP. The campaign was launched to build public support for the implementation of the expensive project. The project demanded sacrifice from all Ghanaians which upon completion would make it the cornerstone of the industrial development of the country. The government's propaganda machinery took the message around the country to explain the benefits of the Volta River Project to the general population. The public relations campaign eventually reached our campus at St. John Bosco's College sometime in 1961. The exchanges that took place between us and the public relations officials was emblematic of the corruption that was taking hold on the country.

The plea by the government for sacrifice was considered as lip service since there was nothing within the ranks of the government and its apparatchiks that they were serious about sacrifice. We asked the public relation officers why the government asked sacrifices from ordinary citizens while senior officers of the government earned very high salaries and perks incompatible with a government demanding sacrifice from all and sundry. We were told that the fat salaries and perks was a demonstration of our freedom as a nation from colonial domination. Our government officials have assumed the positions of the erstwhile colonial masters. Their incomes were spent in the country instead of going to the country of the colonial officials.

In other words independence meant supplanting the colonial masters by new black masters. It was this mentality that has hampered the economic development of Ghana and the other African Countries who took their cue from Ghana. Ghana was the base for other African leaders who were still fighting for independence for their respective countries. They took with them the template of 'success' they observed in Ghana, bribery and corruption of members of the government and other officials of government.

The government and its officials could do no wrong as such there was no accountability in the government at any level. This dearth of accountability may best be illustrated by the infamous purchase of a £3,000 gold bed at a trade show in London in the early 1960's by the wife of a prominent cabinet minister. That indiscretion at the dawn of our independence emblazoned the path of corruption at all levels of society that has not yet abated to this day. The path blazed by the wife of Krobo Edusei became the gold standard of prosperity that we all aspired to reach. Mary Edusei bought a £3,000 gold bed from a trade show in London only a few years after independence.

The price tag of the bed was sacrilegious considering the buyer, the wife of a minister of a poor African country.

The collective jaws of the nation dropped at the at the logic defying conspicuous consumption that made us the laughing stock of the world. This was at a time when the government was exhorting the citizens to sacrifice for the development of the country. Nothing betrayed the hypocrisy of the government than the price tag of a £3,000 gold bed on the front pages of major newspapers around the world. The gold bed was the worse example of the excesses of members of the government of the first republic. The excesses and extravagance of the era can be understood if it is put into context of our country. In the 1960's the price tag would have paid the salary of a senior public servant for more than four years. The salary of a senior civil or public servant during most of the 1960's was £680 a year or ¢1,360 after the introduction of the cedi Ghana currency. The monthly salary of such an official who lived in a bungalow and drove a car was £58 or ¢116. If the bed was not acquired with ill gotten wealth then it meant that our government officials were paid far in excess of their value to the country. After the dust settled on the infamous transaction there was no public retribution for the rank display of wealth by the wife of a government minister from a poor African country.

The lack of accountability for the obscene display of wealth by the wife of a minister from a poor developing country opened the sluice gates for bribery and corruption. It was an example that nobody could make that kind of money and buy such expensive items on his normal income. Bribery and corruption was institutionalized into our national psyche and became an acceptable way of life. Every Tom, Dick, and Harry who could profit from his position in government did so with impunity with no fear of accountability or backlash. Shakedowns by public servants became the order of the day. Bribery and corruption became part of our way of interacting with our government and doing official business and took a firm hold on our collective imagination and has bedeviled and militated against the development of the country as an independent nation.

Bribery and corruption has taken hold of our collective imagination so much so that the military and police who overthrew elected governments over bribery and corruption in 1966 could not keep their hands clean during the period of governance. They were corrupted and by the time they left office they had acquired mansions and were far wealthier than when they came into government. They confirmed the skepticism and widely held beliefs by the general public that the shortest route to wealth in Ghana is through government service. No minister or high government official ever left government service without amassing wealth. We have come to accept that service in government is the quickest way to amass wealth. And one is considered a dupe or an idiot if he left government service without amassing wealth. The one minister in the Nkrumah government who did not amass wealth was considered a dope. Kofi Baako, was the ideal socialist, he truly believed in the socialist dogma of the first republic and lived accordingly, he did not amass any wealth or profit from the spoils of his office by the time the government was overthrown in 1966. Only a few of his countrymen appreciated his honesty and integrity, the majority thought he was a dope to have held office as a minister of defense and left office with almost empty hands.

The culture of bribery and corruption that was sown shortly after independence also doomed Ghana's attempt at capturing the "commanding heights of the economy." The government of the first republic established many industries and factories, but most of these factories and industries failed spectacularly because of bribery corruption. The chief operating officers, known as managing directors, of the enterprises owed their position to party loyalty. The enterprises thus became the piggy banks of the mangers who staffed them with their concubines and cronies. Most of the state enterprises failed because they were not run as businesses but as patronage jobs for the party faithful. The term sugar daddy came into vogue during this era.

Shortage of Consumer Goods

The political and economic development philosophy of the first republic was 'African Socialism'. It was in furtherance of this socialist philosophy that the government established manufacturing industries and trading house to compete with the expatriate trading houses such as UTC, UAC and SCOA. The Nkrumah government bought A.G. Leventis, an established trading house and renamed it Ghana National Trading Corporation, GNTC

Thus was born the Ghana National Trading Corporation. Within a short period of time GNTC became the dominant distributor of every conceivable commodity in Ghana. Endemic corruption soon permeated and took over the legitimate operations of the corporation. Thanks to our socialist leanings and widespread corruption, essential consumer commodities and everything else in between was soon in short supply, store shelves were empty. GNTC as the premier government distribution house became the main importer and distributor of consumer goods for the country almost to the exclusion of the old expatriate trading houses.

GNTC also opened another chapter of corrupt practices in Ghana; black market in the distribution of goods. The powers that be brought their influence to bear on the distribution of consumer goods. The distribution system degenerated into a chit system. The chit was the personification of favoritism and nepotism. Consumer goods were distributed through chits. Those with friends in higher places got a chit that entitled them to a quantity of some commodities or goods from GNTC. The holders of the chits sold them at exorbitant prices and made fabulous profits without ever handling the commodities. The chit thus became tradable commodity. It was not necessary for a chit holder to get hold of the physical goods before selling them; the goods were sold via the chit. The resulting cut throat prices embodied in the chits gave rise to black market which became known as *kalabule*, 'you cheat me I cheat you'. A chit was worth its weight in gold. Those who suffered most from this corruption were the average hardworking Ghanaians who had no friends in high positions of the government.

The black market in consumer goods benefited mostly high government officials and their cronies. And for maximum profitability, commodities were hoarded, thus making a bad situation worse. There were no obvious scapegoats other than the usual rants about saboteurs and neo colonialists trying to undermine the government. As conditions became more and more unbearable; the government public relations machinery manufactured imaginary enemies and saboteurs for the shortages. Thus by 1964-65, the situation was so untenable that the government sought to diffuse the situation by appointing a commission of inquiry to investigate the chronic shortages and the distribution system. The commission of inquiry, it was hoped, would uncover the saboteurs and enemies of the state.

A leopard cannot change its stripes. As the hearings proceeded it soon became clear that the saboteurs and enemies of the state were none other than members of the government, their relatives and cronies. The public hearings unmasked some of the influence peddlers and profiteers. Among them was none other than Mary Edusei, of the gold bed fame. Her name came up frequently during the public hearings. The report of the commission which was released after the coup d'état that overthrew the government in February 1966 was a complete whitewash of the public deliberations. None of the prominent names or influential members of the erstwhile government that came up during the hearings was mentioned in the report. The sanitized report was silent on the role played by powerful members of government in the operation of the black market.

The military coup of February 1966 led by Major Afrifa and Col. Kotoka was a welcome relief. But bribery and corruption had become entrenched, the new military government formed after the coup danced around the edges of the problem without putting in place any effective action or policy to combat it. The mentality that government service is for the enrichment of those who hold the levers of power has continued unabated since the first republic. The architects of the 1966 coup left government fabulously richer and chubbier with all their 'poverty bones' nicely covered up than before they became ministers and high government officials.

POLITICAL INSTABILITY

The government that replaced the Nkrumah government, National Liberation Council, held power for approximately three years before it handed over to a democratically elected government in 1969. The new government was led by Dr. K. A. Busia, an eminent and renowned sociologist, as prime minister. The government of the second republic was a disappointment in one particular aspect: lack of tolerance for free speech. They paid lip service to free speech and did everything to sabotage contrary opinions. Dr. Busia and members of his government extolled the virtues of democracy, free press and free speech while they were in opposition and in exile from the country. But once they became the government they could not live up to the ideals of democracy they championed while they were in opposition or exile.

The members of the government pretended to care about press freedom but made it impossible for any paper with contrary opinion to be published. The government of the first republic nationalized all newspapers and monopolized broadcasting. Dr. Busia and his government kept in place all the powers and restrictions that the Nkrumah government instituted against free press and free speech. As an example of their hypocrisy, the editor of the Daily Graphic wrote an editorial piece that heaped praises on the Prime Minister. He was so pleased with the praise that he went to his office on a Sunday and sent a congratulatory telegram to the editor of the paper, Cameron Duodu. And a few short weeks later when the same editor wrote an unflattering editorial comment about the government, he was fired.

The Busia government was overthrown in another coup d'état after being in office for just about three years. The government of Dr. Busia facing deteriorating economy put in place some austerity measures that made cut backs in the budget including elimination of some privileges for the military and other government agencies. The initial announcement by the coup leader, Col. Acheampong over the airwaves at around five in the morning gave the justification for the coupe as the elimination of privileges enjoyed by the military. But by mid day that first umbrage for the coupe was off the airwaves and replaced with high minded reasons for toppling an elected government by force.

The economy of the country, whether under civilian or military administrations, continued to go from bad to worse and worse. The downward spiral of the economy continued with no appreciable improvements under the various administrations from the sixties through to the nineties. The only thing that was constant was that those who came into government became wealthier than when they came in. The periods of hope and optimism were usually short-lived. The riches amassed by members of governments were enough incentive for any soldier with a gun to attempt to overthrow a government by force. Despite the high minded rhetoric that followed every coup the ensuing members of the government followed the same playbook established by the government of the first republic. They enriched themselves. The culture of bribery and corruption which began during the first republic got progressively worse with each successive government.

As already pointed out the quickest way to become wealthy is through high government service. So despite the high sounding rhetoric and themes of each successive coup in Ghana, the end result was always the same. The enrichment of hungry soldiers and police officers who held enviable positions of unquestionable power, and thus used the levers of power to amass unimaginable wealth by the time they left or were forced out of office. The high sounding rhetoric was nothing more than camouflages or ruse by hungry men with gun and ammunition. Thus after the first military coup of 1966, there was another coup-d'état in 1972; two military coups within six years. The National Redemptive Council government formed after the coup of 1972 metamorphosed into the Supreme Military Council in 1975 with the same basic actors and players. The military government which came into office originally in

1972 was itself overthrown in 1979. But the young officers, led by J. J. Rawlings, who overthrew the government allowed already scheduled elections to take place and the third republic, came into being in September 1979.

The third republic lasted for a little over two years before it was swept out of office by force in another military coup led by Flt. Lt. J. J. Rawlings, Rawlings 2.0. This was the second coming of Rawlings to power by force of arms. I call his second coming as Rawlings 2.0. The elected civilian administration of the third republic was overthrown in 1981. The government of Rawlings 2.0 faced a lot of turmoil at its inception, but it managed to thwart all counter coup attempts, thrived and ushered in a long period of uneasy stability. But before he settled into the long period of uneasy peace he cornered, captured and killed Corporal Jiwa, his nemesis at the house of a girl friend.

Rawlings was in power for over ten years. He later transformed himself into a civilian leader by submitting himself for elective civilian office through democratic process. He won democratic elections twice in the 1990's, and was in office for a total of eight years as an elected civilian president before he handed over to another elected government. Ghana appears to have settled down as a peaceful democracy where changes of government come at the ballot box and not at the barrel of a gun.

Each successive military coup justified their treason by accusing members of the deposed regime of corruption. Their first order of business was to establish a commission of inquiry to investigate the assets of members of the deposed government. But no member of any military government has ever been investigated about their ill gotten wealth with the same zeal as civilians. The Armed Forces Revolutionary Council government under Rawlings 1.0 did not conduct any meaningful investigation into the assets and conduct of surviving members of previous military regimes before they were lined up blind folded and executed in 1979.

The military regimes it turned out were as corrupt if not more corrupt than the civilians they replaced. If anything, they were worse; they were hungrier when they came into office. They built their wealth from scratch. Most civilians had some amount of wealth or respectable professions and trade before they entered into government service. Members of military regimes have the same aspirations and ambitions as members of the government they swept out of office with guns, supplant the previous office holders and the spoils of high office. They scarcely ever had anything new of substance to contribute towards our national weal, they were only interested in the plunder made possible by the gun notwithstanding the condition of the economy. Thus military regimes are by their nature unstable, they come into office through the barrel of a gun but they do not have monopoly over guns. There are always other officers hanging in the wings eager to depose those in power to get at the privileges and spoils of power. They therefore have to be constantly on the watch for the adventurous officers eager to topple them and inherit their privileges. This was the curse of the country that deprived it of the stability necessary for economic development.

Ghana has paid a high price for instability and cockamamie ideologies. Ghana and Malaysia both became independent of British rule in 1957. Singapore broke away from Malaysia in 1960. The two Asian nations have advanced economies while Ghana lags behind economically and socially with underdevelopment. Ghana's progress has lagged quite apart from the faux socialist ideologies but more specifically because of the culture of bribery and corruption. The culture of bribery and corruption sapped our energies and resources for development went into individual pockets. No meaningful accountability system has ever been established with enough moral authority and independence to investigate cases of bribery and corruption against members of sitting government.

Path To College

I was discharged from the Wa hospital on Boxing Day 1959 after almost three months and went home to an empty house. I was very happy when I left the hospital with my bag of Christmas goodies from Father Christmas, Santa Claus, on Christmas day 1959. My heart sank when I entered the house. The house was empty; neither my aunt and her husband, my mother, nor any member of family was home. I was so sad I wished I had not been discharged. If I could have gone back to the hospital for readmission I would have done so. At least, at the hospital I was provided with three meals a day and I had the company of the nurses and the other patients. But as I stared at the bleak and empty house, I did not know where my next meal would come from.

My mother took leave of me about two weeks into my admission for a short visit to my older sister, Cecilia, at Yendi. She took my baby sister Adjoa along with her ostensibly to provide companionship for Cecilia who would then become responsible for the care and education of Adjoa. Mother promised to return within two weeks. She did not come back until after three or four months. My mother was not around when I was in critical condition and on the verge of death. There was no family member to comfort me while I was hallucinating, seeing visions of my death and drifting in and out of consciousness. It would have been comforting to have been able to discuss my visions with a close member of family, but I had to deal with the scary visions without the wisdom of my mother or any family member. I was sustained throughout my ordeal by the hospital meals; I never had any home cooked meals while on admission. I felt abandoned while I was on admission.

When I entered the empty home, my first priority was to gain access into my mother's room. I put down my Christmas goodies on the floor in the courtyard and searched the known hiding places for the room key. I found the key and let myself into our room; I then surveyed the room for any food items that I could live on until a member of family, mother or aunt, came home. I found a calabash full of shea butter, a bowl of ground bean flour, and another bowl of dry beans. The beans, flour and shea butter were all the food I had to sustain me until my mother returned home. I alternated between eating cooked dry beans with shea butter and *kose* or fried bean dough. Although I was advised to refrain from oily and fatty foods at the hospital, the shea butter was the only ingredient I had to flavor the cooked dry beans and fry the bean dough I made from the bean flour. After settling down I turned my attention to my next priority, how to obtain school supplies and transport fare to Navrongo in January 1960. I wrote to my father with the list of the required school supplies on December 27, 1959. I pleaded with him to expedite with the money and supplies and impressed upon him that I was home alone and schools were due to start by mid January 1960.

After I wrote and mailed the letter to my father I had very little to do but wait for either my mother to return from Yendi or my father to send me a box of supplies and money to enable me to go to Navrongo at the start of school. In the meantime I killed time loitering around Wa. The second week of January came and went with no news from either my father or mother. I roamed aimlessly around the streets of Wa like a homeless vagabond. During the third week of January 1960, while walking aimlessly about town I came across one of the teachers at Wa Middle School who by sheer coincidence remembered me and asked what I was doing in town when I should have been in college. I explained my predicament and he advised me to see the clerk of the Wa District Council for help. The next day, I was at the door of the clerk of council's office before he arrived. When he came in, I explained my predicament to him. He gave me six yards of khaki and six yards of calico from stock he had in his office.

The fabrics were enough to make a pair of trousers, shorts and some shirts, but he did not give me any money to cover my transport from Wa to Navrongo. He however informed me that the Wa District Commissioner was due to go to Navrongo on a conference. He therefore advised me to contact the District Commissioner for a ride to Navrongo during his journey for the conference. The District Commissioner agreed to give me a ride after he returned from a trip to Lawra. Meanwhile he directed me to wait for him at his bungalow. Looking back, I cannot imagine how easy it was to walk into the offices of the two most powerful government officials at Wa in 1960 without let or hindrance. I wonder whether in today's Ghana a young man in my shoes could walk into the offices of the two most powerful officials in any district without jumping through many bureaucratic hoops.

But alas the journey did not take place. The district commissioner returned from the Lawra trip late Friday evening and told me that due to unforeseen circumstances, he could make it to Navrongo until the following week. The bubble of my excitement and enthusiasm was deflated at the news but I consoled myself with hope that the district commissioner would give me a ride the following week. Until then I was allowed to continue residing at his residence with his family. I was greatly relieved during the period I lived with the district commissioner. I had practically become his ward and I did not have to worry about how I got my next meal. I got along very well with his domestic staff and family members. Two weeks passed by but the expected journey and ride to Navrongo never materialized. Eventually I resigned myself to the fact that I may never go to Navrongo and made the most of my circumstance. His cook became my best friend in the bungalow. I observed him at his work and never left his side when he was busy in the kitchen. I made myself his unofficial assistant or apprentice.

I was virtually content to live with the DC. I had nothing to lose, I had no idea how to get to Navrongo without any money. I did not have a plan B about job prospects while I was in school as I expected to be in college in the New Year 1960. My prospects for college at this stage was slipping away but I did not know what to do next.

In the second week of February 1960, I got some good news at last. My mother finally returned home from Yendi, and at the same time a box with my school supplies arrived from my father. It had been more than four weeks since the term began, but at last I had the money and supplies needed for school and I could not wait a day longer to get to the school. I decided to take my chances even though I was more than four weeks late.

St. John Bosco's Teacher's College

I arrived on the campus of St. John Bosco's Teacher Training College on a Friday evening after the long journey from Wa. I was directed to report to the principal's office. The principal, Father Pwamang, told me that I was too late for admission. But he was sympathetic to the difficulties that prevented me from reporting on time. The power to admit me at that stage was not solely up to him, he had to consult with members of the school staff. A staff meeting was already scheduled for that Sunday and he said he would consult the staff before coming to a decision. In the meantime he asked a member of the teaching staff who was my tribal kinsman to accommodate me till after the staff meeting. The meeting was very crucial to me as my very future depended on its outcome, it would determine whether I stayed or went home.

Suffice to say I was accepted into residence on probation, though I did not know it at the time. My admission was contingent upon catching up with the rest of the class. I took my place in the school and went on to complete the two year training program successfully. As a trainee teacher I was paid monthly allowance; the admission thus gave me regular monthly income and ushered me into adulthood as I was freed from the need for financial assistance and support from my family. I became financially independent and that could not have come any sooner.

In 1960 Ghana converted from a calendar based school year—January to December, to the standard academic year in the rest of the world. Thus we completed the first academic year in about six to seven months and since I was one month late I completed the first year in about six months or less.

At St. John Bosco's college, I had so much to eat that I forgot the hunger I endured in my first year at Issah boarding school in 1958 and the unpleasant experience of being home alone. The food rations were generous, more than adequate to satisfy the most ravenous appetite. I was introduced to water closets or flushable toilets and showers at the college. The school had two types of flushable toilets. One was the regular pedestal water closets and the other was a flushable pit latrine suitable for squatting instead of sitting. Most of the students were familiar with dug-out pit latrines or easing ourselves in the bush. The flushable pit latrine was the closest to the lifestyle most of us were familiar with. We were at home squatting on the flushable pit latrine. The pedestal water closets were new to most of us and required acclimatization, we were not used to sitting on a toilet. I therefore started using the pit latrine and gradually and tepidly progressed to the pedestal water closets. The regular water closets were cleaner than the dug out toilets because fewer students used them regularly.

Life on the college campus was a luxury I could not have imagined or contemplated. The campus ushered me into the modern era of flushing toilets, electricity and comfortable bedding. I progressed from sleeping on hard cement floor on a straw mat without blanket or pillow to a foam mattress on bunk bed with blanket, bed sheet and pillow. The blanket and bed sheet were part of the list of school supplies. My father would never have dreamed of buying a blanket and bed sheet for me but for the school. And I stood and washed under a shower for the first time at St. John Bosco's college. I was relieved from the drudgery of taking a bath from a bucket so I had no excuse to go for a day without a shower. But I came back to earth when I went on vacation; during vacation I went back to easing myself in bushes or smelly pit latrines, slept on hard floor but on a blanket and bed sheet brought from school and took a bath from the familiar bucketful of water. I lived practically in two diametrically opposite worlds between home and school, school was heavenly.

Over time I became accustomed to living the two incongruous lifestyles between home and school. I lived this incongruous lifestyle from the year I went to St. John Bosco's College then Peki Training College through to the University and after graduation. I was finally able to merge the two incongruous worlds of my life in 1980 when I rented my first self contained apartment at Suame, in Kumasi. Some of the habits I formed during the years of hardship have remained with me. For instance I never slept on a blanket, bed sheet or pillow for the first sixteen years of my life until I went to St. John Bosco's college in 1960. I used to curl my arm under my head as a pillow when I slept during infancy. I have not been able to overcome that habit though I have been sleeping on pillows throughout my life as an adult. The habit I formed during my formative years is still with me.

Honestly, I dreaded vacations because of all the inconveniences and hunger that gnawed at my tummy while on vacation. My vacations were characterized by hunger and food insecurities because I was a bad manager of my money. Campus was a respite; I could not wait to go back to school after vacation. Life at school was much easier than life at home. The difference between home and school was like night and day. Vacations reminded me of where I came from and not to get too complacent with the comfortable life on campus.

SELF CONTROL RANTS

During my senior year at Navrongo, I was paired with an older student who coincidentally was related to the staff member who accommodated me while my fate was being determined when I arrived late on the campus. My new room mate had a

171

lot of real world experience professionally and personally. He was a pupil teacher, the term for untrained teachers, for many years before he came to college.

He was nice and congenial when sober, but he was drunk almost every night. He used to go into town after classes and came back drunk. And while he was drunk he lectured me on self control. He had a mantra that he ranted incessantly virtually into my ears night in night out, *'a man is not a man until he can control himself'*. He repeated this phrase over and over until he fell asleep. The constant repetition every night *'a man is not a man until he can control himself'* used to annoy me. If I had my own way I would have thrown him out or asked for another room mate. I used to murmur asking while he ranted *"Where is your self-control when you cannot be sober for one night?"*. I lived with the smell of alcohol on his breath and his ramblings every night except during examination week when he was sober. I endured his ranting till the end of the year.

In a way, he taught me tolerance; we never had any open conflict or quarrel throughout the year. I bit my tongue and tolerated his babbling on self-control night after night. I never considered his ramblings were worthy of attention since he was not a paragon of self control himself. "How can you advise me on self control when you cannot control yourself", I thought. But I think the ranting was the best thing that ever happened to me. His words on self control sank into my subconscious and affected me profoundly when I faced the world by myself alone after graduation. I did not realize how much he had influenced me until I began life as a teacher

The aphorism on self control that I hated so much became my guiding principle in life. I strived for moderation in my life and exercised self control in my endeavors. When I started drinking alcoholic beverages with friends, I made it a point never to be caught drunk in a beer bar or pito house. I avoided becoming an early alcoholic because I lived by the self control adage that was drilled into me night after night at Navrongo. I learned to know when enough was enough and left my drinking companions behind despite their entreaties when I had enough. Self-control moderated my indulgencies and checked my excesses. When I left the comfort of St. John Bosco's college, it was the gift I took with me. I was subconsciously ready to take my life into my hands through the exercise of self-control whether I was aware or not.

MY TEACHING CAREER

At the end of the school year in July 1961 I proceeded to Tamale hoping to begin my teaching career in September. The Catholic Education Unit in Tamale was my first employer of choice. I made Tamale my first choice because my sister Cecilia was by then residing at Tamale as a staff nurse. She was stationed at the Tamale hospital so I naturally expected her to help me to cope with life until I received my first pay as a teacher. I placed all my hopes of support on her though we scarcely corresponded. I was mindful of the misery and hunger I often endured during vacations and I considered my sister my insurance against starvation until I began earning regular income as a career teacher. At the end of the academic year our monthly trainee teacher allowances came to an end, we were on our own until we began our careers as teachers.

I went to Tamale along with one of my classmates and best friend, Donatus. Donna, as he was popularly known, was a pupil teacher at Tamale before he entered the training college. He was therefore familiar with Tamale and could therefore give me some guidance about life in Tamale. His former landlord assured him of a room when he returned to Tamale. I therefore anticipated sharing accommodation with him until I secured my own. I thought I covered all the bases when we arrived at Tamale to await the beginning of the new school year.

We run out of funds shortly after we came to Tamale. Donna and I were both poor money managers; we could not manage the last allowance we received from campus through our first pay. We run out of money within two weeks of our arrival in Tamale. Our challenge was how to survive from about the middle of August 1961 till the end of September when we might receive our first pay as teachers. My plan of subsisting on my sister's generosity went awry; things did not go quite the way I expected. The first day I met her she suggested that we pull our resources together to buy food stuffs and the like. That was a reasonable suggestion but it was contrary to what I expected of my big sister. I expected her to provide for me without any reservation until I was ready to move on. I needed only temporary assistance; I had no intention of making home with her to share expenses. I did not like her suggestion; I expected the same standard of hospitality our family members extended to one another freely. I could not imagine anything otherwise from my older sister.

I did not accept her suggestion though I did not have the courage to tell her so for fear I would starve, but nevertheless I still felt entitled to take my share of the groceries she stored in her kitchen. I used to sneak into the kitchen when she was at work and helped myself to whatever I could lay hands on and shared that with my friend Donatus. She shared a common kitchen with other staff nurses of the hospital as such the kitchen was open at all times and I went in and out as I pleased without let or hindrance. Her neighbors were familiar with us and that gave me a blank check to go in and out as I pleased. And then one day just as I was about to leave with some food items we collided in front of the kitchen. It was not a cordial meeting as we got into heated arguments, lost our tempers and exchanged blows in front of the kitchen. Some of her neighbors came in between us and were curious about the causes of the fracas, but we were so ashamed of ourselves that we could not give voice to the cause of the scuffles between us and for years none of us mentioned it until well into our old age.

We could not disclose to any third party the reason for fighting; we literally told them to mind their own business. We were raised by a woman who taught us that when you feed a hungry man you give him a burden of defecation. Feeding the hungry was not a big deal though we hardly had enough ourselves we shared the little we had with all comers. I left her house in a huff with righteous indignation. I did not see or communicate with her again for next eight years. We were reconciled after eight years by our younger sister Adjoa. She was the only member of our family who ever heard that the two of us fought over food. No other member of our family ever had a hint of the fight or quarrel. And though we reconciled our relations never had the warmth and spontaneity that existed between Adjoa and me. We reconciled when my sister was by then residing at Sunyani and I was a student at the Kumasi University of Science and Technology.

I was on my own the moment I walked out of my sister's house. I did not have another back up plan, there was no plan B. The numbing hunger that marked my first two terms at Issah middle boarding school came back with a vengeance. I was about two months removed from Navrongo but I might as well have been hungry all my life. The abundance of Navrongo was a distant memory in the face of the starvation that stared at me in the face.

The transition from training college to the classroom as a teacher with a regular monthly pay was the most difficult period of my entire teaching career. Donna and I depended on the generosity of his landlord's household. Sometimes they gave us some leftovers but if there was no leftover we had nothing. We despaired as we counted the days till our first pay at the end of September 1961. In our desperation we became pious and turned to the scriptures for consolation. We were churchgoers with no strong conviction or faith in the scripture. But with no where else to turn we suddenly believed in the promises of God as enshrined in scriptures for comfort. My friend Donna had more faith in the word of God than me. Donna began quoting Matthew 6: 26 *"Look at the birds of the air, for they neither sow nor reap nor gather into barns; yet your heavenly Father feeds them. Are you not of more value than they?"*

We took the passage literally as the promise of God and actually expected nothing less from our heavenly Father to fulfill his promise by feeding us. Are we not more valuable than the birds of the air? We reasoned. Donna used to tell me emphatically, "we would eat before we go to bed. God would not let us go to bed hungry" or God never sleeps. I was always doubtful because I did not see where the food would come from. But eventually Donna made a believer out of me. "As long as God is alive, we will eat before we go to bed" were the encouraging words of Donna when it was late and we saw no sign of any Good Samaritan at our door.

And true to the word of God, we never went to bed hungry. We did not get the food when we thought we needed it but invariably, we had enough to eat every night sometimes with leftovers for the next morning. The Good Samaritans of the neighborhood fed us every night until we received our first pay packets. Our Good Samaritans were the children of the neighborhood who hung around with us during the day. They brought us either leftovers or their own plates to share with us. At least one child brought us food during the night and sometimes up to three children. And when more than two children shared their meals with us we reserved the leftovers for the next morning. Leftovers never tasted as good as the leftovers we got from our young friends at Tamale in 1961.

Some of the children were the former pupils of Donatus during his stint as an untrained teacher at Tamale. We were ashamed to disclose to the young boys who hung with us that we were starving but I guess they saw our desperate situation and by God's grace helped us. The meals and leftovers they shared with us were our manna from heaven. Whether the food was leftovers or fresh from the family of one of our young friends, it did not matter; God's promise in Matthew 6: 26 was fulfilled with us. On a few occasions, we lost hope that our prayer had gone unanswered but we always got something to eat no matter how late. We learned that our time is not God's time neither is our biological clocks the clock for God. My take away from that experience of the promise of God left an indelible impression on me that has guided me ever since 1961. I have known periods of hunger since August-September 1961, but even during my bleakest and darkest hours God never let me go a day on an empty stomach. Matthew 6:26 is a promise of God that He has never failed to fulfill.

At the beginning of the school year in September 1961, I was posted to St. Joseph Primary School on the south side of town while Donatus was posted to St. Ann's Primary School on the north side. During the first few weeks of classes, the pangs of hunger continued to plague me at the school. And then I got my own exclusive miracle of manna from heaven. Once in a while I bought a penny or half penny worth of steamed fresh or green peanuts at school. That was what I could afford while I waited for my first pay. The school kids were fond of me because I did not look any bigger than some of them; they saw me as a friend. They assumed that I loved peanuts so some of them began buying steamed green peanuts for me during morning and lunch breaks. They did not know that I bought peanuts because that was what I could afford. I was glad when they piled peanuts on my table during breaks. What I could not eat at school I took home with me. Thus from the start of the school year I had peanuts for lunch and shared meals and leftovers at night till I received my first pay as a teacher. My lunch and supper were all provided courtesy of school children. God fulfilled his promise to us through the 'mouths of babes'.

I was very popular with my fellow teachers and pupils, but I did not get along with the supervising authorities from the regional office of the education department. As teachers, we were subject to supervised inspections by officers from the regional office from time to time. The supervisors known as education officers came to the schools at random without prior notice to observe the teachers at work. They were experienced teachers who had climbed through the ranks to senior positions in the department. The purpose of their random visits was to observe and advice us on our shortcomings to help us improve our teaching skills. But instead we developed an adversarial and cantankerous relations with them.

I was a newly minted trained teacher with an air of know-it-all. I was already prejudiced against the officers before I had my first contact with any of them. I considered the teaching skills of the supervisors as old fashioned. Most fresh teachers from the training colleges often referred to the experienced teachers and supervisors as "*colo*" or colonial i.e. old fashion with colonial mentality. This pompous attitude did not make for amicable relations between the young teachers and our supervisors.

I had a falling out with the first supervisor who observed me at work. After the lesson was over he criticized my shortcomings openly before my class. Perhaps he assumed that the pupils did not understand what he said but I did not take kindly to the criticism before my pupils.

I was seething with anger over the open criticism and when he asked me to surrender my class for a demonstration lesson I balked at the idea. The demonstration as far as I was concerned was the ultimate insult or humiliation he could inflict on me before my pupils. But I had no power or leverage to prevent him from taking the chalk and blackboard to conduct the demonstration lesson. I decided to frustrate him hoping to make him angry enough to give up on the idea of a demonstration lesson. I harangued him at every turn and used every annoying tactic I could think of to make him loose his cool. In the end he lost his temper and stomped out of the class in anger. My pupils, who did not know any better, cheered me when he stomped out. I had been in the classroom for less than one month when this incident took place.

I won the battle for that day but lost the war with the regional education office; I was practically blacklisted by the office; supervisors avoided my class when they came to the school. I was happy with the outcome thinking that I had won my freedom from unwanted intrusion by the supervising education officers. What I did know was that I was considered an insubordinate and unruly character. At the end of the term, I was transferred six miles out of town to a one-man, one-room thatched schoolroom at *Yong Dakpemyili*. I was exiled from town but I loved it. This was total freedom from supervision or intrusion from pesky senior officers. I bought a bicycle and commuted to *Yong* from Tamale. I was rather pleased with myself because I still lived in Tamale. I was my own boss; no supervisor came to my school for the one term I was there. My newfound freedom was however short lived, at the end of the second term; I was transferred again and this time out of the Tamale urban area. I was sent to Damongo located about twenty-four miles west of Tamale.

I went to Damongo and made the most of the situation. I settled into my new environment and found a lot to like about the town. The first problem that faced me immediately on arrival was the taste of the water at Damongo, the water had a briny taste. But whether I liked it or not, the briny water was the only water available. After about one or two weeks I became accustomed to the unique taste of water at Damongo and drank it without making faces. In 1962 Damongo was the home of a large contingent of the Workers Brigade, a collective farming system established by the government of the first republic and scattered throughout the country. The Workers Brigade were an important component of the working population of the town that made it a very vibrant community. My only regret was the lack of a movie theater but I found other means of entertainment. If the purpose of the transfer was punishment for insubordination then they were not successful. On the contrary the notoriety that made me a persona non grata before my supervisors made me a darling or hero before my fellow teachers. I never had another supervisor come to my class for the rest of the academic year.

Damongo was famous for scorpions. My colleagues at school warned me from the first week to be cautious and look out for scorpions particularly at night. The warning had the opposite effect on me; it made me curios to experience a scorpion sting. I was told that scorpion sting was not fatal; that the effects of a scorpion sting lasted only a few minutes. That description instead of frightening me had the opposite effect of egging me on to look for a scorpion sting as a badge of honor or fraternity with Damongo residents that I could take with me when I left Damongo.

I had my wish a few weeks after I settled down in town. We ate cooked fresh *bambara* beans and were clearing the husks of the beans when a scorpion hiding among the husks stung me on the foot. The sting felt exactly as was described by those who had similar experience. The poison radiated to my groin and armpit. I walked about the courtyard to relieve the pain and after less than thirty minutes the effects dissipated.

RETURN TO TAMALE FROM DAMONGO

It appears my transgressions were forgiven or forgotten by the end of my first full year as a teacher. I had not lived long enough in any community to put in roots, thanks to insubordination. At the end of the year, I sought transfer back to Tamale and my request was granted. I reunited with my friend Donatus again. He had a stable teaching career and residence; he lived in the same house and was still a staff of St. Ann's Primary School. I had gone through three schools and communities. On my return from exile I was posted back to St. Joseph Primary School where I started my teaching career. This time I rented a room in the same neighborhood with Donatus, our houses were only one or two blocks apart. I was mellow by the time I returned to Tamale and never had another confrontation with a supervisor but my prior notoriety persisted. But for the advice of one of my supervisors I would have thrown away a pivotal teacher training opportunity.

I became eligible to take another competitive examination for the second leg of the teacher certification program during my second year as a Certificate B teacher. The training was for the teachers Certificate A and with the Cert A I could teach at either primary or middle school. I began preparing quietly for the examination which was due in the first half of 1963. I was not a gifted student, but my hard work was often rewarded. I was good at cramming, but I could not cram for an examination I did not know the contents. As such, I read some of my old textbooks from Navrongo. General knowledge was one of the subjects of the examination; I prepared for this topic by reading newspapers and periodicals. I formed a life time habit of reading newspapers from the preparation I made for the examination in general knowledge in 1963.

I prepared for the examination by reading for brief periods everyday before bedtime. As a general rule, I read either a newspaper or a few pages of a textbook or solved some mathematical problems. Donna and I were beginning to grow apart; our priorities in life were diverging. My room overlooked the path that Donna took on his way into downtown Tamale. And whenever he passed by my house and peeped through my window he found me sitting behind a table with a book or newspaper in hand. He jeered and mocked me telling me that I should work hard, go to college and leave him behind. And I used to defend myself lamely against the taunts by telling him that I knew I was not as good as he was. "I am not as good as you are so I have to start early to keep up with you" was what I often told him.

We took the competitive training college entrance examination around April or May 1963 and the results were released sometime in July or August 1963. My incremental preparation was rewarded; I passed and was offered admission to the Government Teacher Training College at Peki in the Volta Region. Donna was not so lucky. But I nearly threw away the opportunity for him. I considered postponing going to the college in 1963 so that I could re-take the examination the following year with Donna with the hope that both of us would be successful and leave for college together in the same year. While I was contemplating whether to accept or decline the offer of admission, a visiting education officer to my school helped me to make up my mind. He boosted my ego when he told me that only two teachers from both the northern and upper regions had been offered admissions to the Training College at Peki. He advised me not to throw away the opportunity and I took his advise to heart. I left for Peki in the Volta Region to continue training for my teaching career in September or October 1963.

The time I spent away from Tamale after Navrongo exorcised some of my inner demons. I lost some of my zeal for movies. Tamale had two cinema houses, Rivoli and Victory. Rivoli was similar in design to Hippodrome at Tarkwa, a modern movie theater with terraced seating arrangement and a balcony on a mezzanine floor. I used to go to movies three times on weekends before I was transferred to Damongo. But by the time I returned from Damongo my zeal for movies was dampened, I became an occasional movie fan. I took to movies like a duck to water when I started teaching at Tamale in 1961. I used to go to movies at least twice a day and thrice during weekends. I spent most of my disposable income on movies. I could not imagine living anywhere else because of my love for movies. But by the time I returned to Tamale from Damongo in about September 1962, the novelty of Rivoli and the movies were worn thin.

PEKI TEACHER TRAINING COLLEGE

Before I took the competitive examination I went through two sets of application registration forms at £1.00 each. I bought the first form and made government training college, Tamale as my first choice. But just before I submitted the forms I changed my mind and decided to go out of my comfort zone. I bought and completed a second form and made Peki my first choice. I knew nothing about Peki until I saw it among the list of colleges. And the only reason I chose it was my desire to experience education in the public sector. There were only two *Certificate A* government training colleges in Ghana as of 1963; Peki and Tamale. Peki was then the only obvious choice that fit my new criterion of public education. I was educated mostly in parochial schools; Catholic primary and middle schools and training college.

The school environment at Peki gave me something new to look forward to. I got a new goal in life, a goal I did not have before I arrived on the campus, aspiration for college education. I dreamed of a career that went beyond the Cert A teacher for the first time. A great number of the students on the campus were pursuing home study courses towards the general certificate of education and that was infectious. And in short order I made up my mind to take correspondence courses for the general certificate of education examination. I was burning with desire to start a correspondence course but was hampered by lack of sufficient funds. Meanwhile I started investigating or shopping around for a suitable correspondence college so that I could be ready to go as soon as I had enough money. I obtained and examined brochures from three schools in England: Woolsey Hall, Rapid Results College and International Correspondence Schools, ICS. I settled on RRC. The RRC course materials were all inclusive, no additional textbooks to buy. The college principal, Mr. Annang loaned me an amount of £4.00 to start on the path to my new aspiration. And I received my first set of course materials from the college before the end of the first term.

The Principal of Peki Teacher training college, unlike most college principals encouraged his students to take extra curricula courses to improve themselves. It was widely rumored that he surreptitiously pursued correspondence course while he was a student at a teacher training college that paved the way for him to go to college. He did not want any of his students to go through the same hassles and thus openly encouraged them to do so. I received my first lessons from RRC towards the end of the first term. And when I went on vacation in December 1963, the course materials were my companion for the holidays. I had taken the first step towards the general certificate of education of the University of London, the passport for higher education for none secondary school students.

I worked hard on my course materials throughout the vacation. And I continued to work hard at both the correspondence course and my regular teaching course work. To cope with both courses I dispensed with the homework or test material components of the correspondence courses. I did not submit any written work for assessment, I was content to pay the fees when the installment was due to obtain the course materials but I could not be bothered to squeeze in more study time to submit test materials for grading. By mid year I was confident with my progress and decided to attempt the examination in five subjects in January 1965. I registered for GCE examinations in Biology, British Constitution, English Language, Geography and History.

The results of the January examination were released in April 1965; I passed in four of the five subjects, I failed the anchor subject, English language. No academic progress was possible without English Language. It was the mother lode of the general certificate of education. Without a pass in English the other passes were virtually valueless. When I failed in the English language it had two effects on me. First it dampened my self confidence in English as a subject and secondly it gave me a financial setback as a teacher. Had I passed all the five subjects including English I would have received an upgrade in status and salary. My salary would have been upgraded to the rank or status of a post secondary school trained teacher.

Despite the setback in English language, I was encouraged to consider attempting the advance level GCE in January 1966. Therefore in June 1965 or thereabout I registered to write advance level History and British Constitution and ordinary level English in January 1966. However at this time I was also preparing for my final certificate A teacher examination. I therefore put any preparation for the GCE on hold till after the final teaching examination. We finished with the final Cert A examinations in July 1965 and left the campus a short time later for good. I went back to my old employer, the Catholic Education Unit, at Tamale and was posted to St Joseph's Primary School where I used to teach before I left for Peki. I quickly settled down as a teacher and began earnest preparation for the January 1966 examination.

I had barely five months to cram for the examinations for early in the new year. I turned myself into a hermit or recluse until after the examinations were over. I then kept my fingers crossed and waited for the results. When the results came out in April 1966 I suffered a second consecutive setback, I flunked the English paper again. I could not make any academic or financial progress without a pass in English; I redoubled my efforts to make sure that the third time would be the charm. I expanded my reading list and included work books. I was at a loss to understand how I could pass all the other subjects that were written in English and yet fail the English language paper twice. The examinations were not multiple choice questions but short essays of about ten to twenty line prose.

To ensure that I succeeded on my third attempt I decided to write the English language paper offered by both the West African Examination Council and University of London in 1967. A pass in either of them would be enough to get me over the hump. The only obstacle that stood between me and college admission was a pass in English language. While that was my number one goal it would not have been enough to keep me busy. I therefore decided to take two more subjects at the advance level in Geography and British Economic History together with ordinary level English language.

I had more time to devote to my studies without the distractions of being a full time trainee teacher. For the next six to seven months I concentrated on the three subjects and nothing else. Midway through the period I had a minor setback. I suffered from tummy upsets that caused me to throw up at night. After careful introspection I concluded that the tummy aches and upsets were caused by the dexamphetamine pills I took every night to keep me alert and help me cope with my studies. The moment I made the connection I stopped taking the tablets though it was at a critical time of my exam preparation. But I was relieved of the tummy aches and vomiting and I still managed to keep up with my studies till the examinations were over.

The hard work finally paid off and yielded the desired results; I passed all three subjects including the version of English offered by the West African Examinations Council. My bogey subject was no more a hindrance to prevent me from going to university. A pass in English language paper made me eligible for promotion to a supervisory grade such as an assistant education officer with a salary of ¢1,000. I had in effect become eligible to supervise other teachers and the path to university was wide open before me.

AMPHETAMINE TABLETS

I combined home studies with that of a full time student or teacher; the combination would not have been possible without the boost of energy that I got every night from dexamphetamine tablets. I used to take the tablets before going to bed.

When I started the correspondence courses in late 1963 the only stimulant I knew was coffee and Nodoz tablets. I found that despite drinking multiple cups of coffee and taking nodoz tablets at night I could hardly keep my eyes open or alert enough for studies. Then one day in a casual conversation I asked an older classmate, Mr. Tandoh whether he knew of any aid or drug that could give me enough pep at night other than coffee and *nodoz* tablets. Tandoh gave me one yellow tablet to try that night. The tablet worked like a charm and I was hooked and that was my introduction to dexamphetamine tablets.

I was so naïve about drugs until that day I had never heard of it though it was widely available in corner drug stores. I understood that even ordinary farmers used to take the tablets to boost their energy for work on their farms. Dexamphetamine became my study companion from 1964 until sometime in October 1966 when I stopped using it for health reasons.

For about four to six months a year I took dexamphetamine tablets every night between 1964 and 1966. The tablets used to wake up after about four hours and kept me awake and alert till morning when I left for work. The dexamphetamine was so stimulating one tablet energized me practically for about twenty four hours until I took the next one before retiring for the night. I could not have worked dutifully as a teacher, marking homework at home while staying up at least four hours every night.

I stopped taking the dexamphetamine tablets when I found that it made me nauseous when I woke up at night for studies. I stopped taking the tablets but the tummy aches spawned by the drug persisted for many years. I consulted the local doctors after my examination in January 1967 and was diagnosed with duodenal or stomach ulcer. I accepted the diagnosis hook line and sinker, nursed and nurtured it till it became a phantom illness. I sought remedies and treatments from various doctors off and on for about two decades without satisfactory result. The condition never incapacitated me but it affected my choice of foods from time to time when I thought I had a flare-up. I avoided spicy foods and alcohol during the flare-ups but otherwise lived a normal life. The condition finally cleared up after I had an endoscope probe in 1992 that established once and for all that I did not have any duodenal or stomach ulcer. And from that day I stopped paying attention to my tummy, the phantom condition disappeared without any further attention. It appeared I created a phantom disease and nurtured it over the years refusing to let go until 1992. The phantom menace disappeared when the diagnosis helped me to readjust my mental attitude and that eradicated the menace.

SHORT EXPERIENCE WITH MARIJUANA

Dexamphetamine exposed my ignorance and naivety about illicit drugs. However I was very much aware of the drug which is like a right of passage for youths, marijuana. Until my final night at Peki in July 1965 I had never tried or smoked a joint under any circumstances. My friends and acquaintances smoked pot but I did not. My friend Donna for instance smoked pot. On my last night at Peki I fell into the company of a group of students who were smoking marijuana and appeared to be relishing the pot so much so that I was tempted to try for the first time.

The euphoric expression I saw on the faces of the students convinced me that perhaps marijuana was as stimulating as dexamphetamine the only stimulating drug I knew. I smoked marijuana for the first time expecting an euphoric and stimulating experience. But I became very miserable after I smoked half a joint; my tummy churned while I spat out thick and slimy sputum throughout the night. I was restless and could not sleep during the night from fear of choking with my saliva or sputum. I stayed awake spitting out thick and slimy sputum all night till dawn when I became normal. I dozed off for an hour or so at dawn by then the saliva had stopped flowing. We departed from campus at day break as such I could not find out whether my experience was unique or the common effects of marijuana from the students who shared the joint with me.

I had another opportunity to compare notes on marijuana in 1970 when I was a student at Kumasi University of Science and Technology. My host, Yakubu, was a great fan of marijuana. He smoked pot almost every day and from time to time went to the countryside to buy it for sale in Kumasi. He persuaded me to give marijuana another try, he told me that the marijuana I smoked in 1965 might have been contaminated hence the adverse reaction. I took him at his word and smoked one marijuana cigarette by myself. The reaction from this experiment was worse than the earlier experience. Shortly after the smoke, I felt as if my life was draining away. I felt so weak I could hardly stand on my feet, and just as in 1965, I spat out thick sputum. I was a miserable wretch while the effects lasted. Yakubu laughed at my misery telling me that was exactly the effect and joy of smoking marijuana. Some kind of high! I wondered why anybody would waste his hard earned money to buy misery. As far as I was concerned, marijuana was not worth even a penny or the risk of arrest and imprisonment. My experience from smoking marijuana was so unpleasant I never tried it a third time. Once bitten twice shy.

JILTED MY GIRLFRIEND OVER GCE EXAMS

As soon as I came back from Peki in September 1965, I settled down and plunged into my books and virtually cut off myself from society except when I went to market to buy foodstuffs. I had two main activities to the exclusion of everything else, my work and my studies towards the GCE examination due in January 1966. I considered myself a mediocre student who had to work hard before I could achieve my academic goals. I was thus reluctant to talk or brag about my ambitions, studies and goals whilst I worked quietly for them. I therefore did not discuss or talk about my aims and ambitions to anyone and that included Rebecca, my girlfriend. She was not aware that I had other ambitions and goals on my mind beyond being a Cert A teacher. My ardent desire was therefore to be left alone to pursue my goals quietly. I wanted it to be a surprise to her if I passed but if I failed the examinations she would not have heard it from my lips.

I did not like any distractions from the goal I had set for myself. Every night when I took my pep pill I told myself there is "more time to sleep after death". I hoped to make it up to her when I came out of seclusion from my self imposed hermitage. I tried to impress upon Rebecca that I did not want visitors at night or worse to be woken up from bed. But she was oblivious to all my attempts to make my intentions known without being explicit. As such she visited me anytime she felt like it; and most often I was asleep when she showed up in my room. I lived in a secure large compound house so my door was always open as such I could not hide behind closed door. I yawned and dozed while sitting with her to impress upon her that I was sleepy and could hardly keep my eyes open. But she was unmoved by my antics of sleepiness. Perhaps she loved me so much it was enough for her to be around me without any expectations. But I did not appreciate the interruption from sleep thus wasting the purpose of the drug I took to stimulate me for late night studies.

I was a sitting duck and could not avoid her between October and December 1965 when I was a virtual prisoner in my own room. I bore her interruptions stoically until I completed the examinations in the second week of January 1966. While I was waiting for the result of the examination I started taking evasive actions to avoid meeting her with the hope that she would find my new attitude unacceptable and dump me. I was afraid I would have the same interruptions if I had to prepare for examinations again later in the year. As such I decided to end our relations and the distractions she represented but I did not have the courage to break off the relations with her directly. My plan was to behave like a jerk so that she would leave me alone. I had the notion that girls dumped boys and not the other way. Therefore I did everything I could to let her pull the plug but Rebecca was oblivious to the shenanigans.

I played hide and seek with her taking advantage of my interim freedom to avoid meeting her. I had a strong sense of smell and could sniff her perfume or odor while she about two blocks or more from my house and that often gave me enough time to sneak out of the house through the backdoor of a neighbor before she arrived. But no matter how long I stayed away when I came back she would be waiting patiently for me in my room; my door was open at all times except when I went to work.

I was at my wits end; I did not know what else I could do so that Rebecca would dump me short of telling her off myself. But I did not have the courage to tell her off. So I kept on with the charade for about two months until I could not take the deception any longer myself; I wanted to 'eat my cake and have it'. I desired to leave a small wiggle room for reconciliation if she dumped me. But if I broke off the relations with her there would no wiggle room for reconciliation in the future. I did not want to hurt her feelings, and secondly, I hated to burn the bridge between us beyond repair.

But in the end it was Rebecca who confronted me with her observations of my jerky behavior. She cornered me in my room after she waited patiently for me to return from movies one night. I was unprepared to face her personally and fumbled for words to explain my behavior in a delicate and sensitive manner without being hurtful. What I had sought to avoid for more than two months for lack of courage came to a head. And when she left my room that night, I did not see or hear from her again for about ten years. My fears of a permanent breach with her became a reality. The last time I saw her she was a nurse at Korlebu Teaching Hospital. We literally bumped into one another along a blind alley in Accra. She was startled when she saw me, clutched her chest and yelled, 'my heart'. We exchanged short pleasantries and went our separate ways. And that was the last time I saw Rebecca.

THE TRANSITION BEFORE COLLEGE

Thus far, I had exercised a great deal of self-control over my life while I was preoccupied with the general certificate of education examinations. In furtherance of that goal I sacrificed my girl friend to avoid any distractions. When the results of the January 1967 examination were released in April and I passed all the subjects I became a different animal. My outlook on life changed dramatically; I was proud of my achievements and looked forward to going to the university at the beginning of the academic year in September or October 1967. I lost my head, as all my pent up feelings and desires were unleashed on an unsuspecting world. This was the time I should have reconciled with Rebecca if she were around, but she had moved on and left me to my designs. I did not know her whereabouts. I played catch up on my social life.

My passes in the GCE examinations made me quite popular among my fellow teachers. And I enjoyed my new found freedom and popularity to the hilt. I do not know how the news got around in Tamale but that turned me into a minor celebrity in education circles. My achievement was common place in the south of the country but it was a novelty in the north. Northern adults who earned the high school diplomas at the time did so by competing for admission to the last two years of a high school on a government scholarship to prepare for the diploma. I succeeded on my own without going to the last two years of high school. I showed that it was possible for post middle school teachers to go further in education instead of being content with the Cert-A teacher's certificate. I inspired some of my drinking buddies to take correspondence courses for preparation towards the GCE examination. And a few of them made it out to other tertiary education institutions by the time I was in my second or third year at the university. I dedicated my success to my senior year roommate at Navrongo whose nightly rants of "A man is not a man until he can control himself." Self Control was drilled into me and became my guiding principle after Navrongo. He did me a great favor though at the time I hated him for disturbing my sleep and considered him a nuisance.

In the meantime as I waited for the opportunity to go to the university, I slowly drifted to the wild side of life and began to lose my perspectives on self-control. I am generally a mild mannered and shy person but I took to drinking and womanizing with abandon. I masked my shyness with alcohol; I was drunk most evenings after work and went to bed drunk. I went through a lot of women between April and September 1967 when I left Tamale for University of Ghana.

Although I was happy and proud of my potentials I was also humbled. I was considered an insubordinate teacher though I had not had another run in with a supervisor since my first year as a teacher, but the notoriety lived on.

My fellow female teachers that I had admired from afar because of inferiority complex about the type of company they kept suddenly sought my company. Those within my ambit were content to walk with me after school instead of jumping into cars provided by their rich and influential boyfriends. It came as a surprise to me when I learned that some female teachers admired me for no reason than my notoriety. I also lost my inferiority complex because of my potential status as a senior education officer. My potential salary entitled me to a government car loan that could buy me a beetle, the most popular car for new college graduates and senior civil servants. It was only a matter of time before my promotion papers came through.

I GROW APART FROM DONNA

When I completed my Certificate A teacher training course at Peki and returned to Tamale I renewed my old friendship with Donatus. But I soon realized that time, it appeared had stood still for Donatus. I nearly gave up going to Peki in 1963 in solidarity with Donatus so that the two of us could retake the examination and go to college together just as we had completed Navrongo together. I came back after my course and Donatus was still at the same school and living at the house where we started our lives after graduating from Navrongo in 1961. He had not yet passed the entrance examination for Cert-A college by the time I returned from Peki and his career was at a standstill. His life, compared to mine, had been quite stable. I had been bounced around schools for insubordination until I went to Peki in 1963. He appeared to be content and satisfied; he did not share my ambitious goals though he was a more able student than I was. I failed to persuade him to take some home study courses to improve his chances of gaining admission into Cert-A teacher training colleges.

I offered to pay the cost of any correspondence or home study course provided he completed a registration or enrolment application forms for the purpose. Instead he asked me to find the appropriate forms, pay and enroll him in a course and deliver the course material to him if I was that much interested in his progress. I could have but I was not sure he would even glance at the course material if I dropped them on his laps since he could not find the time to complete a form. He was one person I wished I could have influenced to look beyond the horizon of his immediate limited but comfortable lifestyle. He was not willing to do anything to brighten his prospects as such there was very little I could have done to motivate or inspire him to try something new.

Donna in effect refused to take any action for self improvement. He was a very handsome man and a woman killer. After he refused my offer, we gradually drifted apart. About a year or two later, the Cert-B teacher as a class of professional teachers was phased out. The certificate B teachers who had not been accepted into any Certificate A teacher training college were given short in-service training courses and upgraded to Cert-A status before the Cert B teachers in the education system was finally phased out.

CHRISTMAS 1965

In Ghana of the 1960's dressed chickens in the supermarkets were still a novelty available for the elite or the expatriate community who shopped in supermarkets. Most Ghanaians ate chicken or fowl on festive occasions and did so by slaughtering live chickens or fowls for the festive meal. In 1965, the year I graduated from Peki teacher training college was my first Christmas since graduation and the one in which I had the resources to celebrate a memorable Christmas with all the traditional meals and trimmings. It was the year I bought my first fowl and attempted to slaughter them for Christmas celebration. But I was so unnerved by my failure to slaughter the fowl successfully that I never attempted to slaughter another fowl or for that matter any animal whether big or small. I am the son of a Muslim and I had seen my father slaughter countless number of fowls and sheep. I used to help him with the slaughter so I was quite familiar with the steps my father followed in slaughtering any animal according to Islamic practices. But I had never slaughtered any animal by myself. Christmas 1965 was my first attempt at slaughtering any animal and it was also my last.

As pointed out above Christmas 1965 was my first Christmas since I completed Certificate-A training college and it was the first Christmas I felt I could celebrate it appropriately according to Ghanaian traditions for observing the season. Thus I bought two guinea fowls, bottles of fanta and coca cola, a few bottles of beer, crackers, candies and rice. No Christmas meal would be complete without rice and stew. My Christmas shopping list was complete and by Christmas eve 1965 I was ready to celebrate the best Christmas ever.

I began preparing for my Christmas day meal to share with strangers and children by midday. I set up a small table and assembled all my Christmas goodies on the table; bottles of warm beer, fanta, crackers and candies. Christmas is a time of sharing with all and sundry friend or foe. Refrigeration was a luxury I could not afford in 1965, but I was content to share the warm beer, fanta and coca cola with all comers especially the children that I expected would do the rounds as I had done myself as a child. Asking for Christmas gifts and presents is a time honored Ghana tradition that children indulge in on Christmas day. They put on their best Christmas outfits and go from house to house singing and asking total strangers to share the Christmas spirit with them. By the time the day was over they had candies, biscuits, crackers, soft drinks and donations of monies, candies and cookies from well wishers. I expected to share my Christmas meal with strangers. I boiled some water over charcoal fire to dress the fowls. While the water was on the boil I took my two guinea fowls to the backyard to slaughter. And it was during the slaughter that things went awry.

I took all the steps I had observed of my father when he slaughtered a fowl or sheep. I dug a small hole in the ground as I had seen him do on several occasions, and then I placed one foot on the legs and the other on the wings of the guinea fowl. I put a sharp knife to its throat, slit it and allowed the blood to drip into the hole in the ground. After about a minute or so I removed my feet and the 'dead' fowl sprung life, took to its feet and ran for dear life. I gave chase in disbelief I could not kill or slaughter it. And when I caught it I slaughtered it again and to make sure I was not surprised again I severed the head. But in the process I lost my nerve and could not slaughter the second fowl. I called on the sister of my friend Danso to slaughter the second fowl and help me to prepare the Christmas meal. That was the last time I ever attempted to slaughter any animal for food. From that day onwards others slaughtered any chicken or fowl for a meal or celebration. After marriage my wife did the slaughter of chickens or fowls we bought for food. But when I had to slaughter a sheep as part of giving a name to a new born child the vendor of the sheep slaughtered and dressed it as part of the transaction.

ADMISSION AT UNIVERSITY OF GHANA

I received an early notice of admission from the University of Ghana, Legon on the strength of passing four subjects at the GCE advance level. I exceeded the academic requirement for admission to the university as of 1967. The academic requirements was a pass in two subjects with three as maximum at the GCE advance level. I had four passes and I guess that gave me a leg up on the competition for admission to the university that year.

There was an unexpected surprise waiting for me when I arrived on the campus of the university of Ghana in October 1967. By the time it was over I was cut to size; I lost my confidence and even contemplated going back home. From April 1967 until I landed on the campus I had not read anything of academic value other than newspapers or magazines after I received my examination results. My books went on holiday until I arrived on the university campus. I was academically very rusty when I arrived on campus but I expected to work myself up to speed after lectures. I did not get the time to work myself to speed. Before I could attend my first lecture I had to take placement examinations to win a place in the class. The placement examinations knocked the wind out of my sails. I failed to make the cut in all the placement tests I attempted and as a result I could not find any subject to read, I failed every desirable major or subject I liked. My letter of admission made no reference to any competitive examinations before the start of lectures else I would have cut down on the booze and prepared for them. Failure to make the cut in any subject that was tantamount to failure to make the grade I could not sugar coat my performance in any other way.

The placement examinations were not difficult as such, but I was so rusty that I could not recollect familiar subject materials. I failed to gain a place in the limited number of spaces available for the popular majors or subjects that interested me such as political science and sociology. I was forced into counseling and my academic advisor was surprised at my poor performance considering my GCE profile. I was in a quandary over my abysmal performance. I even contemplated going back home to reorder my priorities and come back the following year fully prepared to take placement exams and secure places in the subjects I really desired. But I quickly dismissed the idea out of my mind, nobody in Tamale expected me to complete a three or four year course in one month. I am not that a genius and I would not know how to explain my quick departure from the campus. I therefore decided to stick it out as long as the university had not given me any dismissal papers. I was given the dregs by my academic advisor, the least popular subjects among the students. I accepted them because I had backed myself into a corner and could not complain. I just hoped that by the end of the year I might be able to transfer into some other disciplines.

However, about a month into the term, I was reprieved from my predicament, I had an unexpected break. I received a telegram forwarded from Tamale that informed me that I had been accepted into the Land Economy program of the University of Science and Technology, Kumasi. The news appeared too good to be true. The fact was that I applied for the course during the college applications period, but I never got any response from the college. I did not receive even an acknowledgment of receipt, so I assumed that my application was either lost in the mail or my grades were not good enough to earn me an invitation for an interview. The telegram therefore came as a big surprise; I had been given a second chance at a program of my own choice. By this time the university had been in session for about a month and I wondered whether my place was still open.

But all the same I decided to take my chances. I packed my bags and baggage and quietly slipped out of the campus without notifying any authority at Legon. By so doing I kept my option to come back open should things not work out. That ended my disastrous brief flirtation with the University of Ghana, Legon. I was saved by the University of Science and Technology from the results of my dismal performance in the placement tests. I had a new lease on academic life at a different institution. I was saved from the prospect of pursuing a degree in subjects I did not really want to one in which I did not know anything about its future prospects. I knew that the Land Economy program was quite new and that was good enough for me, I tend to be excited by the unknown.

THE KUMASI UNIVERSITY CAMPUS

The placement exams were the initial results of the consequences of the unequal development in our education system after independence. Ghana made great progress in primary and secondary school education after independence. Immediately after independence the government under Dr. Kwame Nkrumah expanded primary and secondary school education with the introduction of fee free education. I was given the opportunity to train as a primary school teacher as a result of this program. But there was no comparable expansion at the tertiary level to absorb college level students produced by the increased enrollments at the primary and secondary schools. Thus by 1967 there was an explosion of eligible college level students from the secondary schools but not enough places at the tertiary institutions to absorb them. The placement tests of 1967 were in effect the beginning of rationing at the premier university of the country.

I sneaked out of Legon and headed for Kumasi. Unlike Legon which held a special place in the annals of education in Ghana Kumasi did not have a similar cachet at the time. It was customary for primary and secondary school teachers to conduct excursions to Legon to widen the horizon of their students. Besides most college graduate teachers were alumni of Legon and were wont of talking to us about life at Legon. I was therefore familiar with Legon before I arrived on the campus as a student in October 1967. But I knew very little about the University of Science and Technology, I therefore went to Kumasi on the blind. I had no allusions or previous knowledge of life on the campus and I had no expectations or preference for any dormitory or college housing. I got what I saw. The telegram asked me to report to the university halls, I had no idea university hall was student housing or dormitory until I arrived on the campus.

I panicked a few weeks after arrival when I became aware of some scary aspects of campus life. I despaired at the practice of expelling students at the end of the year who allegedly did not quite make the grade. Every student in effect was on probation from one year to the next until graduation. Failure to make the grade in two or more subjects at the end of any year could result in expulsion from the campus or a repeat of the class if the student was lucky. To avoid the prospect of being "advised to withdraw" at the end of the year, which was the euphemism for expulsion, I stuck my nose into my books and found assurance once more in self-control. The panic was good for my work ethic; whenever I lost the sense of panic or faux confidence I performed poorly though never bad enough to warrant expulsion or repeating a class. Fear was thus a big motivating factor that influenced how hard I worked in any one year.

The department of Land Economy was anchored in the faculty of agriculture. It was customary for the dean of faculty at the end of the academic year and just before the start of vacation, to invite the students to meet the dean where they learned about their performance. At the meeting the dean reviewed the performance of the student with him and by the time the student left the conference he knew whether he had done well enough to return the following year or his life on the camps was all but over. My heart was in my mouth when I stood in line to have my conference with the dean. But I was all smiles when I emerged from the office of the dean, Prof Sey. The dean did not tell me of any grade or mark but he told me that I did 'very well'. And with that I had a new lease on campus life. Some of my flagging and beaten down confidence was restored and when I returned for the second year; the fear of expulsion for poor performance receded. I picked up some of the bad habits that were at the heart of my poor performance in the placement tests at Legon. I began binge boozing at weekends. This time I knew when to drink and when to lay off the bottle. I scrapped through the second year with booze binges. The dean did not hide his disappointment when I met him at the end of the year. The third year had a reputation for being a difficult class. My third year class increased by half with a number of repeat students from the pioneer class. With the fear of expulsion or repetition dangling before me I worked consistently throughout the year to avoid a similar fate. About half of the pioneer third year class were either expelled or made to repeat the class. The fear of expulsion or repeating the third year class gave me the incentive to work hard to avoid either of those scenarios.

I was a quiet student on the campus; much older than the average student who came to college direct from secondary school. I did not have much in common with most of the younger students. There were very few mature students of my caliber on the campus. As such I kept mostly to myself, most of the campus clubs and fraternities were based on alumni of secondary schools and since I was not an old student of any secondary school I was not a member of any fraternity. Outside of the campus there was very little social interaction between a great many of the students and me. My main priority on campus was to earn a degree as a means to an end, win a meal ticket nothing more nothing less. I have never been interested in academic career per se and making it to college did not change that.

My greatest distraction and weakness on the campus was television. I had unfettered access to television and I watched it every night. The television was my constant companion during the crucial test prep period of the third term. My study habits was suited to television. Without any dexamphetamine pep pills I could not wake up during the night to study. But if by midnight I had not fallen asleep then I became wide awake and alert for the rest of the night. Thus my problem was how to stay up until midnight or thereabout when I became wide awake. I slept about three to five hours in the afternoon and watched television after dinner until it went off air. After the TV went off air I sat in the student common room riffling through newspapers and magazines till after midnight when I left for my cubicle fully alert and awake. We were usually under tremendous pressure and stress during the third term of the year as our academic lives were in the balance. And during this period I stayed away from friends and acquaintances for fear of distracting them with idle chatter.

I graduated barely successfully at the end of the four year course. I was greatly disappointed with my final graduation grade. I was a victim of the zeal of the town planning lecturer who created a halo of indispensability and difficulty around his subject and made it appear more difficult than it really was. The failure and expulsions from the course during the third year were due to failure of students not making the grade in town planning. He was obsessed with saturation of the market place by new land economy graduates. He used his subject as the vehicle to put a damper on the number of land economy students graduating every year. Thus he deliberately misrepresented the findings of a panel of judges on my final dissertation. I was not blameless but there is a difference between "correct the typos" and 'your dissertation was rejected'. The latter was the misrepresentation of the former. But for my performance in prior years I would have flunked the final year. I did earn my meal ticket after four years of hard work though I felt I deserved a better grade than I got.

As part of the final year course work, I was required to prepare and write a dissertation on a plan of a residential subdivision to complete the town planning course. Honestly, the statistical portion of the completed and typed manuscript was full of typographical errors which I failed to detect when I reviewed the typed manuscript.

The errors I failed to detect pertained to decimal numbers that were typed as whole numbers. I was hypnotized by my draft manuscript. I explained this to the panel why I failed to detect the errors in the completed manuscript. The typist got the numerals correct but the decimal points were either misplaced or missing. The panel accepted my explanation and instructed me before the lecturer to correct the typos and return it to him. He said nothing to contradict the deliberations and findings of the panel but when I attempted to return the corrected manuscript to the lecturer he refused to accept it on the grounds that my dissertation had been rejected. And as a consequence of the rejection I was asked to wait for an official notification before rewriting and submitting a new dissertation. I resubmitted the same manuscript without making any changes to the original manuscript other than the statistical corrections as I had been told. Besides the statistical errors no other finding was made against the dissertation so I did not know what to add or subtract from the original manuscript. But the harm was done. I barely passed the subject. I was bitterly disappointed by the misrepresentation of the panels' findings by the tutor.

For this and other malfeasance by some of the academic staff I lost faith in the integrity of my degree. I do not know whether I expected too much of our lecturers, but I did not expect the lecturers to take the female students for weekend jaunts. The female students were pawns in the hands of those lecturers who held their academic and future careers in the palm of their hands; they were powerless to resist their advances. I had the impression that some of the lecturers corrupted the academic process for their selfish ends. The process was sometimes rigged to favor specific student when necessary. I remember at one time one of my female classmates was asked to take a make up test in the third year. She appeared for the examination accordingly but was told that her name was not on the list of students scheduled to take make-up test. But nevertheless when the results were later posted on the notice boards she was listed as having taken and passed the examination. Yet all the students who were present in the examination hall witnessed the student being told that she was not on the list. The scandal was rumored around the campus years after her graduation.

DECLINED MY NEW SALARY

I applied for promotion and salary upgrade about three months before I left for Legon in October 1967. The application for the promotion and new salary came through the week I left Legon for Kumasi. My salary went up four fold from less than ¢250 per year to ¢1,000. But I did not start drawing the new salary before I left Accra for Kumasi in November 1967. When I went to Kumasi I did not follow up to have my new salary transferred to me on the new campus. I had never earned more than say ¢25 or ¢30 a month and so I was afraid of what ¢80 per month would do to my psyche. The difference between my new salary and that of a graduate was only ¢360 or ¢30 a month. In other words, I would have made only ¢30 less than my salary after graduation while I was only a freshman. I thought hard and long over the consequences of sudden wealth on my life while a freshman on campus and therefore declined to follow up with the department of education to transfer my salary to Kumasi.

I took advantage of a scholarship scheme that was specifically set up to encourage people from the north to go to college. At independence, Northern Ghana lagged behind the South in the number of secondary school students and college graduates. The Nkrumah government created a special scholarship scheme to encourage northerners, most of whom were teachers, to pursue high school and college education. I applied and was approved for the special scholarship scheme for northerners. I preferred a humble life on campus without the benefit of the income for which I had worked so hard to earn.

A few years after graduation, when my lofty financial dreams did not pan out I questioned the wisdom of that decision and wondered whether I would ever recover the income I gave up at college. I was accustomed to a hardscrabble existence, and I doubted my capacity to be levelheaded with command over high disposable income while a student. The temptations of the sudden affluence on campus would have fueled my alcohol consumption. I guess I never made up the lost income which at the time was only ¢30 per month less than the salary of a college graduate. But it kept me level headed and sane throughout the four year course.

Self Discipline And Alcohol

I grew up in a partial Islamic household, my father was the only practicing Muslim but his faith was pervasive in the life of our household. Thus alcohol did not have any role in our social life. Although like other children of the 1950's I used to collect bottles for sale to roadside recyclers and washed and filled them with water for sale I was never tempted to taste droplets of beer or stout from the bottles. Thus by the time I completed middle school and became a student of St. John Bosco's college I had no experience of the taste of beer or pito. I tasted beer for the first time during my first year at St. John Bosco's College courtesy of some of my experienced and older classmates.

I went sightseeing around Navrongo with some of my mature schoolmates after the bursar paid both the new and old students our first allowance of the year. We went to the market where I bought a pair of canvas shoes or sneakers and flip-flops. Since I was barefooted I wore the shoes as soon as I paid for them and tucked the flip flops under my armpit. We ended our sightseeing with a visit to a local beer bar. The bar pulsated loudly with some of the familiar highlife tunes of Ghana. We sat around a table and ordered some bottles of beer. I felt very awkward like a fish out of water; I had never sat in a beer bar. The nearest I ever came to a beer bar was when I went around bars collecting empty bottles for sale. And for the first time I found myself sitting in the middle of a beer bar with friends; I did not know what to do. I watched as my companions filled their glasses with beer and sipped it with some relish. They appeared to genuinely enjoy the taste of the beer and had great fun doing so. I swallowed hard, but was too timid or shy to lift the glass to my lips. I sat stiffly like a statue and watched them having fun. One of my companions coaxed me to try a sip, telling me it would do me no harm. I gathered courage and slowly lifted the glass to my lips. No sooner had I sipped the beer than I spat it out, wiping the bitter taste from my mouth with the sleeve of my shirt.

My reaction caused an uproar as my buddies burst out into uncontrollable laughter, while I screwed my face wondering what the laughter was about. How could they have so much fun with the bitter stuff? After a few more minutes and more words of encouragement, I took another sip and quickly swallowed it like bitter medicine. And one sip was all it took to make me excited about alcohol. I tapped my toes to the rhythm of the music in the bar. I was instantly transformed from a shy and timid young man into a gregarious talkative. The experience from the effect of my first glass of beer was almost magical, it blew away my inhibitions, loosened my tongue and before I knew it I was tapping my feet in the middle of the bar swaying from side to side to the rhythm of the highlife music. I liked the courage and energy that the beer gave me which allowed me to get over my shyness and timidity. I accomplished two memorable things that weekend; I tasted beer and took the first photograph of my life.

From that first weekend of toe tapping at the beer bar I became a fan of weekend binges with friends. And whenever I drank, the alcohol turned me into a different animal, I became courageous to do and say things I could otherwise not do or say. I was particularly bold chatting up girls and women but shy and tongue tied when sober. Without alcohol I recoiled into my shell and avoided making eye contact with my previous conquests or acquaintances while I was under the influence of alcohol. I felt awkward and embarrassed when I came across a woman I had met while I was under the influence. I felt naked when sober without any alcohol and desperately looked about me for a hiding place away from her glare. I would look away or bury my head in shame doing everything I could to avoid making eye contact. I never engaged in a tête-à-tête with any girl without the influence of alcohol during my early years as a young adult. I could not face myself when I did or said naughty things while under the influence and this was one of the factors that prevented me from becoming an early alcoholic. For instance one time I chatted up and wooed a rich and prominent older business woman while under the influence. When I woke up sober the following morning I could not face myself. I felt so embarrassed by what I did the previous night I declared myself non grata to her house.

I used to be friendly with a classmate of my sister who was a nurse at the local hospital in Navrongo. Initially I accorded her the respect similar to that of my older sister since they were classmates. But as I began seeing her while under the influence I started talking loosely suggestively to her whenever I passed by her quarters while under the influence of alcohol. One weekend I visited her while I was under the influence of alcohol and she entertained me till late in the evening when I became sober. After her intentions for keeping me that long dawn on me, I ran out of her house unceremoniously with my tail between my legs like a frightened puppy. The thought of spending the night in her house scared me to death. That was the end of three months of beautiful friendship. I enjoyed her company and hospitality but as I could not go the extra mile, the friendship foundered. The day she attempted to lure me into bed I panicked and I ran out of her house unceremoniously.

I was a bashful and timid young man when I began my teaching career at Tamale. Although I did not realize it when I left Navrongo, I was under the unconscious influence of my senior year roommate. The annoying phrase he used to drum repeatedly into my ears every night had a positive effect on me once I was out of the protective cocoon of the campus. The test of the annoying phrase came when I began social drinking. The first time I tasted beer I did so in the company of some companions or friends. And when I left Navrongo and began social drinking that became my template for drinking. I strenuously resisted the temptation to drink any alcoholic beverage alone or trap unwitting companions in a bar to satisfy my secrete desires. Craving for alcohol was a sign that I was drifting towards alcoholism while at work or at home. I envisaged that it was an unhealthy habit to seek for friends just to satisfy my cravings for alcohol. And whenever I had a craving for a drink it set alarm bells in my head warning that I was on the brink and thus I went off the drinking circuit or wagon for as long as it took to overcome the cravings or appetite to have a drink. It was contrary to my personal moral beliefs to drink alcohol alone in a bar. The habit I formed as a young adult I have not been able to break entirely in my old age. While I can drink alone in the house I have not been able to overcome the resistance to drink alone in a salon or restaurant.

I hated the stigma of alcohol addiction as that signaled loss of self control and literally loss of ones life to an inanimate object, alcohol. As long as the alarm bells of cravings rang in my head I did not touch another calabash of *pito* or glass of beer until the alarm bells stopped ringing. I knew it when the alarm bells stopped ringing because the craving or urge to drink vanished. The cravings or temptations usually wore off after about three months during which time I did not touch a drink. I went about with my friends and visited all the watering holes with them but refused to touch a drop of alcohol. I was fond of alcohol but I feared addiction even more.

The fear of addiction tempered my drinking habits during most of my youthful years. The iron will power of my youth that protected and prevented me from falling off the alcohol wagon of addiction began to erode towards the end of the sixties to early seventies when my status in life changed, I became a college student and gradually lost a grip of myself generally and alcohol in particular. I did not know when to say 'enough is enough'. I knew no moderation in alcohol consumption, I drank to get drunk. But I came to my senses by 1973 with the realization that I was destroying myself with uncontrolled alcohol consumption. And with that realization I began to look for the phrase or mantra that sustained me during my youth, *a man is not a man until he can control himself.* I came to the conclusion that I was no longer a man and with that realization I began to make amends in my life and abstained from alcohol consumption. I became a teetotaler. for a period of twelve to eighteen months until I went to Australia in 1975. I was literally hypnotized by the many varieties of wines and alcoholic beverages I found on display in the liquor shop windows. I was charmed and enticed to such an extent that I resumed alcohol consumption and drank wine with a gusto for another four months before I stopped again and abstained from any alcohol for another thirty years or more until it became widely publicized that moderate consumption of alcohol was good for the heart. I started drinking wine again occasionally mostly just before bedtime for prophylactic reasons.

As a young teacher fresh from college I was still as bashful and timid in the outside world as I was on campus. During my first term at St. Joseph Primary school a young female teacher on the staff warmed up to me. We were close friends and did a lot of things in common innocently with no any ulterior motive. But it appeared my friend expected something more out of our relationship and when I failed to live up to that expectation the friendship unraveled. I could not jump over a pillow when presented with the opportunity on a silver platter. She dumped me when her repeated attempts for intimacy went unanswered. I was saved from the embarrassment of making up excuses to explain the sudden cooling of relations between the young teacher and me when I was transferred to *Yong Dakpemyili*. I was not man enough to jump over a pillow and was thus dumped unceremoniously.

I was a bashful and timid young man up to the time I went to Peki Training College. My timidity was exposed by a female classmate during the first year. It was the first and last time I had the misfortune of a woman that made direct proposition to date me. Victoria one of my female classmates wanted to date me and boldly told me so. I was taken aback by her initiative and reacted in a knee jerk manner, pretending to be dumb because I did not know how to respond. And when I found my voice I asked incredulously, 'you must be joking'. "Seriously," she said, but my mouth could not say yes to the desire that was burning in my heart. I was from the old school where men are supposed to propose and women to accept or turn down but never the other way round. I could not wrap my head around the fact that a beautiful and sexy woman genuinely wanted to date me, I wondered whether I could live up to the expectations and implication of dating on the campus. The college was overwhelmingly male, the few dating couples on the campus rented rooms in town for weekend trysts. I could not get £4.00 to start a correspondence course without a loan from the principal. I could not afford to rent a room in town and I certainly could not ask Victoria to rent a room out of the campus for our weekend relaxations. I could not accept or reject the proposal, I pretended that she was joking and let the proposal languish until I found her in the in the arms of a courageous classmate.

FOUND MY TRUTH SERUM

I was a chronic liar during most of my infancy. Lies came to me very naturally and I lied as a matter of course whether threatened or not. I lied even when nothing was at stake. The fear of spanking was my primary motive for lying and no amount of cajoling could let me see things otherwise. My mother and other adult family members could not dissuade from lying instinctively without cause. And they tried to wean me from lying through aphorisms, proverbs and other words of wisdom but to little effect. These gems and words of wisdom went through one ear and came out of the other. Children tend to think that they are smarter than their parents, I was not any different. I tried to outwit my parents and elders in whatever way I could. I practiced lying until it became the truth in my mind so that I could outwit my parents and elders. The adage often drummed into our ears at school, 'honesty is the best policy', had no effect on me.

Despite being caught or exposed time and time again I nevertheless thought that I was so smart I could not be caught. And I used to practice how I would lie about specific situation or subject over and over till truth and deception were blurred in my mind and I could not distinguish between the two. When we were children our teachers taught us that practice makes perfect I therefore practiced and became perfect at the lies I planned to say when suspected and confronted about a particular subject matter. My mother and other family members compared my propensity to lie to a blind or near sighted person. While they saw the absurdity in some of my stories, it made perfect sense and logical to me and I stuck to the story line.

Imperceptibly the constant admonition that the truth would not kill or harm me began to seep into my consciousness. I lied as a self defense but by age ten my mother stopped wielding the rod and that reduced the necessity to lie to avoid flogging or punishment. Change was in my future when I arrived on the campus of St. John Bosco's College, Navrongo in February 1960. It was at Navrongo that I finally came to terms with lying for the sake of lying with nothing at stake. One of my classmates was fond of an aphorism or proverb that he used to bandy about on the campus. The aphorism or proverb made perfect sense when I heard it; *"Always speak the truth so you don't have to remember what you said"*. The aphorism hit me like a bolt of lightning. It was another way of saying that the truth shall set me free but in words that I could relate to. I took the saying to heart and made it my own. Truth stands, it needs not be memorized. I recall the stories with minor variations but the gist of the story or subject is never compromised because truth stands by itself, it needs no propping. Of course, truth cannot be absolute, and with age I learned the value of discretion. I might lie to protect somebody from harm or in exercise of "discretion is the better part of valor." Or as the Bible says, "Do not cast your pearls before swine" (Matthew 7:6). I may lie or obfuscate the truth if the obfuscation produces some positive benefit or result. The truth serum let me live like me in joyous abandon without fear of being caught and tripped up in a lie. I lived in the present instead of worrying about my past catching up with me.

FAILING MEMORY FOR NAMES AND FACES

I started becoming reserved and restrained not because of discretion and wisdom but as a result of the erosion of my memory for names and faces as I grew older. I was generally an extrovert and gregarious person during most of my youth. I made and communicated easily with friends of both sexes until I became conscious of myself at puberty when I suddenly turned bashful before girls. My memory for names and faces was so good I never learned how to keep and maintain diaries or address books during my youth and when my memory started failing I could not create and maintain a consistent habit of making entries in journals and the like. So at the age when most of my colleagues and friends made a fetish of diaries and address books I kept all information about my friends and acquaintances in my head and I did not forget them as long as I needed to recall or communicate with them. It was in my thirties that I attempted to keep a journal or diary in the face of my failing memory but my attempts were largely unsuccessful, those efforts were perfunctory at best. The provision of appointment books at my workplace did not alter the situation in any positive direction. At the end of the year the only consistent entry in my appointment book was my name or signature and nothing else. I kept all personal and work appointments and dates in my head or on pieces of paper on my desk. Before I was forced into voluntary retirement that was how I maintained track of my assignments and appraisal appointments. I never made more than two appointments in any one day for fear I would forget some of them if I had too many appointments; I therefore did not make appointments that were more than two or three days in advance. The clear memory I had for names, people and places became hazy and suspect with age but I was set in my ways and despite my efforts to aid my memory with journal or diary entries I failed because I never had the habit or discipline to write consistently for reference at a later date.

I often feel acute embarrassment when a familiar but hazy face smiles broadly at me and worse calls me by name, offers me friendly handshake and I can only stare blankly into his face unable to recall the person behind the friendly smile. For instance I met woman at a supermarket. She called me by name and greeted me enthusiastically but I looked askance and bewildered, I returned her warm smile with a wan smile and screwy eyes, I was lost. About thirty minutes after we parted then it hit me; we were members of the same church. But by then it was too late, I did not have a second chance to show that I was a warm and caring person. I was familiar with her formal wear at church and could not recognize her in casual street clothes. The shame was that I had to meet her in church the following Sunday, I could not overcome the shame and embarrassment I felt within me. At another time I met another church member and again I could not make her out immediately. I have met two members of my church in casual wear at two different locations and could not recognize them though they recognized me and called me by name.

AGAINST THE ODDS

I do not have a spectacular story of success but stories of survival against the odds. The major events in my life happened more by accident and happenstance than by any deliberate policy choice or plan of action. When I set a goal before me, I get unintended results and sometimes pushed into directions or areas I never considered or contemplated.

If genes and DNA have profound influence on our health and longevity then the major events of my life either favorable or unfavorable happened in spite of me. I believe that my life was predetermined by the architects of my being long before I was born and nothing I did could alter the course or change what was preordained. The untimely death of my mother paved the way for me to go to school and changed my fate. My fate would have been similar like my older brothers and sisters, illiterate and uneducated subsistence farmers or laborers, if my mother had not died young. The death of my mother reunited me with a father I did not know existed. Would my father have sought for me in order to send me to school if my mother had not died? I doubt it. My father and mother had no contacts at the time she died. I knew my mother's husband as my father, I did not know he was my mother's second husband and as such my stepfather. Death brought sorrow early into my life but also changed the direction of my later life.

It was a miracle that I stayed the course of education in spite of my dislike of school. Between class three and four, I did everything I could to drop out of school without success.

The fear of being exposed as a truant and disappointing or upsetting my mother was the incentive that motivated me to make the minimum attendance in any year to qualify for promotion to the next class. There were no automatic or social promotions.

I was enthralled with driving. I very much wanted to be like Kwame Atta, our next door neighbor who was a driver. I saw how he and his assistants went about their work at weekends and nothing was more thrilling about their work than the grease and oil stained clothes they wore. Kwame Atta would not have me as an apprentice or driver mate, so I went to the lorry park to find one myself. But none would have me without parental consent. I met the same fate when I tried to get into carpentry. The fear to ask for parental consent to learn a trade was what thwarted my attempts to drop out of school for apprenticeship in a trade.

My professional career was chosen for me by the divine, whether as a teacher or a real estate appraiser. The teacher training college competitive examination was the only one I wrote in the middle school and succeeded. I became a teacher not because I planned or wanted to be a teacher but it was the only opportunity I was given after two previous attempts for secondary schools faltered. The teacher training college was the catalyst that eventually led me to university.

After graduating from college I was disappointed on the job front; I could not obtain a job or employment in any of the departments or establishments that I considered attractive employers. I was forced by the circumstances to accept employment at a department I loathed and a boss I could hardly stand because there was no other viable alternative. But the department and the boss that I could not stand gave me opportunities I would not have obtained elsewhere. I had the opportunity to win a scholarship to study in Australia. Had I been offered a job in any of the departments or corporations I considered desirable I might not have had the same opportunity.

When I was in dire financial straits in 1973 I sought respite from my financial problems by pursuing a one year British Council Scholarship I was turned down for the grant on the grounds that I could complete in Ghana what I wanted to study in Britain. But the very next year I won a three year scholarship for Australia. In place of a one year respite I got more than four years respite. And by the time I returned to Ghana my old financial problems were behind me. I sought and lost a one year scholarship program but won a longer scholarship that proved to be more relevant for my professional development than the one year program would have been.

I was not a great admirer of my father. I never forgave him for abandoning us for another woman. But my life as an adult has been a mirror image of my father. Almost everything I disliked or hated about my father; I have done so inexorably. It is not for want of trying but my best intentions and plans led to the same end. I have followed in my father's footsteps like a beast of burden led to the slaughter.

My Second Marriage

As a young adult I was the darling and admirer of older women. I became sexually active with older women. As a shy young man I was flattered by their attention and ended up in bed with them. I was mocked by my siblings over the texture of my hair but that was what girls and women admired most about me. I hated myself for the curly Fulani-like texture of my hair while women spent fortunes to have similar hair. I did not know that they mocked me over my hair out of envy or jealousy.

As a bashful young man I was more in bed with older women who did not have the same inhibitions like girls of my age group. I did not date older women as such but I allowed myself to be willingly seduced by them. Bashfulness and timidity kept me from bonding with girls and women within my age group until my mid twenties.

During my mid forties or middle age I struggled to date women of my age group. I do not know whether I had some flaws that women of my age group could not stand but which was tolerable by women who were younger than me. I consorted with sugar mummies in my youth but the roles were reversed during my middle age. Middle aged women treated me like a sugar daddy; they were more interested in selling me their love than genuine friendship and companionship. The women of my age group expected me to support them financially. Of course I did not have much disposal income after meeting my obligations to support another family as such I was often dumped. Most of my dates within that category ended for the same reason. I dated only one woman within my age group off-and-on for more than one year. And the affair lasted that long because she had an ulterior motive to keep me hanging on. Her motives became clear shortly after our engagement. Unbeknown to me, she was behind on her mortgage. She lured me to the jewelry store to select an engagement ring. I bought the ring and intended to ask her to marry me at a time and place of my choosing. But shortly after buying the ring she became so anxious to be engaged she could wait and literally wrung the ring out my hands. When we parted after the unconventional engagement I was delighted with the thought that I would have an infertile and menopausal woman for a wife. But I was soon disappointed. The next time I met her she was not wearing my ring. She apparently pawned it shortly after she got hold of the ring. I felt betrayed when I became aware of the situation and was offended; that ended our brief engagement. Maria returned the ring to me about six months later; but it was too late to return it to the jeweler for refund. My attempts to have an infertile partner for fear of fathering more children did not work out.

After the disappointment I stopped pigeon holing myself into specific age groups. I had the knack or luck for women younger than me. My fear about fathering more children was always at the back of my mind but I did not let the fear affect my relations again. I had no problems as such going out with younger companions though I was not very comfortable with them. Going out with younger women was sure to make me end up fathering more children like my father. This fear was the force behind my attempts at dating mature women within my age group.

I met the woman who became my second wife in the early part of 1992. Auspicious circumstances brought us together. Peace was a new arrival in Brooklyn. She was the niece of a close friend in Brooklyn. She came from France where she had lived for a number of years. She was a close friend of my niece in Paris and was aware of me long before she came to New York. She was at her uncle's home alone when I called and left a message for the uncle. That phone call set in motion a chain of events that culminated in our getting to know one another.

Peace delivered my message to Tom, her uncle when he came home. Out of curiosity about the name she enquired who I was. Her uncle brought her to my apartment to introduce me to the best friend of my niece from Paris. That visit led from one thing to another and before long we were dating. Peace was much younger that I was when we began seeing one another. She was the epitome of my ambivalence and conflicted mind about dating younger women. She was younger than any woman I had ever dated. I was at once excited and afraid. I was flattered she even had eyes for me but afraid that if the burgeoning relationship endured my fears would certainly come true. But I did not let the fears come between us, I was not confident that our friendship would endure for long particularly after the euphoria of the chance circumstances subsided. I decided to enjoy her company while it lasted or until she went her way. I am amazed that our relations has endured for more than two decades, I never expected it because of the wide difference in our ages.

Tom, her uncle, was not happy with our blossoming romance and tried through various means of persuasion to break the burgeoning relations. When his attempts failed, he literally evicted her from his apartment and sent her directly into my arms. He hoped that cohabitation with me would discourage or perhaps dissuade her from continuing with the relations. But the move backfired; it accelerated our relations from casual romance to serious romance, from seeing one another twice or thrice a week into early marriage. In as much as I was afraid of the consequences of dating a young woman I was eager to hold on to my treasure despite the fears. I was convinced that the age difference between us would eventually doom the romance and I wanted to strike the iron while it was still hot. I made no secret of my fears and often referred to her as a baby so that when she eventually dumped me I would have the psychological edge that the break up was only a matter of time. She resented that characterization by insisting that she was a mature woman in her own right and that was true. Despite nothing to the contrary I still felt insecure with her. My insecurity led me to discuss my fears with a close friend, Sam. He opined that I was a lucky man; that it was not the likes of me, a poor public servant that won the heart of younger women. 'If I were you I would marry her in a heartbeat before somebody pried her from my fingers'. I put my fears to rest and never second guessed her again.

Peace and I were married in July 1992 after a courtship of less than seven months. The day we were married marked the day the sum of my fears began to take shape. I became my father's image it was only a matter of time before the image was complete. The first time I met my father's young wife I criticized him for having such a young partner. I wondered how my own grown children would receive my new wife. Some of them are only a few years younger than her. Peace assuaged my fears during our courtship that she was not interested in having children of her own. I understood her motivation for not wanting to have children of her own though I doubted it. She is the first child of her mother as such she literally mothered four of her younger siblings. She washed them, cooked and fed them and baby sat them while her mother went about her business. She had it with children and wanted nothing to do with anymore children including having some of her own. But I think motherhood is an instinct and it takes a lot of willpower to stop fulfilling the instinct especially if you are fertile. Before we celebrated our first wedding anniversary she was the mother of a baby boy. So far we are the parents of three boys.

Loss Of Spiritual Tranquility

There is an opportunity cost or everything has a price. We made material progress after we were married. We prospered enough to buy a home of our own within two years of our wedding anniversary and relocated to Staten Island from Brooklyn. In addition to paying a mortgage and all the responsibilities of home ownership Peace enrolled as a student at the Staten Island College. Thus as the sole breadwinner of the family I worked hard at two jobs, a full time and part time job. I used to put in about twelve to eighteen hour days and by the end of the day I was beat up I could hardly observe quiet time for meditation, I could not do any concentration and meditation exercises without drifting into sleep and dreams. While I prospered materially, my spiritual life and yoga practice lagged and suffered. I have practiced yoga and meditation since seventies, but during this period I was often so tired I could hardly keep my eyes open at the end of a long day let alone meditate. I drifted into sleep as soon as I closed my eyes and tried to concentrate and meditate or pray. With the inability to concentrate and meditate quietly, I changed my emphasis from quiet concentration and meditation to loud prayers. I hoped that praying aloud would keep me alert and awake at the end of my day, but despite the attempt at loud prayers I often dozed and fell asleep while on my knees. As time went by my yoga exercises were reduced to perfunctory practices from time to time. My regular concentration and meditation exercises virtually died, but I still held on to fasting about two or three days a week.

Racial Discrimination in School Enrollment

Our first house on Staten Island was in a PUD, proprietary unit development, with a home owners association; Mosel Loop Home Owners Association. One of the selling points of the development when we were shopping for a house was the zoned school of the development. We were told that the zoned school for the PUD was PS48 instead of the school closest to the development. No less than the chairman of the Home Owners Association assured me of the zoned school of the development when we moved into our new home. School children within the development were all enrolled at PS48. The school was said to be a better performing school than the one close to the development.

When I bought into Mosel Loop Owners Association in 1994, I did so purely for value. The home was a foreclosure property; the monthly payment was within my salary as a public servant without the income from my part time job. I did not have a school-age child so the school zoning meant very little at the time. However in 1999, I came face-to-face with the ugly face of racism disguised in the form of school zoning. In 1999 all the white children on Mosel Loop were enrolled at PS48 and a child two doors from me enrolled in the same school, PS48. But when I attempted to enroll my child at the school I was told by the racist principal that PS48 was not my zoned school. In other words there were two school zones for Mosel Loop, one for whites and another for blacks. White children on Mosel Loop were zoned for PS48 while the black children living on the same short street were zoned for another school. If this dichotomy was not racism or racial discrimination then I do not know what is.

I petitioned the department of education for remedy. They promised to investigate my allegations, but in the meanwhile, I was asked to make a choice from a list of schools on the Island with vacancies in the first grade. I chose PS8 on the south shore, a school that was four miles from my home. After a few weeks I was informed that the principal of PS48 had retired. The case languished in the office of the school investigator for months. In the end I was told that due to the retirement of the principal they could not verify historical enrollment of children from the development other than those who were currently enrolled at the school. While the gist of my allegation was confirmed, the retirement of the principal allegedly made it impossible to investigate enrollment of past years. I was not litigious else I would have sued the the education department for racism. Was it a cover up or coincidence that the principal retired only weeks after allegations of racism were made against her? Her retirement prevented the airing of the dirty laundry of the education department.

I was placated with a school of my choice. But why can't every parent have that choice. Nobody should be forced to go to a school he does not want simply because of residence, just because I live in a hole does not mean I do not want to see the sun. The zoning system fosters low performance. If schools could be closed down or perish because of lack of adequate enrolments due to persistent poor performance both the children and the teachers would work hard for the survival of schools, both would have vested interest against disruption when a school is shuttered. Children are like sitting ducks under the school zoning system, if there was real choice in the primary schools failing schools would atrophy for lack of enrollment instead of the mayor or chancellor deciding which bad school closes or opens. That power should be vested in parents by abolishing zoning, let me choose to keep my child in a failing school instead of being compelled by the state to keep my child in a failing school.

Since I was the victim of discrimination or racism I should have asked for transport for my child but I drove him to and from school at my own expense. And as far as I am concerned that is as it should be; the cost of school choice. If I choose to enroll my child at a school in a different borough or location, say near my workplace, I should be prepared to shoulder the responsibility for getting him to school. My residential address should not be the factor that determines the quality of education my child receives. That experience convinced me that the school zoning system; is a tool of discrimination and racism. School zoning should have ended with Brown vs. Board of Education, the decision that ended segregation in schools. But segregation has effectively been kept in place by school zoning; discrimination is not ended simply with mixed races in schools. Zoning prevents interaction between children of various socioeconomic backgrounds during their formative years. It divides schools between the haves and have not's. I live in a free society but I cannot send my child to a school of my choice. The government

ZAKARIAH ALI

tells me where my child can receive education. Where my child goes to school in his formative years depends on my economic status as represented by where I can afford to rent or buy a home. As a resident of New York City I should have the freedom to enroll my child in any school within the five boroughs without let or hindrance. The same program that makes it possible for children to attend middle and high schools out of their borough of residence should make it possible for grade school children to attend schools that are not necessarily tied to their place of residence. By the middle and high school the harm done to children in their formative years is complete. They were denied good education foundation because their parents were poor and could not afford to live in affluent areas where the schools are better provisioned and tend to do better than schools in the low income neighborhoods. At least in New York city we all pay taxes into the same coffers, we should have the liberty to send our children to any school of our choice on a first come first served basis irrespective of address. Our children should not be condemned to poor performing schools or otherwise by the accident of where their parents can afford to live. Poor performing schools would not exist if they did not have children who are compelled to attend them like sitting ducks. If schools competed for our children, such as private schools do, poor performing schools would die for lack of enrollment.

206

IN MY FATHER'S FOOTSTEPS

By the time I was of an age when I could look up to my father as a roll model or example my father was no where to be found. I felt his absence after my father abandoned my mother and siblings for another woman. I was therefore mad at him during most of his lifetime for what I considered as treachery against his own family. I met my father's new wife during the third term of the fifth grade or class five. I did not like her. She was not any older than some of my older sisters. She looked so young I had a crush on her while at the same time I held her responsible for the sins of my father.

When I grew up I resolved to follow a different path from my father. My father was a stingy man who placed most of the burden of raising his children on his wives. I decided to be different by fathering enough kids that I could care for without placing the burden of their care on my wife. I fantasized on a family of only three children. My father had a football team family size; I was determined to be different. But my family plan was in danger of being derailed before I had the chance to start a formal family, I was the father of two children before I ever thought of marriage.

Akuah and Kofi, My Children Before My First Marriage.

When I was bitten by the marriage bug I had an intended girlfriend or fiancée, but I ditched my fiancée, Marie in favor of the mother of my second child so as to keep intact my family plan. My fiancée and I lived in different parts of the country and our relations unraveled after a one night affair resulted in the birth of the second child. I did not marry for love as such but for the sake of a family plan that I tried to keep though the odds were against it. I tried to undo the mistakes I made early in my life by taking the mother of my second child as my partner so as to keep alive my dreams of a family of five.

I scarcely knew Obenewa. I met her shortly after I wriggled out of my relations with Florence, the woman who rescued me from homelessness when I was down on my luck. I sent Florence to a boarding house to get rid of her without putting her out to pasture. I was preparing to leave for Australia by the second month of the New Year when I had a one night affair. Obenewa was the close friend of Grace, Elisha's girlfriend. I accompanied Elisha to her girlfriend. There I met Obenewa and before the night was over I ended up in bed with her. That first night was all it took for me to become a father for the second time. I failed to convince her to abort the fetus. Despite her refusal I had no intention at that stage of having long term relations with her. I was determined to keep her out of my life. When I left for Australia I never communicated with her until I came back on vacation two years later. I became concerned about my image while in Australia. Two children from two women created the image of a philanderer and womanizer. I was concerned about that image because I knew within my heart that I was not what the evidence portrayed me to be. I had also found religion in Australia and it was my new religious inclination more than anything else that ultimately influenced my decision to consider the possibility of making Obenewa my marriage partner. She was a child of God her education level not withstanding.

My first child was born by a woman who cared for me out of the goodness of her heart while I was on my third year vacation at Kumasi. Dora, a kind hearted woman was a cotenant of my cousin Yakubu. She saw that I was starving had pity on me and started sharing her evening meals with us. Her kindness led to familiarity and since she lived by herself it was not long before I jumped into bed with her. By the time the vacation was over she was pregnant. I did not have money to suggest abortion until I went back to school. I failed to persuade her to abort the fetus after I received my book allowance at school. When she refused I walked away and washed my hands. She subsequently traced me to my workplace with the toddler. She called my bluff when I made custody the condition for my parental responsibility. She left the child with me and I never saw her again.

I started thinking seriously of marriage during my second year in Australia. My plan was to go home and come back with Marie. But she was not particularly helpful during the letters we wrote discussing our future plans. For the prior two years our marriage plans appeared to be on track but things took a different turn when I suggested I might bring her with me when I came on vacation. At that stage her priorities changed. Marriage was not her priority for accompanying me to Australia per se. It was an opportunity to further her education. I had no problem against her ambition; I did not want education to be her first priority so that if things did not work out as she expected then I would not bear the brunt of any disappointment. Marriage became the vehicle for Marie's education goals and I just wanted a wife; her education at this stage was secondary. She could not accept my suggestion that she follow me to Australia first as the wife of a student and if education opportunities became available then make use of the opportunity but we could not make it the priority for our relations, our priorities for marriage were poles apart. I doubted whether I could shoulder the responsibility for her education. How would she take it if I could not help with her tuition or otherwise? As a nurse she could make good money in Australia but I was not sure of the cost of further studies.

This was the state of affairs between us when I left Melbourne in January 1977 for Ghana. I hoped that if I met her in person we might be able to iron out our differences. But as things turned out I never gave her the opportunity to explain her rational or for the two of us to hash out our differences. I did not see her when I went on that vacation.

Three days after I landed in Ghana I went to see my new baby who was born while I was away in Australia. When I stared into the face of the new baby the flickers of thoughts that had occasionally crossed my mind were given a face. At that time I said to myself if Obenewa was good enough to go to bed with me she should be good enough as a wife to bear me another child. My thoughts about my family plans tumbled out. When I asked her if she would be content with another child in addition to the one in her arms she answered affirmatively. Once she agreed that she would be content with another child there was nothing else to do than complete the customary marriage requirements of her tribe. The love for my baby and my desire for a better image were factors that influenced my decision. I returned to Australia with Obenewa in April 1978. When we went back I was able to put her through a vocational school for one year at no cost to me, the school was a bonus. Obenewa did not have any plan for education and she did not benefit from it as Marie would have had I known that she could have had free education in Melbourne.

At the end of my studies I went back to Ghana against the advice and wishes of Obenewa. I had a nationalist fervor that prompted me to go back home to serve my country instead of living a comfortable life in Australia. Secondly my failure to obtain an internship position in a private real estate office affected the way I viewed the private sector in Australia. By Ghana standards I made quite good money working in factories and cleaning offices but I did not think that was how I wanted to live the rest of my life if I had remained in Australia. Thus we went back home and started our family. On our return she had a discussion with her older sister who advised her to ditch the understanding we had about our family before marriage. She accepted her sister's advise without bothering to bring me into the picture. By the time it occurred to me that something was wrong I was on the way to my fourth child. I broke Marie's heart for naught and in spite of all my good intentions nothing went the way I planned it. I ended up exactly like a carbon copy of my father. The 'conspiracy' with her sister doomed our marriage the moment she adopted it. I deserted my family just like how my father deserted me and my siblings. When I ran away from my family I landed in New York and eventually started a new family. That brought me to full circle the image and character I sought so desperately to avoid. The way my first marriage ended was eerily similar to the way my father ended his marriage to his first wife. He walked out and never came back, so did I.

We returned to Ghana in 1979 and within a few years after our return my family plan went awry. We had two children in quick succession. I blamed myself for the failure because I practiced the rhythm method of birth control as a product of catholic education. But when she became pregnant with our fourth child it occurred to me that there was more to the rapid fire rate at which we were producing children than miscalculations of dates. I learned that my wife had made a deliberate choice to have more children.

I stopped fathering more children with Obenewa only because I left home. I justified my cowardly departure from home with the excuse that I was forced into an untenable condition, more children than I could comfortably maintain on my income. My departure was cowardly because I kept her in the dark about my travel plans. But the final result between my father and me were very similar. When I walked out on Obenewa I left her with six children; the sixth was my first child from my days as a student. My father walked out on my stepmother when they had five children and I was the sixth child from another woman, the situations were very similar. I left home to seek my fortunes while my father left home for another woman. The children I left behind felt the same way I did when my father left home, abandoned. They felt abandoned because they did not know why their father suddenly disappeared from home. The similarities with my father did not just end there. Obenewa was less than forty years old when I left home; she did not marry again. My mother was breast feeding a baby when my father left home and she did not marry again.

Obenewa has not been divorced according to customary and traditional practices. I have not formally returned or handed her over to her family as tradition requires so by customary law we are still man and wife. If we were of the same tribe the surviving spouse would have been compelled to mourn the dead spouse as if we were still married. Similarly, my father after concocting a phony altercation before he left home, never formally divorced my stepmother. We had our moments of disagreements but Obenewa and I never had open conflict or public squabble. Of course when we faced financial problems I blamed her for breeding a brood far more than our resources could handle satisfactorily. After I left home I could not contrive any pretext to go through the traditional customary divorce proceedings. I was not unmindful of the disastrous results of my older brother's attempt to divorce his wife for infidelity.

In as much as I blamed her imprudence for contributing to our financial difficulties I was still mindful that I was an equal contributor in the make-up of our family size, albeit an unwitting contributor. We were in it together. She could not have had the children without my active cooperation directly or indirectly. I was as guilty as she was. The only difference was that she could have been on the pill and all I did was calculate safe periods, I guess I made many miscalculations. In my culture children are considered an asset. It is therefore unthinkable to seek divorce on the grounds that I fathered more children with her than I could handle. I would have been considered insane to make children the grounds for divorce unless I was prepared to make false accusations. I therefore did not have the courage or reason to mount divorce proceedings according to custom and tradition. We are bound together for life by virtue of our children.

FAMILY CHARACTER

While I do not want to justify my failings and weakness with inheritance from my father I cannot help but notice similar failings and characteristics among some of my male and female siblings and their offspring. The men and women within my family have a tendency to foster broken homes or abandon their spouses and relationships. Of course, I was a child of a broken home on the part of both my father and mother. My birth mother broke my father's heart when she abandoned him when I was barely six months old, and my father in turn broke my stepmother's heart by walking away from us when I was about eight years old.

My older brother had two wives during his lifetime. His second wife as is often the case, was much younger than his first wife. While he had two wives he lived with only the younger woman. His first wife was sent to live with our mother more than two hundred miles from him. And he never visited her anytime during the year. He provided for her physical needs but her emotional and conjugal needs were ignored. Later events proved that indeed a woman does not live by bread alone, the wife eventually had an affair that resulted in the birth of a child.

The child born outside of the marriage was by Dagarti customary practice still regarded as the offspring of her husband. It appears that by Dagarti custom a wife is considered the property of the husband. As such the woman cannot bear a child for another man neither can any man claim lawful paternity of any child born with a married woman. A married woman caught having an affair is grounds enough for divorce. But what if the woman was horny and had an affair because she could not get it from her husband? This was the situation between my brother and his wife. The woman lost her self control because she was denied conjugal visits by her husband.

My brother's request to divorce his wife on the grounds of infidelity was denied by her family. According to our customary and traditional practices, marriage is a union between two families. As such divorce proceedings are held between members of both families. Thus at the formal divorce hearing my brother was blamed for his wife's illicit affair by her family. And at the conclusion of the proceedings the family refused to accept blame and as such denied the divorce. It was asserted or alluded to us that by my brother's refusal to copulate or conjugate with his wife she was forced to find it elsewhere. 'A hungry man would do anything to satisfy his hunger so is a hungry vagina'. They put it succinctly thus 'the food of vagina is penis and the hungry vagina found food when it was hungry'. The tables were thus turned on my brother; he was accused of neglect and blamed for his wife's illicit affair with another man. The annulment or divorce as such was denied.

The divorce was denied my brother stopped sleeping with his wife hence she went astray. And my brother was blamed for his wife going astray to sleep with another man. I guess the divorce was denied despite the obvious because the woman's family was not willing to return the bride price. Had they consented to the divorce they would have been required to return the bride price under Dagarti custom and tradition. But that question was moot and did not arise with the denial of the request. They became an unhappy couple yoked together by custom and tradition neither could undo till the very end.

My brother was devastated and taken aback by the unexpected turn of events. The two were yoked together by force of customary law and tradition despite irrefutable evidence of infidelity for better or worse. The marriage was to all intents and purposes broken beyond reconciliation and the decision did not bring them together. She continued to live with our mother as before her first affair came to light and she had affairs that resulted in the expansion of our family's gene pool through children fathered by other men. And those children are part of our family today.

My older sister, the only one among my older siblings who was educated never formally married. She cohabitated with men for long periods at a time as if they were a married couple. The live-in boyfriends fathered her three children. She was a nurse and as a nurse she was posted to hospitals around the country. It was in that capacity that she was at Yendi in 1959 when my mother took leave of me at the hospital to visit her with Adjoa. And when I decided to go to Tamale at the end of my teacher training course at Navrongo she was the inspiration I chose to go to Tamale. During the period I was in teacher training at Navrongo and Peki, I used to stop by their house whenever I passed through Kumasi on my way to Tarkwa. I was accustomed to them living together as a couple; I did not know that they were not formally married. Hammond used to visit my sister wherever she was posted as a nurse. I knew Hammond as my sister's husband and I used to stop by his home at Kumasi whether my sister was there or not. My sister and Hammond eventually broke up when she was posted to Sunyani

As said elsewhere I do not know whether we have a genetic makeup that attracts us to friends and lovers with whom we become estranged and break up our homes after a few years of marriage or cohabitation. Two of my children have already gone through broken homes or the relations are heading for the rocks.

THE LAST DAYS OF MY FATHER

I do not know how old my father was at the time of his death neither did my father know his own age during his lifetime. He outlived all his contemporaries and used that yardstick to measure his age as two hundred. He never used the equivalent of two hundred in our dialect, but he used to estimate his age as two bags. In the years before and immediately after independence a bag of money was £100. Thus two bags was £200 or two hundred years. My father assumed that if he outlived all his contemporaries who themselves were considered old at their death then he must have been the Methuselah of his generation.

It was tobacco that finally sent my father to his grave. For as long as I knew my father, he chewed tobacco. He died of a condition my stepmother described as as a throat ulcer. And with his history of tobacco use I concluded that the ulcer must have been some type of cancer. I did not see my father before his death and burial. As a Muslim he was buried within twenty four hours after death. I paid homage to him by having a tomb erected over his grave in his adopted home at Charia. When he died he was surrounded by my stepmother, Salamatu and some of her children, my younger half brothers and sisters.

Throughout most of my life in Ghana I feared nothing more than contact poison. My fears may be due to the suffering and death of my mother from poison. I heard numerous stories of the deaths of young men and women from poison while growing up. The Dagarti people generally like to administer poison to their victims through drink or food at festivals, funerals or other gatherings. And some of their poisons are reputed to be so potent that when administered in a say a calabash of pito the victim would be dead by the time the calabash dried up. Thus with the death of my mother at the back of my mind I took the warning to be ware of poison at a funeral to heart long before my father fell ill. I was overly cautious when he died. I went to comfort my stepmother and younger siblings long after the burial of my father. I did everything I could to avoid mingling with the crowd of mourners in the aftermath of his death in which for the sake of courtesy I might have been forced to drink or eat sympathy food and drinks provided for the mourners. It is in such settings that the bad people are in their element where they can target their victims with poison without fear of being found out. I therefore went to the funeral after the mourners had dispersed to their homes and villages. However, I was saved from ridicule and embarrassment for not being at my father's funeral by the exigencies of his religion. He was already buried by the time I heard the news. Had he not been a Muslim the corpse would have been preserved for a few days or until I came around as the oldest surviving son.

My father died about fifteen to eighteen months after the death of my younger sister, Adjoa. The prophetic messages to be cautious at a funeral started soon after I returned from her funeral. The first time I received the message from one of Prophet Tweneboah's ministers I was under the impression that I was being warned about a past event but the prophet reiterated that the funeral was still to come. But I never associated it with my father until he fell sick. And when he fell sick and was near death the warnings of caution during a funeral became consistent at every church service. I was warned that if I ate or drank at a forthcoming funeral, that would be the end of me. By the time my father died I was afraid to show my face among a crowd of my kinsmen. And when I finally went to the funeral I went with my own seer for guidance.

I had reason to fear poison. I saw the pernicious effects of poison early in my life and the fear has never really gone away. The fear was always at the back of my mind when I interacted with my fellow tribesmen even at an age when kids and youths of similar age behaved without a care in the world, I had inhibitions. I threw caution to the wind when I was in the company oof strangers but I looked about me with a wary eye when I was in the company of my kinsmen or tribesmen. If I did not know any victim of poison the warnings would not have resonated as much as they did. But I was able to put a name and face on the warnings and that obviously influenced my cautious behavior and reaction to news of my father's death.

The final funeral obsequies or rites of my father rested on me as the oldest surviving son. I had older sisters but the final funeral rites was my responsibility. Fortunately it is one customary rite that has no set time limit. Among the Dagabas the final funeral rites are not meant as a second round of mourning and weeping but a joyous occasion celebrating the life of the departed. At the final funeral obsequies food and drinks are provided to the guests or celebrants by the host and are therefore expensive undertakings. My stepmother died after I left Ghana and so I combined the final funeral rites of my father and mother together. It was ironic that the woman who long suffered as an abandoned wife was forced to mourn the man who abandoned her in his lifetime. Their final funerals were held or celebrated together. It appears that the more than thirty year gulf that was between them was abridged at their deaths.

Wrestling The Devil

The problems that nearly doomed my successful graduation from college was but a shadow of the things to come.

The problems followed me when I left the campus. My job prospects which seemed bright before I left the campus suddenly dimmed after I was let go by the first employer that offered me a position during recruitment at the Public Service Commission.

Work In Public Service

Most of the employment opportunities for newgraduates were in the public sector. Thus about three months after we left the campus we were invited to the offices of the Public Service Commission to meet representatives of our prospective employers. At the meeting the various corporations and departments gave us a presentation of the nature of their work and what role the land economy graduates would play in the establishments. The Public Service Commission was a one stop shop for most public service jobs. Thus if any of us failed to obtain employment through the office of the commission then the going would be very rough for that individual. Opportunities in the private sector were very few to none as the real estate industry and profession was in its infancy. Most of our peers who were trained in Britain worked in one or two departments until they set up practice after retirement. But by the time we came out of college the opportunities were brighter. At the meeting in October 1971 all the relevant corporations and government departments were represented. We listened carefully to their presentations asked questions particularly about salaries and prospects for advancement.

After the presentations were over we jostled over one another to attract the attention of the representatives of the various employers present at the meeting. And some of the representatives were also trying to recruit favorite individuals among the new class of graduates, those who had interned with them during the course.

The lands department where I had interned the prior three years tried to attract my attention but I looked away and turned my attention towards a corporation that offered me new opportunities though I had no previous experience with them. When I turned away from the lands department I turned away from certain financial security. The department, as its name implies, administers government lands with responsibility for title registrations. The clients of the department are generally the cream of the society and they tip generously when they have transactions with the department. After three years of internship with department I was sure I could have financial security if I chose to work with them. But I threw in my lot with the Tema Development Corporation. The Tema Development Corporation was responsible for the development and administration of the Tema township but I had no idea of the internal workings of the corporation. I think I like the challenges of the unknown and I guessed that I could be better off in one area, housing. Thus I was one of three new graduates who were selected by the Tema Development Corporation. I was ecstatic but my previous benefactors were upset with me. But within two to three weeks my impulsive decision came back to bite me. My excitement and exuberance were misplaced; I had banked on the wrong horse. My happiness turned to grief on the day I was supposed to report to my new employers to begin the paper work prior to starting work. The head of department informed us that due to budgetary constraints, they could afford to employ two of us. The three potential employees comprised of two men and a woman. The corporation decided to keep the woman and the man who had interned with them in prior years. I was therefore let go. I was crushed and devastated by the turn of events.

I was on my own after I was let go. The doors of the public service commission where I could have chosen any employer were closed. I therefore had no choice but go back meekly to lands department and ask to be taken back. The department did not reject my application outright they frustrated me until I stopped going back. I was kept hanging on without knowing my fate one way or the other for up to a month. I hung on for close to a month and went to the department at least once or twice a week but was told each time to return after a few days. I went back time after time without ever receiving a definitive answer. Gradually I came to the conclusion that the department was toying with my life or paying me back for turning down their earlier offer at the public service commission. I was suddenly uncertain of myself and saw hunger and starvation looming before my mind's eye; I became desperate. I went the rounds to the other potential employers who were present at the offices of the public service commission in search of new opportunities. All my desperate efforts ended in vain, like the lands department, I got no offers.

I made several futile visits to several departments and corporations except the the one place where I knew there were vacancies, the ministry of local government. I kept the ministry at the back of my mind as the employer of last resort even as I made futile attempts in search of new job opportunities. The turning point in my futility came after I was snubbed at the office of the State Insurance Corporation. The State Insurance Corporation was my last hope or gasp. They were not represented at the public service commission job bazaar but I was aware that Inusah, one of my college seniors was employed there. So I decided to see if I could make a good case to the personnel manager to add me to the fledging division of Inusah. I went to the personnel manager's office bright and early and was waved to a seat by his secretary or receptionist without a word. I guess she was used to a lot of desperate people like me going to the manager's office in search of work. I sat before the receptionist for close to an hour, I was invisible to her because she never lifted her countenance once to find out what brought me to the office. I felt humbled and humiliated at the office of the State Insurance Corporation and when I left the office I went straight to the ministry of local government where I knew there were job vacancies begging for people to fill them. All my frustrations and humiliations ended at the ministry of local government. I was hired as a valuation officer that very day pending completion of civil service paper work for new employees. I realized my miserable and pathetic condition when I left the office of the state insurance corporation. I had no uncle, friend and did not know anybody in a place of influence who could at least me help to get the attention of some potential employers. I had brought the situation on myself and the solution was within reach and had been there all along while I searched fruitlessly for work elsewhere.

I was initially reluctant to work at the ministry because of the fear that I would never obtain appropriate professional designation or recognition for work experience at the ministry. The head of the valuation division was not a professional associate of the Ghana Institution of Surveyors, the professional body for Quantity Surveyors and Valuers. As such the ministry was not recognized as a training ground for young graduates who had intentions of professional affiliation with the Institution. It was this fear of professional acceptance of work experience at the ministry that was at the heart of my reluctance to work at the ministry until I had no choice. The ministry was represented at the public service commission but apart from one Mensah who was sponsored by the department they left practically empty handed. Nobody volunteered for work at the department. We were afraid of being stuck in professional limbo with little prospects for future private professional practice. But those fears were rendered moot when my back was against the wall and hunger and starvation stared at me in the face, my very survival was at stake. My present need took precedence over my future professional prospects. Survival outweighed everything else, the dead have no prospects. The certainty of monthly pay packets was more precious at that juncture than any prospective future valuation practice.

BLIND PURSUIT OF STATUS SYMBOL

Once I was ensconced as an officer of the ministry of local government with secure monthly pay my fears of hunger and misery dissipated as if it had never happened. I turned my attention to the perks of a senior civil servant; chief among them was a government loan to buy a car. Had I been employed and sent to my home region I might have been dreaming of a government bungalow. But in Accra I was a small fly content to pursue my dream of status symbol with a car loan. The car market was in shambles but nobody could have convinced me that buying a car only a few months after college was a bad idea. The car was the ultimate status symbol of the middle class. I was eager to demonstrate that I had arrived with the ultimate symbol of the burgeoning middle class, a car. A government job and car loan was the guaranteed route to the middle class. The amount of loan I could obtain was based on my annual salary. And the only qualification necessary for a car loan was for my boss to concur that I needed the car for the efficient performance of my official duties. I did not have to worry about that aspect of the loan because my work actually required a car or some means of transportation. My priorities in life at that time were skewed to the absurd, while I was dreaming about a car I never gave any thoughts to housing or a place to lay my head at night. I was content perching with my niece Regina and her live-in boy friend, Gad. The pair lived around the east side of Nima police station. The moment I knew the maximum loan I could obtain for a car then I jumped into the used car market.

I shopped for a car from the numerous used car dealers dotted around Accra. Used cars were the only vehicles available on the market except for government ministers and a few well connected individuals who could obtain import licenses to import new cars for personal use owing to a deteriorating economy and the dearth of foreign exchange. To prevent the economy from grinding to a halt the government liberalized the importation of cars to any person or business who had their own sources of foreign exchange to import vehicles into the country. By this time in the development of the country a black market in foreign currencies was already developing due to shortages of consumer goods and restrictions on imports. The liberalization of imports led to the flooding of the market with used cars of every make, age and model.

This was the state of the auto market I plunged into fresh from college and nobody could have convinced me otherwise. I learned to have my head in the right place the hard way. The merchants were only interested in importing whole cars, they gave short shrift to parts to service the numerous used cars that were imported into the country. The part shortages spawned a lucrative auto parts smuggling racket in the country. The new breed of smugglers brought in spare parts from neighboring countries mostly from Nigeria and Togo. It appears that most of the smuggled parts were counterfeit or cheap imitations especially the parts from Nigeria. When I plunged into the car market I was unaware of this aspect of the market until I was neck deep into car ownership when I came face to face with the problem of procuring parts to service my car. I was so bent on buying a car I doubt whether anybody could have reasoned with me to bide my time before jumping hand and foot ignorantly into a market about which I knew very little. I lulled myself into the belief that my car would be self sustaining and problem free. The only thing that could have saved me from myself would have been a denial of the car loan. And that individual who denied me the loan would have made an enemy for life.

I was oblivious of any real or imagined potential problems of car ownership. My only experience with cars was seeing Kwame Atta service some parts of cars in the courtyard of the tenement house we all shared. The next thing that was upper most in mind was driving; I craved driving ever since childhood. I could literally taste the excitement of driving as I shopped around for a car. I never test drove any of the cars I inspected or had their engines cranked. I shopped for my ideal car by sight, examining the paintwork and interior. I did not give a second look to any car with poor paint work or drab interior. I was able to test crank the engine of the car only after it was paid for and the keys were given to me. I had a false sense of security on the cost of running a car. Civil service car owners were paid maintenance and mileage allowance. The potential value of these allowances lulled me into a sense of security that the cost of running a car would be minimal. I did not see any disadvantages or downside to owning a car.

My application for a loan was approved and processed in record time considering civil service bureaucratic minutiae. And by the third week of December 1971, I was the proud owner of an Austin 1800. I did not know it was a front wheel drive car when I bought it but it would have made no difference because I did know the significance of the type of drive train.

I knew next to nothing about cars when I bought my first car. I examined it from the exterior only during the transaction and was able to open the hood to look at the appearance of the engine and battery after I paid for it. I then climbed into the car started the engine briefly and shut it off lest it takes off inadvertently. I wonder what recourse I would have had if the engine did not start or the engine and battery were grubby or even not quite road worthy after I paid for it. The check was made payable directly to the vendor. Fortunately the car passed my lame inspection. I had nothing else to do but contemplate how to get a driver instructor to help me until I became a competent driver. My car was big and roomy without a hump in the middle of the back seat. But I had no idea it was front wheel drive. I guess it must have been the next generation front wheel drive car after the Mini. It was a bigger version of the Mini Cooper but with a different name plate. I was pleased with my new toy; it was neat inside and outside. There were very few Austin's or Morris, scions of British made cars on the road by the 1970's. The scarcity of the make and model of car made it more appealing and attractive to me. I was proud driving around in a car with few peers on the road. I felt special being one of a few owners who drove around in a large and roomy car. I grinned from ear to ear when I sat on the front seat. My joy knew no bounds; I felt as if I had won the hand of Miss Ghana or the most beautiful girl in the neighborhood that I always ogled but was afraid to ask her out. But she was all mine. My only problem was that I could not show off my new girl, I did not know how to drive. I needed a driver; I made no prior arrangement for a driver even as I was nearing the end of the transaction. The fact was that I was new in Accra and I did not know any driver who could introduce me to a driver or at least recommend one to me. In the Ghana of the 1970's there were no formal driving schools, one learned to drive professionally through apprenticeship or through a hired driver instructor when one bought a car. I was in need of a driver instructor to drive me around until I passed my driving test.

The excitement and euphoria surrounding the car transaction was comparable to the excitement of a child who has just been given a new unwrapped toy; I was giddy with excitement. The car rekindled my interest in auto repairs as I fantasized about servicing my own car. I was as excited as a child in a candy store.

I had almost become a car owner before I thought of getting off my perch with Regina and Gad. I needed a place of my own to live independently of them. I contacted a rental agent to find me a suitable rental accommodation. The agent obtained a closet size room at the boys' quarters or outhouse of a young bank executive's home in the Pig Farm neighborhood of Accra. It was the first offer I got and I accepted it. I accepted the room as a temporary accommodation until such time that something better came along. The room was big enough for a twin or single bed and a table. Houses in Ghana or rooms did not have closets; the well heeled used custom made portable closets. But the house was ideal for a new car owner eager to protect my investment and pride. It would be parked behind a six foot high perimeter fence wall with steel gates. I moved into the room with nothing but a small suitcase. I stuck nails on the door and window sills to hang my clothes. I started life as a fresh college graduate in a room that was smaller than my college cubicle. It was an inauspicious beginning.

My Financial Downfall

I took delivery of the car on a Thursday afternoon in the middle of December 1971 or thereabout. I had finally arrived I thought. I had gone from perpetual poverty, hunger and deprivation into a new social class. I twirled the car keys around my index finger practicing how to show off my status as a car owner. I climbed into the driver's seat and inserted the key into the ignition hole cranked it and shut it off. That was the extent of my experience about driving, but I was satisfied that I could crank it without let or hindrance; it was my own car. For the next fifteen to thirty minutes I was stuck in the car with nowhere to go but to check the minute details of the interior as I sat in the car lost in my own thoughts. I examined every inch of the interior of the car, from the sun visors to the seats and steering wheel to the center arm rest on the rear seat. It was the first car I saw that did not have a hump in the middle of the rear seat. What I did not know was that I had bought a front wheel drive car, the latest technology in automotive engineering. The lack of a hump at the rear fascinated me but I had no idea why it was different from other cars. As I sat daydreaming in the car I was woken from my reverie by a knock on the car. The intruder asked me whether I needed a driver. How did he know? I thought. That was what kept me rooted on the street across from the dealer's lot.

I sat up erect and answered affirmatively, that was exactly what I needed but I did not know how to find or go about finding a driver. He disappeared and returned after about fifteen minutes followed by a young man that I recognized as an employee at the dealership. I hired him as a driver-instructor. The terms were affordable and reasonable, he would drive me to the office in the morning and give me driving instruction after work.

I had my first driving instruction on the first day after my new driver-instructor finished with his work for the day. He enthusiastically praised me for buying a good car, though flattered I did not expect anything less. He could not bite the finger that fed him by speaking ill of the dealership. However I did not need his opinion to confirm what I could see with my own eyes. Before we took off on our first driving lesson he gave me a piece of advice or wisdom that in hindsight became my real driving instructor. He advised me to assume that all road users are insane and to expect the unexpected at all times. An insane person can dash across the road without looking; you have to look out for him. Look out for the insane driver who runs red light and flouts road signs. I was forced by circumstances to venture onto the open streets without my instructor the next day; that gem of wisdom was my driving instructor and kept me safely on the road until I became a proficient driver. Since that day I have imparted the same gem of wisdom to every new driver I have ever been associated with; whether family or friend. My driving instructor on the first day taught me how to take off and stop. I was thrilled with the first one hour driving instruction. I drove home with my instructor the first day and he duly picked me up the following morning for the office. After that I did not see him again until the next Monday morning when he showed up in my house, I fired him and dispensed with his services. I survived the weekend without him and I presumed that I could go on without him. I therefore had only about one hour of formal driving instruction before I took my fate into my hands.

My driver instructor gave me an hour driving lesson and we drove from the office to Pig Farm together. The following morning he picked me up promptly to the office as agreed. But he was no where to be found during the evening. My office hours were over by four o'clock and I waited for my driver for the next two to three hours. By six thirty the ministries were very quiet. I sat in my car alone at the office parking lot waiting for my instructor. I began to fret and when he did not show up after seven o'clock I gave up hope. At that time I knew I was on my own. I considered leaving the car at the parking lot and catching *trotro* home. That would have been the prudent and sensible thing to do. However before leaving for the lorry park I decided to attempt going over the previous day's driving lesson. I had the large parking lot all to myself, there were no moving traffic to pose any danger to me. I held my breath, started the car and slowly shifted the gear into first. Slowly I disengaged the clutch and the car began to move slowly without jerking or sputtering. I drove to the end of the parking lot without fully disengaging the clutch. At the end of the lot I was able to stop, make a U-turn and drive to the other end. After the first round I congratulated myself. I drove slowly up and down the large parking lot on just the first and second gears. After about the fourth round instead of parking the car as I had intended I decided to venture onto the dark quiet streets of Accra. The ministries area at that time of day was like a grave yard, my problem lay on the stretch of road through 37 Military Hospital and traffic circle.

Bravo! I congratulated myself when I was done practicing the previous night's lesson. I was ready to venture from the empty parking lot to the open road. I mentally mapped out the route to my home before I eased the car slowly into the thin night traffic. I drove slowly on first and second gears from the ministries through to the airport road. I drove past 37 Military Hospital and around the traffic circle turned westward towards Pig Farm. I breathed a big sigh of relief when I reached the gas station opposite my house that also served as the mini passenger van or *trotro* station. I reached home at about eighty-thirty to nine or thereabout. I nose parked on the street without attempting to drive through the gate of my house lest I bump into the gate. I was happy I drove home safely by myself; I did not want to take any more chances.

I was on my own over the weekend; the driving instructor did not show up either. I continued practicing the driving lessons solely by myself without the benefit and guidance of an instructor during the weekend. I even did the unthinkable for one learning to drive by himself without a driving instructor. I drove through the maddening traffic of Pig Farm through Accra New Town while under the influence of alcohol late Saturday afternoon. When I woke up sober on Sunday morning I was alarmed at my bravado. I got goose flesh when I reflected over the insanity of driving under the influence of alcohol along one of the busiest roads in Accra. I swore never to repeat the mistake again; drive under the influence.

I survived the weekend without the services of a driving instructor. I was therefore ready to take my fate into my own hands after the weekend. I preened like a peacock and fired my instructor when he showed up on Monday morning. I drove around the streets of Accra like a veteran for the next six to eight weeks until I obtained a driving license in February 1972. Boy, was I glad the day I was handed my driver's license. I have never parted company with my first driving license over these many years.

I had no idea of the extent of trouble I would encounter with my car. I did not know I was driving a car with the latest technology that the ordinary run of the mill mechanic was not conversant with. The front wheel drive was new and unfamiliar to most auto mechanics of Ghana in the early 1970's. The auto workshops located on vacant lots and along roadsides that most ordinary car owners relied on for repairs because of their low cost did not know about front wheel drive mechanisms to repair the car; I relied on the official dealers. The unfamiliar drive train coupled with the dearth of parts was the death knell of the car and the cause of my financial downfall. The gear lever or stick was connected to the gear box by three spring cables. The original connector gear cables gave me about four to six months of satisfactory service. It was all downhill when the original cables broke down. The shortages of spare parts did not exempt the dealerships, they never had any of the shifter cables in stock. I was therefore forced to supply the cables obtained from smugglers at exorbitant prices for installation by the dealers. The spring cables were not durable, they broke down after only a few weeks though I used to spend a fortune to buy and install them. .I was compelled to rely on the expensive labor charges of SCOA, the official dealership for want of a viable alternative. The labor rates of the dealership often exceeded by far the cost of the shift cables. But I continued to rely on them until I learned that some of their mechanics had their own workshops where they did repairs after hours and on weekends. From that point onwards I stopped going to the dealer's workshop. The mechanics provided me as competent a service as the official workshop but at cheaper labor cost or charges. I had low cost mechanics but the woes and durability of the parts were still the same. I had the same problem whether the cables were installed at the dealer's workshop or at the wayside workshop.

The main problem with the car was the shifter cables. I never had more than three weeks of satisfactory service from any set of cables. The three connector spring cables worked together; the gears could not be engaged or function if one of the cables was defective or broken. I used to scrimp and save for about three months to buy and install a set of cables. But each set of new cables that were installed gave me only about two to three weeks of driving satisfaction before I packed the car and began another round of scrimping and saving. Thus for a period of about twenty four months I worked for the car, my lifestyle revolved around the car. I used to starve and scrimp for about three months to save for installation of new gear cables but used the car for approximately two to three weeks. The cables never lasted any longer than three weeks maximum. It was therefore never on the road long enough to earn me the maintenance and mileage I counted on to defray the cost of running the car before I bought it.

The gear cables were the weak link with the car. The gears prevented me from enjoying the car and earning the maintenance and mileage allowance I had counted on before I bought the car. But I was wedded to the car and despite all the pain I could not let go. How could I let go? I was married to miss Ghana or the beautiful girl in the neighborhood, I did everything I could to satisfy my girlfriend. I willingly went hungry so that I could save to sink into her and all to no avail. The only joy I got from the car were two to three weeks every quarter, the rest of the time I grieved and starved. But I must confess those two to three weeks, when the car was on the road, were heavenly. They were what I lived for, I wished for more. I chased the mirage hoping that the next time she would give me more time, but that was never to be. The car for a period of about two years defined who I was and dictated how I lived, communicated and interacted with acquaintances, friends and loved ones. It was the bane of my existence, my heart ached but I could not let go. I starved and deprived myself of everything that made life worthwhile just to have the company of Austin. During the two years that I tried to please Austin the only luxury I allowed myself was two or three bottles of beer at the end of the month and a full meal, a meal that included gravy or soup, meat or fish. Otherwise for the rest of the month I subsisted on dry foods such as roasted plantain and peanuts. I never had the luxury of enjoying my pay unhindered for any one month without worrying about money for Austin so that I could sit in her laps for two or three weeks.

Despite the unending problems with the car I could not let it go, I was emotionally attached to it and my only problem with it was the gear shifter. Thus I was always optimistic that the next batch of cables would be more durable than the last but that never happened. I was drifting into insanity without knowing it.

If insanity is defined as doing the same thing over and over again and expecting different results, then I was definitely insane for about two years. I was insane because I sank every penny into a car that was roadworthy for only a few weeks at a time while I starved to make that happen. I was insane and addicted to the prestige and status of car ownership. I was so blinded with my obsession for the car I did not see the harm I did to myself both financially and physically. The cost of maintaining the Austin 1800 became a ruinous addiction I could not resist obliging when I had any money in my pocket, i.e., my monthly pay packet. I worked to pay the smugglers and the mechanic. I paid through my nose to feed my obsessive addiction; while every facet of my life deteriorated or disintegrated from neglect. I visited my car brooding eggs on the side of the road about once in a week while I scrounged for the money to buy and install new gear cables.

I strove to maintain the status symbol at all cost. I neglected my loved ones and avoided friends and relatives who might have talked some sense into me. I pinched my pennies to spend on the car while I neglected to pay my rent. My rent fell into arrears and it became difficult to pay the current rent together with the arrears. I could not, in all honesty, disclose to my loved ones or friends that my financial fortunes had taken a hit and was unraveling due to my obsession to keep and maintain a car. I went to college in a fanfare and I expected a great deal from myself. There was no way I could embellish or sugarcoat my financial meltdown to disguise or hide my failings or otherwise. As a result I cut everybody out of my life. I hoped that in time my financial situation would stabilize and improve to allow me to emerge from the shadows into the sunshine. But the problems only got worse.

I was a pathetic figure of my former self. The maintenance and mileage allowance I counted on to help me defray the cost of ownership never materialized. The car was never on the road long enough to justify the payment of maintenance or mileage allowance. The allowance could not be justified because I never used the car for work to earn the allowances. And I was my own worse enemy; I did not have good relations with my boss. If I had good relations with my boss he could have overlooked the problems with the car and allowed me to draw the allowances to help with the cost of repairs. Meanwhile, as a condition of the loan, I was forced to maintain a comprehensive insurance on the car even though it was off road most of the time.

MY FINANCIAL MISERY EXPOSED BY PICKPOCKET

After more than twenty four months of an uphill battle, I had enough and decided to surrender. I made up my mind to sell the car for whatever I could get for it and pay the proceeds to the government to reduce my debt load on the car. It dawned on me that my life would be better off without the car; I could be quite comfortable with the remnant of my monthly wages after deductions for the loan. I had regained my sanity or did I?

My determination to keep the appearance of success was the cause of my financial misery. Instead of riding to office comfortably in my own car, I rode in crowded mini passenger vans (*trotro*) to and from the office. It was punctuated for about three weeks every three months or so when I had brief satisfaction driving my car. Financial and material success eluded me as I clung to the shadow of a middle class life with all the attendant problems. I was on the verge of losing my room and only saved from homelessness by a prostitute that I picked up while drowning my sorrows in a bar at the end of the month.

I lost any semblance of self respect after the extent of my financial downfall was exposed at the *trotro* or mini passenger van station. One morning I attempted to board the minivan to the office, the one cedi fare was the only money I had to my name until the next pay day. As I hustled with other passengers to board the van in the morning rush hour, I kept a firm grip on my back pocket protecting the fare. I checked my pocket frequently to ensure the cedi fare was safe in my pocket before I took the van. I was afraid that if my pocket was picked I would be unable to pay the fare at the end of the journey. To save myself from such shame and embarrassment I could not let go of my back pocket. I was guarding myself from shame and the wrath of the driver mate if my pocket was picked. I carried no wallet for fear of pickpockets; I carried any currency notes in my back or shirt pocket. When the next van was ready I rushed with other passengers to board and before I climbed aboard the van I checked my back pocket again and just before I took a seat in the van I checked my pocket one last time before taking a seat. I froze up just before I sat down, the fare had mysteriously vanished from my back pocket between the time I boarded the van and just before I attempted to sit. The fare vanished before I could take a seat. Under the circumstance I had no choice but to get off. I started to make my way towards the entrance while other passengers were still struggling to board the van.

At this stage the driver's mate or assistant asked me whether I had lost something. I answered yes, inaudibly, ashamed to raise my voice lest I betray my pathetic financial position to the world. I told him in a quiet and feeble voice that my one cedi fare had vanished from my pocket. What I did not know was that as the mate stood watching the passengers getting into the van, he kept an eagle eye on the hangers-on who mingled with the rush hour passengers for the sole purpose of picking their pockets. I was an easy target because I kept a hold on my pocket as if I was carrying a ton of money. In one instant that it took me to remove my hand from my pocket to support myself into the van the pickpocket picked me and I never felt it. The driver's mate or assistant turned to a young man pretending to be hustling to board the van and asked him to return the money. When he hesitated in denial, the mate dipped his hand into his pocket and brought out my crumpled and miserable looking cedi note.

He then asked triumphantly, "Is this your money?" I whispered yes ashamed to raise my voice. The driver's mate returned my crumpled cedi note to me and after that he and the other weary passengers turned their frustrations and wrath against the poor man, he was beaten mercilessly. I could not bear to watch as he was being beaten by the crowd for stealing a cedi so I quietly slipped out of the scene. I walked to the office and from that day I never took another mini van or trotro to the office, I was too ashamed to show my face at the mini van passenger station again. I walked the eight miles round trip each day and never rode another *trotro* after my financial position improved. The silver lining in this episode was that I was forced by embarrassment and shame to walk to the office regularly shunning the mini vans and as I became used to walking I also appreciated the benefits of walking. I came to genuinely enjoy walking and I have never stopped walking since that morning in 1972-73.

SAVED FROM SHAME OF EVICTION

The love of my car put me in a financial bind. I was in danger of losing my room because I could not pay my rent. My landlord gave an eviction notice, pay up or get out. At the end of that month I went to the Moon night club located around the Nima traffic circle to drown my sorrows with a few bottles of beer. While I was going through my monthly binge drinking I wondered how to deal with the pending eviction. It is said that God works in mysterious ways his wonders to perform, I had fallen as low as I could and could fall no further. I prayed for God to have mercy on me for the first time and He did. He gave me another opportunity to start my life over. My help and salvation was right there at the night club with me snooping around for a client for the night. The woman of the night was the angel God sent to rescue me from imminent shame and homelessness. Her name was Florence. I shared some beer with her and before the night was over we were in bed together at her Nima home. I was her client for the night except that instead of taking her to my place I was at her home. I never left for another twelve months. I had very little worldly possessions when I moved in with Florence. I picked up my suitcase and the few clothes hanging on the door and window sill stuffed them into my suitcase and left. I left during the absence of my landlord, I walked away from my rent arrears. Florence was the answer to my prayers; she saved me from the disgrace of certain eviction from a cheap room and for the next twelve months gave me shelter. She lived in a slum, there was no running water or toilet in the house but I had a roof over my head.

Florence brought some measure of stability into my life; we became a two-income couple. Florence saved me from the starvation diet I had hitherto subsisted on. I ate home-cooked meals every evening, the kind I used to eat once or twice a month. That removed the need for lunch from my dietary needs; I ate one quality meal a day and an occasional snack for lunch. Florence gave me companionship and stability and, in a way, helped me to come to my senses. I was anchored in a home environment no matter how humble the home. Nima was the largest and worse slum in Accra with open sewers. In looking over the conditions of my life I was worse off as a college graduate than when I was a post primary or middle school trained teacher. The optimism I had including even denying myself the luxury of higher income on campus were all for naught. I was in a home that was worse than any home I had ever lived in since I left my village for Bogoso as a five year old. Though my life was very miserable I had no self pity, I blamed myself for everything that happened to me. To cope with the lack of toilet in the house I used toilet at work during the week and on weekends I made use of toilet facilities in bars and hotels. Despite all these shortcomings I was better off than before I met Florence.

I found a buyer finally for the Austin 1800 at a giveaway price of less than half the amount I paid for it a few months after I moved in with Florence. I had a brief period of lucidity and clarity of mind and intended to return the proceeds to the government to reduce my loan burden. But while I was walking from Nima to the office I came across a used car lot with a blue Alpha Romeo Spider 1600 on display. I do not know what came over me; I branched into the car lot to look at the cars on the lot. And just before I stepped off the lot I casually enquired about the price of the Alpha Romeo. Before I knew it I was driving out of the lot in the Alpha Romeo paid for with the proceeds of the Austin 1800 I had intended to return to the government.

I was not any wiser from my previous experience and I was setting up myself up for more misery. I drove out of the lot in a blue Alpha Romeo coupe with big smiles on my face. The Alpha Romeo was on the road for about one month, and I could have continued driving it for many more months. But the shiny blue coat of the car hid the defects behind the shiny paint job. When I cruised along the streets of Accra I was followed by a trail of smoke. I took the car to a workshop on my own volition for assessment of the causes of the smoke. The mechanic diagnosed the cause of the smoke as busted piston rings; he recommended an engine overhaul to replace the rings and seals. I should have walked away with my car but I did the unthinkable again.

I parted with money for the mechanic to buy the parts from Togo to overhaul the motor. I assumed that he was competent enough to overhaul the engine; Alpha Romeos have been on the roads of the country for a long time though their numbers were very few but I assumed that the mechanic was competent to do the repairs he recommended. My assumption was a big mistake.

The mechanic brought the parts from Togo and worked on the engine for a few weeks. Meanwhile when I looked under the carpets I found the floor was rotted. I engaged the services of a welder on the same lot with my mechanic to fix the rotted floor. I hoped that by the time all the works were completed, the bodyworks and the engine overhaul, I would have a strong and a serviceable car that I could enjoy for years. I used to stop by the workshop located along the Accra Overhead Bridge road at least once a day on my way home from the office. I used to walk along that route to and from work. The mechanic finished with the installations of the rings and seals after about four weeks and invited me to be at the workshop when he re-started the engine.

It was a great let down; the motor turned over when cranked but otherwise could not come to life. Thus began another three months of futility to fix the Alpha Romeo by parting with more money for every part that the mechanic required to complete the repairs and bring the engine back to life. I had travelled this road before and I thought I learned my lesson from the first experience but apparently I did not. However, I was circumspect the second time around. I was not as foolhardy as the first time, for I had a live-in girlfriend to support. That alone was enough for me to evaluate the money I was putting into the car. I stopped putting in more money and asked the mechanic to make do with the supply of parts he had bought over the prior three months. I watched him struggle several times to restart the engine without success. A new battery did not help, the engine cranked or turned over but otherwise never started. After several futile attempts my daily visits became weekly, then monthly and finally I forgot about the car altogether. The car was a total loss; I could not sell it for salvage value as that kind of market did not exist in Ghana. If it were on wheels I could have gotten some money for it but not while it sat on rocks.

The mechanic, it turned out had never worked on an Alpha Romeo car but assumed that as a mechanic he could work on any car. That might broadly be accurate but just as some of us have our idiosyncrasies and quirks some cars might also have their quirks and oddities; a knowledge of the oddities and quirks helps in servicing those cars satisfactorily. My mechanic did not know the quirks and oddities of Alpha Romeo cars and hence he could not restart the engine despite all his efforts. I paid the welder for his work but the car never got off the rocks on which it was placed for the welding.

At one time I considered towing the car to another workshop to try to salvage it but that would have continued to prolong my misery. I dismissed the idea quickly out of mind to save myself from more financial misery.

Thanks to Florence, the financial burden of trying to fix the Alpha Romeo was not as great as the Austin 1800. I wasted my hard earned money for about three months and gave up the fight and never looked back.

I abandoned the Alpha Romeo in the latter part of 1973 or early 1974. I reckoned that my life since I graduated from college was a total flop financially and socially. I failed miserably in every facet of my life. The only material property I hankered for as a status symbol became a mill stone around my neck that almost dragged me below the waters. Actually I felt liberated after I abandoned the Alpha Romeo and never looked back. I learned to live within the limits of the remnant of my income after deductions for the car loan and insurance coverage on a car that sat on rocks. I pinned all my hopes of ever driving another car on a scholarship or fellowship that would take me out of my country to a western country for at least one year. My hopes were realized when I won a scholarship to study in Australia around the middle of 1974.

I left for Australia in 1975. By the time I came back the loan was fully amortized through pay roll deductions over the five year term of the loan. I did not get any worthwhile benefit from the loan. The loan was a total bust; it was like a bad dream or nightmare that led me along a dark winding road into penury or servitude. Over the thirty to thirty six months that I theoretically owned a car I do not think I enjoyed the use of the car up to an aggregate of nine months. I did not get the maintenance and millage allowances that I had counted on to reduce the cost and the burden of maintaining a car. The car payments and repairs thus created a big black hole in my personal finances that turned me into a pauper for more than two years. My life was turned around in a positive direction after Florence took me in literally from the street.

BREAKUP WITH COLLEGE SWEETHEART

Nothing illustrates my financial unraveling and descent into insanity more than the circumstances that caused the breakup with Frances, my college sweetheart. I was quite a confident, proud and optimistic person with a sunny and can do attitude in life prior to my abysmal financial undoing. My personal and financial life became a quagmire shortly after I left college. I lost my confidence and sunny personality and became a nocturnal creature afraid of the sun. I secluded myself from familiar associates and friends because of shame and embarrassment. I was ashamed of my financial and personal debacles and afraid to bare my mind and soul to reveal my tortured personality. The person who bore the brunt of my personal failings the most was Frances. My life after college was worse than before college when I was a post middle school teacher working hard for a better life. Everything was rosy then. I stopped corresponding with Frances to create the illusion that I was too preoccupied with other things to write. But she bombarded me with letter after letter expressing her frustrations over my silence. I remained stoically silent. I did not write falsehoods and deliberate deceptions. I wished I could still write the sweet nothings I used to write while I was in college but those would be deceptions because my life was a mess. I hoped that my silence would frustrate her enough to stop writing and end my tortured misery. My plan eventually worked to perfection. She heard rumors that had no basis in reality but which nevertheless relieved me of guilt. In a society where rumors were part of how we got information about important and mundane things, she attached great importance to the rumor and responded to them. She heard that I was not corresponding with her because of anger over her dating activities at her school in Tamale. She vented her frustration about the rumor and asked me whether I could in all honesty deny dating in Accra. At the time I was overwhelmed with my personal and financial problems and struggled to keep my head above water. I was too ashamed to bare my soul to reveal my self inflicted financial wounds.

My wishes were thus handed to me on a silver platter. She had formed an opinion about my silence and I took no step to disabuse her mind about the rumor. The false rumor thus became the truth as she knew it. I bit my tongue and maintained my silence. I guess she took her frustration to an early marriage or may be it was the way our romance was meant to end. Her vented frustration confirmed that she had indeed betrayed my love. I did not reply to that letter either and made no attempts to tell her otherwise. I loved her, but my feeling of shame, embarrassment and inadequacy was more than I could bear. She was disappointed and I guess that affected her performance in her final year, she did not do as well as she could have done.

Ten years after we broke up we met in Accra, reconciled and became faithful friends. The old sparkle was still there but we had commitments we could not overcome. By then we had about eight or ten children between us. She was a divorced mother of five and I was a married father of four. We remained good friends until right up to the day she passed away in her sleep on Christmas Eve 2009. She went to her grave without ever knowing that I set her up for our relations to fail.

FLORENCE IN VOCATIONAL TRAINING SCHOOL

Florence and I had positive influence on each other. We brought stability into each other's life. While we lived together, she led a stable life in which she gave up the street life. We lived as a couple for about one year. At the end of twelve months I was ready to move on to begin life anew. I wanted to pick up the pieces and start life afresh as a single man and to try to get back some of the old sparkle of my life, optimism and sunny personality. I was very appreciative of the stability she brought into my life when she rescued or helped me when I was at the lowest ebb of my life. But I was not yet ready for permanent family life. The marriage experimental was over but I was in a bind because I did not have the heart to throw her away like an old rag doll.

Florence introduced me to her family and other relatives as her live-in boyfriend and was eager to hold on to that facade. I owed her a debt of gratitude and was prepared to help her put her life together without going back to the streets. If there was anything I could do to help her with life without me, I was prepared to do it as long as it was within my means. Fortunately I knew the principal of a women's vocational training school at Madina, a suburb of Accra. I sought and sponsored her for a catering course at the vocation school. I did not see her again from the day she entered into the boarding house of the vocation school though I remained her official guardian until she graduated from the school.

We never saw one another again. I maintained contact with her through the school for as long as she was a student at the school. I was her official guardian and I dutifully paid all her necessary expenses including pocket money. It was a three year training course and by the time she completed the course I was in Melbourne, Australia. I continued to support her while I was in Australia until she completed the training course. Her progress reports were sent to me in Australia. I do not know what became of her after she left the school but I hope she found peace and success after the vocational training.

I WAS MY WORSE ENEMY

I fell out with my boss within six months after I began working at the ministry of local government. I had a professional prejudice against him as such I did not see eye to eye with him about anything professional. It was akin to my first year as a teacher when I thought that my supervisors were old fashioned with colonial mentality. The fact was that my boss had no practical valuation or assessment experience. He had been working as an administrator from his inception at the ministry and had never done a single property assessment in his professional life. Thus I felt that he did not have enough practical professional experience to instruct or impart to me. I was fresh from college and had no professional experience; I was eager to have some relevant professional experience. I had interned with the lands department; but I could not build on that experience. I could therefore not accord him any professional respect whether he deserved it or not. I was contemptuous because he was not an associate of the Ghana Institution of Surveyors and thus a hindrance to my professional development and future prospects. I concluded that since he had no experience outside the narrow confines of administration at the ministry he could not help me in professional development. I was frustrated about my future professional prospects and I expressed my frustration by being disrespectful and impetuous towards him. And I paid a personal high price for my attitude and behavior towards the boss. Thanks to civil service rules and regulations he could not fire me but he could make my life miserable. And he did. My boss could have overlooked the long periods when my car was off road while I scrimped to save for parts and repairs and allowed me to draw maintenance allowance to help me with the repairs. As it was I drew very little maintenance allowance because the car was never on the road for up to a month continuous to justify the allowances. He had no reason to do me a favor, but for my big mouth and empty pride life could have been a bit easier during those desperate two years at the ministry. May be I would not have walked away from the Alpha Romeo if I could have earned maintenance allowance, I would have been encouraged to tow it to another mechanic. If I could only smooch or stroke his ego a little, my life could have been a bit more tolerable than it was and there was nobody to blame but myself. I was full of empty pride to kowtow to him to make life easier on myself. In my life nothing ever came easy without complications.

The ministry or department had professional development programs that were provided by western donors. The donors were predominantly British and Australian governments. The valuation or assessment division of the ministry was set up with the advice of an Australian expert so most of the fellowships were donated by Australia. I was the first in line for any fellowship award if one became available. But my attitude did not encourage my boss to ask the donors for any fellowship that would have benefited me considering that we were constantly at loggerheads. I needed a fellowship or scholarship so badly it was in the forefront of my mind even as I was at loggerheads with him. New graduates who were sent to the ministry by the public service commission also anticipated these fellowships for their professional development. I was financially strapped but I lacked humility to entice my boss to do his part by requesting donors for fellowships. I could not do that by myself, I did not have the credentials to act on behalf of the department without explicit permission from my boss. Due to the rancorous relations between us the other officers suffered the same fate like me. The number of fresh or new graduates sent to the department increased over time and they all had the same concerns, dim professional prospects. But they did not show open disdain or disrespect towards the boss as I did.

Because of the poisoned relations between the boss and me, I became a stumbling block against the pursuit or implementation of any staff development program through a fellowship or scholarship scheme. In the course of time my boss sought to bypass or sideline me legitimately without exhibiting hostility or bias. Thus in 1974 my boss found the best opportunity to neutralize my seniority. I was encouraged or rather pushed to compete for an open scholarship through the scholarship secretariat. The scholarships that were administered by the secretariat were open to the general public as opposed to departmental staff development programs that were limited to staff of the particular organization.

I was put in an awkward and untenable position. I saw the potential pitfalls of applying for an open scholarship with the general public and I did not like my prospects. In a society where influential people count a lot in such matters there was no guarantee that I could even make the shortlist of applicants invited for the interview. If I did not make the shortlist I could not compete for a place. And my boss could genuinely sideline me on the grounds that I had an opportunity and blew it. I considered that the odds were against me making the cut but nevertheless I submitted a completed application form that was approved or countersigned by my boss to give it an air of an official application to improve my chances of making the shortlist.

Luckily, I was shortlisted and invited for the interview before a panel of scholars. I impressed the panel enough to win one of the scholarship awards. And the award was more satisfying because I won it by my own efforts and I knew my fate long before the official results were released. The chairman of the panel was a dean of faculty from my former college; university of science and technology. The chairman was proud of my performance and conveyed the results to the head of the land economy department and some of my former lecturers. A chance encounter with some of them on the streets of Accra gave me the information that I won one of the places at the interview long before I was officially notified. The former lecturers who gave me the unofficial results also told me that the panel adjudged me as the best candidate. I was a disgruntled former student and that bit of information coming from some of the very lecturers who nearly derailed my graduation gave an air of 'I told you so'. The alleged result of the interview confirmed what I suspected, that I was indeed cheated out of a good final grade. The fears I had before the application process was laid to rest; I won a merit based scholarship instead of a department sponsored fellowship.

By October-November 1974, time had become my enemy. I could not wait to depart for Australia; I was in a hurry to leave my financial troubles behind. In February 1975, I left Accra by Ethiopian Airways through Durban, South Africa for Melbourne, Australia. My prayers for a respite from my financial woes were at last answered. The scholarship was godsend; I had the chance for a fresh start in life and hoped that by the time I returned to Accra my auto loan would have been fully amortized. And I would start over on a clean slate; debt free. I continued to draw my monthly wages in addition to any scholarship allowance while I was away. That enabled me to meet my responsibilities in Ghana. God gave me another opportunity to begin my life anew, and this time; I was determined not to mess it up. Australia, I hoped, would give me a second opportunity to believe in myself again.

FRESH START DOWNUNDER

My program of studies was not very demanding academically. I was not studying anything new as such except a few subjects. The nature of my studies considering my background was almost like a revision or refresher course. I have never been interested in an academic career and so a higher degree has never been on my radar screen. I would have pursued a higher degree if it was required by my profession. I therefore considered my program of studies as part of my professional development which when completed would qualify me for associate membership of the Australian Institute of Valuers. And by the time I returned to my country I would have earned designation from the Institute. There were two new subjects in my program that bothered me greatly in the first year, statistics and computer science. Without a good foundation in mathematics the two gave me a lot of headaches. I appreciated the Basic computer programming language that was introduced to me but it gave me no experience or any expertise in computers. The personal computer was not yet born or at least not widely available in 1975 Australia. I never saw a personal computer until I came to America. Since I did not have a rigorous and time consuming academic program; I had a lot of time to devote to my personal development.

Hand held calculators were also in their infancy. I bought my first electronic calculator to help me with statistics only to be told shortly before the exams that calculators would not be permitted at the examination. I bought my first hand held calculator specifically to help me with statistics in 1975. But I was very skeptical about the accuracy and reliability of the electronic calculator in 1975. My skepticism saved me from certain failure in the statistics examination when about a week or two before the examination we were warned that calculators would not be allowed in the examination. The skepticism about the reliability of calculators indirectly helped me to pass the statistics paper. Due to my ignorance and skepticism about the potentialities of calculators, I did not trust that my calculator was accurate and dependable so I used cross check the result of the calculator by working through every problem manually the old fashion way. I trusted my brains more than the calculator. The product of problem that was displayed within fractions of a second sometimes took me more than one hour to slog through it until I was satisfied with the results displayed almost instantly on the calculator. I studied statics along two tracks, with my manual brain power and a calculator. I solved the problems manually to satisfy myself that the calculator was dependable and reliable. The skepticism in the end was my savior in the statistics paper. Throughout the first year that I used an electronic calculator I never took the results for granted. These days I cannot even do a simple multiplication or additions without an electronic calculator. Had I trusted and taken the results of calculators for granted as presently I would have flunked the statistics paper when the calculators were disallowed at the last minute.

I scrapped through the computer science and statistics courses at the end of the year. I was very rusty at the beginning of the first semester in February 1975. And after I scrapped through the computer and statistics paper I began to get a bit more confident particularly after the computer and statics courses were out of my way. I was on familiar grounds after the two subjects were out of the way. I began devoting more time to my extra curricula activities and skipping classes from time to time.

I practically became a student in name only during most of the first semester of my third and final year. I skipped classes on the assumption that I could cram to pass any examination within two to three weeks. But I think I deluded myself. I failed the second appraisal course that semester. I was surprised that I failed and had the audacity to ask the head of department the reason for flunking the subject. I expected him to tell me where I did not do well so that I could put in more time in those subject areas. But after he examined my records he retorted 'you don't attend classes and you expect to pass'. I considered the flunking a blessing in disguise. I was not upset in the least other than bruising of my ego. It was an opportunity to extend my stay in Australia by at least another semester. The subject was not offered until the following year. That gave me enough time to hustle for money to acquire my dream toy, a reliable new or used car for Ghana. As a result of flunking one subject in a semester my graduation at RMIT was pushed back a year.

MY FIRST SUMMER DAY

I arrived in Melbourne at around two o'clock in the afternoon and by the time I was checked in at a small hotel in South Melbourne it was about four o'clock in the afternoon or thereabout. I was told that dinnertime was six o'clock and so I decided to take a nap until dinner time. I woke up at about six o'clock according to my watch but the sun said otherwise. I became confused and perplexed by the bright sunshine outside my window. This cannot be and I glanced at my watch again. I could not reconcile the time on my watch with the amount of sunlight; I concluded that my watch inexplicably went haywire while I slept. The sun cannot be that high in the sky at six o'clock in the evening I surmised, therefore my watch must be wrong. I could find no logical explanation for the apparent paradox because the sun cannot be wrong. I went back to bed for anther ninety minutes or so. But when I woke up I was nowhere near the solution of the paradox than when I woke up earlier. The sun was still shining brightly outside my window. I was more confused. My stomach was beginning to rumble so I went down to the dining room. The dining room was closed for the day. Dinner had been over for more than an hour and the kitchen staff was gone. It took a few days before the riddle of the sun was solved during my orientation. I arrived in the Australian summer. It did not occur to me that I was not in tropical Africa or Accra where the sun sets by six o'clock. Suffice to say I went to bed hungry on my first day in summer down under.

I went through a week of orientation during which I was taken through the basics of navigating Melbourne. By the end of the orientation I knew the whereabouts of my college, the public transport system, the busses and trams and how to move from point A to point B. I bought a street map. After the week of orientation I was cut loose by the relevant government department. I checked the local papers and found my first rental accommodation. I did not move far from the small hotel where I was housed on landing in Melbourne. My first housing experience was also my first experience of mixed living arrangements. I shared a house with three men and a woman. I assumed that I was being offered a room by a couple. But I had hardly settled down before I was given a weeks notice by the woman to find another place because she was relocating. I realized then that contrary to my assumptions all the men were subtenants of the woman.

It took about six weeks before I settled down in familiar surroundings, roomy house. I had accommodation with another woman in Carlton when I left South Melbourne. I guess I would have had ideas if I had not had one or two weeks of living in a mixed household. I would have had a dirty mind but I was more interested in learning about my new society from my new landlord than rifling through her pants. I guess the three months before I settled in a roomy house where I was comfortable was part of my education and introduction into the Australian society by the divine. If I had lurid thoughts towards my landlady I would have had to compete with her dog for her attention. I heard anecdotes while in Ghana about the pet loving nature of the white man, those anecdotes came alive before me in Melbourne. My landlady was a dog lover who had a large dog. I had no idea of breeds of dogs at the time but it was a very large dog. My landlord was a kind hearted woman who used to share her meals with me. But I did not like the meals she shared with me as much as the one she fed her dog. My landlady used to feed her dog with fresh cuts of parts of meats that used to make my mouth water. She did not feed her dog with canned or dry dog foods, she fed her dog with fresh meats that I would never have given to a dog. The parts she fed her dog were the preferred parts of meats that most Ghanaians bought for food. These were the bone-in parts of animals sold in our markets. I used to salivate as I watched her feed her dog with shanks of sheep, feet, tripe, head and other bone-in meats. I would have taken the bone-in meats to the boneless steaks she shared with me. I had not yet started preparing my own meals and relied on the generosity of my landlord for food. I learned from her that the meats she fed her dog were sold in pet food stores and not at regular butcher's shops. She got her supplies from pet food stalls at Victoria market, a kind of farmers market. I could not wait to move out of her house to start preparing my own meals with the cheap meats from pet food shops. This was a cultural difference between my landlord and me. I preferred bone-in meats while she preferred boneless meats. My preferred meats were her dog food. I would have liked to chew on the bones, suck up the marrow and finally throw the spent bone to the dog. I would have loved to share the meats she bought for her dog instead of the boneless steaks and vegetables she shared with me.

During my third month in Melbourne I moved to a roomy house. I do not know exactly what prompted me to leave the home of my first benefactor but I guess I was anxious to be on my own. I was more comfortable in the roomy house setting than with with my previous landlord. She rented me a room in her house but otherwise I could do nothing on my own. With the roomy house I was on familiar ground, it was practically the only type of housing I was familiar with. I was comfortable sharing a kitchen and bath with others than sharing a whole house but without the freedom to the kitchen as I pleased. I wasted no time before I went to Victoria Market to survey the pet food stalls. I was mildly surprised, to say the least, about the varieties of tropical foods on sale at the market. Most of the familiar food items I could buy in any market in Ghana were available at Victoria market. The farmers market became the only place where I bought all my groceries. The pet food stores provided me with all the meats I needed for food. I progressed from buying meats from pet food stores to banding together with other African students to buy goats or sheep directly from farmers. The farmers slaughtered, dressed and cut up the animals as we desired. In this way we got every part of the goat or sheep we wanted including the intestines, head and feet. We bought matured sheep or mutton instead of lambs.

HYPNOTIZED BY MATERIAL ABUNDANCE

When I left Ghana in February 1975 for Australia I was happy to leave behind a society where every conceivable commodity was in short supply. The lines for commodities were endemic and influence peddling was part of our commercial landscape. I was amazed, to say the least, on the abundance of every conceivable commodity or merchandise stocked in all types of shops. I was used to pleading with merchants or standing in line to buy a few items of a commodity. But in Melbourne I was practically lost amidst the display of prosperity and abundance of every conceivable merchandise in the stores. I used to wonder whether the merchants were able to keep track of the uncountable items in their shops. I was lost amidst the plethora of material goods. As far as I am concerned globalization has been in full swing since the seventies. I became a discriminating or discerning consumer in Melbourne. In Ghana I did not have the luxury of choice; I bought whatever was available that I could lay hands on to meet my needs. I came of age at the time when black market in consumables was taking shape and the shops were already experiencing shortages. Discriminating or selection was a luxury I did not know before I went to Australia. In Australia I learned value shopping, but mostly I shopped from the discount shops that carried merchandise from Asian countries. My favorite shops were K-mart, Woolworths, Coles and Target.

And when I had money burning a hole in my pocket I shopped at Myers basement for discounted merchandise with made in a western country labels. My value selection was based on known labels from my youth, thus designer merchandise meant that they had say made in USA, England or Germany etc. on them.

I was overwhelmed and lost in the sea of abundance of material prosperity. Nothing I ever read or heard about prosperity in western countries did justice to the real thing when I landed in the midst of a prosperous western country. I guess I was overwhelmed because of where I came from, not my country, but my personal journey through life. I was thrown into a wonderland or dreamland. Everything I could dream off or conceive of was available in super abundance, nothing was left to the imaginations, the only limitation was money. In my country of origin I could have the money but unable to lay hands on what I wanted. But nothing intrigued me more than liquor shops. I had never heard or read about stores dedicated solely for sale of booze that were not drinking bars. Alcoholic beverages were part of general merchandise from where I came. Liquor shops seized my imagination. At the time I landed in Australia I had been off alcohol for over one year. But I was hypnotized by liquor shops with their arrays of bottles and packages in display windows. I could not resist the temptation to sample the fanciful packages of wines in those display windows. I was not very familiar with wine so I was eager to break my self imposed abstinence. It was only a matter of time before I ended my abstinence. I was not a fan of hard liquor and I did not fancy beer. I was already familiar with the taste of lager and pilsner beers. My interest in wines was piqued by the unknown-wine. Thus the curiosity of the unknown was the driving force behind my eagerness to taste or try wine. I itched for the taste of wine but my conscience still bothered me about breaking my abstinence. I waited for the excuse or an opportunity to drink without guilt. That opportunity came within two weeks of moving to a roomy house and I lost the inhibition of disturbing or inconveniencing my landlord. I was invited to my first student party.

I went to my first student party and was plugged into the Australian society. The student who drove me to that first party clutched a bottle of wine and encouraged me to do likewise. It was a 'bring your own grog' party. Every patron brought his grog or alcoholic beverage to the party. All the bottles were assembled on a table and each person could drink from any bottle on the table. One was not limited to the bottle of wine or beverage he contributed for the party. The organizer provided small items such as ice and peanuts. I tasted wine and that first glass of wine in over a year had the same magical effect on me as the first glass of beer I drank as a sixteen or seventeen year old young man. The glass of wine loosened my tongue, made me garrulous and I think good company. By the time the night was over I had made friends and went home with the names and telephone numbers of some of the female students at the party. I was ready to date a white woman for the first time. The party was literally my introduction to the social life of Melbourne. By Australian standards, I was an old man among young boys and girls. I was over thirty years old and most of the students were in their late teens or early twenties. But age difference was not a barrier to building friendships of both sexes. The race factor made it impossible for me to make reasonable guesses about the age of my young friends and neither could they make reasonable guesses about my age. The female students were not particularly discreet about their ages thus to avoid the appearance of cavorting with underage girls I did not shy from asking about the ages of my dance partners at parties, I never knew when a casual dance partner could become a date.

I was anxious to go out with some of the women I met at the party but I was also apprehensive about arousing the jealousy of their escorts. I discussed my dilemma with a Malay friend at college. Mr. Leong, who had lived in Australia for many years, was literally my tutor on the mores of the Australian society. I was freed from all fears and guilt by the time I appeared at the next party. Thanks to the magic of alcohol I was uninhibited in my relations; I necked and smooched openly at the party. I accepted an invitation from my first date to her place. I was in tune with the youths of Australia and I played along without inhibitions of race or age except going out with the underage. But from my very first interaction with the youth I was interested or eager to exorcise the fear that had haunted me for almost twenty five years, when I was unnerved at the sight of a white man and failed my catechism test in grade three.

I lost my first date within a short time for no apparent reason. I thought I had done something so heinous she dumped me. But I learned sooner than later that it was part of the dating scene among the youth. The loyalty of ones date could not be taken for granted. But by the time I was dumped by my first date I had exorcised the fear of the White Father that had haunted me since the third grade. My first date was a learning experience. By the end of my evening I had been closer to a white body at less than three feet, the approximate distance between me and the White Father who gave me the catechism test for baptism. I had never been any closer to a white person since the third grade. I overcame my childhood fears and jitters forever; I concluded after getting to a white person that my childhood fears were unwarranted and were borne of ignorance. But I have never forgotten the chill that went down my spine when I stared at the green eyes of the White-father who sat in front of me that Saturday afternoon. I also discovered that age had not changed me that much. I still used alcohol as a crutch to get into the good graces of the opposite sex.

Alcohol or wine gave me courage, made me less self conscious and helped me to craft an image of an outgoing person at social functions. I jumped into the *BYOG*, bring your own grog, culture and until I settled on my own favorite wine I never went out twice with the same brand of wine under my armpits. The weekend parties served two purposes in my life. The parties were the venues where I interacted with the Australian youths and met my dates. Without the parties it would have been very difficult for me to date in the open since I was often sober and rather timid in the open. Secondly I satisfied my curiosity about wines through the parties. I knew next to nothing about wines, I bought wines based on the price and the fancy packaging. For instance I was initially fascinated by the taps on large casks of wine and bought them for their novelty.

I was cheap and used my cheapness to my advantage when I dated. I discovered that dating revolved around food and drink. I am not accustomed to eating out in restaurants and I watched my pennies so I made African cuisine my calling card for dating. And it worked every time because the youths were open minded and willing to try new cuisines. I invited friends and dates to experience African cuisine or dishes prepared by me. I prepared the meals with bone-in meats I bought from pet food stores so as to provide what I considered as an authentic Ghanaian dish. My Australian companions that I invited for dinner at my house came with bottles of wine though I often asked them to dispense with that formality. I was eager to show the cultural differences between the Australian and the Ghanaian. As a Ghanaian I did not expect my guests to contribute for my hospitality. I hosted my companions and friends as a typical Ghanaian; I provided the food and drinks and expected my guests to drink, eat and have fun at my expense. But I did not turn down any contribution. I was happy to spread the culture and traditions of Ghana.

On The Verge Of Alcoholism

My social life was dependent on alcohol. I had no life without alcohol. I had satisfied my curiosity for wine but in the process I had become dependent on it to spice up my social life. The consumption of wine at weekends gradually degenerated into drinking on most evenings after classes. I drank wine with or without friends for about the next four months. I drank wine with enthusiasm as if I was making up for loss time, for the many months I abstained from alcohol. I found excuses galore to drink and every social event was an excuse to imbibe wine. I met a Ghanaian couple in Australia, Chris and David, who had been in the country for about three years before I arrived. They used to provide me information on parties and gave me rides to the parties. They were thus my source and chaperons to parties at weekends. But they began expressing concerns about my drinking habits when they observed the increasing amounts of alcoholic beverages I could consume at a sitting. I was a shy and bashful person and alcohol gave me Dutch courage and made me appear to be fun and jovial than I really was; I mingled without being self conscious and made friends with ease while under the influence. But without alcohol I was a wimp. I was gregarious and talkative but inclined to be reticent when sober.

After about four months of making hay with wine I was ready to get off the alcohol bandwagon. I dated my first girl while under the influence of alcohol and drank my last glass of wine with a date. The sister of my last date just before I went off the alcohol bandwagon gave me a headache I should have relished. The younger sister of Joanne, my girlfriend, courted me openly or at least tried to go out with me. I found the proposal flattering but I had two inhibitions. She was sixteen and I was afraid of statutory rape. There were widespread rumors swirling in the Gold Coast in the 1950's that one of our illustrious sons was jailed in Britain for statutory rape, he was alleged to have gone to bed with a willing sixteen year old girl. Although I never read or saw it in print during my infancy; I never forgot the story. And thus when I found myself in a western country, the rumor about statutory rape of long ago was my guide. Secondly it was against my tribal morality to sleep with two sisters. It is quite common for a younger sibling to be infatuated with the date of an older sibling. But infatuation should not become an open proposal. I was therefore very suspicious of her true intent. Was she trying to set me up for a fall? I wondered. As an expression of my love for Joanne I informed her about her younger sister's conversation with me. Surprisingly she gave me the green light if I was interested. I declined to take the bait on the ground that it was against my cultural morals. It is considered a taboo for a man to go to bed with two sisters in my tribe and I honored my cultural tradition. This incident took place at about the time I was thinking about quitting or abstaining from alcoholic drinks. I wondered whether the teenager liked the bashful and timid me or the pretentious me. In any case I concluded it was time to put the pretence aside and be me, quiet, shy, timid and concentrate on my yoga practice.

When I picked up my first bottle of wine, it was easier to indulge my new habit without straying far from home. There was a liquor store at the corner of the street from my home. I visited the shop once or twice a week for a big bottle of wine. I preferred the liter size bottles because I finished one in about two days or more. By the third month I could finish a liter bottle in one afternoon between the time I returned from school and went to bed at night. For about the first few weeks I sought for the best agreeable wine with my palate. As such I did not buy the same wine twice until my preference settled on sherry as the most palatable wine for my palate. Sherry is higher in alcohol content but sweeter than most. For some inexplicable reason I found that I could tolerate wine better than beer. And as the days passed, my capacity or tolerance for wine increased. Despite my capacity or tolerance for wine consumption, one thing was patently clear to me; my joints were stiff in the morning. I was into the practice of yoga and the stiff joints were a hindrance to my progress. It was incongruous to practice yoga every morning while consuming a lot of alcohol. The dichotomy was not lost on me. I gritted my teeth to limber up every morning because I used to drink myself to bed. I reasoned that if I had enough will power to go through the postures in the mornings despite my stiff joints then I could summon the same will power to return to my state of abstinence before I came to Australia. Also anytime I drank a glass of wine I sought for cigarettes, I could not drink a glass of wine without triggering the urge to smoke. So over the three to four months that my capacity and tolerance for alcohol was increasing the number of cigarettes I smoked was also going up. I was getting addicted to a deadly combination of toxins at the same time. Twin habits I did not have before I came to Australia. Was my nascent addiction due to the euphoria of being hypnotized by a prosperous society or hidden desires that were kept under wraps due to my financial condition? My smoking was also exacerbated by the fact that cigarettes are sold only by the pack. In Ghana I bought one or two cigarettes when I felt for a smoke, in Australia, like all western countries, cigarettes are sold by the pack, so as long as I smoked I bought cigarettes by the pack of twenty at a time.

I had become an unwitting victim of material abundance in my new society. I was in danger of losing my self control over alcohol and tobacco. I smoked when I drank, thus to control smoking I had to curtail alcohol consumption.

One thing that I found common to both Australian and Ghanaian youth was the smoking of marijuana or hashish. I tried marijuana twice, the first time in 1965 and the second time in 1970. I did not like the effect it had on me and so I never tried marijuana again. And I was determined to let it stay that way. Marijuana or hashish smoking was an integral part of any social gathering of the youth. Parties often started with dancing, wine and beer drinking and by midnight the dance floor began thinning out and the patrons gathered in small groups at different areas of the party venue, usually a house. This was literally a break for hashish as part of the party ritual. The members in the group began with lively chitchats among themselves and eventually the hashish was wrapped lit and passed around from one person to the other. This continued until about three to four joints has been smoked. And then everybody in the group fell silent in a sort of dream or hypnotic stupor, each person lost in his own thoughts. That was the aspect of marijuana I never understood. On the two occasions that I smoked marijuana my stomach churned and I spat out thick sputum. I could not sleep while the effects lasted. But when the party patrons finished smoking the marijuana the fun of the party died. Although we still hung around till dawn but the energy and vigor of the party was never the same after marijuana breaks. I have never understood the allure of marijuana but the breaks created the perfect atmosphere for necking and smooching in dark alleys and empty rooms around the venue, most party goers after the marijuana were too drowsy to be bothered. Poaching another's date was easier when the date was drowsy under the influence of marijuana.

After four months of swilling alcohol almost every day I found the courage to try to become abstinent once more. Thus in the first week of July 1975 I took my first tentative step towards the goal of abstinence and stopped drinking and smoking cold turkey.

How I Overcame My Addiction

Around the middle of June 1975 I began flirting with the idea of abstinence from wine or alcohol consumption to ease the pain from stiff joints when I did yoga exercises in the mornings. I also wanted to assure myself that I still had what it took to be a man, self control; I learned long ago that "a man is not a man until he can control himself".

I decided to inform Joanne, my girlfriend, at dinner on the day I intended to go off the alcohol bandwagon. I did not know how she would take it or whether it would affect our relationship. So far our relations revolved around alcohol, smoke and sex. That weekend instead of having dinner at home as usual we went to a cabaret show at the Melbourne Hilton, one of the few times that I dined in a restaurant. At the end of an enjoyable night, I disclosed to Joanne my decision to turn over a new leaf and try life of abstinence without alcohol and take control over my life. "This was my last glass of wine, from now onwards I am done with wine and cigarettes", I concluded. She in turn informed me she had been contemplating about breaking up with me and this was perhaps the best time for us to call it quits. The setting was just right for both of us to go our separate ways amicably. We held each others hands as if we were afraid to let go. Joanne drove me to my house and disappeared into the starry night and that was the last time I saw her. I still have fond memories of her and she is still one of the few individuals from my past whose full name I can still recall but not that of her teenage sister.

The breakup was a blessing in disguise for while I struggled to abstain from alcohol and tobacco, maintaining my self discipline would have been almost impossible had Joanne dropped in on me while I was struggling with my inner demons to stay off the alcohol bandwagon. I never set eyes on Joanne and her little sister again after I started frequenting the old party venues till the day I left Australia.

Over the next three months I became a recluse, I secluded myself from all social activities except school. I had no telephone so I contacted no one and vice versa. I disappeared from the face of the earth; I avoided my acquaintances, friends and the weekend party circuits where I was most likely to face temptations of alcohol and tobacco. Adopting a hermit like lifestyle was necessary while I struggled to deal with my addiction. Returning to the flow of things would have exposed me to the temptations when I was still very vulnerable. Hiding from social activities other than school was therefore necessary to minimize the temptations of coming face to face with my vulnerabilities, alcohol and smoke. I fought very hard just to stay in my room after school and on weekends without being tempted to walk to the corner for a bottle of wine or across the street for a pack of cigarettes from the deli. My home was within a block of a liquor store and a deli located diagonally across the street from my home. The proximity to the shops magnified the difficulties of maintaining self control and will power to stay away from alcohol and cigarettes.

I fought myself constantly during the first four weeks of abstinence from wine and smoke. I used to crave for a glass of wine at about the time I used to come from school and drank myself silly in my room. But I bit my tongue and resisted the temptation to walk across the street for a pack or the liquor shop at the street corner for a bottle of wine. I drank for only about four months since I came to Australia but this addiction was more difficult to kick off than when I was in Ghana. In Ghana I could not afford to drink beer everyday, I used to binge drink for a few days after every payday or whenever I came by some money. But in Australia I could afford wine and cigarettes from my allowance without being affected financially. The affordability helped to turn me into an addict within four months. The determination to free myself from alcohol and tobacco began to bear fruit by the third week. My cravings for wine began to taper off and I began to be freed from the grip of alcohol on my imagination.

243

Surprisingly by the end of the fifth week the cravings for alcohol had almost gone away, but the urge to light up seemed to grow stronger with each passing day. I won my battle with alcohol after approximately six to eight weeks but the war with tobacco was not that easy to conquer. The urge to smoke remained quite intense after the urge for alcohol subsided. About twice a day over a period of approximately four to six weeks I fought the temptation to walk across the street to the deli for a pack of cigarettes. On several occasions the craving for a smoke was so strong that I went out of the house and walked to the deli across the street for a pack. But my good angels always pulled me back at the last minute just before I stepped into the deli. While I stopped short at the entrance of the deli I could not turn around and go back home. I remained standing at the entrance and gazing lustfully at the rows of cigarettes in the deli. One part of me would urge me to just walk in and get a pack while another part of me would urge me to go back home. I used to walk up and down the street between the deli and my roomy house like a mad man while two factions within me urged me to either indulge my cravings or be a man and take control of my life. The warring factions within me were silenced after I plucked some courage and disgust with myself, entered my room and stoically stayed there uneasily till the next day when the war within started all over again on my return from school. I kept going through this wacky routine of marching to and fro between my house and the deli for about another two to four weeks. The day I came from school and was not tempted to walk to the deli was the day I practically won my battle over tobacco and began to take control of my life. My better angel always won out throughout this period against my demons. I never entered the deli; I always pulled back at the last minute before the final step. Sometimes I felt disgusted with myself as I walked like a crazy person back and forth between my house and the deli, almost spell bound by my desire for smoke.

Two and half months after I started the fight for self control to abstain from alcohol and nicotine I was finally at peace with my self. I was not dragged out of the house to march across the street reluctantly again. But I was not confident that I could withstand temptation when exposed to it. My better angels always pulled me back at the last minute to prevent me from succumbing to the temptation but it would be a different story if I was in an enclosed atmosphere where wines and smokes flowed freely. I therefore continued to keep myself away from my former friends and associates for about another two months or so before I took the first step to reenter the youthful world of parties, wines, cigarettes and marijuana.

I gingerly reentered the lions den of wine and tobacco at the end of October 1975. I was confident that I had overcome my twin addictions of alcohol and tobacco, I could withstand any temptations that came my way except that I never counted on the attitude of those who knew me only as an alcohol dependent pretender. I assumed that my old friends and associates would welcome me back into their fold. I couldn't have been more wrong. Initially I was enthusiastically welcomed until they found that

I did not touch another glass or cigarette. Suddenly I was an anathema to most of my old friends and associates before I went off the party circuits. I was avoided like the plague when I tried to mingle with my old acquaintances and buddies. I had no idea why they kept shifting their positions when I got closer to them. I used to be part of the informal groups that formed midway through the night at parties for marijuana breaks and chitchats. I was tolerated among them despite not participating in marijuana or hashish smokes with them. When the joint got to me I passed it on without a drag. But when I returned from my seclusion I could not find a group of boys willing to let me into their midst. Whichever group I tried to associate with literally dissolved before my eyes and left me sitting alone. When the group dissolved they reassembled a few feet away just that I was not part of the new gathering. I put on airs when I came back and tried very hard to fit in. I acted with some bravado as if I was still on the bottle, but I could not persuade the boys that I was still the same person. The girls were more forward looking but when the groups moved they moved along with them. The boys saw through my pretence. The strange thing was that the girls I used to know virtually disappeared from the face of the earth; I never saw one at any party until I moved away from the scenes.

The old familiar faces avoided me like the plague. I was flummoxed by the attitude of my known buddies and I could not explain their weird attitude towards me. I was a pariah for two consecutive weekends before I had the courage to confront some of them for answers about their new attitude towards me. I was surprised when I learned why I was given the cold shoulder. It was alleged that I was too clean for them to be around me. "You are too clean for us to be with you"; was the curt but short answer. "What do you mean?" I asked. "You do not drink, you do not smoke, we do not have anything in common with you anymore. We feel dirty when we are around you."

I became a persona non grata because I gave up my addictive bad habits. I never expected to be ostracized for overcoming bad habits. I never anticipated this problem and was not mentally ready when it hit me. I grasped at straws looking for answers. The best answer I could come up with was to placate my friends and take up smoking again. I regarded smoking the lesser of the two evils. But that was not good enough; I remained a pariah to my old buddies and I was not prepared to become my old self to patch up relations. I was under the mistaken impression that since I did not consume any alcohol I could quit smoking at will. I became a light smoker, smoking only about three to five cigarettes a day. But my addiction to nicotine caught fire again much to my surprise. I became addicted to nicotine despite smoking less than half the amount of my previous habit. Contrary to my expectations, I could not quit the nicotine habit when I attempted to do so. It was more difficult to quit the second time than the first. This time I struggled with the addiction for over five years before I was able to find the courage and will to quit again for good.

FRATERNITY WITH THE GAY COMMUNITY

It was during this confusing and turbulent period of my life that I met Elizabeth, a young and beautiful woman at a weekend party. She was a breath of fresh air; she neither drank nor smoked, we made quite good company together. She did not feel dirty to be around me. I hitched my wagon to her's and she introduced me to another world; that was different from the narrow world of student parties, alcohol and tobacco. Elizabeth introduced me to a world I did not know existed, the gay community in Melbourne. We went to a night club one weekend instead of the usual student parties and gatherings. This nightclub was unlike any club I had ever seen, men danced and smooched men and the women smooched women. I was bewildered and perplexed; I had never seen such a spectacle before. When we were students we used to dance bone-to-bone because there were not enough girls or women to go around. But I had no experience of any situation where the sexes kept to themselves and smooched each other. I was confused at the spectacle particularly since they all appeared so deliriously happy and danced with joyous abandon. A man enthusiastically tried to embrace or drag me onto the dance floor but I instinctively pulled away from him as I had my own partner. And although Elizabeth danced with me at the club we were the odd couple at the nightclub.

I was confused and perplexed with the nightclub scene. I did not understand the peculiar scene. It was contrary to everything I knew about bars, clubs and interactions between men and women. The problem was that there were no interactions between the sexes. I stood with screwy eyes surveying the spectacle. I was saved from further confusion by Elizabeth who took me to the club. Elizabeth and I were the odd couple that night but I enjoyed myself because I did not realize the oddity of the situation. It did not occur to me that we were an odd pair at the club. The men who wanted to dance with me respected my resistance and left me alone. I did not know on which planet I was that night. I mingled and chatted with both the men and women at the club and at the end of the night was not any closer to understanding the nature of the club. The club members drank hard, danced hard and smoked profusely, everything at the club went overboard but I loved the unconventional company.

I had so much fun at the club that the following week I tried to go back to the club, but I was refused entry. I did not know why I was not allowed entry; I concluded that the club must be a private club that was not open to the general public. My escort must therefore be a member of the club. The following week I was able to get into the club with Elizabeth; I went to the club several times with her but was never allowed in without her. Despite the odd situation I still did not know I was among queers for several weeks until I deduced that the men were homosexuals, but I did not know what to make of the women. I was aware of male homosexuals but I had never heard of the female counterpart or equivalent. As of 1975-76 I had not yet heard the word lesbian and did not know they existed until I came to New York in the eighties.

I felt like a fish out of water on my first night at the club. The world I knew was turned on its head or turned upside down. I do not know whether Elizabeth realized my ignorance and naivety, she never discussed or explained the queer and unconventional club atmosphere to me. But over time I came to the conclusion that the men were homosexuals but I did not know what to make of the women. I made friends with some of the men and they used to drive me around the homosexual club scenes. I never associated Elizabeth with my homosexual companions though I got to know them through her; she was heterosexual as far as I was concerned. I had no reason to think otherwise though she shared a studio apartment with another woman and I slept in the same room with the two women.

I enjoyed the company of the male homosexuals. I never understood why women at the club would not even glance at me let alone dance with me but they were friendly and easy to talk to. After I came to USA and became familiar with lesbians then I rationalized that Elizabeth must have been bisexual because of the type of nightclub doors she opened for me. For the period that we dated and was introduced to the gay scene in Melbourne it never occurred to me that she was anything other than heterosexual.

In Ghana homosexuals existed in the shadows. And most often we used to associate homosexuals with white men. When a white man was fond of the company of boys or men he was often rumored to be a homosexual. Black homosexuals like the one who molested me during infancy, existed in the shadows and masked their orientation by conforming to the mores of the society. They pretended to be heterosexual and one would never know their sexual orientation by their lifestyles or the company they kept. It is not unusual or a sign or indication of sexual orientation for young men and women to hold hands on the streets. I had a rude awakening on the connotation of holding hands with a man when I attempted to hold hands with Mr. Leong on RMIT campus in Melbourne.

I found the company of homosexuals in Melbourne very exciting. I built a cadre of homosexual friends with whom I hobnobbed at weekends bar-hopping from one neighborhood to another. I was gratified that it never bothered them that I was straight. I was a heterosexual in their midst and furthermore it did not bother them that I did not drink any alcohol or smoke marijuana. My gay companions drank, smoked cigarettes and pot, but they accepted my nonconformity without more. I found their company rather refreshing. The gay community in Melbourne was more open-minded than my straight friends.

My association with the gay community of Melbourne in the mid 1970's influenced my attitude towards homosexuals in New York during the heady days of the AIDS epidemic in the ninety's. During that period I was a housing inspector of the city of New York. Housing inspectors used to work in pairs in some communities or neighborhoods of city of New York. It was common for warning notices to be posted on the vestibules, doors and floors of houses where an aids victim was housed. When we were sent out to inspect houses for code violations in which such notices were posted some of my work colleagues used to be scared to enter into such a house. But owing to my former association with gays in Melbourne I did not have such qualms, particularly when the disease was said to spread through exchange of fluids. The victims I came into contact with were often ostracized by their landlords and society. Some of the landlords I guess took steps that were perhaps meant to hasten the death of the victims. Utilities were often cut off to their apartments or rooms and needed repairs were often ignored. I was not afraid to enter into the presence of aids victims. Indeed on a number of occasions I sat beside the victim lying helpless on a bed. I saw the victims in the eyes of the gay men I roamed around the streets and night clubs of Melbourne in the 1970's.

QUIT SMOKING FOR GOOD

Over the next several years I fought many losing battles to quit smoking the second time. From the latter part of 1975 when I resumed smoking, I gave up smoking umpteen times but relapsed each time. I could not find the same will power that enabled to stop drinking and smoking on the same day in July 1975. On several occasions I psyched myself for inspiration by crushing a pack of cigarettes and throwing it into the garbage bin only to dive back into the bin an hour or so later to salvage some of the crushed cigarettes. And I never succeeded in going for more than one day without smoking at least one or two cigarettes. I do not know whether it is in the nature of addiction; I found several excuses to continue indulging my addiction. My chief excuse for my indulgence was that I smoked only a few cigarettes per day and that was not that bad. But whatever justification I gave for smoking, I did not like or enjoy the habit, it was not fun and yet I could not resist the allure of smoke.

I hated the taste of nicotine in my mouth so much so that I could not smoke without a gum or mint candy in my mouth and yet all my attempts to quit the habit always ended in failure. I did not have the same willpower or incentives of my youthful years when I could stop drinking while going around the bars with my drinking buddies. As the years rolled by I lost some of the powers of will that enabled me to avoid becoming a youthful alcohol addict and the older I grew the more difficult it became to summon willpower.

I returned to Ghana for good in September 1979. By then I had not touched another bottle or glass of wine for over four years. The economic condition of the country was worse than when I left. The queues for consumer goods were longer than before. Some goods were rationed or distributed through our workplaces to ensure that ordinary workers with no powerful and influential friends or relatives in the corridors of power were not priced out of the market for essential consumer commodities. The endemic shortages and the queues for consumer goods gave me the impetus and will power to quit smoking.

I found it absurd that I had to stand in line to buy life sustaining food items and also stand in line to buy cigarettes that are hazardous to my health did not make sense. This was the catalyst or inspiration that I needed to summon enough willpower to stop flirting with the cancer sticks. Due to the constant shortages we were often tempted to buy commodities in bulk whenever possible. I therefore resolved that my next bulk purchase of cigarettes would be the last cigarettes I ever bought.

About two weeks after my resolution I purchased a carton of cigarettes from the stock that was distributed at my workplace. The carton gave me the perfect opportunity to implement my plan to quit smoking. I had ten packs of cigarettes to use as a bait for my secrete plan. I hoped to quit smoking for good by time the carton of ten packs of cigarettes were finished. My plan was to overcome my cravings for cigarettes by exercising self control while seeing cigarettes at all times. Therefore I put the cigarettes at places where I was most likely to see them as I went about my daily chores. I put about five packs in my car because I was often on the road, three packs in the office and two packs at home. If I was able to control myself up to the time the ten packs were finished without one touching my lips I would have slayed the nicotine demon for good.

I overcame my cravings for nicotine by the time the ten packs of cigarettes were finished. I gave the cigarettes in my car to security officers at checkpoints at the many road blocks around the country. The cigarettes in the house and office I shared with visitors. It took about six weeks to give away all the cigarettes one or two cigarettes at a time. And by the time the ten packs ran out I had no craving for cigarettes. I have not puffed another cigarette since I gave away the last of the ten packs of cigarettes in 1981.

African Students Union-Melbourne

There was a small community of Africans in Melbourne in 1975 who were mostly students, the majority of whom were southern Africans. Economic migrants from Africa were virtually none existent until the latter part of 1975 or early 1976 when a few Ghanaians and Nigerians started trickling in from Europe. The first such migrants were a group of Ghanaian seamen that jumped ship in Melbourne in the latter part of 1976 or early 1977. The life and soul of the African community centered on the African Students Union. I was introduced to the African community and thus the African Students Union by David and Chris, a Ghanaian couple were already in Melbourne for more than three years before I arrived. The African Students union was under the control and influence of two Zimbabwean brothers, Charles and Simba, they were the life and soul of the union. The union was in effect the public relations outfit or propaganda arm of ZANU in the campaign for the liberation of South Rhodesia or Zimbabwe.

The African Students Union was used as the propaganda arm or mouth piece of the Zimbabwe African National Union for the liberation of Rhodesia from white minority rule. Simba and his younger brother were so articulate about the evils of white minority rule that those of us who were hitherto fence sitters became enthusiastic supporters. The oratory of Simba captured the imagination of the Australian youths. The union created the infrastructure that enabled the African students to interact with our Australian counterparts that were not related to booze and parties. They gave us the forum to meet Australian youths outside of our own institutions. The Australian youths we met at these functions were more friendly and open minded than most of our classmates or schoolmates. The two brothers, Simba in particular worked tirelessly for the liberation of Rhodesia by organizing fundraisers for the struggle. He used to be the principal speaker at these functions. The students union was in effect the mouthpiece of the Zimbabwe African National Union-ZANU. The union was supported by the youths of Australia and they were at the forefront in fundraisers and symposia on the liberation of southern Africa. In a way Simba aroused patriotic feelings and a higher consciousness in the African students who robbed shoulders with him and he succeeded in making us virtual ambassadors or activists for the liberation struggle. When Steve Biko was killed by the white apartheid regime of South Africa in 1977 we had almost a week of activities devoted to the memory of the murdered patriot with our

Australian counterparts. The Australian youths demonstrated to us that the liberation of southern Africa could not be accomplished without the support and goodwill of the white people whose racial counterparts or kinsmen we sought to overthrow. Through the auspices or the work of Simba the wife of Robert Mugabe paid a visit to Melbourne in 1976-77. A symposium or meeting was organized at which she gave us an update on the liberation struggle. The meeting was overwhelmingly white. The white students or sympathizers outnumbered the Africans at the meeting.

The number of Africans in Melbourne were so few that of necessity we were bound together as a close knit community. We were so few we knew one another and everyone. The African migrants who started tricking in from Europe were mostly Ghanaians and Nigerians. And as might be expected the new arrivals were also introduced to the students union but their priorities as economic migrants were different from the student activities and politics. The dilution of the student body with none students meant that our politics could not be as monolithic as it was, we had different interests and priorities particularly on ideology. The basic tenet of the union, the liberation of southern Africa from white minority rule was unchanged and remained the same. While the new arrivals were sympathetic to the liberation struggle they were not enamored to the ideological leanings of Simba which was at the heart of the ZANU propaganda and any talks or lectures that he gave. A fissure in ideology among us began to simmer under the surface. The new arrivals were not inclined to jump on the ideological bandwagon of Simba. The ideological differences simmered but did not affect our participation in the activities of the union. The simmering however boiled over when Simba used the forums of the students union to express support for the murderous regime of Cambodia. Those of us who were not ideological purists frowned on the open expression of support of mass murders in our name. That was how some of us saw Simba's open support or adulation of Pol Pot for the mass murder of the people of Cambodia. It was unconscionable that any sane person would condone and approve such atrocious and heinous acts in the name of ideological purity. I was hitherto generally indifferent and passive at our meetings and symposia while Simba waxed about his political ideology. But I objected to the use of the student forum as a platform for the expression of support for political murders in Cambodia. And for the first time I began speaking out at our forums. And once I started talking I could not stop. By this time David and Chris had long left for Ghana. I became the next unofficial chief of the Ghanaian community. I provided the same type of support services that David and Chris extended to me when I was new in Melbourne to the new arrivals. I gave support to both Ghanaian and Nigerian arrivals. The political ideology was tearing at the heart of the unity of the African students union. The Southern Africans were on the same side as Simba ideologically but the West Africans differed with him ideologically. Thus Ideology became the virtual dividing line between the West Africans and the Southern Africans. I was content to blow steam at our meetings without more. But some of the West Africans were incensed and felt so strongly that they urged me to break away and spearhead the formation of a splinter group.

Simba would not have been that strident on his ideology if the youths of Australia did not support him. They were obviously fascinated by socialism and showed their support through donations to the cause. Our Australian counterparts were mesmerized by socialism, it was a romantic concept which most may never see or experience in their lifetime. They could donate and support theoretical socialism but I doubt that most would be that supportive if they had lived through the atrocities of Cambodia or of the other socialist countries of the 1970's. I lived through the socialist experiment of Dr. Kwame Nkrumah during the first republic of Ghana. I guess I saw the good and bad side of the experiment. I had free education up to university level because of the socialist policies of the first republic. But for those policies my education would most likely have ended at middle school level. But thanks to the education infrastructure put in place by the first republic I had free college education even as I had the luxury to turn down the opportunity to live like a king on campus for fear of what a large income on campus would have on me. I was not affected by the dark side of socialism but I witnessed the pernicious side of the Nkrumah government when it was overthrown by force. The emaciated bodies of a retinue of political opponents detained without trial or any judicial process were paraded before the local and international press. The local press was largely silent during the years of the detentions but through rumors and BBC, knowledge of the detainees were widespread. And as a citizen, I was directly impacted by the economic collapse of the country from corruption, influence peddling and bad policy choices. I could not romanticize socialism despite the benefits I obtained from the socialist policies of the Nkrumah regime. I believed that the Australian youths who were the main backers of Simba would be less sanguine if they knew the actual practice of socialism and would have been displeased with his support of Pol Pot. My speeches or utterances at our forums were cautionary tales about practical ills of socialism. I did not have any of the oratory skills of Simba, my motivation was to sound warning about my experience of living through a socialist experiment. I could not change many minds except the West Africans who sided with me.

The Ghanaians and Nigerians were eager to disassociate themselves from the African students union as it existed under the leadership of Simba. At heart I remained loyal to the union and I was not interested in creating schism within the union. Firstly I knew my own weaknesses, I had a poor performance record in leadership positions. I was a sort of rabble rouser good at arousing passions, but unable to sustain the interests and passions that I kindled. I have idealistic tendencies and thus inflexible and often unable to deviate from the original aims and objectives of a club or society to reach a goal if that required compromise. There are two political parties and their various incarnations in Ghana, the CPP of Kwame Nkrumah and the UP of Busia. During the political campaign leading to the second republic in the late 1960's a number of new and old politicians decided to chart a third course different from the incarnations of the CPP and UP. They called it the third force or third way. I aspired to play a role as a student member of the third force and was eager to take part in student politics for the third force. Unfortunately the third force fizzled before it got off the ground because the leaders were so egotistical or megalomaniacs they could not decide on the leader of the nascent political party. That squabble killed the third force and that ended my political aspirations. Many students who were aspiring for roles in the third force transferred their activism and loyalties to one of the incarnations of the old political parties. But I was so disappointed with the breakup of the third force or third way that I could not transfer my loyalties or support to the incarnations of any of the old guard or political parties. With my weaknesses at the back of my mind I concluded that it would have been easy to break up or form a rival union but I could not sustain the interest and enthusiasm that prompted the breakaway faction. I therefore stopped active participation in the activities and meetings of the union. I felt that it was only a matter of time before Simba returned to Zimbabwe if the political climate in that country changed. And when that time came two ineffective and competing student unions would exist in Melbourne neither of them big enough to have any influence. Simba and his brother left Melbourne when Zimbabwe was on the cusp of majority rule that ended white minority domination.

Simba and Charles left Melbourne about eighteen to twenty four months before Zimbabwe achieved formal or official majority rule in 1980. After majority rule was attained none of the open hostility that Simba often expressed against the white settlers became a policy of the new government. On the contrary the settlers were encouraged to stay and help with the development of the new country. The fierce oratory against the white settler minority gave way to pragmatism in building a new nation. The policies of the new nation were more pragmatic without all the limitations of an inflexible socialist ideology. I assume that ideological talking points of Simba in far away Australia, was the official ideological leanings of the Zimbabwe African National Union-ZANU while it was struggling for majority rule. Maybe the talking points were more an expression of frustration with minority white rule than a real intent to establish a socialist utopia with all the destruction and dislocation that it would have entailed. Simba, it was understood, became a deputy minister in the new Zimbabwe government.

Zimbabwe, after independence was a success story with a strong economy. It appeared that Zimbabwe escaped the curse of African Socialism. African socialism was characterized by dictatorships, corruption and anemic social and economic development. I was so impressed with the economic development of the country that I applied for a commonwealth fellowship as a real estate appraiser in the new country. I hoped to renew acquaintances with Simba and Charles if I won the fellowship. By the time the fellowship was approved I had left Ghana in search greener pastures in New York.

Zimbabwe after more than thirty years of virtual one-party rule has succumbed to the curse of African socialism. Everything that can go wrong has gone wrong because of power grab, the bane of African Socialism. I do not know what it is with African leaders who turn to autocratic rule and behave like traditional chiefs or kings when they lose popularity or when their term of office ends. They arrogate to themselves an air of indispensability as if without them their country would grind to a halt. Mugabe and ZANU-PF have clung on to power at all cost and like all African socialist countries an otherwise buoyant economy went into precipitous decline.

ENDOWED WITH PROPHETIC DREAMS

I took my childhood spiritual experience into adulthood. I was inclined to be suspicious and within two years after I left middle school I began paying attention to the tenor of my dreams and nightmares. When I was in the primary school I used to be tormented by scary and unpleasant dreams and nightmares. Then in about the third grade I learned to pray at night before going to bed. As a catholic school student my prayers were the Lord's Prayer, Hail Mary and Hail Holy Queen. The nightly prayers freed me from the scary and unpleasant dreams and nightmares until I became a student at Navrongo. It was at Navrongo that I tasted my first glass of beer and subsequently began binge drinking at weekends. I began experiencing unpleasant dreams and nightmares again. As time went bye I started suspecting that the nightmares were connected with my hometown. I became suspicions that these nightmares occurred after I spent vacation in my hometown. But I did not make any definite deduction or association until about 1962. After I graduated from Navrongo College in 1961 my frequent travels around the country on vacations came to an end. I went home only once during my first two years after completion of St. John Bosco's College. The only travel outside my teaching station was a trip to my hometown while I was stationed at Damongo in 1962. On my return to Damongo I began having scary nightmares in which I was chased about by scary bulls or other scary creatures and in those dreams or nightmares I was often saved from apprehension or capture by flying away or climbing tall trees. The ability to fly or climb tall trees in my dreams always saved me from capture or apprehension by beasts and scary entities encountered in nightmares. After I came to a conclusion that the nightmares ensued after visits to my hometown I stopped going home for any visit for over seven years. And during that time I was relatively free of frightening or scary nightmares. But in 1969 , while a student at the Kumasi University, I went home on vacation along with two friends, Delimini and Lankono. During the visit all the fears that previously kept me away from my hometown became a reality; I was hospitalized for three days. During the vacation I slept with Lankono and one night while we were in bed I ghostly figure, the type of ghost figures that haunted me during my infancy, came through the open door and jumped into my bed with me. The effect of being in bed with a ghost was immediate. Following this incident I went to my mother and while resting on my bed I saw a vision or scary nightmare in which I saw a dark woman at the door of my mother's room beckoning to me while breathing fire through her mouse and nostrils and flames shooting from her eyes. I guess she must have been the she devil coming for my soul and if she had succeeded this story might never have been told. The experience of that night landed me at the Wa hospital with an inexplicable health condition that hobbled me for more than one year. I was admitted in hospital on five different occasions with the same health condition but every diagnostic test came back negative.

My personal beliefs and faith were shaped more by my personal experiences than what my class teacher or catechism teachers taught me or heard from the pulpit. I learned about the power of prayer very early in my life at about eight or nine years old due to nightmares. I used to have a lot of scary nightmares during infancy and I found that when I prayed before going to bed I did not have those scary nightmares. I therefore formed a prayer habit from about the second or third grade and I never stopped praying before bedtime and as long as I prayed I did not have spooky and scary nightmares in which large bulls and other creatures or entities chased me on land and in the air. As a result of this early experience prayer resonated personally with me and has a special place in my heart. But my prayer habit broke down when I went to St. John Bosco's College as a young adult in 1960 and discovered alcohol. I began binge drinking on weekends and started missing or skipping my nightly prayers. The results were immediate, though I did not realize it at the time, the nightmares returned with a vengeance. I lived with the scary nightmares until I stopped paying visits to my hometown in 1962 and the scary nightmares came to an end. I did not know it at the time but my fondness for alcohol affected my spiritual wellbeing.

As indicated above the events that culminated in my admission at Wa hospital for three days and five subsequent admissions at the college hospital began in the room of my college buddy, Lankono. I had not been home for over seven years as such I had no room for myself in my family house when I went on vacation in 1969. I would have had to sleep in my mother's room if Lankono did not accommodate me in his room. Lankono and my family's home were located at the same Zongo neighborhood. One night I tossed and turned about in bed unable to sleep mostly due to the warm and humid weather. Both the door and windows were wide open for cross breezes but the air was very still until after about midnight. The room was so uncomfortably warm that Lankono gave his bed to me and slept on the floor. The atmosphere began to cool down after midnight when cooler air and breezes began blowing through the door and windows. I became drowsy and about to drift into sleep when I saw a dark ghostly shadow or spirit come through the open door. The ghostly figure jumped into bed behind me. As soon as it hit the bed, I started shivering and trembling and gasping for air. As I trembled and gasped for breath it occurred to me that death was imminent. I told myself that I did not want to die in my friend's home and have my body carried across town to my family home for funeral and burial. I did not want to inconvenience my family and my friend's family if I died in his room. I was not afraid to die but I did not want the burden that would be placed on others if I died at the home of Lankono. With that in mind I woke my friend and told him point blank that I thought I was going to die and he should help me to get to my mother to die there. I told him what happened and he comforted me that I would not die.

Lankono walked me home to my mother. I shivered, trembled and gasped for breath until we entered my mother's room in the dead of the night. My mother gave me her bed while she and Lankono kept vigil over me. We were waiting for daybreak to go to the hospital. Meanwhile I drifted into an uneasy sleep still shivering and trembling on the bed like a wet dog. I had slept only briefly before I saw a black woman with fire shooting from her eyes, nostrils and mouth like a dragon attempting to come through the door with outstretched arms. I tried to shout or cry for help but nothing came out of my mouth. My mother sensed that something was wrong from how desperately I thrashed about in bed woke me up. I felt a tremendous sense of relief when I woke up and the image of the fire breathing woman has captured my imagination ever since that night. The image helped to put a further strain in my relations with a relative who tolerated me but never really liked me. For some unknown reason I never trusted her piety and we never liked one another. After I came home from the hospital and until she passed away our relations was forced politeness towards one another.

At dawn, Lankono accompanied me to the hospital. All this while the shivering and trembling had shown no signs of easing as I walked slowly to the hospital. But as soon as we walked through the gates of the hospital the symptoms that had tormented me all night suddenly vanished. Suddenly all the shivers and trembling stopped and I felt completely normal, all the symptoms inexplicably vanished. The whole episode now appeared like a nightmare from which I just woke up. I was at a loss for words to explain to the charge nurse the condition that brought me to the hospital. I fumbled for words to explain my condition without appearing foolish or silly and as I struggled for words I broke down in tears. I was admitted for three days and treated for malaria.

My condition appeared normal while I was on admission, but the condition deteriorated after I was discharged, I did not shake and shiver like before the admission, but instead I had heart palpitations and eerie sensations of my blood racing through my arteries and veins. The eerie feeling of my blood rushing through me as if it would gush out of my orifices and finger tips was very scary. I had never felt or sensed my blood circulating let alone circulating at breakneck speeds through me. I felt these sensations only at night when I became drowsy and as was about to drift into sleep, the sensations used to scare me from sleep while they lasted, otherwise I was almost normal during the day. At night when I became drowsy and was about to drift into sleep then suddenly my heart would start beating wildly and followed by the sensation of my blood racing through my body at maddening speeds. The heart palpitations and the sensation of blood rushing through my arteries often scared me out of my wits and made me wide awake. I could not wait for vacation to an end so that I could go back to the campus and consult Dr. Bannerman, the college hospital physician. And as soon as I got back to the campus I rushed to consult him, expecting a miracle or at least an explanation for the inexplicable condition.

I reported at the college hospital expecting that Dr. Bannerman and the college laboratory would diagnose my condition and provide me with appropriate treatment. I was admitted at the college infirmary for five days while a battery of diagnostic tests were done. All the tests results came back negative, I was normal and so I was discharged. I was given a prescription of tranquilizers, Phenobarbital tablets, to take before bedtime. Over the next twelve months I was admitted at the same hospital on four other occasions but the result of every test that was done with the knowledge and technology of the sixties and early seventies came back negative. The only remedy I had to cope with the condition was the tranquilizer tablets, Phenobarbital. But I was eager to lead a normal life as much as possible without fear of the condition hanging over me; as such I did not take the tablets unless absolutely necessary. I hated taking the tranquilizer tablets for prevention purposes. I took the tablets after my efforts to control the palpitations and sensation of blood circulating at tremendous speed through me failed. The irregular manner in which I took the medication prevented me from becoming dependent on the Phenobarbital tablets.

Over the next twelve months I was afflicted with rapid heart beats or palpitations at bedtime followed by the scary sensation of the velocity of blood through my body. As the year progressed the condition or symptoms became worse, I tried to sleep as normally as possible without taking tranquilizers but on many occasions when I tried and failed to sleep through the condition for more that two hours then I was compelled to take the tranquilizers as my sleep aide. The tablets calmed my heart palpitations and helped me to get some sleep under those circumstances.

I was hospitalized with the same condition the last time in June 1970 shortly before the college broke up for the long vacation. I chose to spend the vacation at Kumasi for my internship at the local lands department so as to be close to the college infirmary in case of a crisis. I had frequent attacks during the holidays; I do not know whether the condition was exacerbated by alcohol because I continued to drink socially during the vacation. The heart palpitations and the eerie sensations of my blood racing through me occurred only around bedtime when I became drowsy with sleep and because if this peculiarity I began questioning my sanity. I wondered whether the condition was real or psychosomatic and phantom illness that existed only in my mind. I could not understand why the heart palpitations occurred only at night and not during day time. Secondly I wondered "how is it possible that I have a debilitating health condition that cannot be detected by the tools of modern medicine?" Perhaps the conditions or symptoms existed only in my mind and that was the reason the tools of modern medicine could not make a diagnosis.

I enjoyed my vacation as well as I could under the circumstances. But every night when I felt blood racing through my body and my heart beating rapidly I could find no satisfactory explanation for the phenomenon and started to blame myself that the symptoms and conditions existed only in the confines of my mind and finally I concluded that I had a psychosomatic and phantom illness and therefore decided to ignore and pay no attention when the condition occur. By this time I had been suffering the condition for over one year.

The day I made up my mind to ignore the condition I had a very severe attack that night as if my body was trying to tell me that the condition was real and not a figment of my imagination. But despite the severity of the condition that night I paid no heed and refused to go for my bottle of tranquilizers as I would have done under such circumstances. I gritted my teeth and lay still and dared the devil to do its worse. I surmised that if the palpitations and the blood rush were real as I felt them then the blood would ooze out of my orifices and gush out of my finger tips. I clenched my jaws and repeatedly told myself that the condition existed only in my mind, it was not real. I kept repeating this to myself as my heart beat wildly and I felt blood racing through me. Eventually I drifted into an uneasy sleep without any sleep aide.

I began to mend after that night in August 1970; I never took another tranquilizer tablet to stabilize the condition when it occurred. The frequency and intensity of the attacks began to ebb and I ignored any attack from then onward until the condition petered out without any further attention or treatment. I refused to feed the condition with fear so it petered out. Whenever the condition struck I simply said it was not happening for real, it was my mind playing tricks on me. Suffice to say that by the time I went back to School in October 1970 I was almost cured and was in much better shape than when I left for vacation that year.

Throughout the one year that I struggled with the condition it never occurred to me that an evil force was behind the condition despite how the condition began. What I knew was that I overcame the condition more by the power of the mind or auto suggestion than through medical intervention. That incident taught me about the power of the mind and willpower and that there are more things in this world than meets the eye. My personal experience of a ghostly figure and a nightmare that landed me in the hospital with an inexplicable health condition that lasted for more than one year shows that there is more to this world that meets the eye.

In our traditional African or Ghanaian societies a lot of unfortunate events and inexplicable things happen for which we cannot find logical explanations and attribute them to sorcery and witchcraft. Some of the things are such that one could not draw any other conclusion than sorcery, the supernatural or witchcraft. For instance the brother of one of my best friends, Thomas died after a nightmare. He had a nightmare in which he was tied up sitting on a tree and as he attempted to free himself from the ropes that bound him he lost his footing and fell headlong on the ground and at the precise moment he hit the ground he fell from the bed that he shared with Thomas, his younger brother. His neck became swollen and he died of a broken neck a few weeks after falling from his bed. And Thomas, despite his brilliance, could not keep a job because of drunkenness. When I came across him again in the 1980's he was jobless having been fired from his position as head of department due to absenteeism and drunkenness. I was just recovering from my satanic problems and so I understood the nature of the problems that faced him and helped him by offering him a job in my department at AESC. But I was forced to fire him a few months later when he relapsed, became a drunk and was often absent from work. After I fired him I took him into my house for six months and helped him with fasting and prayers until he sobered up again. I then took him back in my department and he eventually became the officer in charge of the department after I left Ghana. And in a similar mysterious incident, one of my female relatives broke her leg while waiting for a bus at a bus stop. The broken leg was attributed to sorcery or witchcraft and was set and treated through prayers at a spiritual church.

I am of the opinion that our past and our present are intertwined. The mortal and the immortal live together in the same space just as good and evil live together in the same space. People with the gift to see and interact with spirits do so in this physical realm; the spirit must therefore exist in another dimension of our physical world.

As a person with some amount of western education I should not be that superstitious or frightened about dreams and nightmares but for my personal experience. It is difficult if not impossible for me to deny my personal experiences even though some of those experiences do not make logical sense. For instance, how could I be experiencing heart palpitations unable to sleep but my vital signs when checked were always normal even as my heart and blood raced through me. My mother died from poison that was introduced into our pot of water. The whole family ate the food and drank the water but it was only my mother, the target of the poison who was affected. During the course of my life I have sometimes wondered whether my childhood experiences were the result of an overactive imagination but for certain inexplicable things I cannot explain away.

THE BREAKUP WITH FRANCES REVEALED IN A DREAM

In 1962 I was sitting in front of my home with some friends one Saturday afternoon when an itinerary fortune teller singled me out to read me my fortune. During the fifties and sixties nomadic tribesmen from Upper Volta, Niger, Mali and other countries in the Sahel region used to visit Ghana during the dry season. They used to roam around our towns and villages begging for alms and telling fortunes. It was one such person who singled me out from my colleagues while passing by our house. He provided me with a brief summary of my future, he told me that I was pure of heart and mind wished no person any harm but in the future as I made progress evil forces would work for my downfall. Then he asked me to give him a shilling so that he would read me my fortune gazing into a bucket of water. I was skeptical about fortune tellers so I asked him to read me my fortune first and then I pay for the reading. He refused and walked away. About ten years later when I was going through financial turmoil I remembered the words of the stranger and wished I had paid the one shilling to have had my fortune told, events in later years gave credence to the short but cryptic message in 1962. Coming events are sometimes revealed months or years before they occur. When I was a student I had a dream about my college sweetheart shortly before a great misunderstanding between us. We resolved the misunderstanding but broke up after about another year. At the time I did not understand or perceive the ramifications of the dream until years after we broke up and went our separate ways. I used to exchange letters and photos with Frances about once or twice a month. She was a final year high school student at St. Francis Girls Secondary School at Jirapa and I was a final year college student. We planned through our correspondence to get married as soon as we found our feet after graduation.

In this prophetic dream I received a letter from Frances in which she enclosed her picture. I eagerly tore open the envelope and removed the photo, but as I tried to look at the face in the picture she turned away from me in anger. At that particular time in our relations we had never had any disagreement or quarrel so I did not know what to make of the face in the picture. Three days later I received a heart wrenching letter from her. She wrote that she was breaking up with me because I was not a Christian, specifically a Catholic. I was a baptized Catholic at the time. I sought the counsel of my best friends Delimini and Lankono. They advised me to send her a copy of my baptismal certificate to prove that I was a baptized and confirmed catholic. Her next letter plunged another dagger into my heart. She was not impressed with the baptismal certificate and insisted that we break up. I was unable to persuade her so I kept my peace and nursed my heartache. I pined away with heartache and misery. I became a miserable wreck and searched my mind and heart for the real reason behind the break-up and could find no reason for her sudden change of heart.

That was the state of affairs between us when one Friday I returned from lectures and was told by security that a visitor was waiting for me in my cubicle. The visitor was none other than Frances. When I saw her I had mixed feelings, I was very excited and ambivalent at the same time. I was uncertain about her intentions; my confidence was shaken as a result of the recent misunderstanding that arose between us. I wondered whether she had come to tease and torment me just when I was beginning to get over our breakup. I was at a loss for words; I did not know what to do with myself—laugh, cry, or jump for joy I did not know. I was ambivalent while my heart raced widely with excitement and joy.

We talked all Friday night and all day Saturday. We talked of sweet nothings and even made plans for our future together. The long talks revealed the motivation behind the letter that threatened breakup with me. It was supposed to be a psychological test to assess the depth of my love or fidelity. The test was a lesson from some of her tutors who were mostly nuns. I do not know whether I passed the test or not. When I sent her the baptismal certificates and could not persuade her I gave up. If I was expected to be persistent then I failed. As far as I was concerned the test wrecked my heart; the heartache ended only when she unexpectedly came back into my life with a visit to me on campus. But I think the squabble might have left a blot on my heart. That blot left a little bit of distrust or uncertainty about her in my heart and might have contributed to our eventual breakup from which despite friendly reconciliation we never really recovered.

Frances was more thoughtful and looked forward to our future together. That was one of the purposes of her surprise visit. She had not given up on me despite her letter while I was a broken man. She therefore sought for the opinion of the man with whom she intended to spend her future about her next career path. We discussed the options before her, a two year sixth form course leading to university or two year post secondary teacher training college. I liked the post secondary school training college option because that meant an early marriage while the sixth form would postpone any marriage plans by another three years until after university. But I was ambivalent about my preference. Our recent turbulent history briefly as it might have been reminded me that the affairs of the heart can be fickle and fleeting. I did not want to influence her career path based on our future plans together, a future plan that as far as I was concerned was uncertain. At the back of my mind I imagined being vilified in the future if she became a post secondary school teacher instead of a university graduate and our relations unraveled. I therefore left the decision up to her promising to support her with whatever decision she made. She decided on the university education route by going to sixth form to matriculate. We broke up in the second year of the sixth form course. Although I blamed our eventual breakup on my financial downfall; I wonder whether the relationship was destined to end the way it did.

POWER OF THE CROSS

When I returned to my country from Australia I believe I was more enlightened spiritually than when I left. I struggled to maintain my spiritual equanimity against all the distractions that came with the deceptive appearance of wealth as represented by the type of car I drove around town. Despite the distraction and my own foibles I remained steadfast in my heart about the love of God and relied on Him for direction and guidance in my life. I blamed God when I found myself in compromising situations because he allowed them to happen. I wished the situations had never happened or occurred even while I was enjoying the fruits manifested by the condition.

The direction of my future spiritual life or path came to me in a dream during one of those nights when I was compromising my marriage vows with another woman. I had returned from a pleasure trip to the home of my host in Accra with Tosh, my female companion when I had the dream. In the dream I found myself standing alone in a dark room when I overhead voices discussing how to kill or take my life. They lamented that all their past attempts to kill or take my life had all ended in failure because I always called aloud the name of God and His name always neutralized their evil deeds and intentions. They reached a consensus among themselves that the best way to deal with me was to neutralize the source of my strength, prevent me from proclaiming aloud the name of the Lord.

As soon as they came to conclusion on how to overpower me by preventing me from calling aloud the name of God my tongue began to expand and swell in my mouth. As my tongue expanded and filled my mouth I began to choke up and gasp for breath. I was in great distress choking with my own swollen tongue. I could not speak or call on the Lord to save me because my mouth was filled with my swollen tongue. I was dying but I knew that my salvation lay in the name of the Lord if only I could utter the name of the Lord I'll be saved but I could not. I repeatedly said to myself "if only I can call the name of Lord I will be saved" I was on the verge of passing out when suddenly a bright light lit up the room from behind me against the wall in front of me; then a small table was placed beside the wall, and the table was covered with a large red table cloth. And finally a large gleaming gold cross similar to crosses used in Catholic Churches on ceremonial occasions was placed on top of the table. As soon as the gold cross appeared on the table I got well. The shortness of breath and the swollen and expanded tongue that was choking me to death vanished. I woke up sweating and panting for breath from the dream. I gave thanks to the Lord and knew from that moment that when I was in trouble and helpless salvation would come from the cross. My unknown enemies in the dream were once more vanquished by their old nemesis; the name of God as represented by the cross prevailed over them.

At the time of this dream I was not affiliated with any church. I had not been to any church since I returned from Australia. I felt it was not in my place to clamor for a church at that stage, God in his own time would show me the way. I drifted from the Catholic Church in search of spiritual satisfaction or something that I felt I was not getting from my church. And when I took up yoga meditation I sought for the love of the one God. I started on the premise that God was not a Christian, Muslim, Hindu, Jewish or for that matter any of the parts of God we call God. I wanted the whole experience. As later events proved I could indeed become enlightened with the love of God but when I came under satanic attacks, the nebulous God I served deserted me; I was saved by the cross.

About one year after this dream, a series of events unfolded in my life and in the end I was as helpless in reality as in the dream. The dream showed that God was the source of my strength and power against my enemies. And just as in the dream the source of that power and strength came under concerted attack by the devil. For a number of weeks or months I could not concentrate and meditate on the name of the Lord or pray. That ability was neutered and effectively taken away from me or denied to me. Once I could not concentrate, meditate or pray I became a sitting duck ready to be taken down. I was living in sin mostly by cheating on my wife but despite my personal foibles I found time under difficult and inconvenient conditions to observe quiet time in the morning and evening. All the while, praying for a place so that I could move my family from Kumasi to Accra. Luckily a brother of one of my best friends, Elisha gave me a place in his house until either he moved out and gave me the whole house or I had another place. I was happy I had a room to myself where I could meditate and pray without interference or disturbance. But I could never meditate or pray effectively in my new room due to cobwebs and itches. When I made attempts at concentration and meditation I felt cobwebs crawling on my face and arms. The first day I had this experience I returned from work with some insecticides. As soon as I came home I cleaned and sprayed the room from corner to corner with insecticides in my attempts to rid the room of any spiders. But after cleaning and spraying the room the cobweb attacks continued, I felt cobwebs crawling on my face and arms during prayers and meditation. And that was the only time when I felt the invisible cobwebs on my face and arms. I examined every nook and corner of the room for spiders including an orange tree in the courtyard. I took a broom and brushed the leaves of the tree to rid it of any spider webs that might be on the tree. After all said and done I was still attacked by the cobwebs during prayers and meditation. I found no cobwebs on my person but I felt them crawling over my face and arms. As I was unable to find the source of the cobwebs I decided to close my mind and persevere through with my prayers and meditation. And just when I was beginning to concentrate and pray or meditate through the cobweb sensations then I came under a different set of problems, itching and scratching my body. The cobwebs were replaced by irresistible or uncontrollable itch over my whole body. As soon as I readied myself for prayers and meditation and entered into quiet contemplative mood then suddenly I itched all over my body, I scratched my body from head to toe as if somebody had poured poison ivy over me. I had an earful when I consulted my colleagues at the office. I was told that the cobwebs were tools of sorcery and witchcraft. The cobwebs were an indication that I was being tied up with ropes or twines represented by the cobwebs through witchcraft or sorcery. I was advised by my coworkers to seek immediate help before I was driven into insanity. Although the threat of insanity appeared to be an exaggeration; but come to think of it I was already on the edge of insanity. I was already untangling invisible cobwebs in my room and looking for the invisible cobwebs and spiders on a tree in the middle of the courtyard. Only an insane person would inspect and clean the leaves of a tree standing in the courtyard to get rid of cobwebs on his person in the room. I could imagine myself walking about the streets of Accra untangling invisible cobwebs from my face. Anybody seeing me doing that would have considered that I was insane; I guess the insane do not know they are insane and that would have been my lot. To make a long story short the cobweb attacks and the uncontrollable itch were remedied through prayers and ritual baths of a Christian Pentecostal Church pastor. She prayed for me and blessed water for me to take a ritual holy baths for seven days. She also confirmed the stories my coworkers told me at the office that the cobwebs and itch were caused by witchcraft or sorcery against me.

LIFE AND ENTERNITY

I began my spiritual journey of self discovery by praying for enlightenment on some basic truths of my being. I meditated and prayed for enlightenment and understanding of the meaning and significance of eternal life. If I could find no satisfactory answer or understanding of eternal life then the basis of heaven and hell, the reason we toil to live by faith would be in vain. My spiritual enquiry through concentration and meditation gave me personal satisfaction and physical benefits. But that could not justify spending hours a day to increase my self awareness if there is no life after death. If there is no life after life then perhaps our religion is in vain. As already said I have been a skeptic on matters of faith I believed in my senses. I saw demonstrations of survival of life after death every Sunday at church but that could be chicanery and I remained as doubtful as Thomas when his colleagues informed him of the risen Christ. I sought for validation within my heart and soul as in Matthew 7-7 *"Ask, and it will be given to you; seek, and you will find; knock, and it will be opened to you."*

As I went about my daily chores the puzzle of the eternal soul of man was always at the back of my mind. I turned over the puzzle in my head in every which way hoping that perhaps in one unguarded moment God might give me a flash of inspiration that would bare the truth a tiny bit to give me an insight into the puzzle. Every living thing has a definite beginning and an end. How can man be both eternal and mortal at the same time? For a time I made it the theme of my concentration and meditation hoping that one day I shall have an insight during meditation. The bible tells us that we are created in the image of God and yet we die but God is said to be eternal and never dies. Genesis 1:27 *"So God Created man in His own image; in the image of God He created him; male and female He created them".* The same bible tells us that despite our being made in the image and likeness of the eternal God our days on earth are numbered. Psalm 90:10 *"The days of our lives are seventy; And if by strength they are eighty years, Yet their boast is only labor and sorrow; For it is soon cut off and we fly away.* Understanding the eternal soul of man became an obsession and eventually I got a slight inkling of the truth in a dream. The dream revealed the enigma of eternal man. Dreams have been my line of communication with God ever since infancy. God thus communicated the puzzle of mortal-immortal man in a dream or nightmare. The dream gave a slight insight into the puzzle that I had been struggling with for over two years. I understood that the physical body has a limited lifespan but the spirit within lives on; it cannot be killed or murdered by the hand of man. That was comforting. The dream confirmed the veracity of the demonstrations of survival after death during Sunday church services.

The dream captured my imagination and was embedded in my subconscious, it is one of a handful of dreams that I can still remember as clearly as the night I had the dream. In this dream I was walking through a dark alley when I was suddenly surrounded by unknown assailants. The men wore long robes like characters from the Mamelukes movie and were armed with long swords. They had murder on their mind because without any provocation whatsoever they set upon me and attacked me from all sides with their long swords. There was no room to escape or run. I felt the sharp pointed swords go through my flesh like a butcher's knife through beef or carving knife through a loaf of bread. As I bled and my life began to ebb away, it flashed through my mind that the assailants were killing my physical or mortal body but not the spirit within; in the dream it occurred to me that the real me within was untouchable. They could not harm or touch the real me; the spirit that dwells within. And then I told them in defiance that "if it is the body you want you can have it". And with that I handed over my limp body like a rag doll to them and stepped backwards out of the mortal body. And then I woke up sweating but happy to be alive safely in bed with my heart pounding. The dream taught me about the eternal soul of man and the possibility that an enlightened person can consciously surrender his body or consciously exit his body at the end of his days on earth.

The spirit of man is therefore eternal and indestructible; the body may be destroyed in a jiffy, but the spirit lives on eternally. Death is therefore the end of one journey and the beginning of another. Without the first one the second cannot be born. Methuselah had to live on this earth for over nine hundred years before he inherited eternity. Unless we die we cannot inherit the eternal. One cannot inherit eternity without first surrendering the physical body that ties us to the physical world as we know it. Death and immortality are intertwined; they are two sides of the same coin.

I was raised in a household of conflicting faiths. My father was a Muslim and my mother was animist. And by virtue of education in a religious school I was inclined towards the Christian faith. But I had more in common with my mother, my father left home by the third grade and my mother was the only person I could relate or discuss entities I saw around the house. Those personal experiences taught me that there is more to this world than meets the eye. I struggled to reconcile my experience with the doctrine of the Christian faith that was taught at school. For most of us spirits exist only in the pages of fairy tales, the pages of the bible or traditional lore.

But to me spirits were very real. I saw them and I interacted with them virtually everyday during most of my formative years. I experienced the pernicious power of the spirits of idols when I intruded on their privacy. The power of the idols that were supposed to protect my family property was turned on me when I saw them innocently in their private moments. So I know from first hand experience that spirits have powers that can be used for good or bad and evil purposes. Spirits can influence our lives whether we know it or not.

By the time I was in Form II or the eighth grade my conversion was almost complete but my skepticism had also began. I had virtually forgotten the childhood experiences with spirits since my spiritual sight faded away entirely by the fifth grade. That was also the period when I began asking the questions that have been at the forefront of my life since Form II. I went back to my people after more than eight years and on my return participated in many idol worship at which animals were sacrificed by members of my family. By this time I had an air of know it all, I sneered and mocked at them in my heart over their ignorance. But in my heart I felt differently, I was reminded of the past spirit encounter and interaction and thus not unmindful of the spirit and power lurking behind the idols. I took part in the sacrifices and ate the meat that came from the animal sacrifices. I also witnessed a very unique animal sacrifice with an uncle in my grandmother's village. Thus far most animal sacrifices that I had seen, the sacrificial animals were slaughtered. This was the first sacrifice in which the idol took the life of the sacrificial chicken without the offeror first slaughtering it. At the start of the sacrifice I was very skeptical, as I had been since returning from the south. I arrogated to myself enlightenment and wisdom and mocked them in my heart that they were ignorant for making the sacrifices and implied that the sacrifices were only a means of adding meats to their diets. I thought my uncle was deluding himself by expecting the idol to take the life of the animal; he would squeeze the neck of the chicken to kill it and pretend that the idol accepted or killed the bird. This was my general attitude towards my people, their worship of idols and animal sacrifices; I mocked and derided them in my heart.

I watched with deep skepticism every move by my uncle when he began the sacrificial offer to the idol. He began the sacrifice by unburdening his heart to the god and when he was done he squeezed the legs and neck of the chicken together and hit it hard against the small mound at the front gate. He aroused my ire by this action and I murmured to myself that he was squeezing the life out of the bird in the name of the god with his strong hands. I watched in dismay as he desperately tried to squeeze the life out of the poor fowl but it refused to die. Try as hard as he could the bird would not die. Had the bird died, it would have confirmed my deep skepticism of the hypocrisy of the sacrifice. After he failed to kill the bird he returned it to the chicken coop and went out to consult oracles for the causes the gods rejected his sacrifice. The oracles told him the reason for the rejection and he remedied the condition before he resumed the sacrifice again. The second time around he did not squeeze the chicken half as hard as the first time and I saw the quick anal movement of the fowl signaling the end. My skepticism mellowed but years later it occurred to me that if the spirits nearly killed me, then they could also take the life of a chicken.

Gradually and with the wisdom of age I understand why the God of the Jews forbade them from making idols. The idols we make assume a spiritual life of their own. And God said plainly that He was a jealous God, He does not want competition from any lesser gods. And it became clear to me over the years that just as our physical world is structured according to class or influence, so is the spirit world. The God we serve as Christians is at the pinnacle of the spiritual power structure hence He was able to save me time and again from lesser evil powers. I believe from my journey through life that there is an omnipotent God that has dominion or power over all lesser gods. But for that God I would not have lived to see my eighteenth birthday let alone live to be more than sixty years. There were many times when I came close to death but somehow some power beyond me, always pulled me from the jaws of death and from the hands of my enemies. But I am also a product of the conflict of the faith that was part of my upbringing. I have not been able to accept or come to terms with the Christian concept that they have monopoly over heaven. The emphasis by some sects of Christianity that the God of love and compassion would condemn those images of himself who have not accepted the name of Christ as their personal savior would be condemned to fire and brimstone is not compatible with a compassionate and merciful God. I have never been able to accept that my animist mother and Muslim father were condemned to hell because they were not Christians. And according to the propagators of this teaching abiding by love or other Christian values are immaterial as long as one has not confessed that Christ is his lord and savior without more. God is made out by these teachers to be a petty dictator like Idi Amin or Stalin that delight in the cult of personality. Is God that petty? No. When I started on an active spiritual journey or enquiry I worshipped the almighty and omnipotent God of all creation without distinction of faith. All faiths and religions are but a manifestation of the same God. God is one but mankind has cut him up into little bits for our own glorification. Despite my concept I could not disassociate myself from Christianity, it is the only faith I have practiced. I never prayed a day as a Muslim and I never worshipped or made any sacrifice to an idol. I maintained my association even as I sought answers for my doubt and skepticism.

I learned to pray by the third grade as an antidote against nightmares. As a Catholic school student most of my prayers and devotions were to the Holy mother. And she saved me from the nightmares. And when I was cursed after I stole cassava from a farm Mother Mary saved me from the curse when I appealed to her for help. The Holy Mother was therefore the center of my devotion from infancy to adulthood. I have never stopped reciting the Hail Mary though I do not remember the last time I set foot in a Catholic Church. As long as I say the Lord's Prayer I always end them with the Hail Mary. When I began my spiritual journey in search for the truth, I worshipped at Christian Churches but I never considered myself a member of any church. I was a freelance Christian. And God used me to serve him in a healing ministry at Christian Church in the late seventies though I was not a formal member of that church.

The power of the mind can be harnessed to bestow great spiritual insight and power on any individual that has the discipline to pursue the goals through concentration and meditation. That individual through concentration and meditation can realize his image as God. We are made in the image and likeness of God, the discipline of the mind through meditation can crack open lightly the door to the infinite, the image of God. I gained or attained some level of spiritual enlightenment and power after single minded dedication in concentration and meditation for about three years. However I was helpless and vulnerable when concerted efforts were made against me by sorcerers and witchcraft. Although I maintained my association with Christian churches my devotion was no more to Christ or Mary but God. Spiritually I had nothing to fall back on when the iniquitous made it impossible for me to carry out my devotion to God.

RE-DISCOVERED YOGA IN MELBOURNE

I became interested in yoga during my final year in college when yoga postures by a Ghanaian master used to be published in a weekly newspaper, *The Weekly Spectator*. The newspaper was my formal introduction to the discipline of yoga. I had a wish list and a lot of dreams when I was in college but after graduation my dreams and wishes were squelched before they ever took off. Thus my interest in yoga practically died after graduation; I failed financially and materially and my life crashed and burned before me. My financial problems overwhelmed all my personal ambitions and interests. The carefree life I had on campus was replaced by the anxieties of eking out an existence outside the comfort of the college walls. My optimistic and sunny personality became dour and brooding filled with the anxieties of holding on to any semblance of life befitting a college graduate of the early seventies in Ghana. I did not have the means or the peace of mind to devote to other activities and interests beyond keeping body and soul together. In 1974 I took the unprecedented step of walking away from my car, the cause of all my financial misery. That singular act freed me and taught me the pitfalls of attachments to material property. Finally I got the means and peace of mind to resume the practice of yoga under guidance of an actual yoga teacher.

I started taking yoga lessons about three years after graduation from an Indian master at Asylum Down in Accra. I became quite adept at the postures or assanas. The teacher was impressed with my progress and invited me to join an advanced yoga class that included meditation. The invitation came at the time my mind was all focused on my forthcoming trip to Australia. Since I was preparing to leave for Australia early the next year I did not honor the invitation. I decided to pick up my practice in Melbourne, Australia.

Accordingly as soon as I settled down in Melbourne I bought a small paperback book on yoga from the college bookshop; *Yoga over Fourty*. That book served all my yoga needs from postures to meditation for the next three years. But as I got more adept at the assanas and meditation I bought other books on the subject. But none of them was as well illustrated and easy to follow as *Yoga Over Forty*. The following year 1976 I came across *Autobiography Of A Yogi* by *Paramahansa Yogananda* from the bookshop of the church where I worshipped. The book introduced me to *Self Realization*

Fellowship and I became so enthralled with the life of the Yogi that I subscribed for lessons from the Self Realization Fellowship in the latter part of 1976.

In Melbourne I was as free as a bird. I had no care in the world and was as carefree as during the days I was a student in Ghana. The conditions were conducive and ideal for me to have other interests and passions other than worrying about keeping body and soul together. For the first time in over four years I had no anxieties about my sustenance and did not have to worry about my next meal. Thanks to student allowance, I had the financial resources to support myself without fretting about work or income. I came to Australia with definite material goals in mind but they were years in the future, I decided to enjoy myself and let the future take care of itself. I therefore did not let my material ambitions intrude on my present.

My light academic program virtually gave me a free hand in pursuing my extra curricula interests without the academic work or my interests being adversely affected. The yoga practice started earnestly at about the same time that I became greatly interested in drinking wine and going to wild parties on weekends. My drinking, which began as curiosity for the taste of wine, went from weekends to daily binges within a month. On most evenings I got drunk after school. But despite drunkenness on most nights I did not let alcohol interfere with my physical exercises or yoga practice in the mornings. I never missed a day of practice though my joints were stiff on most mornings. The physical exercises, it appeared also improved my tolerance for wine but the joint stiffness made the morning exercises a chore as such I gave up the bottle.

Once I gave up the bottle I had very few distractions from my yoga practice and exercises during the week. At weekends I went to the usual parties but I was less welcome than before I gave up the bottle. I became quite agile with the assanas and became flexible and pliable. Yoga became my virtual religion on which I spent about two to three hours a day depending on my class schedule. I learned the art of relaxation and could go limp and almost breathless during practice. From yoga assanas I added the other leg of yoga, the yoga of the mind, raja yoga with guidance from *Yoga Over Forty*. As my virtual religion I read books on yoga to further my understanding of the subject similar to the period I read the whole bible so that I could hold intelligent discussions with members of the Jehovah Witness sect when I encountered them. In addition to the Upanishad and Bhagavad Gita I became acquainted with other esoteric books such as the Egyptian and Tibetan Book of the Dead. My favorite Gita translation was a Penguin Classic by Juan Mascaro. I have carried that translation with me since I bought it more than thirty years ago. In the course of time the meditations had the same beneficial effect on my mind as the assanas had on my physique, the priorities of my social life changed. I shifted from bar hopping to group meditations, séances and divinations with church going colleagues. My associates and companions changed from bar and party hoppers to meditation and divination hoppers. I hopped from one meditation site to another in search of spiritual excitement. I became familiar with mediums, taro card and palm readers at the various venues I went from week to week. I was already a regular church attendee at churches where proof of survival was demonstrated every

Sunday thus I was in tune with that crowd. I participated in the study and practice of various methods of divination from those who were good at them and taught us, the wannabes. At these meetings I learned and tried the basics of automatic writing, Ouija Board, palmistry and taro card reading or channeling and medium techniques.

My meditation practice eventually went from once a day to twice daily, morning and evening. I had never been consistent and persistent at anything over any length of time but I was consistent and persistent with yoga over a long period of time without tiring of it. I practiced concentration and meditation at least one hour in the morning and evening. Thus over time physical and meditation yoga became easier, the assanas became easier and entering into concentration and meditation mood became easier as well. I obtained a measure of control over my restless mind and was able to concentrate on any object of my meditation. The twice daily meditations affected my socializing; I spent less time on socializing when I went out to any mundane social event. The concentration and meditation exercises virtually controlled my social life. I stopped staying out at any social event beyond midnight. I returned home from any event before midnight so as to have ample time to meditate and still get enough sleep. Meditation was like a drug that had the tendency to make me wide awake after it was over or put me into a quiet and contemplative mood. I was absorbed in my own mind during and after meditation and began to enjoy my own company. I enjoyed the peace and quiet that descended upon me after concentration and meditation and liked keeping my own company without disturbance or interference. I became self centered and for the first time I actually craved for quiet and solitude. Gradually I stopped making the rounds to the group meditation sites. And with that ended the various divination experiments. I kept and often played or referred to the Chinese book of changes as my diviner. It was alleged to be one of the most reliable or accurate writings on divination though I never quite understood it.

Eventually Elizabeth and I drifted apart with the change of direction in my life and associations. I frequented a small church around downtown Melbourne that held demonstrations of survival after death every Sunday. The demonstrations piqued my interests in spiritual matters and I made associations from the church and became interested in channeling and medium techniques. My initial aim when I participated in group meditations was to study the techniques or become a medium. Those early weekend outings were thus spent in exploring the theory and practice of survival after death to allay my skepticism or get an actual experience myself to confirm the legitimacy of the demonstrations and dispel my doubts.

I found the demonstrations of survival or the doctrine that life continues after death very comforting. The tenet that after death one crossed over with his carnal mind but without the mortal remains was assuring and intriguing. I yearned for an experience from a departed spirit I could recognize to confirm that indeed life as we know it continues on the other side. I took part in group experiments to contact spirits of the departed. It was this group that exposed me to the various methods of divinations mentioned above and the discovery of the Chinese book of changes, *I Ching*. I was initially mesmerized with channeling or spirit mediums and longed for the ability to channel spirits and become a spirit medium.

I do not remember exactly how it happened but I found myself in the company of an Australian Aboriginal social activist. My involvement with social activism was another manifestation of the change in the direction of my life. I followed her to some of her meetings and interacted directly with aborigines. Some of the aborigines that I met were intrigued to see an African and there were those who had become so radicalized that they wanted nothing to do with anybody they considered a lackey of the white man. I became familiar with the problems of the Australian Aborigine that helped to dispel the unfavorable opinion I formed about them before I ever met an aborigine in the flesh. I had the privilege to meet, sit and chat with some Aborigines and heard first hand stories about their problems and survival in a white dominated society. I was invited to an aboriginal country and western music festival in the countryside outside of Melbourne by the activist. I saw or came into contact with the largest gathering of aborigines.

During the various conversations and discussions I had with them we came to the conclusion that indeed the African had much in common with the aborigines though we might be continents apart. Africans and Aborigines have common colonial heritage. The only difference between Africans in the tropical regions and the Aborigines was the level of settlement by the white colonialists. Tropical Africa was not settled by the white man because of the scourge of the mosquito. But in the semi tropical regions of Africa the problems of those Africans were very similar to the Aborigines. The indigenous populations were shunted to the sidelines of society. The original or first settlers of Australia were criminals and the behavior of the original settlers towards the indigenous populations was as criminal as their criminal reputations. They deliberately attempted to wipe out the indigenous populations. In today's world they would have been charged with genocide or crimes against humanity for what they did to the aborigines. The Australian Aborigine became a minority in his own homeland and was settled in the equivalent of Bantustans or reservations and consigned to life on the margins of society. It is no wonder that to the aborigine a good white person is a dead one.

The music festival was the largest gathering of aborigines at any one place that I came across while in Australia. The festival had a dual purpose; education and entertainment. On education the festival was used as a rallying cry for the youths to stay in school. I was taken to the festival because the activist thought that my story might be encouraging or inspiring to others. I did not consider myself qualified to advise any person but my own journey through life was fraught with problems as the life of many aborigines. But if I could find myself in Australia then it was possible for the aborigine to make it in their country even though they might hate the white man's culture and education, but that is the reality. I told some of my hosts that the difference between me and some of their youthful dropouts was education. I managed to stay in school against all odds because my mother would not have it any other way. Left to my own designs I would have dropped out of school by the fourth grade. Some of the people who sat around me nodded their heads in agreement. But for education I could not have afforded the plane ticket to Australia let alone make a living there. I made it to Australia by virtue of education and not by the size of my father's wallet.

For a few months I was happy to be involved in social work, and I liked my role as a side kick to the social activists. I served as her cheer leader among her people. I tried to impress those I met that discrimination is a fact of life; that even among the aborigines there might be tribal discrimination. Some tribes might consider themselves better than other tribes. I suffered from discrimination from my fellow countrymen but I learned to live with it. You cannot force another person to have a positive opinion or impression about you but you can work to have a positive impression or opinion about yourself. I developed a thick skin endured and fought against discrimination and gradually won grudging acceptance from some of the very people who looked down their noses at me. The white man respects success and you would win grudging acceptance and respect from the white man if you succeed in school. Then their fallacies about your innate abilities would be exposed. But you reinforce the prejudice by dropping out of school and turning to the bottle for company.

I led quite an active life in Melbourne. Apart from my engagement with aborigines I took ballet dancing lessons, did a radio program, and acted in a television commercial for soap but my main focus from day one was spiritual discovery. Yoga was the path I chose for my spiritual renaissance and renewal.

I underwent some sort of renaissance when I landed in Australia in 1975. I chose the path of self-awareness or spiritual awakening as a route to contentment and material prosperity or success in life. "Seek ye first the kingdom of God and all other things shall be added unto you" (Matthew 6:33). I was convinced from the outset that if I became spiritually aware material prosperity would follow.

Owing to my background and experiences I was always fascinated and interested in mysticism and the occult. At St. John Bosco's college my favorite books were biographies of saints from the school library. I found their lives so compelling that I could not tear myself away from reading them while a student. I was fascinated by their extraordinary mystical powers that enabled them to do things that were above and beyond the capability of the average mortal being.

FLICKERS OF SELF AWARENESS

The practical benefits of consistent and persistent practice of concentration and meditation was the attainment of peace and tranquility in my life. The things that used to rattle me and set my heart racing did not seem to have the same hold on me anymore. As already said I began to enjoy quietude or solitude happy to be left alone to be lost in my own mind. From the enjoyment of silence, or as is often said 'silence is golden' I found my dreams begin to manifest into physical reality within a few days of the dreams. Most of these dreams were mundane but it was nevertheless exhilarating to stumble across an event or situation that I saw in a dream a few days prior. Some of my dreams that manifested before me used to amaze and confound me. Sometimes I recognized or remembered the dream immediately as soon as I saw the event unfold before me but on many occasions the realization hit me long after the event has come and gone. The manifestation of my dreams into reality prompted me to keep a journal for dreams to help me to track and remember the sequence, the length of time before any dream manifested into reality and then to discern the dreams with prophetic or valuable messages from the rumblings of the mind. The journal was the closest I ever came to keeping a diary but it was devoted solely to my dreams. The purpose of the journal was to jog my memory to remind me of my dreams But I was unaware that along with the dreams was the development of my intuition until an unfortunate accident opened my eyes and I stopped taking my hunches or intuitions for granted. The hunches were my subconscious or super conscious mind sending me messages that I later characterized as the voice of God or my guardian angel. I was saved from several pitfalls and unpleasant situations that could otherwise have been tragic. The unfortunate accident set a bench mark in my mind that began my personal relations with God by listening for his voice in the silence of my mind. I dubbed the quiet and unobtrusive intuitions or hunches as the voice of God or my guardian angel.

When I left Ghana for Australia I 1975 I went with one overriding goal, a car by the time returned to Ghana. The car was the center of my life and had a hold on my imagination. I considered a car as essential to my self esteem and affirmation of my status in society. I resolved that by the time I returned to my country I would go with either a new or reliable used car. But I put this goal on the back burner and sought spiritual enlightenment through yoga meditation. I sought spiritual awareness believing that if I found the kingdom of God within me then all other things shall be added. *Matthew 6:33 "But seek first the kingdom of God and His righteousness, and all these things shall be added to you"*. I assumed that if I found God and his righteousness I shall also find material prosperity, after all, God is the alpha and the omega. By the middle of 1977 my perspective on the car and material properties in general began to shift in line with everything else in my life. Possession of a car and other material properties ceased to hold on my imagination as symbols of my success or social standing. I never reckoned that God was the ultimate prize but once I found Him nothing really mattered again. In time I came to rationalize the car for its true purpose, a utility to move me from place to place. The car lost its allure as the center of my life and a symbol of my success and social standing. This new attitude towards the car liberated me in much the same way I was liberated when I walked away from my junk car a couple of years earlier. I decided to enjoy whatever material properties or largesse God brought my way and let go when lost or used up without any attachment or regret. I realized that my contentment and happiness should not be dependent on external things but should emanate from within. I found contentment and true happiness when I let go my obsessions. I freed myself from voluntary servitude to the material world. As my attitude of non attachment firmed up and seeped into my consciousness my financial prospects began to move in a positive direction. In 1977 the year I made my first foray into earning extra income towards my material goals the results were almost disastrous. I was so anxious to keep a job that was above my physical abilities that I got hurt on the job. By 1978 with quiet and tranquil attitude and improvement in my intuition I had a devil may care attitude towards my ambitions. And the more it appeared that I did not care the more material prosperity came my way.

My fortunes started changing for the better as I began going through attitude adjustment from the latter part of 1977. The following year I had enough confidence to wade into the used car market again. I guess I was trying to exorcise the ghost of the misery the used Austin 1800 gave me in Ghana. I wanted some self assurance that the problems I had with the car were due to lack of reliable parts and were not caused by any sorcery or witchcraft. After obtaining a Victoria State driving license I bought a used British car that was far older than the Austin 1800 that made my life so miserable in Ghana. The car was rear wheel drive and surprisingly, despite its age, it did not give me a lot of headaches. I bought a repair manual and was able to install front and rear drum brakes and set the points on the car. At least for those brief moments I had some personal satisfaction of repairing a car, a yearning I had since infancy a yearning that has never really gone away.

Transformation Of My Life

I was poor but I did not know exactly how poor I was. Poverty did not seep into my consciousness to adversely affect my outlook on life. My family did not have any of the popular gadgets I looked on enviously in the rooms of our neighbors. As already pointed out my parents had no furniture of any kind other than a bed; when necessary we sat on the short stools that my mother sat on for cooking. And thanks to the tropical weather we lived most of our lives in the courtyard; when we came out in the morning we did not go back until sleep time. There were certain things of which I was ashamed but poverty was not one of them. I was ashamed to be sent away from school for not paying school fees on time. I would have been forced to drop out of school if my family could not pay my school fees. As it was my fees were perpetually late and from time to time I remedied the lateness from my own resources. I would have been ashamed to wear torn uniform to school and fortunately I never did. My khaki school uniform was always nice and crisp, but apart from the khaki uniform I never had much of anything. A draw string shorts was the only other clothing I had. But the draw string shorts was the standard casual wear for most boys in Gold Coast during the fifties. My shorts was often filthy but that was not due to poverty but to my personal hygiene habits.

I learned the value of work very early in life. I did chores for others for which I was paid and later on sold water in bottles at the local lorry park. The money I earned from activities filled some of my needs or wants as a child; I was even able to make up my school fees from time to time. I had a lot in common with kids of my age, we did similar chores for others and I sold water at the lorry park with competitors my age. But I knew I was different because my schoolmates would not let me forget that I was a northerner or *pepe nyi*. The ethnicity that showed that I was different was plain for all to see, my father wore Islamic cassock and my mother had prominent tribal marks on her cheeks. And most of my older siblings had marks on their faces or cheeks. Tribal marks were a common feature of most northerners during the colonial era. I did not have tribal marks but that did not matter to my schoolmates, I was mocked for marks I did not have. I did not consider my parents poor, as far as I was concerned they were stingy and tight fisted. The fact that we did not have furniture, radio or gramophone was due to their illiteracy not because of their poverty. Whatever they considered necessary they bought or provided for it. I did not feel I was poor as such but that I was different from other kids. Poverty while it is real and can be degrading is also a state of mind and I was lucky that despite the obvious lack of a lot of things while growing up I never considered myself poor.

Despite the fact that most families of the Gold Coast did not make very much the stark poverty exemplified by malnutrition or kwashiorkor was not common. I never saw them at Bogoso or Tarkwa where I spent most of my childhood and I was not a particularly robust and healthy child. I went to the clinics frequently. These anomalies or deficiencies in the diets for infant children came after independence the result of the demonstration effects of our new political elite. The basic diet of the average Ghanaian was rich in vegetables and fish was very cheap in the Gold Coast. But after independence our new rulers flaunted their new found wealth to the envy of their countrymen who scrambled to imitate their lifestyles. They popularized baby formulae. The nouveau riche of independent Ghana demonstrated a new kind of lifestyle, they showed that it was cool to feed our babies with '*Lactogen*' baby formulae at the expense of the old healthier diets we used to feed our infants. The formulae became a fashionable statement for our new mothers who displayed it prominently in public as a sign of affluence or level of civilized living. The formulae were expensive by our income standards thus a can had to be made to go further than recommended. The baby formula was thus diluted with water and the babies fed the diluted formulae were practically undernourished. The diluted formula amounted to feeding the babies with water flavored milk. For solids, instead of meals rich with greens, we fed them rice and watery stews or margarine. Thus within a few years after independence the attempts to keep up with the Joneses had a devastating effect on our infants who were fed the new fad diet. They started appearing at our clinics with the characteristic signs of malnutrition, distended tummies. Is it any wonder that kwashiorkor, the name coined for malnutrition, is a word from a Ghanaian dialect? Kwashiorkor was caused by 'trickle down economics' or demonstration effect of a corrupt political system.

Ignorant Ghanaians were misled by a corrupt political system that was put into place shortly after independence from colonial rule. It was made fashionable and desirable to feed our infants with western foods we could ill afford. Until I graduated from college and fell spectacularly from grace, I was not conscious that I was poor as long as I could work and meet my basic needs. But my confidence in work and rewards was shattered when I could not make ends meet though I was working and making a good income by Ghana standards.

I was driven to the edge of insanity by a combination of bad luck, ignorance and poor choices. And for the first time in my life I felt the sting of poverty and want. Although I was working and making quite a good income I could barely afford a good meal. I was still struggling to find my footing in life when I arrived in Australia. I started life down under anew by learning to recapture a positive attitude while losing the mentality of poverty and want that had characterized my life after graduating from college. I started my life in Australia with religion as my first focus by seeking the kingdom of God first and foremost through concentration, meditation and prayer hoping that when I found the kingdom of God, all other things shall be added unto it.

With religion as my focus and the center of my life I made enough progress in my chosen path and midway through my second year I underwent a quiet transformation of attitudes and habits. The transformation freed me from myself. My mind and efforts became God centered or self actualization instead of the mundane and cravings to satisfy and gratify my desires and wants. Self actualization or God centeredness became my ultimate goal.

I did not renounce the world or become an ascetic or gave up the material goals I had when I landed in Australia. I was still the same individual with the same desires and needs but I was not controlled by my desires and obsessions. I became confident that in time my essential needs would be met by God though I had no idea how that would be fulfilled, but I stopped fretting and worrying over them. I had effective control over my desires and have never allowed them to control the essence of my life again. I am content with whatever I have and have very few longings and desires or wants.

The practical effect of the changes that came over me was that I gained a measure of control over my mind. My fears and anxieties exist within the confines of my mind and as I gained a greater control over my mind my fears and anxieties melted away. I realized that apart from my physical aches and pains and in harmonies everything else exists outside of me. My perception of the world controls my interaction with it. To gain control and tame my mind was to gain control over my anxieties my fears and expectations. The regular and constant practice of concentration and meditation over a period of time gradually tamed my restless mind and gave me a measure of self control and freedom. I tamed my fears, anxieties, expectations and desires and I became the architect and engineer of my happiness and misery. I stopped feeling sorry for my past failures. The poverty and want that overwhelmed and made me financially miserable for more than two years was self-inflicted. I sought for contentment and happiness from without and never found it. I lacked self-confidence and sought affirmation of my social standing from the validation of my peers and consequently did dumb things. I hankered for recognition for that which I was not, prosperous, by clinging to material things which only sunk me deeper into depression and poverty. Finally I freed myself from the prison of my mind and walked away from the source of all my anxieties, fears and misery. I became the master and captain of my own ship when I ultimately went through an attitude adjustment.

Unforgetable Experieces From Melbourne

Australia was the first time I went outside the boundaries of my country, I was fascinated by the country and took advantage of the opportunities that were offered me and made the most of the opportunities. I lived a full life and I have never come to duplicating my total life experience since I left Melbourne in 1979. I led a balanced material and spiritual life in equal measure. I became interested in physical fitness in Australia quite apart from yoga and for a brief period was obsessed with it. Apart from regular yoga exercises I rode a bicycle around Melbourne on my daily chores, something I would not have dared to do in Accra because of traffic fears. Embarrassment from a pickpocket prompted me to start walking to office from Pig Farm. I did not walk to the office from the love of walking but I was forced into it by the shame inflicted on me by a pickpocket. I was obsessed with fitness in Australia; I walked, jogged and rode a bicycle around the streets of Melbourne because I wanted to not because I was compelled by circumstances or events beyond my control. I was such a fitness nut that at one time I was mistaken for a world class black athlete when I was seen jogging around a park opposite my apartment building. In 1977 or thereabout there was an athletic meet in Australia involving Kenyan runners and when I was spotted running in the park passersby's stopped to look at me. I was embarrassed by the mistaken identity but not ashamed.

The streets of Melbourne were so safe for pedestrians that that young lovers could hold hands and kiss in the middle of a pedestrian crossing oblivious to the traffic tie up in both directions waiting on them to cross. The first time I came across young lovers holding up traffic I thought they were nuts, but the pedestrian was king on the streets of Melbourne. It is noteworthy that my unfortunate riding accident did not involve a moving vehicle but a parked and stationary car. I was knocked off the bike by the door of a parked car that was swung open as attempted to pass by.

Ballet Dance Exhibition

One of my earliest physical activity apart from yoga exercises was ballet dance lessons. I mingled with college, secondary and grade school students for the dance lessons. When the opportunity for ballet lessons was presented to me I could not not refuse the opportunity to meet a cross section of Australian youths. It was an opportunity to learn something that had nothing to do with my studies or profession. I had no idea of the dedication and discipline required for success in the art form. When I had the opportunity to try it I accepted it as part of my obsession with physical fitness. The school was housed on the second floor of a large warehouse like building outside the center of Melbourne. The lessons gave me an opportunity to meet Australians who were not within my normal circle of acquaintances. I interacted with grade school children, college students and men and women of various walks of life. The ballet lessons gave me an opportunity to assess my progress in yoga. The dance was the first time I did any exercises with other people outside the confines of my roomy house. Doing exercises with kids and young men and women some of them less than half my age showed me the physical benefit I got from my dedication to yoga. I never really knew the extent of the control I had over my body until I mingled with the dance students. I was surprised at the extent of my physical agility when compared to my younger dance students.

I considered the lessons as an extension of my regular physical exercises or yoga practice and I hoped that when I returned to my country I would continue to apply the lessons in my daily exercise routine. I took the ballet lessons for about two years. I discontinued only after my wife came to join me in Australia and my attention shifted to other opportunities that came my way. But long after I stopped taking formal lessons I continued to apply some of the exercises in my daily routine while in Melbourne until I went back to my country and my intentions unraveled. I liked the discipline and dedication of the dance form and appreciate the profession of career dancers. Some of the old and retired dancers that I met intimated that though their bodies were wracked with arthritis which they attributed to the rigor of their profession they would do it all aver again if they had to start all over again.

Jeannette, the ballet teacher, gave me the only opportunity I ever had to participate in a dance exhibition at Monash University Theater or one of the universities around Melbourne. It was my one and only appearance on the stage in a theater. For that brief period I basked in the lights that were trained on me during the dance exhibition. Although I was agile and flexible but I do not think I was that competent to be on stage with some of her best students but I guess I was included because I was the only black student in her class. But for whatever her motivation I had the time of my life and a lasting memory. For once in my life I was the recipient of cheers and claps, I was not only a spectator but also a performer. I was an object of curiosity while the exhibition lasted, there were very few of us in Melbourne in the mid to late seventies. I still cherish the memory of my brief performance as a ballet dancer before spectators.

Extra In TV Commercial

The first opportunity came my way when I was only a few months old in Melbourne, it was a bit part in a television commercial on soap. I was one of the supporting cast and that was the only time I ever took part in any theatrical event whether on stage or before cameras. The dance exhibition in which I took part was before a live audience but there were no cameras. Melbourne gave me the only experiences involvement in a theatrical or acting event, it was brief but I cherish the memory.

My first attempt at acting in a school play was also a bit part while I was a student at Peki Government training college in 1963-65. During the final year the English Tutor decided to put on a drama show as part of our final year graduation activities. The drama was based on a play by Wole Soyinka, The Trials of Brother Jero. The drama was about the temptations of a married church minister; the dialogue contained some erotic dialogue. The play was all set to go, the costumes and props were completed and the stage was set. Then we held our last dress rehearsal before the principal. The play was cancelled after the dress rehearsal, the principal disapproved of the erotic dialogues in the play. We were all mature students, some of us were fathers and grandfathers, I never understood the principal's rational for cancelling the play. We were a public institution so I do not know whose sensibilities he was protecting by denying us the forum to show our acting talents to our classmates and colleagues. Thus the only opportunity I ever had to take part in a school drama was taken away at the last minute.

The cancelled drama, The Trials of Brother Jero was the closest I ever came to taking part in any school drama or play until I found myself at the Newport Railway Museum taking part in the shooting of a television commercial on a brand of soap I have never seen-Lime Fresh. The shooting at the Newport Museum lasted virtually the whole day. The excitement of being on camera wore off by the end of the second hour because of the constant repetition. We kept on shooting the scenes over and over again until we became tired and bored. The main actors were two twin sisters brought in from Sydney. My bit part was to ride in the vintage train wagon dressed like a calypso dancer or performer, smile and wave my hands at the trees.

It appears the commercial might have been shot for the New South Wales market because I did not see it before I left Melbourne more than four years after the commercial was shot. The role I played paid me the largest one day pay I ever received to date. I was paid three hundred dollars for a day of waving my hands in a vintage train wagon at trees. I was bored and beat up by the end of the day but when I saw the figure of $300 I was quickened and the tiredness melted away. The one day pay was more than my one month pay in Ghana so obviously it was a big deal for me and it was also more than the largest weekly wage I ever earned while in Australia.

RADIO BROADCAST EXPERIENCE

I had never seen or stepped inside a broadcast booth and I never dreamt I would ever see one let alone make my voice heard over radio. The nearest I ever came to a broadcasting house was when I passed by the offices of the Ghana Broadcasting Service on the way to the airport or thereabout. So to be invited to make a radio program about my country over public radio in Melbourne was beyond my wildest dreams. It was something I had never thought of, imagined or ever visualized, it was beyond my comprehension. While I delighted in talking about Ghana at small meetings and gatherings this was the biggest opportunity to talk about my country to a wider audience. The best part was that it was not just one hour but five hours over five days. It gave me the opportunity to finesse the history, culture and geography of Ghana in another country relying on my background knowledge and experience. I was eager since the first day I landed in Australia to learn about my host country and suddenly I was provided the forum to tell them about mine.

I had no writing experience of any kind other than normal essays and school assignments. But with the guidance of the producers I wrote five one hour length stories about Ghana that was delivered live over the public air waves. In the end I was able to write and present the five part series live without being prerecorded. I saw the inside of a broadcast booth for the first time ever. The effort was voluntary without any remuneration whatsoever, but the experience was worth more than money. That was the first and last time I saw and sat inside a broadcast booth or studio, the experience was worth its weight in gold. I had a rare opportunity ever granted to a citizen of another country to broadcast cultural and propaganda materials over the public airwaves of the host country. I wonder whether Ghana would grant such an opportunity to a citizen of another country without previewing the broadcast material. My material was not prescreened or previewed by any higher official, they had no prior knowledge of my broadcast material. I gained an insight into the workings of radio, an experience I could not get in my own country or for that much anywhere else unless I had a celebratory value.

SHORT HOLIDAY IN HOBART

The first two years of my stay in Australia was the most adventurous. During that period I went on a road trip to the capital territory, Canberra, Sydney Opera House and Sydney Harbor Bridge and a boat trip to Hobart. One trip I never attempted even though the tab would have been borne by my host was a trip to snowy mountains for skiing or just sight seeing to experience snow. My wife went on one such trip to the mountains in the winter but I felt too queasy to ride up the mountains for the spectacle of cold and snow. Of all the excursions and travels around Australia my trip to Hobart stands out in my mind because it lasted about a week. Most of the other trips were day trips and remain hazy in my mind. The trip to Hobart was sponsored and paid for by my host, the government of Australia as part of my scholarship. The scholarship program paid for all my excursions around Australia and even paid for me to return to my country on vacation. I married Obenewa during my vacation in 1977 and they paid her plane fare to come to Australia with me. The government took care of every aspect of my visit to Hobart including arranging with a host family to house and show me around the city. The host family took me around Hobart and showed me the places of interest in the city and its suburbs.

I went to Hobart by boat, I fear water and apart from crossing the Volta River by ferry I would not step into or wade into water beyond my buttocks voluntarily. Some phobias do not make sense and I guess my phobia of water is one that is illogical. I suppressed my phobia once I was on the boat but I never lost sight or bearings of the location of the flotation devices on the boat incase I need one in an emergency. The excitement of speeding down the runway and watching the world speed by or grow smaller is missing in a boat it is replaced by being a speck in the middle of the sea with the port of departure a world away. I let myself relax and enjoyed the ride.

Of all the sites my host family showed me around Hobart, one stands out in my mind, the museum dedicated to the last original inhabitant of the island. Tasmania appears to exemplify the criminal element of the first settlers of Australia when the indigenous populations were hunted down and killed like wild animals. And nowhere are those atrocities more clearly exemplified than Tasmania. The indigenous people of Tasmania were wiped out like some wild animals. The museum pieces were all that was left of the indigenous population of the island.

As one who regularly goes to church I had a unique church experience at the church of my host family. The churches I frequented in Melbourne did not serve communion. The Brotherhood Church of Hobart was different from the churches I frequented in Melbourne in that aspect; it served the Lord's Supper. The communion was served with regular bread rolls instead of wafers or unleavened bread. The rolls were passed around in a small wicker basket, each member broke a piece and passed it on. The wine was served in small vials; I felt the effect of the alcohol in the communion wine. Up to that time I had not tasted any alcohol or wine since I gave up the bottle in the latter part of 1975; for one who could drink a liter of wine in an evening it showed that my system had cleaned itself of any vestiges of alcohol. The church lived up to its name; it did not have dedicated pastors. Each brother is a pastor. The pastoral duties rotated among the brethren from week to week.

Spiritual Awakening And Awareness

In retrospect the hints of spiritual awakening or awareness began when I began going through a change of my attitudes and habits by questioning the wisdom of my attachments and obsessions with material possessions. Those questions led me to make a complete about turn in reassessing my priorities in life. These questions and doubts did not come easy. I replaced one obsession with another; materialism with passion for spiritual development and awareness. I was consistent and persistent in the practice of relaxation, concentration and meditation whether in the privacy of my home, public place or work. Concentration and meditation became a habit and whenever I closed my eyes I switched into concentration and meditation mode automatically. Closing my eyes at any location became almost synonymous with concentration, meditation and prayers. The other indication that I was on the path to a greater awareness came when I began questioning the purposes of group meditations, divination techniques and desire to be a medium or channel for discarnate spirits. I questioned the wisdom of channeling, spirit mediums and spirit communications in general. The discipline required to become God aware is the same to become a channel for earthbound and ignorant spirits. It occurred to me that channeling for spirits was an awful waste of time. Time that should be used to get to know and contact God within instead of chasing earthbound spirits who want to make themselves heard but who might not necessarily know any better than me. Shedding the body or mortal remains, I conjectured, does not necessarily bestow power or wisdom. I became disenchanted with the very idea of spirit mediums or my body temple as their channel of communication with the living. I thought that any spirit that cannot communicate with the living except through the body of another is not worthy of reverence. The doubts and questions raised in my mind eventually led me to break with the weekend group meditations and practice of divination techniques.

Just about the time that I began having doubts and questions about channeling or spirit mediums was about the time I began seeing ghostly figures or shadows in the church during demonstrations of survival after death segment of the order of worship. But by this time I had lost the initial euphoria and excitement on the demonstrations by the mediums. As such I found it difficult to accept that the ghostly figures were spirits. Though I did not see them until much later, I attributed the figures to light and dust formations caused by the drawn curtains during the segment. The practice had not changed, I had changed and suddenly I questioned everything. The figures must be my eyes playing tricks on me, I concluded, why are they not there until the curtains are drawn. It did not matter that the curtains were always drawn and I started seeing the ghostly figures lately, the skepticism remained. Although I was skeptical about the ghostly figures nevertheless I looked forward to seeing them every Sunday. That led me to express another skepticism, supposing the shadows and dark figures were real spirits, where would my own spirit be while I channeled other spirits. Would I be estranged from my spirit during the period of channeling? What would happen to my spirit in the unlikely event that the channeled spirit decides to make my body its permanent home? Demon and spirit possession while rare in spirit communication is nevertheless a possibility. Nothing I saw and heard allayed my fears, doubts and skepticism about the practice of channeling or spirit communications.

Thus far the only reliable guide I had on my yoga practice was the paperback *Yoga Over Forty*. And then in 1976 I came across a copy of *The Autobiography of a Yogi* in our church bookshop; I became a member of the *Self Realization Fellowship*. I incorporated the lessons on concentration and meditations techniques of the Fellowship into my daily routine. The literature of the *Self Realization Fellowship* became an integral part of my studies. The Self Realization Fellowship became my guru. It is said in yoga that when a pupil is ready a teacher comes along. I guess I came across the literature of the Fellowship when I was ready. The Autobiography of a Yogi brought reincarnation into my consciousness for the first time. Some events and places recounted in the book seemed familiar though I had no reason to feel a sense of familiarity about lands and places that had no historical or geographical connection with me. It took more two years after I read the biography to set foot on Indian soil. As I continued with my yoga and meditation practice I began to touch the God within through informative and prophetic dreams and flashes of insight and awareness about things I had no previous knowledge.

The doubts and skepticism I had in my heart about spirit mediums eventually led me to abandon the practice and break with the church altogether. I had been going to the churches for about three years and never once got a prophetic message or shout out from the other side of life, but the week I made up my mind to sever relations with the practice I got a message at church. The gist of the message was that I had abandoned a path of spiritual development that would have yielded fruits within a short period of time and brought comfort and solace to many. And the dark figures and shadows I had been deriding as dust and light formations vanished from my view during the demonstration of life after death segment of church services. I stopped seeing the figures though the subdued lighting and drawn curtains were the same. The disappearance confirmed that at least some spirits might have been present in the church during the demonstrations perhaps clamoring to be heard or channeled by a medium. It also confirmed my personal belief that the spirit world is as much stratified as the physical world. When I changed my mind about spirit communications I was no more on the same wavelengths with them, I removed myself from their sphere of influence and severed the channel of communication that was developing. I never saw another ghost or shadow figure in the church during the demonstrations until I moved away and ended association or contacts with the church.

I began going through my personal transformation in the latter part of 1977. And as I began reassessing the priorities of my life I also started having dreams that had relevance about my life or were perhaps meant to enlighten me on path of spiritual development. This phase was followed by hunches and intuitions about trivial and serious things that could have direct impact on my life either negative or positive. But I never associated any of these events as an indication that my chakras or spiritual centers were opening up. I had different expectations of spiritual development or awareness. I did not expect a gradual change and transformation of attitude and perceptions, hunches or dreams as signs of awareness or enlightenment. I expected something more dramatic such as clairvoyance, clairaudience or bold visions and not dark and ghostly shadows. None of these happened. I was still expecting my eureka of enlightenment or awareness moment when an avoidable accident brought everything about the change that was going on within me to a head and gave me a practical measuring rod of spiritual awareness or God consciousness. My expectation that spiritual enlightenment or self-awareness; would manifest through revelation of some supernatural event such as a vision of celestial figures in the heavenly realm never paned out.

The dramatic expectations blinded me to the positive changes that were taking place within and without me. I was more at peace with myself than at any other time in my life, healthier and full of vitality. Without knowing it my inner peace, tranquility and contentment reflected on my countenance for those who had eyes to see. One morning I came across two nuns on the sidewalk near my house just after my morning prayers and meditation who complemented me on my luminous countenance. The peace and tranquility within me illuminated my countenance though I was not aware of the glow but the glow attracted the attention of the nuns and prompted them to start a conversation with me. They told me that my countenance glowed from the distance as we walked towards one another from opposite directions and prompted them to speak with me. I never saw them again. I was excited when I reflected over the exchange and as far as I was concerned it was a sign of encouragement to continue what I had been doing by people of God.

I never got my moment in the sun of enlightenment or awareness but I do know that I surrendered myself to God. And in that surrender I felt everything was possible. I was emboldened, liberated and with an unbounded sense of optimism. And I was still waiting for my moment in the sun when I found myself in the back of an ambulance on the way to the emergency room after the accident involving a bicycle and a car. The emergency room physicians sent me back home on the back of another ambulance with some tablets for my pain and assured me that no bone was broken. My perceptions and expectations of awareness were finally altered by the unfortunate accident. I realized after that day that the Divine had been communicating or talking to me but I was not listening. The accident opened my mind on how God communicated with me in silence. I began to listen and pay attention to His silent voice. That accident gave me the yardstick to discern the voice and wishes of the Divine from my carnal and mundane thoughts in the stillness of my mind. The accident established a benchmark in my heart and mind of the virtue of remaining calm, quiet and serene at all times even when involved in bedlam. It is when I was calm and serene that the voice of God was loud and clear. I recognized the voice of God in the calm waters of my mind; I could not hear His voice through the noise and clamor of my mind. Serenity is essential to hear or discern the voice of God.

My expectation of the dramatic and spectacular were not met exactly as expected but my dreams and hunches over time became very dramatic. My hunches saved me from situations that could have been tragic or even fatal if I had not listened and paid attention to the voice of God that emanated from within me. Some of the unfortunate events that were averted or prevented through hunches, intuitions or the voice of God from within are recounted below. But I guess that at the time I was expecting to see visions I was past the age of visions. The Book of *Joel 2:28* "*I will pour out my spirit on all flesh, your sons and daughters shall prophesy. Your old men shall dream dreams, Your young men shall see visions*". Thus by this passage my expectations were met exactly as God intended. I saw visions in my youth even including the one in which I saw my dead body being carted to the morgue at about age fifteen or sixteen. And as a mature and grown up man I dreamed dreams and the dreams were as informative and prophetic as any vision could have been. I saw visions in my youth and dreamed dreams as an adult just as God intended it to be. My expectations had been met though I was unaware at the time.

The practical benefit of surrendering myself to God was that my life took a very positive turn in ways big and small. Once I surrendered myself to God I stopped worrying about the things that used to rile me and made my blood boil. I realized that in spite of all my worries I was not able to alter an iota of any event or condition in my life. And so I did not see why I should flog myself after surrendering my life to God. From the moment of surrender I was never disappointed and when things did not go as expected I had better alternative or God told me why or just asked me to bide my time. My problems did not go away or vanish but I saw myself from a different perspective and that altered the nature of my problems.

The car I eventually bought when I was about to return home was practically chosen for me. It was a car I had never considered as financially feasible or within my social class or status. When I was getting ready to buy a car I considered only the most common cars I knew on Ghana roads. I was anxious to avoid another debacle with exotic or scarce car. The cars that were on my radar screen were: Datsun (Nissan) Toyota, Mazda, Peugeot, Rover and VW. It never crossed my mind to enquire about BMW, Mercedes Benz or Volvo though I was following their commercials in the local media for entertainment. I sought quotations from the manufactures of the above cars but none of them even acknowledged receipt of my letter for a quotation. I was stumped. Then out of the blue I had a hunch. Why don't you try Mercedes after all you have been dreaming of a diesel car. I wrote to Daimler Benz and within two weeks I received a quotation with directions on how to place an order through their dealership in Melbourne.

When I placed the order for the Mercedes 200D in the second half of 1979, I did not have the full purchase price but I was optimistic that by the time I emplaned for Ghana I would have the money to make full payment. On the day I left for Ghana I had fully paid for the car and even had a rainy day fund of more than $6000 left in my account. That amount could have bought me a house, but home ownership had not seeped into my consciousness. I had no history of homeownership in my family neither did I know any homeowner so it never occurred to me to use the extra money to buy a house. It took about another three to four years to come to that threshold.

When Daimler Benz was about to ship the car they requested for an extra payment of thirteen dollars or so before shipment. By the time I sent the extra payment the government had standardized the makes and models of cars that could be import into the country and Mercedes Benz was not one of them. They had eggs on their face. If they had not held up the shipment because of a measly $13 I would have beaten the deadline. But I decided to assume the risk of seizure for importing a restricted car and asked them to ship it anyway. I did not know where else to turn for another car. All the manufacturers I contacted earlier did not reply to my letters. I took delivery of the car without problems when it finally arrived.

The changes and transformation of my life sometimes took unexpected turns and some things happened slowly and imperceptibly. During this period I noticed by accident that some of my utterances whether intentional or unintentional were manifesting into reality like the fulfillment of the words of a prophet. The unexpected realization that my utterances could have legs a few days after they were uttered became an unanticipated burden I did not quite know how to handle. I remembered the story of Peter and Ananias in Acts 5:1-11. Although I did not expect that my utterances would have similar potency, it served as a cautionary warning and made me mindful about what I said to my wife, friends and acquaintances even during unguarded moments. If I had such a gift while I was wallowing in financial misery in Ghana I would have wished myself the world. But this time I felt the gift or realization was a burden than something to celebrate or cherish. I therefore became guarded about what I said and avoided frivolous and loose talk. I was already predisposed to be quiet and reticent and this unexpected gift did not help. The fear of unanticipated or unexpected consequences made me more quiet and reflective.

When I returned to my country my physical and spiritual life took a downturn, I lost my self discipline and most of the qualities that made me God centered. I had a family with a lot of distractions and responsibilities that I did not have in Melbourne and as such my spiritual life was adversely affected by my responsibilities of parenthood. Despite the loss of most of the spiritual qualities the one quality that I did not lose was inner peace and calmness. I maintained calm disposition and as a family man I refrain from uttering careless words, curses and profanity as much as humanly possible.

LARGE EXTENDED FAMILY

I come from a large family of both my immediate and extended family. At the start of my own family life I tried to limit my family to three children but I ended up with a family size as large as my father's. I grew up as a member of an extended family and was grateful for the help and support inherent in the extended family system. Although I benefited greatly from the large extended family network, I took the help and caring for granted and did not appreciate it until maturity. As a child I took the hospitality and help given to me by disparate extended family members as a matter of course and at the beginning of my adult life I never thought of reciprocity or returning some of the favors I enjoyed as a child but instead aspired to live a like a western family. That was my aspiration until I went to Australia and was able to compare the two systems the nuclear family vis-à-vis the extended family. As a result I gained a new appreciation and perspective on the extended family and my place in it. I appreciated the caring and safety net built into the extended family system. We are practically our brother's keeper as members of the same disparate family members.

I am proud of the culture and the mores of the tribe that gave me being and nurtured me. The more I have been removed and away from my tribe the more I have come to appreciate the essence of my culture. But my fear of the prowess of my people in poisons has not diminished and as such I avoided some of them for self preservation, the same reason estranged me from my hometown as a young adult. I have experienced enough nefarious deeds to be wary and keep a safe distance from my people whenever possible.

LIFE AFTER LIFE

I have made several references to demonstrations of life after death or spirit communication. And below I provide how I became enchanted with it before I became a skeptic and ended my romance with spirit communications after pursuing spirit communications for three years just when it appeared I was making progress in the concept. I was taken by storm the first day I entered a church and saw demonstration of what was termed as life after death for the first time in the open and not in a dark and spooky room. never heard or seen anything like it in any form other than rumors. To compound my confusion the church functioned like any Christian denomination with readings of the bible, sermons and everything else one would see in any normal Christian congregation or denomination. The only difference was the segment at the tail end of the service that dealt with demonstration of survival after death. The emphasis was the survival of life as we know it but without the mortal remains. I was forced to face my prejudice against my people or kinsmen from the perspective of my Catholic education background.

I came across the church by accident the first Sunday I went out searching for a place of worship. It was the first church I stumbled upon and I never looked back, I was hooked. I looked forward to the weekly demonstrations hoping that someday the two most important people known to me on the other side of life might bring me some comforting message. I went to the church week after week hoping for that moment when the spirit of my mother or younger brother would reveal themselves to me in an open church. So I kept going week after week hoping for that moment when proof of life after life would be validated in my own life and make a disciple of me.

During the last two years of my elementary education in my home environment I heard of stories about a village near Wa that was famous for channeling the spirits of the dead or spirit mediums. They allegedly channeled or used spirit mediums to help the living deal with the sudden and inexplicable deaths of loved ones and relatives. By the time I came back to my hometown as a teenager after almost a decade I had forgotten that I ever saw or interacted with spirits. I was a converted catholic still seeking baptism. As such I was prejudiced against the very idea of spirit mediums or spirit communications. I considered the practitioners of spirit communication or spirit mediums when I heard stories of the practice at *Duon*, a village near Wa. I considered the practitioners and their clients as pagans or heathens. I pitied those who went to the village to consult the mediums as ignorant idol worshippers. Of course nobody ever took me to the village of *Duon* to see or experience their practice but that did not prevent me from condemning them out of ignorance. Their reputation and exploits in spirit communications were legendary and widespread in the surrounding villages and towns. They were reputed to help people deal with grief, particularly those who lost loved ones suddenly. It was said that the mediums of *Duon* brought up the spirits of the recently departed to communicate with the loved ones they left behind to obtain closure. Where the death was allegedly caused by poison the spirit revealed how and where the poison was administered. I believed that the practices were fakes perpetrated by charlatans against an ignorant and unsuspecting people. That was the opinion I held of the spirit mediums of *Duon* until I went to Australia and found practically the same concept practiced in a 'civilized' Christian country. I was forced to confront my own ignorance and prejudice borne from indoctrination to believe that everything White was civilized and everything Black was backward and uncivilized. The basic principles and results were essentially the same, communication with spirits of the dead. People allegedly went to *Duon* to bring closure at the sudden deaths of loved ones and relatives. And that was what kept me returning to the church week in and week out looking for that moment in time when I might also receive a comforting message from beyond. I guess I faced my own ignorance and prejudice.

For about three years I was obsessed with the concept and practice of spirit mediums. I sought the company of mediums to impart their skills or direct me on how to become a spirit medium or channel spirits. I took part in group meditations and séances moderated in private homes by mediums at weekends for more than a year. During that period I tried every tool of a medium to communicate with the spirit of the dead such as Ouija board, automatic writing, tarot cards or crystal ball. But none of these tools brought me any closer to my objective of a spirit medium. I did not lose faith in the philosophic underpinning of the practice; I doubted that it was in the form as demonstrated at church by the mediums. I speculated that perhaps my mother or brother might have reincarnated or moved to higher spiritual planes and could not be bothered by the emotions of earthlings. Either that or the demonstrations themselves were false and chicanery playing on our emotions and mindset or expectations.

While I was running around the homes of mediums at weekends seeking for the skills of a medium I was also practicing raja yoga at home. I did not see any contradiction between the two, I thought that my meditation would enhance my chances to become a spirit medium. The discipline of meditation or mind control was as necessary to become medium as to become God centered or conscious. The discipline of the mind was the prime objective between raja yoga and spirit mediums. The church gave me a different social diversion and focus. Instead of running around bars and booze houses as hitherto I found a new avenue to profitably spend my weekends. Thus I spent more of my weekends taking part in séances, meditations, divination or spiritual readings instead of bar hopping.

After more than two years of fruitless efforts I began questioning the wisdom of spending valuable time chasing after spirits. As already said this was about the same time when my efforts were perhaps beginning to bear fruits, when I started seeing ghostly figures in the church during the demonstrations of life after life. I do not know whether my skepticism was due to sour grapes or because of the attitude adjustment I was going through about the same time. But I became very skeptical and doubted whether the ghostly and shadow figures I saw in the church during the demonstration hour were actual spirits. Without knowing it I was on my way out. I changed residence and neighborhoods but the basic premise of my skepticism did not change.

My changing attitude and transformation perhaps marked the beginning of my spiritual renaissance, awareness, enlightenment or God consciousness.

During my search for spiritual renaissance and development I did not obtain any practical advice from an enlightened and knowledgeable individual to deal with real world problems I was likely to encounter. As a result I was ill prepared for the problems and temptations that confronted me when I returned to my country. First my family responsibilities became a distraction, I never had to deal with family when I was in Australia. The responsibilities and social temptations distracted me from following the path of discipline and devotion I charted for myself while in Melbourne. I did know how to balance family life and worldly distractions and temptations with spiritual life.

In a way I reaped the fruits of the choice I made as a young adult. When I was a student at St. John Bosco's College I became interested in the life of the ministry, but I chose family life over the celibate life of a catholic priest. I wanted family life while I yearned for the contentment and serenity of the ministry. And when I returned to Ghana I was overwhelmed by responsibilities and temptations with the result that I fell from grace and lost my poise.

THE HEALING TOUCH

Fear and necessity led me to the accidental discovery that I was gifted with spiritual healing powers. The fear arose from my ignorance of the healthcare system in none emergency situations at night. I used the system twice in emergencies only and never used the system for routine medical care. To make matters worse the situations that required routine medical care occurred at night and were ameliorated by daytime. Thus when my wife got ill at night I was forced to nurse her and help her get through the sniffles. Obenewa and I relocated to Thornbury from Brunswick in the winter of 1978. Our first home in Thornbury was a studio apartment on 99 Smith Street where we lived for approximately few months. The studio apartment was the first self contained residential unit any of us had ever occupied. It was a novelty to have a bath and kitchen literally in the same room. We were already thinking about our eventual return home at the end of my studies. We thus began buying and storing some of our necessities in our apartment. The studio as such was becoming a little cramped. We upgraded to a mansion by our modest standards of roomy houses. We moved into a one bedroom apartment. Compared to the living conditions we were accustomed to living in our country, 112 Ballantyne Street was a mansion. It was our first taste of life in an apartment or flat with a separate living room and bedroom.

It was on Ballantyne Street that the health problems of Obenewa led me to discover that I had a gift for spiritual healing. I do not know whether it was ignorance or frugality but we did not upgrade our small portable one bar radiator to one large enough to heat our new living quarters. Houses in Melbourne are not centrally heated, at least the type of house we could afford to rent were not centrally heated. Thus while our living room used to be reasonably warm our bedroom was like an icebox.

We used to preheat electric blanket and crawl into a warm bed but stepped into the cold room if we woke up in the night for any purpose. The heat in the living room was not enough to affect the bedroom as such it was very cold in the middle of the night when one of us got up to use say the bathroom. We stepped into a cold frigid room from the warm bed and scrambled to use the bathroom and back into bed as quickly as possible. We used to dress warm around the house and used our small radiator and the heat from the stove to keep the living room warm during the day. Our weather related problems occurred late at night when the apartment became very cold. I endured the mild Australian winters quite well but Obenewa did not tolerate the cold as well as I did and used to suffer from cold weather related sicknesses at night.

On the nights she came under the weather I found myself acting or playing the role of her nurse. I administered over-the-counter cold remedies to her as if she was a baby. And when the cold symptoms struck in the middle of the night I was often forced to wake up to offer any help I could. She suffered from colds most often while we were in bed. I helped her with some cold remedies such as cough mixtures and pain killers. At that time my knowledge of over the counter cold remedies and pain killers was limited to APC, Codeine and cough mixture. I did not know of such remedies as Tylenol PM or any such over the counter medication. Thus anytime she fell sick I gave pain killers or cough mixtures routinely and then one night out of the blue, I laid my hands on her while half asleep and she got relief without my having to get up to give her the usual remedies. That night I was fast asleep when I overheard her coughing in my sleep as if I was dreaming. And while in that dreamy state a bible verse or quotation came to me thus; *"These are the signs that shall follow them that believe, in my name when they lay hands on the sick they shall recover"* Mark 16-17. And with the verse ringing in my dreamy and sleepy mind I stretched my hand over her half asleep and she quieted down and slept like a baby for the rest of the night.

When we woke up in the morning I remembered the application of the bible verse and its effect on Obenewa during the night though she was not aware that I laid hands on her according to the bible. That was the first time it ever occurred to me to lay hands on her as in Mark 16:17. I doubt whether I would have laid hands on her were I fully awake, I would have continued with the tried and trusted remedies of pain killers or cough mixtures. Suffice to say she was healed that night in the name of Jesus Christ. And from that day I prayed and laid hands on her in the name of Jesus Christ whenever she became sick. I stopped giving her the usual medications and relied solely on prayer whenever she fell sick. And I would never have considered practicing spiritual healing or laying hands on any person outside our apartment had not a prophet or messenger in our church told me openly that I had a gift for spiritual healing.

Since we moved to Thornbury I had not been going to Church. But for some unknown reason I began searching for another place of worship. I found a small stone brick church by the side St. Georges Road as I drove up and down the street. It was therefore the natural choice when I was looking for a new place of worship. The small stone brick church was known as the *Heart of Spiritual Truth*, HOST. The church was similar to the churches where I used to worship before I relocated to Thornbury except there were no demonstrations of survival after death. Instead of demonstration of survival after death they practiced spiritual healing and prophesying during that period. I was quite comfortable in the new church; the congregation was as friendly as members of my previous places of worship.

We had been part of the congregation for barely two or three weeks when I was given a message by the prophetess or seer on duty in the church that Sunday that I had a gift for spiritual healing. She then asked me why I was not using the gift for the benefit the congregation. "Is it because we are white?" She quipped. I was surprised by that quip and stammered for words to explain myself but before I could find my voice to explain that this was something I found by accident she had moved on to the next member. I had never considered the possibility of spiritual healing or seen myself in the role of a spiritual healer beyond my home; it therefore did not occur to me that anybody could benefit from the accidental discovery that laying my hands on my wife often relieved her. So despite the message I did not become emboldened to join the ranks of the spiritual healers in the church. But the following week the leader or church elder invited me to help the spirituals healers.

Thus far my only experience in spiritual healing was limited to my wife. Therefore when I was asked to help I could only follow the example of the spiritual healers in the church. I stood behind a chair like the others and waited for the first person to take the chair so that I could lay hands on the person. But I was practically ignored and as I was about to give up when the church elder saw my predicament and came to my rescue. He took the chair in front of me and I laid my hands on him in the name of Jesus as in Mark 16: 17. I did not actually touch him; I suspended my palms about an inch from his hair or person for about one to three minutes. And when he got up he gestured with his hands a sort of hallo effect on his head and announced to those who were curiously looking at him that it felt 'peaceful and relaxing'. After his gesture and pronouncement the other members of the congregation followed his example. From then onwards I practiced the laying on of hands every Sunday without fail. In time I became the only spiritual healer of the church as the other itinerary healers stopped coming to the church. The healers and prophets of the church were like itinerary preachers but instead of preaching they healed and prophesied. I was a regular member of the church as such they came to rely on me and ignored the various weekly visitors. I became the reliable fixture on Sundays and stood on my feet for hours after normal church service laying hands on the members who waited on me. And I could not leave until I laid my hands on all who waited patiently for their turn.

I was the only black man or minority in the church so I do not know whether my color made me an object of curiosity because shortly after I began serving as a spiritual healer I noticed an increase in the church attendance. It was mostly the increased number of new visitors that kept me in the church hours after the formal service ended. Apart from my color I do not know what else attracted people to me; as I said very little during the healing session. I did not speak until spoken to and considered myself merely as channel or instrument of God with very little to say about the process. It was therefore not in my place to play doctor by asking questions, my duty was to lay my hands in the name of Jesus Christ and let God do the rest. During the healing session I used to feel some tingling sensation in my spine or warmth in my hands but I had no idea where the sensation and warmth came from. While I never asked anybody about their problems one lady volunteered to me that her condition was much better since I started laying hands on her.

I never asked questions but from the beginning I did not need to ask. I used to pick up the mental or physical conditions of the people within my body as I laid hands on them. That feeling or sensation used to help me to concentrate or pray for the relief of the conditions I felt in me. I entertained this feeling for only a few months before a scary condition prompted me to pray against sensing the health and other problems of others in my body. One Sunday I picked up an acute backache during the healing session that literally followed me home from the church. Prior to that Sunday the sensations passed in and out of me as the people came and went from the chair. But this feeling persisted long after the person left the chair and I went home feeling the backache. As long as the feelings passed in and out of me as the people left my healing chair I did not care but once a condition remained with me long after I went home I got scared. I had no control over the sensations that passed in and out of me so I prayed that God should take away the sensitivity and he did within a period of about one month. I stopped sensing the problems of "my patients" in my body as I laid hands on them.

The weekly healing sessions were both tiring but also invigorating. I used to feel tired standing on my feet but was invigorated shortly after I completed the healing session and went home. I was glad that God found use or a way for me to serve my fellow man and I had a lot of satisfaction from the service. I enjoyed it and was thankful for the opportunity that God gave me to serve others; no matter how humble, it felt good to give of myself instead of always receiving. And I gave of myself in the name of Jesus Christ.

The highlight of my healing services at *The Heart of Spiritual Truth* (HOST) was in June or July 1979 when the church hosted the anniversary of *The Australian Spiritual Healers Association*. The church was filled to capacity with both new and old visitors. When it was time for healing I assumed that the healing would be restricted to members of the spiritual healers association and as I was not a member of the association I stayed out of their way. But the members of the church pulled me to take a chair among them. I became the center of attention as soon as I took a chair among them and almost everybody, new and old alike waited on me while members of the association were ignored by the congregation. Thus a scramble for 'patients' ensued at which some of them asked me to keep my hands off some particular individuals because they either accompanied them to the church or were past 'clients' or 'patients'. God allowed me to shine, among the Spiritual Healers Association during what should have been their moments in the sun, though I was not one of their members.

The spiritual healing was my humble contribution to the tapestry of the human family which for a brief moment in time God provided for me to bring some comfort and solace to a few members of the human family. I found during the laying hands in the name of God that it was easy to fall prey to temptations of the flesh. Working in the name of God did not shield me from temptation; on the contrary the temptations are accentuated as God and Satan vie for influence within the same space. There were mutual attractions between some members and me but I did not talk during healing and thus never established any channel of communication that Satan could have exploited.

When I was in Melbourne I was in constant contemplative and meditative mood and thus God centered. As such I had enough will power to resist the temptations that led to my spiritual downfall when I went back to my country. I was also conscious that any scandal would have reflected poorly on my country.

DIVIDED BY FAITH UNITED BY LOVE

Faith is the great divider of our world. It is the one element which at once energizes us and at the same time creates a less than charitable attitudes towards those who do not share our faith. The dogma of faith I was taught was incompatible with my family life. I grew up into the Christian faith by virtue of Christian education. But the one great concern I had about my faith was the implication that my family members who did not share my new Christian faith were bound for hell or fire and brimstone. I was conflicted with the implication that my family was bound for hell because they were not Christians. There were no rigid boundaries of faith in my family. My father did not foist his Islamic faith on his family; otherwise I would not have been educated in a Catholic school. He left me to choose my own path of faith without imposing his faith on me. That was the general tenor in my dysfunctional family. We were united by love as a family. The acrimony and divisiveness of faith was not a part of my family heritage. The dysfunction and estrangement within my family was a function of our flaws and weaknesses as the sons of Adam but not because of our faith. My doubts and skepticism grew out of the implication that my animist mother through no fault of her own was bound for hell. The more I grew into my faith the more I became skeptical. My mother was not perfect but I could find no reason to imply that she was bound for hell because she had not accepted Christ as her personal Lord and savior. She did for me what Christ commanded us to do, love one another. Love has been lost in the clamor to profit from the divisiveness of faith. Faith today is big business that has nothing to do with the salvation of the sinner. The faith of the new age is more interested in profiting from us by its emphasis on our differences instead of our common humanity through the love of God, love that has no color or boundaries. Most faith based churches are business enterprises that stoke fear and divisiveness, for it is in our divisiveness that they profit. The line of succession in these church businesses is not any different from any family based business; they are passed from father to son as if the family has monopoly of the Holy Spirit. The sad part is that we the foot soldiers claw and commit atrocities against one another while the church leaders laugh all the way to the bank. Their lifestyles are not any different from the life style of successful public enterprises. We are unwittingly the enforcers for the family dynasties.

The three religions of the patriarch Abraham have both been a blessing and a curse for humanity. They brought civilization to remote corners of the world but along with civilization and spread of their faith came the sword. And the sword of faith has been the bane of mankind since the dawn of civilization. Our development and progress has not diminished our penchant for violence arising from our brand of faith. If anything the divisions and violence has accentuated with time as we have made tremendous material progress. Our blessings and curses have gone hand in hand.

The three religions pride themselves on being religions of love and peace but one would not know it from the actions of some or our leaders and members. Love and Peace seems to be far removed in parts of the globe where we need it most. Faith is the dominant theme in those parts of the world where we justify our atrocities and violence against one another in the name of God or our faith. Most of the things we do against one another would be humanized if we but lived by the perception by which we like to describe our religions; love and peace. Those are the missing ingredients in our modern day discourse. The interests of our parochial and temporal leaders are served when we are divided by faith than united by love. The constant turmoil in our world is caused by the divisions fostered by our differing faiths even when it appears that we belong to the same faith.

The Christian religion that I follow in its many manifestations has lost its essence. Many of the churches have become virtual businesses; particularly the so called faith based churches. They are dominated by greed, avarice, power play and get rich quick schemes geared at making their founders rich in the name of faith. Love, the essence of the Christian religion is shuffled aside and if we lived by the commandment of love the world would be a much better place. Therefore if we lived by the great commandment the world would be a better place. I grew up with an understanding that my church was the one true church or faith that set me apart from other churches. I was a member of the only true church, all the others were pretenders. It appeared that by the tenets of my faith I did not have much in common with other Christian denominations until much later in my life. Skepticism eventually led me to come to the realization that by the great commandment I had a lot more in common with all than I was led to believe. I have striven to live by that edict though my attempts are most imperfect but amidst the imperfection I find I have more in common even with those who look down their noses upon me.

In Matthew 22:37-40, 'Jesus said to him, *"You shall love the Lord your God with all your heart, with all your soul and with all your mind. This is the first and great commandment. And the second is like it: You shall love your neighbor as yourself. On these two commandments hang all the Law and the Prophets."* By the words of Christ Love is the standard of Christian conduct and relations with other members of the human family. But I guess living by love is not as sexy as faith. Otherwise I don't understand our infatuations with faith almost to the exclusion of love. We are told by the author of our faith that all the commandments, laws and prophesy are dependent on love and yet love is virtually a footnote when it comes to our relations with one another and God. Why have we made faith the center of our relations with God and with one another? Perhaps it is because while no denomination can claim monopoly over love they can claim. No religion can claim monopoly of love but each can exploit a branch or point of faith for maximum divisiveness and financial gain. Faith without love is nothing (1 Corinthians 13). It is everything! People of faith are not necessarily people of love. Would I fulfill the demands of my faith and the law through love? The love that should be the guiding principle in our relations with God and one another is not because love is not divisive. Love does not demand of me to become a second Christ but simply to see the common humanity in all and do unto others as I would they do unto me. No man of faith wishes hell on his loved one even when we know that our loved ones have lost their way we are still compassionate to forgive the sins and faithlessness of our family members. It is another man's child who is an infidel and unbeliever who deserves to be in hell or killed but not my child. The people of faith have no compunction condemning others and heaping coals of fire on them. While the proponents of faith are more than willing to heap fire and brimstone on others they more forgiving of the foibles and weakness of members of their family. Faith negates love, debases and dehumanizes those we see as different so we can commit atrocities against them without any guilt. If my salvation or path to heaven or eternal life lies in the destruction of another then I do not want that salvation or association with that god.

Love for my mother caused me to question my faith from infancy. I could not see inside my mother's mind or heart but I knew that she loved me and sacrificed a lot for me. I was not a child from her womb but a child of her dead rival. Therefore when I was taught that except a man accepts the name of Christ that man cannot enter into the kingdom of heaven I questioned the tenets of my faith. Did I deserve heaven more than my mother who made it possible for me to have the Christian faith? In my mind's eye I could not see my loving mother going to hell because she was not a member of my faith. Whether I became a good and faithful Christian or not, I do not know but I know that I became a loving Christian whose faith did not estrange me from my mother because of her differing faith. I grew up knowing in my heart that love, the great commandment, is the path to eternal life.

I guess the basis of my faith was challenged when I came into contact with The Jehovah Witness sect at Bogoso in the eighth grade or Form II, they steered me from relying on catechism books for the tenets of my faith to the bible. I began reading the Bible so that I could hold my own when my faith came under attack during bible discussions. During my youth and early adulthood members of the Jehovah's Witnesses and to a lesser extent the Seventh Adventists helped me to come to terms with my faith and overcome the divisiveness inherent in the faith and dogma I learned in school. They challenged the tenets of my faith with quotations from the bible that exposed my ignorance on questions of my faith. That challenge led me to read the bible and formed my opinion on my faith. The opinions I formed were sometimes different from the popular narratives or the dogma and lessons I was taught. The Apostle Thomas was often portrayed in an unflattering light for doubting that Christ had risen. But I was greatly inspired by Thomas and followed his example in asking questions about my faith. I was inspired by the example of the doubting Thomas. Despite Christ chastising Thomas about his doubts and skepticism, Jesus nevertheless revealed himself to Thomas and made him a believer. If it was good for Thomas to see the Lord before believing it is good for me too. Thus I believe only that which I have seen and experienced; 'seeing is believing'.

I do not know whether my mother is in heaven or hell. But wherever she is in the great beyond, she is there because of what was in her heart and not because she shared my faith in this life. If she lived by love then I have no doubt that she must have found favor with the Lord. Love enables us to see one another as part of the tapestry or quilt of humanity. She gave practical meaning to love. I do not know whether she ever saw the inside of a church or a mosque until her death. She converted to Islam in her twilight years but if the example of other converts in my family hold true then she prayed only at home. The nearest that anyone can come to the truth is to be consumed by love in all its manifestations. Perhaps if we recognized that we are all part of one human family—whether as Christian, Islam, Hindu, or whatever faith we follow—loving those who do not share our faith would become easier. We would be united by love and not divided by faith.

ESSENCE OF MY FAITH

"Blessed are those who have not seen and yet believe" (John 20:29). This is the quotation that has been drummed into our heads time and time again to believe without seeing what they tell us. But Jesus did not condemn Thomas, on the contrary he said to Thomas: *"Reach your finger here, and look at My hands; and reach your finger here, and put it into My side. Do not be unbelieving, but believing".(John 20: 27)* Christ exhorts his followers to believe without seeing, but he did not condemn Thomas, he blessed those who would believe without putting him to the test. But he took pains to satisfy his doubts and misgivings and made a true believer out of him. And I believe that God still satisfies the doubts and the misgivings of the Thomas's among us. Jesus Christ despite chastising Thomas still satisfies the doubts and misgivings of the doubter and skeptic. This is the essence of my faith, the bible is said to be the word of the living God and if so then the living God still fulfils the promises of the bible. I believe in the power of fasting and prayers from experience not because my teacher or preacher told me so. And Matthew 17-21: *But there is no means of driving out this sort but by prayer and fasting.* I experienced this truth in my life, I saw the human face of Satan in broad daylight after fasting and prayers. Thus I believe that when I pray for salvation through fasting and prayer I expect that God who delivered Daniel and Esther in their hour of need will deliver me in my hour of need. God has never failed me. Miracles still happen as of old.

It is only in matters of faith that we are exhorted to believe blindly without proof. Are we afraid to test the premise that if we had faith as a mustard seed we could move mountains?. I ask questions and expect answers in accordance with the bible or scripture. Matthew 7: 7-8. *"Ask and it will be given to you; seek, and you will find; knock, and it will be opened to you. For everyone who asks receives; and he who seeks finds, and to him who knocks it will be opened."* The doubtful and skeptic believer is more faithful and loving Christian than the blind and slavish believer who follows and abides without question the teachings of his pastors and leaders. It is the blind and slavish follower who is both the bulwark of the faith and the one easily manipulated to commit atrocities in the name of the faith. The faith of the skeptic believer might even be steadier and stronger when tested than the slavish follower.

My faith rests on my personal experiences of the truths inherent in the bible. I do not believe that the truths of the bible endure only for the Christian or Jewish but for all who seek redemption or salvation from God. There are no two ways to truth no matter how we manipulate or make it malleable to suit our purpose, truth stands and it stands for the Jew as for the Gentile. The sun shines on the saint and the sinner and so both the sinner and the saint would find the truth when they search for it in whatever language or dialect they speak.

God is omnipresent and omniscient and He is so ubiquitous that we take Him for granted. I know and see God every day in the eyes of my fellow man. I cannot profess love for God and yet hate my fellow man, the image and likeness of God.

FORTUNE SMILES ON ME IN MELBOURNE

As already noted when I landed in Melbourne I virtually had a long list of material things I intended to buy on return to my country. I also had another goal, resume or take up again the practice of yoga I began in college but was forced to abandon due to my financial problems and resumed only a few months before I went to Australia. So prior to 1977 I took no steps towards fulfilling my material ambitions. I felt there was enough time ahead of me to meet my goals before I returned to my country. Thus, as soon as I landed in Melbourne, I took up yoga practice. I busied myself with yoga and spiritual studies while trying to find out what my new community had to offer. The only job I did during the first two years was a few weeks of cleaning offices after lectures. I was like a country boy come to the big city. Everything I found in Melbourne was magnificent beyond compare in my eyes. I goggled at the offices I cleaned, which at the time I thought they were luxuriously furnished compared to my office in Ghana. In the early part of 1977 I dipped my toes into the Melbourne job market. I found my first job through the local papers. It was a per diem job unloading containers at a warehouse near the port. I was a day laborer for a little under two weeks before a job related accident ended my first foray into the labor market. The day jobs were assigned on a first come first served basis. I used to get to the recruiting site by 5.30am and took my place in line. I used to count myself lucky when I made the cut because I did not have the size or brawn to do the assigned job without help. The jobs were usually over by ten or eleven o'clock in the morning and I went back home happily with my day's wage. But in the second week my string of good luck came to a screeching halt through an accident on the job.

On the day of the accident I should have thrown in the towel when I found that assignment was more than I could handle. The job that day involved the unloading of

400lb drums of bitumen. The drums were so heavy that I could not tilt one an inch on its edge without help, but I needed the money and I was not willing to go without the money. My fellow day laborers were kind and generous and asked me to get out of their way. They were kind and generous to a fault, they were not resentful; they just wanted me to get out of the way so that they could do finish the job on time without interference. But I felt guilty to be a bystander and earn the same amount of money as those who did the back breaking job so I tried to help in anyway I could. I was helping to tilt a drum onto its side when the drum keeled awkwardly out of control fell on the floor bounced up and landed on my right foot.

The heavy drum busted my right toe open. I hopped about in pain with blood dripping through my sneakers. I was rushed by an ambulance to the emergency room at Queen Victoria Hospital. An x-ray examination showed no broken bone just the soft tissue of my right toe busted open. The wound was dressed and I was sent home by another ambulance with instructions to return after three days. Meanwhile I was heart broken over the potential lost wages as I could not work. I could think of nothing else but the lost wages due to my injury. But I got the surprise of my life when I went back to the hospital on the third day; the staff informed me about something called workers compensation. I did not know anything about workers compensation but it was music to my ears when it was explained to me.

The staff helped me to complete the necessary paperwork for the workers compensation. I grinned from ear to ear at the prospect of earning income for doing no work. Suddenly, I forgot how sorry I was about the missed opportunities and rather wished that the wound would take long to heal. I wanted to mine my busted toe to draw free wages or compensation. As I nursed my wound, I counted my wealth for each day I was on "sick leave." The accident was fortuitous and godsend. I obtained workers compensation for three or four weeks. When the hospital took me off the injury list I did not go back to the day labor lines again. Indeed I did not attempt to do another job till the following year.

My first attempt at odd jobs for extra cash nearly ended in disaster but I learned something new, workers compensation. I also became knowledgeable about the labor market, the labor department where I could search for jobs in the future or apply for unemployment benefits if necessary. I came out of the shadows into the labor market. Previously I thought that because I was on scholarship I could not work on the books without jeopardizing my scholarship allowance.

In 1978 Obenewa became a part of my life in Melbourne and I was approaching the end of my stay. But I was still floundering for the money needed to meet my financial goals before my eventual return to my country. I intensified my efforts in 1978 and got my next job through the labor office. I got my first fulltime job in a brake and clutch remanufacturing shop located in Coburg. I was excited about the job because it brought me close to my childhood dream job of an auto mechanic; I was happy I had a job that had something to do with autos. My duty was grinding down asbestos linings on brake pads, shoes and clutches to tolerable sizes. It was a humdrum job but I was happy doing a job connected with cars and pretending I was working as an auto mechanic. But within three months I left the job for fear of the dangers of asbestos which was in the news at the time. The health dangers of asbestos trumped my childhood fantasies. That was the first of many full time jobs I did for brief periods at a time to accumulate money to meet my financial goals. The full time jobs turned me into an absentee student; I missed many lectures at crucial periods and the absences adversely affected my academic performance.

As I hustled from one factory to the other my meditation and concentration was also impacted. But I adapted my prayer and meditation routine to fit my work life. I meditated for a few minutes before I left for work in the morning and during my coffee and lunch breaks I practiced concentration and meditation techniques at any quiet and secluded spot I could find at the workplace. . I scarcely ate or snacked at work and I did not socialize much at work as such I used my breaks for concentration and meditation purposes. I saved all my earnings towards my financial and shopping goals for my country. I was more than satisfied with my wages since I did not depend on them for my day to day living expenses. And the minimum wage in the seventies was indexed every year to the consumer price index (CPI) so I guess the wage was a livable wage. I was not familiar with the concept of the working poor in Australia in the 1970's, the annual adjustments of the minimum wage kept pace with inflation.

I was disappointed when I failed one of the major subjects, but happy because the flunking potentially extended my stay in Australia by at least semester or until the subject was next offered. My stay was automatically extended by at least another semester until the subject was next offered again. I did not like the stigma but the potential material benefit of an extended stay felt good. To avoid another academic debacle, I switched over from day to night work so that I could have regular student life during the day. My class hours were no more than three hours a day in 1978 so I had enough time to rest. Towards the end of 1978, I had saved enough to meet some of my basic material goals. I imagined myself in a new car instead of a reliable used car.

With enough money in my savings account I began shopping for my ideal car by following the motoring press, auto reviews and car commercials. My desirable car was any of the popular Japanese makes and models that were common on Ghana roads in the seventies. These models included Datsun Z or 1600, Mazda 1800 and Toyota Cressida and Corolla. The auto market in Ghana offered me limited choices and I was also eager to avoid repeating the mistakes I made in the early seventies. But in the end my dreams and shopping list did not matter, I ended up buying a Mercedes Benz 200D which was never on my shopping list for reasons of class and status. I would have loved an Australian configured car but Ghana changed over to driving on the right in 1974 and Australian cars are configured for driving on the left. Importing a car configured for driving on the left would have cost me extra tariffs and taxes.

As I have already noted, the car I bought was chosen for me. During the period I was shopping for a car anytime I settled on a car I got a prophetic message at the Heart of Spiritual Truth church to bide my time. But the week I made up my mind to order a Mercedes I was literally congratulated by the seer or prophet on duty in the church that week. The gods conspired against me from buying any other make of car as I never got any competing quotation. Apart from the car I also ordered domestic appliances from Phillips Electronics in the Netherlands just before I left for my country for good. Australia brought me into the middle class and gave me a façade of success; I had a refrigerator, freezer, range and television; items that were a pipe dream in Ghana as I could never afford them on my income. My dream of a middle class life became a reality after I returned from Australia.

Fortune smiled on me in 1978-79 and although I worked at minimum wage jobs in factories I earned enough money to fulfill all my financial and material goals. I made enough to buy a brand new car and domestic appliances from top manufactures of the day. The turnaround in my fortunes or luck may be illustrated by a disappointment that turned fortuitous and made me an unexpected income from internship. A private real estate firm agreed with the college to have me as an intern at $30 per week. But the company, after an interview, turned me down partially as a result of my own casual and unprofessional attitude. The next internship opportunity that I got paid me handsomely, I was paid almost ten times the $30 I would I have made from the private real estate office. The income from the internship exceeded my wildest expectations and made it possible for me to meet and exceed my financial goals beyond my imagination.

WALKING WITH THE LORD

I learned how to distinguish and discern my intuition or the voice of God the hard way. Below are the particulars of the accident that gave me the bench mark or mental road map to discern my hunches, intuition as the voice of God from the din of my mind. The discernment gave me timely warnings and prevented and protected me from falling into some pitfalls that could have been tragic or even fatal. The accident provided me an indelible mental roadmap on how to walk with the Lord. I recognized and discerned my intuitions as the wish of God and walked with Him at all times. And as long as I walked with the Lord all was well. Once I learned to distinguish my hunches, intuitions or the quiet voice of God from the myriad jumble of thoughts going through my mind at any one time despite my attempts at mind control, I followed the Lord no matter how silly, trivial or inconsequential the directive. In walking with God I avoided many perils and pitfalls that could have had an unfortunate and tragic ending. Listening to the voice of God emanating from within me gave me a sense of confidence and assurance that the Lord was always at hand guiding me with His infinite wisdom. I did not therefore second guess that feeling or His wisdom even when it conflicted with commonsense or the obvious.

1. <u>Accident on a Bicycle</u>. This was the accident that established the benchmark or roadmap for walking with God, it taught me how to pick out the gemstone from the base material, the voice from all the noise, I became an obedient child and complied or obeyed whatever was asked of me no matter how nonsensical. In May 1978, I was riding a bicycle along Brunswick Road on my way from a second hand shop a/k/a opportunity shop to a farmers market along Sydney Road. The road apart from being the main thoroughfare between Melbourne and Sydney was also the main strip shopping mall where the farmer's market was located, it was the shopping area of the Brunswick Township or neighborhood. The road was therefore busy at all times carrying all manner of traffic. As I rode towards Sydney Road that afternoon, I had a nagging feeling or an inner voice urging me to avoid riding along Sydney Road to the market. I therefore decided to take a parallel street to my destination but I stumbled onto Sydney Road before I could branch off on an alternative route. I guess I should have turned around or gone pass Sydney Road for an alternative route but I rather decided to ride cautiously along Sydney Road to my destination. After all the market

was located beside the road, the incentive to ride along Sydney Road was therefore greater than seeking an alternative route.

I rode slowly and cautiously along the road following the direction of traffic with oncoming traffic on the opposite side of the street. I kept an eagle eye on the parked cars lest I should find myself beside or in front of one as it took off. I watched out for the cars taking off or attempting to park along the street as I rode along. I was less than two blocks from my destination when my world was turned upside down. I saw ahead of me a man open and enter a parked car. I assumed that the driver was about to take off so I slowed down to avoid getting too close to it when it took off. But it did not take off before I came parallel to it and had almost gone past it when suddenly the driver side door was swung open. It was so sudden I could not react to avoid it. I was sent crashing down almost in the middle of the roadway, as I crashed down I looked up and saw my life flash before me, a tram and bus slammed on their brakes and screeched to a stop as the oncoming vehicles scrambled to take evasive action to avoid slamming into the vehicles in front of them. The tram, the bus and the oncoming traffic stopped just in time. But it appears the real danger was the traffic behind me but fortunately all traffic came to a stop in time. I was rushed to the emergency room of Queen Victoria Hospital. The x-rays again were negative, no broken bones. I was therefore sent back to 755 Park Street, my home. Twice within two years an ambulance has carried me to and from the hospital after an injury. I was sent back home at about four or five o'clock in the afternoon and I sat in my room alone hungry and wracked with pain. I was in so much pain I could not drag myself to the kitchen to get food or snack from the refrigerator. I was wracked in pain and had not eaten all day but I was so helpless I could not drag myself to the kitchen and felt so sorry for myself that I wept. As I sat there drenched in my tears I realized for the first time that life is indeed very fragile. I came face to face with my mortality; I lost the innocence of youth that day. The accident literally opened my eyes; I realized that death is only a heartbeat away. If I had taken a different route to the market I might have avoided the accident but I might not have gained the mental roadmap. I made a mental note of the inner voice that urged me to take a different route to the market. And that mental note became my roadmap or yardstick; I called it variously as the voice of God, guardian angel, hunch or intuition. And from that day I learned to pick out my genuine intuition or voice from all the noise and chatter going through my mind at any time wherever I was. Life was never the same again as long as I held on to that voice I walked with the Lord.

That accident seared into my memory the still voice of God or intuition. And I have not suffered a similar incident or had another close call. Over the years I averted many potential perils and pitfalls by following my intuitive hunches or the voice of the Lord in my endeavors. The car owner was a business owner along the strip mall; I received $3,000 insurance compensation for my pain and suffering a few months before I left Melbourne for good.

"But the fruit of the Spirit is love, joy, peace, longsuffering, kindness, goodness, faithfulness, gentleness, self-control. Against such there is no law" (Galatians 5:22).

2. <u>The Internship Bonanza:</u> The joy of God consciousness is not that you are immune from disappointments and heartaches but when they come the man at peace with God weathers them better than his counterpart who is not so anchored in higher consciousness or God. I have already alluded how my disappointment in an internship position became an unexpected bonanza beyond my wildest imagination. I was crushed when I was turned down by the real estate office and took the rejection very hard. When I was asked for an interview I thought the results were a forgone conclusion and was not mentally ready for the disappointment that followed my rejection. I thought that the interview was a mere introductory formality with a predetermined result. I did not approach the interview as a job seeker out to impress a potential employer. I went to the interview dressed in casual summer wear but I was devastated when I was rejected and felt very sorry for myself. I sulked and felt worthless, 'if I could not even win a pre arranged internship position then what chance did I have for professional work if I decided to make Australia my home'. While I sulked and brooded with despair the voice of the Lord comforted me telling me to "cheer up there is a better opportunity on the way".

After those assuring words I put the debacle behind me and went about my business and looked forward to the college to arrange for another office for me to do my internship. About two weeks after the fiasco, I was asked by the college to report to the Valuer General's Department for an interview on a Thursday afternoon. I went to this interview appropriately attired and looking very professional. The Valuer General's department was among other functions, the supervisor of assessors of the various local authorities. I was accepted and began my internship at the office the following Monday. To my utter delight and surprise, I earned about $500 take home pay every paycheck or $250 per week. The new position was indeed a better opportunity both financially and professionally. The work of the Valuer General Department was more relevant for my job in Ghana and the experience I gained from the office was applicable and transferable to my job as an assessor in Ghana. The rejection, in effect, was a blessing in disguise.

3. <u>The Miracle Cure From Warm Milk:</u> In September 1979 I left Melbourne with Obenewa for Ghana through Bombay/Mumbai and South Africa. Due to turbulent weather we missed our connecting flight from Bombay/Mumbai to South Africa. The next scheduled flight was three days away so Qantas airline accommodated us at a Hotel in Bombay. We took advantage of the free boarding and lodging to sample foods with unfamiliar names on the menu. And that experiment nearly cost me my life. I ordered an Indian dish for dinner which comprised mainly of fish and vegetables. The meal was delicious but also very spicy. As an African who eats no meal without pepper I thought I could eat any spicy food without any problem. But I learned that day that all spicy foods are not created equal. The meal though delicious was so spicy I literally had to douse the flames on my tongue with fire extinguisher every now and then until I finished every scrap of the meal. It was hotter and spicier than any meal I had ever tasted, despite that I did not expect the reaction that followed shortly after the meal.

I was struck with diarrhea less than an hour after the meal and I started running to the bathroom. The intensity and frequency of the diarrhea increased with each round of going to the bathroom and at one time I thought I had contracted cholera. I called for help from room service and was brought some two small pills which I guess might have been Imodium AD pills. I chewed the pills for quick results and washed them down with water for quick and maximum effect. But the pills did not have any effect on the diarrhea and I continued emptying my bowels of watery stools. Next I asked for a doctor and was told none was available on Sundays. The diarrhea only got worse and my physical condition began to deteriorate. I felt very cold and my muscles began cramping and twitching uncontrollably. All my muscles including my facial muscles began contracting and twitching. I was cold even though it was hot and sunny outside; I crawled under blankets too keep warm. The blankets did not give me any respite from the cold, I still shivered and twitched from muscle cramps under the beddings.

As I shook like a wet dog under the pile of blankets, I had a sudden eerie feeling that I would not make it alive out of Mumbai. The thought of death itself did not scare me, but I rather felt sorry for Obenewa who would be saddled with a dead body in a foreign country. I wondered how she would deal or handle the unexpected emergency considering her level of education and expression in the English language. I felt pity for her for the burden and responsibilities that would be thrust upon her should I succumb to the diarrhea. I imagined she would be hassled and overwhelmed with funeral arrangements for my burial in Bombay or arrange transport for my corpse to Ghana. I felt I would have been overwhelmed under such an emergency despite my education level and the more I thought about the conditions the more I felt sorry for the inconvenience my death would place upon her. As the scenarios played through my mind, there was nothing I could do but pray for God to spare my life. I prayed for forgiveness of my sins and for my salvation not just for my sake but to spare my wife the ordeal of having a dead body on her hands in a far way India.

I meditated and prayed quietly while quivering in bed, and then I had a hunch or the voice of God spoke to me; "Ask for warm milk." Milk! It did not seem right. I am lactose intolerant; milk bloats me up and causes me to have diarrhea. Indeed when I am constipated I use milk as laxative. I wondered how milk could help me with diarrhea. But without any further hesitation I called for warm milk as instructed. The hotel brought up a small ceramic kettle of warm milk. I poured a glassful and as I began to drink the first glass of milk I began to feel heat and warmth radiating through my body. And within thirty minutes after the first glass of milk I felt warm under the pile of blankets and broke out in sweat, I crawled out from under the blankets. The effect of the warm milk was instantaneous and miraculous, it radiated heat through my body the moment I began downing the first glass. The muscles spasms, shivers and twitches vanished and I felt completely normal within an hour. It appeared the diarrhea and the muscle twitches had never happened, I regained my strength and went on to enjoy three days of bliss and sightseeing around Mumbai. We departed Mumbai for South Africa en route to Ghana the following Wednesday. Since the incident at the hotel room in Mumbai I have been a bit leery about eating very spicy or hot foods whether African or Indian.

4. Self Inflicted Aches and Pains. I formed an unconscious habit during the two years I spent at Issah Middle Boarding School of tensing my body parts unconsciously. Without knowing it I bore the brunt of the hunger, deprivation and the bullying at the school on my body. It was most likely that the disability must have been going on for most of my life but it became apparent and adversely affected me during the two years I was at Issah. I used to suffer from stiff neck like CSM caused by aches and pains in my neck and shoulders, I could not move my head or upper body freely with a stiff neck. I guess the aches and pains and the stiff neck was my way of eliciting sympathy from my fellow students for my woes at the school. I formed a habit and unconsciously carried the habit with me through my teaching career up to college and beyond. The aches and pains were worse during the period I was in great financial distress after graduating from college. Once in a while I took an aspirin or APC otherwise I bore my aches and pains stoically. It was so pervasive I did not even realize most of the time that I was in pain. The aches and pains were part and parcel of my make up or personality. And this was practically my condition when I landed in Melbourne in February 1975 and started regular yoga exercises. One of the first lessons I learned during relaxation techniques was self examination or introspection. I had never previously considered self examination as solution of any personal problems. Self examination or introspection was a part of my initial yoga exercises and led me to discover the cause of my aches and pains as emanating unconsciously from me. I realized that I tensed my neck and shoulders most of the time without being aware that the muscles were tensed. The constant tensioning of my neck and shoulders caused the nagging aches and pains in my neck and shoulders.

When I realized that I was unconsciously causing aches and pains on parts of my body through unnecessary muscle tensions the next stage was to learn to let go and relax those muscles. The self examination or diagnosis and relaxing the muscles during exercises was easier on the exercise mat than away from it. It was not easy to maintain a relaxed posture away from the exercise mat. So I had to learn to be self conscious and on the lookout for signs of relapse or tension as I went about my daily chores. When I relapsed due to diversion of my attention I returned to the state of relaxation as soon as I became aware. It was virtually a constant battle between awareness and unawareness between the conscious and unconscious mind. When aware or conscious I relaxed my muscles but otherwise tensed them when unaware and unconscious. The difficulty was keeping one eye on my body even as I went about my daily chores without betraying that I was self conscious. As I began to replace my unconscious tension with conscious relaxation the constant aches and pains gradually began to ease but it has been a constant battle between attention and inattention. The aches and pains I experienced earlier in my life were not arthritic but were caused by unconscious reflexive action of tensioning my body parts. The unconscious reflexive actions of tensions were replaced in the course of time with conscious relaxation of the body parts where I felt aches and pain the most. I learned to be self conscious without being self absorbed to the neglect of my surroundings. And it took quite sometime to teach myself to be self conscious and observant while interacting with my surroundings. In time it became easier to spot the tensions in various parts of my body and took remedial action to relax or let those parts go to prevent any buildup of tension in my system to cause aches and pains.

5. <u>Averted Potential Accidents:</u> When I returned to Ghana from Australia I led a very hectic life for about the first three years or more. For most of this period I lived and worked in Accra while my family lived at Kumasi. I was therefore constantly on the move between Accra and Kumasi, I used to pay visits to my family at least once every fortnight.

One Sunday afternoon while on my way back to Accra from Kumasi the Lord prompted me to pull over to the side of the road. I looked behind and in front of me as far as the eye could see and saw nothing unusual or any other road user to prompt the urge to pull over to the side of the road. I was alone on that stretch of the road and was about midway up a hill. I shrugged and pulled over to the side impatiently. I drummed my steering wheel with my fingers to kill time and watching out for what God had in store for me this time. I was in the middle of nowhere and had hardly parked on the roadside for for less than three or four minutes when I saw coming over the horizon two large articulated trucks barreling up and down the hill running side-by-side. The two articulated trucks racing along the road none willing to yield to the other to pass. As a result they occupied the entire roadway as none could overtake the other. If I had not pulled over to the side of the road I would most probably have come upon them near the apex of the hill or they would have suddenly descended upon me with not enough time to maneuver out of the way to avoid being crushed like an eggshell. I avoided an otherwise potential tragic or fatal accident by pulling over when asked to do so though there was no visible reason to stop by the side of the road.

5B. A few years after this incident I had a similar experience on the streets of Brooklyn while operating a car service in the summer of 1989 or thereabout. I was cruising along Bay Ridge Blvd when I had this sudden urge to pull over to the side of the street. I took shelter under a shady tree to shelter me from the hot summer sun. I fretted as I sat under the tree wondering what prompted the lord to ask me to pull over. But I did not have long to wonder when I heard a loud explosion, one of my rear tires exploded while I waited under the tree; the tire was practically blown to shreds. I called the base of *Your Car Service* on the citizen band radio to report that I had a flat while I proceeded to replace the tire with the spare. I changed the tire under the comfort of the shade instead of doing so under the blazing summer sun. I smiled smugly and thanked the Lord and after I changed the tire called to report that I was back on the road and ready for work.

That day was not one of my lucky days because I lost the other rear tire in a similar explosion but with a different outcome. Later that evening, at around nine o'clock, I got a fare order to an address in Sunset Park. I decided to take the Brooklyn-Queens

Expressway to the destination. But as soon as I climbed unto the expressway from Sixth Avenue the Lord asked me to get off at the first exit ramp I came to. My first exit was the 60th street exit, I therefore decided to get off on the when I got to the 60th street exit. But when I got to the ramp I found that traffic conditions were light and moving rather briskly. Thus instead of getting off the expressway on the 60th street ramp I decided to drive to the next ramp on 38th Street. And as soon as I went pass the 60th street ramp I heard another loud explosion.

I was barely a hundred yards from the ramp when I heard the explosion but it was too late to make amends. I could not reverse or make U-turn on the highway back to the ramp, I was forced by the circumstances to continue along the expressway for more than one mile on a flat tire to the next exit. I drove slowly with blinking lights to 4th Avenue through the 38th street exit ramp. That was the first time since my bicycle accident in Melbourne that I did not do as I was prompted because I thought the conditions did not warrant getting off and I paid dearly for that disobedience. I lost both the fare and the tire. I could not take the passenger to his door though I took him close enough to his destination but he refused to compensate me for my troubles. I went home early that day burdened by debt of replacing two tires.

6. Difficult Child Birth: About three months before Obenewa gave birth to our second child God warned me several times to be careful otherwise she would die during child birth. Every morning during my meditation hour as soon as I closed my eyes and turned inward the warning came "be careful else your wife would die during child birth". This was the first time God gave me a warning without telling me how or what to do to avert the peril against the pitfalls ahead of me. I knew nothing that is more powerful than prayers and as long as I prayed I did not know what else I could do differently. I meditated and prayed regularly for the mercy and salvation of God. I was so confident I took it for granted that the warning would never become a reality. I could not imagine God allowing a tragedy of that magnitude to happen after warning me about it. Why would he warm me if He had no intention to avert the tragedy?. The general tenor of my prayers reflected my faith and optimism through such expressions as: "as long as God lives that cannot happen". "Only if God is asleep", "God never sleeps" or "God is alive". I placed the fate of my wife in the capable hands of the Lord and waited on Him to prevent the tragedy. The cautionary warnings came to me over the three month period before she was due; every morning as soon as I closed my eyes and began meditation the voice rang in my ears "be careful else your wife would die during childbirth".

Obenewa went into labor and was admitted at the *Komfo Anokye* Hospital on the night of April 11th 1980. I stole a glance at her chart the following morning when I visited her and noticed that it was marked two fingers. I did not know the meaning and significance of two fingers so I was not alarmed when the chart was stuck at two fingers for six days. I was optimistic when she was admitted and expected that the mother and child would be home within three days. But the three days stretched into seven days and there was no sign that the ordeal was near solution. And every morning while she was on hospital bed, I still got the same messages as soon as I closed my eyes for meditation and prayers in the morning, the voice rang out "be careful else your wife would die during child birth." I had no idea what else I could do beyond prayers and the Lord never told me anything otherwise. On the morning of the seventh day my faith was put to the test, that morning the warning had an ominous tone or ring to it, "I told you that if you are not careful your wife will die". This time the warning affected me, I was alarmed and for the first time I felt that Obenewa's life was really in danger. Despite the ominous tone I was still confident that God would prevent the tragedy from becoming a reality. But when I left her bedside I was distraught because her chart showed no signs of improvement, it was still stuck at two fingers. I did not know the significance, of two fingers but it not auger well, to have two fingers for seven days. As I left her bedside for the office I could still hear the voice ringing in my ear "if you are not careful your wife will die." As I made my way to the office from her bedside I could still hear the voice ringing in my ears "if you are not careful your wife would die". But I had no clue how to avert or prevent the tragedy that appeared to be unfolding before me. I had one overriding thing in my heart, a quiet place to pray and commune with God. I needed a quiet place where I could commune with God without disturbance or interference if I hoped to prevent the tragedy. And I could not find or think of any place quieter than my office.

I got to the office very early that morning before any member of staff and went into my office and locked the door behind me. I sat down comfortably closed my eyes and went into deep concentration and meditation. I prayed and meditated deeply as never before for the mercy and salvation of God. So far I had never asked God what to do to avert the tragedy. I always took it for granted that He would take care of the problem and for the first time I asked God what to do to prevent the calamity that stared at me in the face. I did not know how long I had been praying and meditating when I saw a rare vision of a man bearing a heavy load on his head. The man was lean, thin, emaciated and wearing only a loincloth; he staggered under the weight of the heavy load on his head. I watched him stagger and wobble towards me with the load and when he came close to me he heaved the load and it landed in my laps. The vision was so real that I jumped up when the load landed in my laps and found myself standing in the middle of my office. I felt a great sense of relief and at that moment I knew that the Lord had answered my prayers and saved my wife from the calamity. I knelt down and thanked the Lord.

As soon as I got up from my knees I heard a knock on the door, it was *Abotsi*, one of my fellow officers. He sympathized with me over the length of time my wife was in labor. He suggested to me that we seek help from some of the popular charismatic church pastors in Kumasi. But then he added, "Since you arrived in Kumasi your faith has always carried you through your problems. But I think you may need help with this unusual condition". When he finished, I told him that "all will be well. God has taken care of the problem".

By the time I returned to her bedside that evening she was the mother of a healthy baby girl, Lamissi. It appears she gave birth shortly after the vision I saw at the office. I was glad that the ordeal was over and enquired when I might take mother and child home. I was told that the placenta had not been discharged, the danger was not yet quite over but the staff showed no sense of urgency though it had been over six hours since she gave birth. I showed no sense of urgency either, she was out of immediate danger the rest was just a matter of time, I concluded. But deep down I felt some unease because I was aware of fatalities caused by placentas but I remained optimistic that God would work another miracle. My confidence and optimism in God was realized when He worked another miracle during the night.

The placenta had not been discharged by ten o'clock, it had been more than ten hours. But about that hour an off duty gynecologist driving by the hospital decided on an impulse to go into the maternity ward. He enquired whether all was well, the nurses answered affirmatively, but just as he turned around to leave one of them remembered the condition of Obenewa and informed the doctor. When he was shown the patient he asked the staff to prepare for surgery. Meanwhile, he examined and checked her vital signs looking under her eye lids for signs of anemia. According to Obenewa, while the doctor was examining her, she overheard him grumbling and mumbling to himself that he did not know what prompted him to stop at the hospital. Obenewa's vital signs were satisfactory so the doctor put on surgical gloves, reached into her and pulled out the placenta without surgery. She was instructed by the nurses to remain still in bed, but she was famished, she had eaten nothing all day. So she tried to reach into her bedside locker for a snack and blacked out from the exertion. When she came around, she was lying on the floor with the snack beside her. She picked up the snack from the floor and ate it while still lying on the floor. She was admonished by the nurses for disobeying their instructions and that it would have been her fault if she had died. Obenewa was discharged two days later.

"God is love and he who abides in love abides in God and God in him" (1 John 4: 16). "God is a shield to all who trust in Him" (2 Samuel 22:3). Despite the dire warnings and premonitions during the last three months of my wife's pregnancy, my faith and optimism never wavered. I never doubted for a moment that God would allow the warnings to become a reality. And throughout the period that I was struggling with the warnings I never gave a hint to Obenewa. She became aware only after the ordeal was over.

I do not know whether it was sheer coincidence, but the dire warnings started about the same time that my mother-in-law was brought in from the village to help Obenewa after child birth. She showed no obvious or visible concern or any sense of urgency when Obenewa was in the hospital. She did not receive her grandchild warmly and did not appear to share our happiness and joy after the ordeal was over. Her frosty relations with Obenewa and the new baby gave me the impression that she was not pleased with the happy ending; she would have preferred a different ending.

7. <u>Timely Warning Saved Lamissi:</u> One Friday afternoon at around 4.30pm I began tidying up my office to leave for the weekend. I was just about to leave the office for the weekend when out of the blue the Lord asked me to leave for my family at Kumasi. So without any further ado, I hopped into my car and headed for Kumasi. I arrived in Kumasi just before eight o'clock. The house was quiet but otherwise nothing was out of the ordinary. I asked my wife whether there was any problem around the house or with any of the children. None, she answered. But I did not see Lamissi which was quite unusual. She used to be the first person to meet me at the gate whenever I came from Accra as if she knew or expected my time of arrival. She was sitting alone in the living room playing with her favorite toys. She smiled at me but did not jump into my arms as she was wont to do. About two hours after we went to bed I heard her moaning in her sleep. She was on fire when I touched her. I gave her fever remedy but the medicine was effective for only a few minutes before her temperature shot up again.

I kept vigil over her throughout the night, robbed and sponged her with cold water and covered her with wet towels at about every thirty to forty minute interval until dawn when we left for the hospital. Ghana, throughout most of the eighties, was in turmoil due to political instability and economic dislocations, armed robbery and violence were rampant in many of the population centers of the country. The hospitals and clinics lacked adequate supplies of drugs and medicines, the doctors wrote prescriptions for the patients to buy from the private drug stores. Under the circumstances it would have been futile to drive to the hospital only to be given prescription which could not be filled till daybreak. We reasoned that it would have been dangerous and fruitless to go to the hospital in the middle of the night as it would have been impossible to fill any prescription at that hour.

When we were about two blocks to the gates of the hospital she went into convulsions, her eyes were turned into her head with only the whites visible while she twitched and sucked her lips like a toothless old woman. The condition scared me and I accelerated through the gates of the hospital looking for help. And who did I see on entering the hospital? The off duty gynecologist who saved the life of Obenewa during the birth of the child. We rushed towards him and as soon as he saw the condition of the child he took her from us and rushed with her into the hospital with my wife behind him. Meanwhile he quickly scribbled a prescription for us to procure from the private drug stores just as I expected. I dashed madly around Kumasi in the early morning hours in search of an open drug store to fill the prescription. It was too early; no store was yet open for business but I could not stay at one spot waiting for business hours. I rushed around for two to three hours before I found the first drug store that was opened early for business.

Thanks to the doctor, who as a staff of the hospital was able to obtain the necessary drugs to stabilize her condition while I was dashing around trying to fill the prescription. By the time I returned with the prescription she was out of danger. I don't know what would have happened if we had not met the doctor on entering the gates of the hospital. It took about three hours between the time I entered the gates of the hospital and procuring the prescription. And if I had not obeyed the silent voice of the Lord I do not know how Obenewa would have copped with the emergency. The story had a happy ending; we went home with our baby and the prescription to continue treatment if her condition changed again.

8. Thwarted A Purse Snatcher: When we arrived from Australia in September 1979 there was a popular revolutionary government in power. The government, known as the Armed Forces Revolutionary Council was led by Flt Lt. J.J Rawlings. The members of the government comprised mostly of young idealistic commissioned and none commissioned military officers and they turned the country upside down during the brief period they were in power. The heroes of past coups and soldier politicians were accused of bribery and corruption, lined up and executed summarily. Next they turned their attention to the women traders of Makola market leveling accusations of hoarding and profiteering against them. The AFRC government, in its zeal to clean up the country and rid it of the evils of bribery and corruption, hoarding and profiteering razed the market to the ground. The demolition of Makola market, apart from the execution of past soldier politicians, was one of the most sensational actions of the AFRC government in its attempt to introduce accountability and probity into the nation. The demolished market overnight became a tourist attraction for Ghanaians from all walks of life. Nobody believed that Makola had actually been razed to the ground until one saw it for himself, for as we say in Ghana 'Seeing is believing'. We flocked to the demolished market site in our thousands and gawked at the demolished market with the women transacting their business atop the rubbles and ruins of the market.

A few days after arrival I strolled to Makola market to see for myself the handiwork of the Armed Forces Revolutionary Council government that the venerable market had indeed been demolished. I jostled for space or standing room on the packed sidewalks clutching my passport and some dollar currency notes intended for payment of tariffs and taxes on my unaccompanied baggage. As I craned my neck over the heads of people for a view of the demolished market, my guardian angel in an emergency tone asked me to lift up or raise my hands. And at once I raised both hands above my head and as my hands went up somebody stumbled into me almost knocking me off my feet. God is indeed omnipresent; while I was busy jostling for space among the teeming crowds for a view of the debris of the demolished market a thief was scouting me and getting ready to pounce at the right moment. He pounced and lunged at me to snatch the passport from my hand at the same time that I raised my hands above my head. He missed and grabbed at air lost his balance and bumped into me. By the grace of God I thwarted the attempts of a thief to snatch my passport and dollar currency notes that would have made it difficulty for me to pay tariffs and taxes and prove that the unaccompanied baggage was mine. I was saved from the snatcher just in the nick of time. I gave thanks to the Lord, smiled at the thief and went about with my sightseeing without uttering a word to him.

7. Arthritis Remedy The Hard Way: At the ripe old age of forty-four, I found my knees swollen with fluids swishing from side to side when depressed. The condition

reminded me of similar condition that afflicted my mother and led her to drink liniment sold to her by a quack doctor for remedy. At the time my knees doubled in size I was a struggling undocumented alien in New York and legally nonexistent. I worked as a security guard at a Brooklyn hospital under another person's name and social security number. The job had no benefits of any kind but I was happy making a nickel above the minimum wage to keep body and soul together. Being a security guard at night in a hospital had its benefits and rewards; I had access to doctors, nurses and lab technicians of the hospital. What I lacked in official benefits I got through friendly relations with the hospital staff. I had good personal relations with the doctors and nurses and none of them ever turned me away or refused to answer honestly my health related questions. I did not know I had allergies until I was given a diagnoses at the hospital. I stopped eating raw unprocessed honey for over twenty years as a result of itchy ears and throat whenever I ate honey. But I did not know why honey had that effect on me; I only observed that when I ate honey my ears and throat became itchy. It was an eye opener when I was informed I had allergies. I often consulted the doctors and nurses informally and received free diagnostic tests from the laboratory as requested by a doctor. I was told I had allergies after a blood test at the hospital. After all said and done, I knew that I had allergies and arthritis. My prescriptions were filled free by the hospital pharmacy, but that was not my concern; my concern was the fear of becoming pill dependent for an incurable condition the rest of my life. I was haunted by the memory of my mother's knees and I did not like the prospect of depending on pills for the rest of my life to deal with the condition.

The knees of my mother were deformed from the effects of arthritis. She had a condition we called K-legs because when she walked her knees tended to knock one another. I considered that the conditions were perhaps inevitable but I resolved to do all I could to delay the onset of the deformation and popping pills for a few more years.

When I was diagnosed with arthritis and allergies I lived in a closet size room and was relatively free of any immediate family responsibilities. I used to practice hatha yoga and meditation morning and evening and fasted about three days every week. I also used to practice concentration and meditation techniques at my desk when I was idle. I meditated and prayed for divine intervention on my swollen knees. Then one morning during my concentration and meditation exercise I had an inspiration that I should apply some pressure to the knees and that would relieve the swollen condition. At that instant I had no clue how to apply pressure on my knees that was any different from what I did during my regular yoga exercises.

The solution of how to apply pressure on my knees came to me while I was was going around the hospital on my regular nightly duties. I was required to go around the hospital at intervals of one hour clocking in at designated stations in the course of the night. So while I was going around the quiet corridors of the hospital alone it occurred to me that I could squat up and down as I moved from one station to another. And that was exactly what I did. I squatted up and down playfully during my hourly rounds about four to five times a night, from midnight to dawn. I stopped the squatting exercises around dawn when the morning workers such as the kitchen and cleaning staff started streaming into the hospital.

By the end of the fifth night my knees were so sore I could hardly walk. The weekend gave me a two day respite during which I rested my knees. By the time I returned to work on Monday night I was ready to resume my squatting exercises.

I noticed a slight improvement in the condition of my knees after the weekend and was thus encouraged to continue with the squatting exercises when I went back to work. But by the morning of the ninth day I was so sore that when I staggered home I decided to rest my sore and painful knees until the pains eased naturally. I did not want to take any pain killer for the sore knees since they were self inflicted for a purpose, to heal my swollen knees. It did not become necessary to put myself through the same grueling and torturous exercise again. The swellings were practically gone and the knees almost back to normal size by the time I was relieved of the sore knees. I saw no reason to continue torturing myself; the extra pressure exerted on the knees by the squatting exercises had produced the desired results for which the Lord recommended it. And I have been relatively free of swollen or deformed knees for more than twenty years. I guess my aim of delaying the onset of the chronic condition and the inevitable treatment of popping pills for a few years was realized.

MEMORIES OF SPIRITS FROM INFANCY

I have made several allusions about seeing and encountering spirits during my infancy. I had a turbulent co-existence with spirits from about the age of five until the sight faded away at about age ten or eleven. I say coexistence because they were imposed on me, I did not choose to see them, indeed I was scared of them most of the time but I had to live with them. Those six years eventually influenced and shaped my beliefs and faith. During that period I saw spirits in various guises, some of them were ghosts and shadow figures lurking on dark moonless nights while others were so lifelike I did not know I was seeing things that were not really there. On a number of occasions I talked to them, mistaking them for my mother or other relatives, and when they did not talk back I moved on. On the other hand the shadow and ghostly figures used to strike fear into my heart and made my life miserable at night. The experiences and memories have dogged me all my life, from my first day in the classroom at a Catholic school where I was introduced to Christianity to the present. Throughout the elementary school I was interested in occult, magic and the supernatural. When I went to Australia and saw channeling of spirits by mediums in an open church it reopened the lingering memories and set me on a three year quest to become a medium until I lost the fascination and turned my attention from the spirits without to the spirit within.

I was about five years old when I encountered dwarves unexpectedly in the bush for the first time. I saw a group of dwarfs literally materialize from nowhere playing under the fruit tree on which I sat gorging on the fruits. I did not know that they were not human beings and was apprehensive and surprised to see them under the tree as they were when they saw me sitting above them. I was puzzled about how they came to be under the fruit tree without being seen or heard. The experiences and the turbulence that engulfed my life from time to time led me to the conclusion that all spirits are not created equal, they differ in power and influence similar to the power and influence of mortal beings. There is a power structure in the world of spirits just as there is a power structure in the physical world; the spirit world is just another dimension of our physical world. I lost the ability to see and interact with spirits as a result of deliberate action by my father but the sight faded gradually over time until I lost it completely by the fifth grade. The memories lingered and faded in and out of my consciousness and directly or indirectly influenced my faith and eventually aroused my interest in spiritual development.

As already said I was conflicted right from the very beginning of my introduction to Christianity. The logic of western education and religious studies implied that my experiences were illogical and physically impossible or heathenish. The sight of little people in the bush that chased me over land and under the earth was not only illogical but impossible or that I was delusional. I miraculously eluded apprehension and capture by malicious spirits that chased me over and below ground but this experience was not compatible with the concept of miracles in Christianity. At the time of this incident I was not even aware of the name of Christ or of any formal religion beyond the traditional religion of my people. If I were from a Christian household my escape would have been celebrated as miraculously deliverance from God. But I was made to feel that my experience was not possible, matter cannot disappear below ground. I was either delusional or worse evil. It was not possible logically to run below ground and so I doubted the experience but the memory lingered and I was reminded of the reality of the encounter by a peculiar physical mark on my body that resulted from the encounter. Thus I never discussed or talked about my spiritual experience with my peers or schoolmates for fear of ridicule. And over time I tended to forget about those childhood encounters until, sometimes out of the blue, the experience plays like a video before me to remind me of my past. The memories reappeared and never faded again when I came across spirit communication or spirit mediums in a church in Melbourne. And for the first time I could freely discuss or talk about spirits without fear of ridicule. As a young adult there were times when I regretted my father's intervention to rid me of the seeing eyes but I never asked for their restoration or whether that was even possible.

In Australia I conducted an experiment with a lady friend that I used to meet at group meditation sites. The result of our experiment proved that out of body travel was possible. Out of body travel was one of the concepts we used to explore at the group meditations. We wagered in an experiment to find which of us could travel out of body to the abode of the other. I experimented with out of body travel during my concentration and meditation hour. I tried mental projection of my image to her place. The next time we met she excitedly told me about how I appeared as an apparition in her bedroom while she was in bed. She said that she froze with fear at the sight of what looked like an apparition of my image appearing from the wall into her bedroom. I was surprised by what she said because I did not know that the mental image I projected during my meditation hour materialized successfully at the intended target. Her report convinced me that out of body travel is possible though it requires a lot of dedication and self discipline. Saints and people of God are able to do such impossible feats of magic because they are very dedicated and disciplined individuals. The difference between the saint and ordinary mortal is the extent of their dedication, devotion and discipline.

The result of the little experiment together with my childhood experience of running below ground gave me an understanding of the passage in John 8:59. I understood the passage to mean that Christ could vanish at will during his ministry. That he deliberately allowed himself to be captured and crucified out of concern and love for his disciples. He could have disappeared as he had done many times during his ministry when they went to arrest him. With dedication, devotion and self discipline one could attain Christ like qualities and perform similar feats. *"They took up stones to throw at him but he was not to be seen; and he left the temple."* Jesus was able to dematerialize his physical body at will to elude his enemies. *John 15:13 Greater love has no one than this, than to lay down one's life for his friends.* Christ paid the ultimate sacrifice for love by surrendering himself to his enemies. If he could elude capture during his ministry then he could have eluded his captors as he had done many times during his ministry. But he surrendered to love and allowed himself to be captured and killed by his enemies and that is why he is God and we are not.

MAN IS THE FACE OF GOD AND SATAN

For a number of years I dedicated myself to yoga concentration and meditation hoping for a glimpse or revelation of God. I did not have a mantra per se but I had a short prayer that I repeated over and over during meditation; "Lord reveal thyself, enlighten and illumine me." Then one day during meditation it occurred to me in a hunch or feeling that God was already revealed as me. Suddenly the passage in Luke flashed through my mind and I understood the real meaning and significance of the passage. *Luke 17: 20-21 Now when He was asked by the Pharisees when the kingdom of God would come, He answered them and said, "The kingdom of God does not come with observation; nor will they say 'See here! Or See there! For indeed the kingdom of God is within you".* The quotation did not resonate immediately until a few days afterwards. And when it did resonate it awoke me to the realization of the ubiquity of God, God is omnipresent and so ubiquitous that we take him for granted. If the kingdom of God is within me then He must be in every man, thus to see God is to see man. We are with God all the time without ever realizing that he is always a heartbeat away or the heartbeat itself.

The realization that God is within me was tantamount to looking for something that was hiding in plain sight. God is always present and so obvious He is taken for granted and once that realization dawned on me I never saw my fellow man in quite the same way again. The face of man is the face of God that I see every waking hour, to persecute man is to persecute God. A few years after this realization I had rude awakening of the incongruous nature of man when my life was turned upside down in Ghana. I saw a wonder that could only be described as Satan's own miracle. The power of Satan, after I fell from grace, manifested as hell in my life. In one instant I saw new underwear I was preparing to send to customers at the market for sale changed into old underwear instantly while I looked on helplessly. I knew from the moment of the transformation that it was the work of Satan but it took weeks and months of fasting and prayers before Satan was revealed in the flesh. The revelation showed me that Satan also has the face of man. God is ubiquitous but Satan is more cunning, he lives among us in various disguises as friend, family or trusted colleague. Satan hides in plain sight wreaking havoc against us without arousing any suspicion because most often we know and trust the satanic agents. In my particular case the satanic agent was a trusted family friend that I never suspected. Nobody ever saw Satan descending from the clouds with horns and flames blazing from the eyes and nostrils just as no man ever saw God coming down from the heavens. God and Satan dwell within us. The line between good and evil is very thin. The man we adulate today as saintly may be vilified tomorrow as satanic. One of the early religious lessons we learned in the primary school was the notion that man is made in the image and likeness of God. We learned that Lucifer or Satan was a fallen angel who took all his powers to hell and thus as capable of duplicating what God can do. God and Satan are spirits and dwell side by side but it takes a lot of dedication and devotion to unearth the obvious Satan within our midst.

I felt blessed when I realized that God is within me. I surrendered myself to the will of God, His wish was my wish and He blessed the words of my mouth and manifested them into reality even when I did not intend them to come alive. God accepted the words of my mouth and the meditation of my heart and gave meaning to them. I became humble, cautious and guarded on what came out of my mouth. I never had the experience that was akin or similar to my infancy but I realized that I am one with God, I am a child of God. Years after this realization I fell from grace and on occasion crossed the thin line between God and Satan by gratifying my body, the temple of God. But I never lost sight that God dwells within me even if I was not worthy to call Him father or His ambassador at all times.

CHRIST THE MAN

As I continued and dedicated myself to the practice of concentration and meditation I gained some control over my mind and it became possible to enter the inner recesses of my mind. I sometimes got different perspectives or understanding of some passages of scripture or teachings that were different from the popular interpretations or narratives. I obtained one such perspective on the temptations of Jesus Christ during meditation and prayers. The popular interpretation or narratives that I grew up with was that Satan appeared before Jesus Christ as an evil entity and tempted Him on the morning He completed forty days of fasting and prayers in the wilderness (Luke 4:1-13). The revelation I received in the form of a vision or mental picture during meditation was different from this popular interpretation or narrative of the story. I perceived Jesus as a man who was sitting alone in the wilderness the morning he completed the forty-day fast but had not yet broken fast. He was human and as such he faced the same inner temptations all humans face when we are fasting or hungry. I saw him sitting famished atop a small hill in the middle of nowhere. He looked about him and wondered why not turn one of these stones into food. He picked up a stone held it in his hands but he gave up on the idea of transforming stone into food telling himself that his powers were not for trivial purposes. Thus he abandoned the idea; the temptation came from within himself just as any human being. Man is tempted by man but there was no man present with him in the wilderness, and as he himself said, we will not see God descending from the heavens and so vice-versa we will not see Satan descending from the heavens blazing with fire and brimstone. Similarly he pictured himself flying or floating like a bird through the air to his disciples and friends but again dismissed the temptation or wish from his mind as that would have been a misuse of his powers as son of God. Service to God or spiritual enlightenment and temptations go hand in hand, Christ was a man that dwelt in our mortal and physical world, He was therefore subjected to all the temptations and desires all mortals face. The difference between him and us; was that he was able to rise above the temptations and desires. There was no entity with horns that stood before Christ and asked him to prove his mettle or demonstrate that he was the son of God. Satan played his games within the confines of Christ's mind just as our temptations play out within the confines of our minds. Any person of God long before succumbing to any temptations goes through mental struggle and torture before the actual fall. We fall and succumb to temptations or withstand them first in our minds and Christ faced similar temptations in our mortal world.

The mind of man is the battle ground of God and Satan, good and evil; it is where all the warring for our souls, attention or alliance goes on. Satan comes in the form of greed, jealousy or lust and God comes in the form of goodness, accountability, probity and the urge to help others. We cross from one side of the thin line between the two sides on any single day as we go through life. The fall of a man of God, from my experience, is due to lust or gratification of the flesh. Greed might play a role but the ego and lust are the temptations that mostly lead to a fall from grace. I survived some temptations and fell many times. Christ overcame his satanic impulses as a hungry and thirsty man sitting alone in the wilderness. And the men and women we revere for their saintly qualities are those who overcome their satanic impulses and sacrifice a lot for the good of their fellow men. Those who cross the thin line to the left side of the aisle and find the lure so strong they are sucked into the lifestyle while maintaining a façade of life on the right side of the aisle are our disgraced priests, pastors and other men of God. We live or die by our own sword of the mind and not by Satan as a separate entity dragging us against our will to perdition.

For one to overcome the world, one has to overcome his inner demons. And most of us fail when confronted with the pleasures of the flesh. Jesus was man and God, he had desires, he slept, ate and dreamt like any mortal man and felt temptations like a man; he did not succumb to the desires of the flesh. I succumbed to temptations of the flesh and fell from grace in the eyes of God and man. Jesus as man struggled with common desires of the flesh. The revelation of Jesus as a man who faced similar temptations and desires gave me a personal relationship with Him. I relate to him at the human and spirit level. I comfort and console myself that Christ knows and understands my frailty as a man. He forgives when we confess our frailty and ask for help and forgiveness.

On another occasion I was meditating on the agony and suffering of Jesus Christ before crucifixion when for a brief moment I was carried through time to the garden of Gethsemane. I was sad and lonely as He was in the garden with his disciples; he was tormented and tortured within his soul while his disciples could hardly keep their eyes open even as he admonished them to keep watch. Jesus agonized over the pain and suffering he saw ahead of him, the thought of a hiding place with his disciples where they could not be found crossed his mind. He could conceal himself in plain sight but that was also not an option because he told himself that it was for this purpose that he came into the world. And when the soldiers led by Judas entered the garden of Gethsemane to arrest him; I panicked; my heart beat wildly with fear as I watched the panicked Jesus trying to rouse his disciples from sleep, telling them *"Rise, let us be going. See, my betrayer is at hand."* (Matthew 26: 36-46). At this juncture my heart beat so wildly I was aroused from the meditation.

As flesh and blood, Jesus must have felt the weight of what lay ahead of him. As a man, he must have been tempted to let the cup pass, and for that brief moment when his heart beat with fear, I was with him across time. The mind is the portal to our soul; we are influenced through the mind which contains the sum total of our being.

ARMED ROBBER IN PAST LIFE

Is reincarnation myth or fact? I am ambivalent and uncertain about reincarnation though I had an unforgettable dream once that revealed that I might have been a notorious criminal in a past life. Most of the stories and literature I read or heard on reincarnation were very important in their past lives such as rulers, kings, queens, princes and other high class members of society. And those who were servants or slaves were privileged servants or slaves who served royalty, generals and war heroes or powerful members of the society. Scarcely did I ever hear or read about the past life of anyone who was a common man or woman or criminal. It appears common people or low class members of society do not reincarnate. It appears that it is only the privileged from past lives that reincarnate into the present to continue living their glorious lives. Common men and women of the past such as indentured servants and slaves who led a humdrum and mundane lives do not reincarnate and if they do their present lives are not any different to afford them the time and peace of mind to bother with regression into a past that might have no relevance to their present struggle of keeping body and soul together. It is those who have comfortable lives in the present who can have the luxury of trying to regress to the past. The vast majority of us live such a humdrum life that we could not be bothered about reincarnation because it has no bearing or meaning for our present lives. I saw a few television programs in which some people under hypnosis recalled their past lives, where they lived and how they hid in underground chambers and bunkers during periods of upheavals, persecutions or wars. Some of those hypnotic revelations led to discovery of some underground bunkers and ruins of houses.

While in Australia I had the luxury to consider the possibilities of a past life. Reincarnation had never excited or interested me; it had no bearing of any significance to affect my present life for me to waste time and effort to find out about a past life that could not make my present life any better help to alleviate my present struggles in life.

I contemplated reincarnation from time to time during meditation exercises without ever expecting anything from the periodic exercises but one day I had a dream that altered my perception. The dream pointed to the possibility that I might have existed or lived in the mid 1800's in the Indian city of Calcutta. In that dream I was a notorious criminal whose life ended ignominiously in the outskirts of the city. I was the leader of a gang of armed robbers and was a good horseman. We pillaged and robbed the communities and villages on horseback. I was ambushed together with some of my gang members while crossing a stream on the outskirts of Calcutta. I was shot in the ambush, fell off my horse face down and drowned in the shallow waters of the stream. The dream if true might perhaps explain my fear of water in my present life. I was also vey tolerant for thieves as a young adult. When I started teaching in Tamale I met one of my middle school bullies who by then was a thief, he took me to his room several times to show me his exploits. One of my Issah middle school classmates, Yelliu thrice stole from me but I could not turn him away the next time he visited me.

IMPLAUSIBLE ESCAPES OR VANISHING ACTS

During my first two years after middle school I had some experiences that up to date I cannot logical explain them. It was within that period that my nightmares led me to stop going home on holidays and vacations for up to seven years. There must have been a guardian angel or spirit that took care of me during my age innocence until I was matured enough to take care of myself both physically and spiritually. On two different occasions I run away or vanished from threatening conditions where I got frightened, panicked and when I came to my senses I could not explain or remember how I ran away from the threats. And in an unrelated situation I understood the conversation between two people in a language I did not ordinarily speak or understand while I was asleep.

1. In the first incident I was on my way to Navrongo from Tamale after vacation with my father at Tarkwa. Midway along the journey I dozed or fell asleep in the truck and while asleep I overheard a conversation or dialogue between two men sitting behind me. They spoke in a dialect or language I did not speak or understand and yet in that nether state I understood everything that was being discussed or said between them. As I listened to their conversation in my dreamy state I became excited that I understood a foreign language I knew I did not ordinarily speak or understand. I thus became curious to know the language or dialect that was being spoken behind me. In my sleep it occurred that if I saw the particular individuals I might be able to guess the language they were speaking. I literally therefore kicked myself up but as soon as I woke up I saw them but could not understand a word they spoke. I tried to go back to sleep hoping to pick from where I left off but I could not go back to sleep and when I succeeded in dozing I could not understand them again. I have wondered what I tapped into during that trip but have been unable to duplicate though on some occasions I picked up snippets of foreign languages when asleep on a journey. Traveling is the only time I am likely to fall asleep among strangers.

2. The second incident took place at Rivoli Cinema in Tamale during my first year teaching experience. I took to the movies like a duck to water when I went to Tamale and found a modern cinema house similar to the one I used to brave my fears at night to patronize in 1955. The excitement of proximity to cinema was palpable, I used to go to the movies almost everyday during my first term as a teacher at Tamale, sometimes twice or thrice a day.

One Saturday afternoon I was at the movies with my friend Donatus, when midway through the movie we saw what seemed like fire on the screen or as if the screen was on fire. Pandemonium broke out in the theater at the sight of the screen on fire. The people jumped out of their seats in panic and rushed for the exits. The exits were soon clogged with people falling and trampling over one another to get out of the theater. Donatus remained cool calm and collected while I squirmed in my seat. I looked to him for cue about when to join the exodus out of the theatre but he remained calm in his seat while the exits were clogged by panicked patrons. Suddenly, I panicked, lost my nerve, bolted out of my seat and headed for the clogged exits. When I came to my senses I was walking towards the movie house from about two blocks away.

I have no idea how I got out of the theatre, by the time I got off my seat the exits were already clogged and packed with panicked movie goers. I did not remember how I leaped or trampled over the patrons already packed like sardines at the exits. I ran out of the theatre for about two blocks before I came to my senses and realized that I was running on the street, stopped and retraced my steps. The entrances were still clogged with people still struggling to get out when I went back to the theater. I waited in the courtyard for calm to be restored before I went back into the theater. Donatus was still sitting where I left him in panic; and I wondered how he could have remained so calm in the face of the mass hysteria. Apparently he had a similar experience a few days earlier and therefore did not panic. He explained that the fire on the screen was from the projection room. If there was any fire at all it was in the operator's room but did not have any effect on the theater itself. I have never ceased wondering how I made it out of the theater when the entrances were already filled with shrieking people trampling over one another to get out before I panicked and rushed for the same exits.

The last incident took place while I was on my way to Damongo from Tamale in about April 1962. Again, as on the road to Navrongo, I fell asleep or dozed off in the vehicle. I was rudely awoken from sleep by the sudden cries of fear and hysteria by my fellow passengers and when I came to senses I was walking to the van from about one to two hundreds yards away from the direction we came. The van had come to a stop at the edge of a precipice, prevented from going into the ditch by a sandbank. The driver and his mate were standing by the truck. Later they got out a tire rod and jack and changed one of the front tires. I learned later that the van blew a front tire and driver struggled to maintain control of the truck. The cries that woke me were in response to the heroic efforts of the driver as he tried to control the truck as it zigzagged along the road. I did not remember how I stepped over the three rows of passengers ahead of me and got out of the truck before they did. I got back to the truck before the passengers got off for the flat tire to be changed.

The Rivoli Cinema and the Damongo road incidents have one thing in common, fear and panic. Fear and panic triggered unconscious reflex actions that made me ran away from threatening situations without being aware how I got away. During my youth I attributed the escapes to some unknown supernatural power that spirited me away when I felt threatened and panicked. I turned these events over several times in my mind but I have not been able to figure out how I overcame the obstacles and got away in the panic situations. It is also possible that I might have been lithe enough to wiggle and worm my way out of impossible situations without being aware how I did it.

ASPIRATIONS OF MY CHILDHOOD

The man I became and the professions I followed were happenstances dictated by circumstances and conditions beyond my control. I never understood the role or influence of role models in the life of children until recently when on reflecting about my childhood fantasies I realized that my childhood aspirations were dictated by my surroundings. I could not imagine conditions, lifestyles, work or profession outside the purview of my experience. My worldview during infancy was very limited and as result my aspirations were limited as well. I had a very limited worldview on jobs and professions, I did not know much beyond manual labor and craft trades and I could not imagine or visualize myself doing anything when I grew up than driving or auto repairs.

In 1949, the year I left the northern territories for Bogoso in the Gold Coast Colony, there was not a single house at either Duohi or Nyagli, where I lived, that was roofed with corrugated iron sheets, the symbol of affluence and the well travelled man of the north in those days. So Bogoso with its open drains and wide dusty-gravelly streets, when compared to the villages I left behind was out of this world. The modest lifestyles of my neighbors filled me with awe and wonder and for many years I ogled their possessions and wished to emulate their standard of living when I grew up. Their treasured possessions were wireless radios operated with large battery parks and a hand cranked gramophone. The family had no furniture so my experience of any room furniture was what I gleaned through the doorways of my neighbors. The first time I saw and felt room furniture was in the sixth grade or thereabout. One of my relatives was a domestic servant or cook in the bungalow of a senior expatriate mine official at Tamso. I saw how the white man lived, the gleaming white cushions, refrigerator and the food they ate. The white man's potato tasted awful compared to the sweet potato that I knew. My worldview was limited to the experience of my immediate environment. On education for instance my experience was limited to the ten years of primary and middle school and until the eighth year I did not know about secondary or technical schools. I could not imagine anything beyond my immediate environment and when my horizon widened I did not see myself in the new world. My world was a world of manual labor and artisans as such my professional aspirations during most of my infancy were driving and auto repairs.

My father was not much of a role model in my life. He left home just about two years after I got to know him as my father and the next time I reunited with him about three years later he was not the same man I knew before he left home. I tried to drop out of the primary school to become an apprentice for carpentry, driving or auto repairs and failed. The carpentry fell out of my favor after I was rejected, but my fascination with driving and auto repairs persisted for many years, despite rejections of my application for apprenticeships. No other job or profession had a more powerful hold on my imagination than a driver or auto mechanic. I did not know any white collar workers beyond say clerical assistants and they did not attract me.

The standard housing in the Gold Coast was single room occupancies in compound house setting. I never experienced anything different during my childhood until I completed college. I saw bungalows of the expatriate mine officials located on the hills of the gold mines overlooking Bogoso and later Tamso but I never went near one to aspire to live in one or any self contained housing. When I went inside a bungalow in the mid fifties I did not think I belonged, that was a white man's house and the only reason I had access was because a cousin was a servant in the bungalow My limited worldview during infancy may be illustrated by a comment I made to a relative when I was in the sixth grade. I boasted to an older female relative that when I grew up I will invite her to live a life of luxury with me. My concept of a luxury house was a two room tenement house popularly known as chamber and hall in Ghana, and a bed with kapok cotton mattress instead of a straw mattress. I could not imagine or visualize any accommodation greater or superior than 'chamber and hall'. The 'chamber and hall' was a variation of the single room housing; this was a room and an enclosed verandah. The enclosed verandah was the hall or living room and the chamber was the bedroom. Bungalows and other self contained housing were occupied by expatriate colonial officials and high government officials. These types of housing were provided either by the government or by the mining companies. From the late sixties when my prospects through education began improving I upgraded my aspirations to a government bungalow. Modern home ownership was not within my worldview or experience. No member of my family or relative owned a home in the south although every boy when he came of age literally built his own home with the help of his community. I did not grow up in that environment so homeownership was not part of my world, my world was roomy house. The homeowners I knew, such as our landlord at Bogoso, were rich men with command of financial and material resources I could not imagine.

I used water closet and slept on a foam mattress for the first time at St. John Bosco's College at Navrongo in 1960. Life at St. John Bosco's College was a luxury compared to where I came from. The college used to provide us with entertainment by showing us movies on weekends at the open air theater. The movies we were shown were cartoons or exploits of the Canadian Mounted Police. Two of our tutors were Canadian nationals, Father Lincout and Father Perrault as such we were treated mostly to Canadian movies. After independence a new class of furniture based on springs and foam cushions and interior spring mattresses were introduced and promoted by the government of the first republic under Dr. Kwame Nkrumah. The new class of furniture was made by Industrial Development Corporation, one of the first industries established by the Nkrumah government after independence. The armchairs and sofas consisted of springs and foam cushions and were more comfortable than the old town hall chairs with cotton or straw cushions on *wawa* wood board base. They became the most sought after furniture for every young man. The IDC furniture was freely copied or imitated by local carpenters, the imitation chairs and sofas were cheaper than similar ones made by the corporation. The IDC furniture and their imitators were however beyond my means when I bought my first set of chairs in 1961-62, I bought the cheap imitation chairs with cotton instead of foam cushions. It is ironic judging by western standards that I could afford only custom made clothes and furniture, ready made clothes and furniture were for affluent customers. I bought my first ready made furniture in Australia for Ghana. Ready made furniture had reputation for superior craftsmanship and I could not afford them when I came of age and started my working life from the early sixties until the mid seventies when I left for Australia.

It is also ironic that throughout my infancy I aspired to become a driver or auto repairer but ownership was beyond my imagination, car ownership was outside my world experience. Most of the drivers I knew and heard about were hired by wealthy owners. Owner drivers were few and tended to come from rich families, most drivers worked for rich car and truck owners. For instance my landlord at Bogoso bought a truck for his son when he became a licensed driver. Auto ownership entered my lexicon for the first time around 1965, the year I obtained passes in four subjects at the general certificate of education. That was the first time I was able to imagine and visualize myself as a college educated graduate. And with that I had new set of goals and aspirations that hitherto had not crossed my mind such as car ownership and self contained housing or bungalow. By this time I had almost given up my aspirations for professional driving or auto mechanic. I aspired for college education as a means of improving my life but I did not aspire to go beyond a bachelor's degree. I left that aspiration to those who came after me. I told myself that I was the first from a largely illiterate family to go to college; it was up to those who came after me to aspire for higher degrees or goals. I paved the way through hard work for the others to follow.

I did not have any ambition greater than my immediate world when I was growing up because I did not know any better than what I saw around me at Bogoso. When I went to Tarkwa I was like a giant among midgets, my fifth and sixth grade class was seen as a great milestone by my kinsmen. Most of them were illiterate mine and sanitation laborers who appreciated my literacy and reading skills limited as it was. My dreams and goals in life were shaped by my environment. That my life differed from my childhood experience was accidental or destiny. My life is made up of a series of accidents and happenstance that together make me the person I am today. I seized opportunities that came my way while others I wanted slipped through my fingers through no fault of mine. When I had financial difficulties in the early seventies I put my faith in a scholarship program as a way to turn my life around but I was not interested in a second degree unless it was the only opportunity available. In the end I won a scholarship that was virtually tailor made for me.

I returned to my country in triumph after more than four years in Australia. Every material goal I ever had became a reality. But within a few years after my return I was nearly driven to financial ruin for the second time in my life. If the devil had a hand in my financial meltdown at the beginning of the decade, this time the devil met its match. I was a bit more enlightened and although the devil brought me to my knees I learned that through fasting and prayers all things are possible. Through fasting and prayers I overcame the spate of misfortunes, bad luck and the numerous problems that confronted me. Throughout most of my life I never attributed my personal misfortunes and problems to influences beyond my control even when it was obvious. This was the first time in my life when I could find no logical explanation for the things that happened in my life. How could I find a logical explanation when new babies' underwear were transformed into old underwear before my eyes on the morning I was set to deliver them to customers. That event sent me seeking for spiritual help for the third time since my return from Australia. Before this I always had at the back of mind that most of my past problems were due to poor choices but in the light of the recent events of my life I was forced to conclude that some of my problems and difficulties were caused by forces beyond my control. I did everything correctly but watched helplessly as my life went downhill. But I had the last laugh when the agents of the devil or sorcerers were exposed before my eyes in the same way that the new underwear was transformed before my eyes. There was no subtlety in either case, they were raw and to the point. Fasting and prayers between three and five days a week became the most potent spiritual weapon that I learned to wield against satanic forces. I learned that while I could touch the nebulous or nameless God within me I was no match against satanic powers bent on my ruin without Christ. Fasting and prayers became a substitute for my regular concentration and meditation exercises. Fasting and prayers had the same calming effect like meditation and made me triumph over evil and satanic forces against me. Fasting and prayers helped to draw me closer to God on the wings of Christ instead of just my inner light.

The intuition or the quiet voice of God or my guardian angel which had led me through many stormy waters dimmed as my self discipline in meditation took a hit due to work and family responsibilities. Besides, I succumbed and tripped by sensuous temptations that came my way and gave an opening to Satan to wreak havoc in my life. But fasting and prayers opened different spiritual doors of the fruit of spirit before me. Fasting and prayers had the effect of intervening before God to save me from myself. I have been at peace with myself through since I found peace and tranquility through concentration and meditation in the mid seventies. But after I became a family man my powers of concentration and meditation was adversely affected. I longed for the quiet and serenity I enjoyed before I became a family man. It was then that I realized the wisdom of celibacy demanded of Catholic priests, without that requirement I would have probably chosen the life of the pulpit. I chose family over turning myself into eunuch for the sake of the gospel and I have replaced that peace and tranquility with love of family.

When I decided to seek greener pastures overseas my back was practically against the wall by virtue of the whip lash I had endured from the devil. I did not know exactly what I wanted except to make ends meet and take care of my family. My aim was to provide some basic frame work for my family so that they could have higher aspirations than I did when I was growing up. While I was in Ghana I tried to educate my children in private schools but the outcomes were rather disappointing. So disappointing that when I had the opportunity to sponsor two of them for studies in Cuba I demurred because I felt they would not have been good ambassadors for the country. It is a decision I have lived to regret. My other aim was to work at one place long enough to earn a pension. I was a middle aged man but I did not have any savings or source of dependable income I could rely on for support in old age without having to depend on my family. I have met that aim by qualifying for social security. My social security check, meager as it might seem in the USA, would be enough for me to adequately take care of myself if I were to return to my country of origin.

I migrated to America with modest aims and goals as such. And when I became self employed I did not know much about the workings of the social security system otherwise I would have paid more of my self employed income into it instead of writing off most of the income as expanses. I started limiting my expense write off when I read about a self employed truck driver who was denied disability benefits because he used to write off all his income as expenses without making contributions to social security. I had a job with the city and could have continued working at the city job for the rest of my working life. But it is not in my nature to stay still at one place for long periods of time and certainly not the rest of my working life stretching over twenty to thirty years. In spite of my aims and good intentions I rolled along into self employment after less than fifteen years with the city but that was my longest stint at any job.

There is opportunity in every misfortune in life if we look for it or as it is said there is light at the end of every dark cloud. That is the way I characterize the beginning of my appraisal practice in New York. When I was trying to dip my toes into the profession no appraisal company was willing to give me a shot to prove my mettle particularly in narrative appraisal reports. On one or two occasions I could have had some opportunities if I was conversant with form appraisals. I tried to get into the profession through real estate sales but my sales career was short lived because I did not get the appropriate support and cooperation from my Broker and mentor. I could have done well as a sales person because within two weeks of joining the sales team of the Real Estate Office on Flatbush Avenue I had a potential listing in East Flatbush. The white broker who was supposed to train me was afraid to go into East Flatbush, the saleswoman he assigned to me as a mentor found an excuse that prevented her from taking me to meet the property owner. The property owner would have given me the listing if an experienced person had accompanied me to meet him. After this incident I became discouraged and stopped going to the office. I turned my attention to the Appraisal Institute Courses after I became a car service operator. My fortunes as a real estate appraiser began to turnaround after I completed the courses and examinations of the Appraisal Institute. I had my first trial appraisal assignment from Rossman Appraisals on Long Island in about October 1989. After the trial assignment he kept me busy until after the Christmas holidays in 1989. Rossman gave me the practical experience that helped me to obtain a full time appraisal position with TRW-Real Estate Loans Services. The office was located at Plainview. My boss at Plainview used to wonder how I could successfully complete the courses and examinations of the Appraisal Institute when I could hardly complete an error free residential appraisal report. I was not accustomed to form appraisals and I used to have a lot of omissions on the form. The Real Estate Loan Services was later divided into two office locations, the Plainview office on Long Island and a Brooklyn office located at Bath Beach on Bath Avenue. The Bath Beach office was under the supervision of one Stan Timari. I worked well with Stan until I started working with the city around the middle of 1990. I do not know Stan's motivation but he fired me allegedly for not being at home to answer my phones in the afternoons though I never missed a date on any assignment. When I resumed practice in about 1992 the market was beginning to change. The troubled neighborhoods of New York City were on the verge of gentrification. I did appraisals in Harlem long before the Harlem renaissance. Fear of the so called violent neighborhoods resuscitated my career. The white appraisers were either frightened or reluctant to venture into the so called violent neighborhoods of New York City such as Harlem, Bushwick, Bedford Stuyvesant or East New York. These were the neighborhoods where I had most of my initial appraisal assignments. I had a full time job as such I used to inspect my subject properties and sale comparables after my full time job. I went into the neighborhoods in the evenings at a time when non residents were hurrying or itching to leave before sundown. I used to drive and walk around the streets inspecting taking pictures of properties till dark when I could not take a picture even with a flash. During most of the nineties I was more afraid of a gunshot from a jittery policeman than violence from a crack head.

The only time I ever came close to any danger occurred in broad daylight at a Harlem subway station on 110th Street and Lexington Avenue. I was waiting for the A train to downtown Manhattan. I stood near the south entrance of the platform all alone when a young tall gentleman entered the station through the same south entrance. As soon as he entered I was prompted to keep some distance from him. I moved towards the center of the station. He surveyed the station saw that we were the only two people at the station and sensed or saw a crime of opportunity. I kept walking as I had been prompted and did not wait to become a victim. I continued walking at a steady pace towards the north entrance. The gentleman also kept a steady pace towards me, I quickened my pace and was about to strut or double my steps when I perceived that he was gaining on me and just then another person entered the station from the north entrance where I was going. As soon as the gentleman saw the entry of the third party he stopped dead in his tracks and gradually retreated to the far end of the station. I took a deep breath and stood by the new gentleman who did not know that he had probably prevented a crime of opportunity.

WALK WITH THE DEVIL

When I set foot on the soil of Ghana in September 1979 on return from Australia I felt an eerie and weird sensation like a worm that crawled up from the base of my spine and went out through the crown of my head. I turned to my wife and told her that I thought something. I did not know what had been taken from me but I presumed that my spiritual healing power might have been taken away as unexpectedly as when I realized I had the power.

I was shortsighted and over optimistic before I left for Australia in February 1975. I gave up my roomy house at Mataheko to spite the woman who eventually became my wife. Obenewa was pregnant with my child but she refused to abort the fetus when I asked her. I was therefore displeased with her decision to keep the child I decided to sever relations with her. And to show her that despite carrying my baby there was no future between us I surrendered my roomy house. If I had allowed her to stay in my roomy house while away it would have given her hopes that we had a future together. In spite of my attempts to sever relations with her and even refused to have any correspondence with her, she became my wife two years after I left for Australia. And thus when we came back we had no home to go to. But luckily when we landed we were met at the airport by my office colleague and friend Elisha, who offered us his room at Alajo, a suburb of Accra and moved in with his wife at Kokomlemle. Two days after we arrived my fears that my spiritual healing powers might have been taken from me were confirmed when I was unable to calm or help a sick child of one of our new neighbors. Obenewa brought the baby into our room for me to lay hands on it after she heard the child crying in distress. I had already lost confidence or faith in my ability to do spiritual healing due to the creepy sensation I felt at the airport. When I saw her cradling the baby in her arms I told her "it will not work, the power was taken away at the airport". But I went through the motions anyway, laying hands on the baby and just as feared, I could not help the child. The tingling and warm sensation I used to feel when I laid hands on people in Melbourne was missing. I was dense with no feeling of any outflow of energy or power from me. After a few minutes I returned the child to Obenewa still crying and wailing, I was unable to calm him down. The hands that used to send people into deep sleep or relaxation within a few minutes could not calm down a crying baby. I was doubtful before I left Melbourne that I could practice spiritual healing in Ghana. I did not have any of the characteristics of the typical faith healer in Ghana. I was not a minister or preacher, seer or prophet. But I did not expect that I would lose the gift the way it happened, a tingling sensation or feeling that arose from the base of my spine and went out through the crown of my head when I landed at the airport in Accra. Obenewa never asked me to attempt healing another person again not even my own family, I even forgot that I ever practiced spiritual healing. But a few years later the sight of a lean and emaciated lady touched my heart and moved me to try spiritual healing again with help of fasting and prayers.

A few months after our arrival we departed for Kumasi. I returned for a short visit on one weekend and stayed again with Elisha at Alajo. On that Sunday morning I decided to visit a kinsman at Amrahia agricultural experimental dairy station along Accra-Dodowa road. While driving out of Alajo I saw a young woman in her Sunday best and a bible in hand waiting for a bus or trotro at a bus stop to go to church. I offered her a ride and as soon as she sat on the backseat I went on heat like a dog. I was surprised at myself. I did not believe or expect that reaction or sensation of myself; I had never felt that way before. I therefore had to let her off the car before her destination to prevent myself from succumbing to the temptation. That was the precursor of the future that lay ahead of me though I did not recognize or accept my own hidden desires and vulnerabilities on gratification of the flesh.

I was able to weather the temptation that day by letting her off midway before her destination. But it was only the beginning. I had a vulnerability that I did not recognize. The cars I bought in the early seventies were never on the road long enough to teach me how to handle advances from the opposite sex who might show an interest in me only because she might be in need of transportation from one place to another. In a developing country such as Ghana, car owners often tend to attract attention because of the dearth or lack of adequate public transport facilities. That was my quandary when I became a car owner; I was ill prepared for the temptations of the privilege of car ownership. I was not prepared for sensual temptations that came my way as a result of the privilege though I rarely ever attempted to leverage my privilege car ownership into sensuous affairs. And that stance served me very well and kept me on the straight and narrow as long as the opposite sex was not bold enough to engage me in flirty conversations or exchanges. And that was basically how I began having affairs and cheating on my wife. I fell or misconstrued the friendly or flirtatious and suggestive conversations of my female passenger into sensuous affairs. In Ghanaian society it is almost a taboo for a woman to take the initiative to woo or date a man so flirtatious talk was seen as an invitation to treat. Thus even though I liked to believe tat I was holier than thou I could not resist to respond to the flirts of a beautiful woman. I was often flattered or too vain to resist the flirtatious initiatives of a pretty woman to woo her in my own way.

My First New Car

I returned to Ghana from Australia with an air of prosperity, I bought every material thing that was on my wish list before I left for Melbourne. I came with a new car and every material property I could only have dreamed or envied before I left for Melbourne. I was also a new man literally and figuratively different from the man I was before I left. I was disciplined and had a new perspective on life with a fervor for prayers and meditation, qualities I had lost in adulthood before I went to Australia. I was a disciplined practitioner of yoga exercises and meditation. But the distractions and inconveniences that confronted me on my return threatened my disciplined lifestyle and yoga practice. I was content and happier than at any time of my life; I had learned to use and enjoy material properties without emotional attachment to them in my heart. That was a trait or quality I sorely lacked and paid a steep personal emotional and material price in the early seventies. I tried as much as possible to continue living a disciplined life though the distractions and inconveniences got worse and became more difficult to have equanimity. The admiration of the opposite sex was a new distraction I did not previously have before I had the privilege and veneer of prosperity. I was mindful of the demonic and nefarious deeds of my people and kept a wary eye to avoid being victimized by demonic forces despite my new found faith in God. I was cognizant particularly of their prowess in concocting and delivering poisons to target victims.

I took delivery of my new car from the port and completed custom procedures in the first week of November 1979. Later events in my life proved that the Mercedes Benz 200D was both a blessing and a curse. I was happy that I was the owner of a new car though I did not have the cachet and resources befitting the ownership of an expensive or luxury car; for instance I could not afford the premiums for a comprehensive or full insurance coverage. I could only afford liability insurance or third party fire and theft. It would have taken my entire monthly pay packet to pay the premium for comprehensive or full coverage with nothing left to subsist on. The day I took delivery of the car effectively marked the beginning of my fall from grace.

On Transfer. To Kumasi

I tried for two months to obtain another accommodation after our return without success and I could not inconvenience Elisha indefinitely. I therefore asked my employer to transfer me to one of our regional offices where I felt it might be easier to find suitable accommodation. I was thus transferred to Kumasi and placed in charge of the regional valuation office. About two or three weeks after I completed customs and registration of my car I set out for Wa en route to Kumasi. I decided to visit my parents and reacquaint with Kofi, whom I had not seen since his mother gave him to me in 1973, before going to Kumasi. I left for Wa in the first week of December en route to Kumasi.

I was given custody of Kofi when he was less than two years old and at the time I did not have suitable accommodation in Accra. But fortunately Regina, who was a teacher at Labadi, was preparing to go on vacation to Wa, cared for him for a few days before she sent him to my mother. I therefore never lived with Kofi for even one night before I sent him to my mother. I tried to blackmail Dora, Kofi's mother through her motherly instincts, but the attempt failed. Dora came to my office sometime in 1972 for child support. But instead of giving whatever modest support I could provide I asked for custody of the child expecting her to refuse my demands and give me an excuse to deny support for the child. Instead she called my bluff and handed the child to me at the office the very next day. I was therefore caught unprepared but I had to accept him meekly with nothing more to say. I suddenly became a father when I was not ready for fatherhood; I was exploring for ways to avoid my parental responsibility by asking for custody. I do not know what I would have done with Kofi without my mother's help.

The wisdom of buying a diesel motor car became apparent during the long journey to Wa from Accra. During most of the seventies and eighties there were sporadic shortages of gasoline or petrol in the country, but diesel fuel was often in abundant supply throughout the country and was also cheaper than gasoline or petrol.

Diesel fuel was the lifeblood of the country's trade and commerce and was available in any small village where there was a corm or flour milling machine. No expensive infrastructure was required to sell diesel, a drum and a hand cranked pump was the only equipment needed to sell diesel.

I drove almost nonstop from Accra to Wa, a distance of about four hundred and fifty miles over a twenty four hour period. We stopped only to refuel or buy food or snack or feed Akuah who was reunited with us before we left Accra. We drove through the night from Bamboi to Wa. We passed through Bole around midnight or thereabout and from that hour until dawn we saw lights and tongues of flames flying from place to place under the cover of darkness. The flames are reputed to be witches and wizards gathering at covens in our small towns and villages. The fires and flames are a common sight on dark moonless nights around our towns and villages in the northwest of Ghana. They are most often seen on large baobab trees similar large trees near our towns and villages. We saw the nocturnal flying flames as we passed through towns and villages along the road. The flames burned in trees while some of flames darted from tree to tree through the darkness. The flames are normally visible with the naked eye though the spirit of the evil spirits behind the flames can be seen only by one with seeing eyes or seer. If we were walking through the towns and villages we might have taken shelter in one of the villages till daybreak out of fear of the nocturnal flying flames. The flames cannot be mistaken for fireflies because they are bigger, brighter, faster and do not blink like fireflies.

If there is anything like a witch's coven; then I guess the baobab tree or similar such large trees around our towns and villages might be considered as witches covens. They seem to be a phenomenon in that part of northern Ghana. The flames converge on large trees without singeing the trees. From the experience of my personal struggles with evil I concluded that the power of evil to affect and influence me was more psychological than real. I was under the assumption that the only evil that could touch me was contact poison and I took precautions in my life to prevent it. I held those beliefs until the early eighties when my beliefs were profoundly challenged. I was assailed by forces beyond my control and brought me to the edge of poverty and starvation The revelations that came to light altered my perceptions and I discovered my spiritual inadequacy that made me vulnerable to demonic and satanic forces. I was helpless against the ill winds that blew against me and my assumptions and beliefs were put to the test.

When I was a student at the University of Science Technology I had a friend and namesake who was also from Northern Ghana. We had similar health conditions that could not be diagnosed or treated by conventional medicine. We had similar beliefs about sorcerers and witchcraft in our families. And we used to meet in the student common room to compare notes on our health conditions and lament about demons, sorcerers and witchcraft within our families wreaking havoc against our health and potentialities. We were both afflicted by heart conditions that could not be diagnosed for effective treatment. When we became familiar with one another he had already repeated a class as a result of his illness. He used to go home for treatment whenever he had crisis or flare ups from his illness. The last time he went home during one such crisis was 1970 and he did not come back, he succumbed to his illness; incidentally that was the year I recovered from my mysterious illness but in spite of the demonic nature of my illness I did accept or dwell upon demonic circumstances as cause of my condition. I construed the illness as psychosomatic.

We arrived at Wa, our final destination at dawn, all the flying flames we saw during the night disappeared towards daybreak. We stayed with my sister Vida and her husband Bob Millar at the Wa school for the Deaf for approximately one week before I went to Kumasi to assume duties. I met Kofi for the first time since I sent him to my mother at about age two, he was by then an eight years old kid.

BECAME IMPOTENT AFTER A NIGHTMARE

My faith was sorely tested shortly after I began work at Kumasi. I won the first battle of wills with the devil when my wife gave birth naturally and safely to a baby girl after seven days of labor in the hospital.

My next problem came upon me unawares, without any warning or premonition, after a nightmare. I was warned about three months about the dangers ahead of my wife before the event. The premonitions gave me the opportunity to pray against the disaster. I did not get any hunch or intuition about any pending serious incident in my life. Three days after a nightmare I became impotent. At the time Viagra had not yet been invented and impotency at the prime of my life would have led to the breakup of my marriage if that was the intent of the devil. We had been married for less than three years when the devil attempted to take away my dignity and manhood.

The dream or nightmare portended death or funeral but there was a silver lining in the nightmare which gave me hope that the final result of whatever happened to me would not be fatal or permanent. In this nightmare, I dreamt I was dressing after a shower; I put on white underwear top and bottom and followed that with a black shirt. I was then about to put on a black pant or trousers when a large powerful black bull demolished the wall and charged into the room. I ran out of the bedroom for dear life with the bull behind me and finally I scurried up a tree. The bull was left below the tree huffing and stomping its hooves in anger or fury when I woke up. The outer symbols of the dream pointed to a pending major catastrophe but with a little saving grace or silver lining beneath the ameliorate the catastrophe. The silver lining was the white underwear in the nightmare and I did not finish the full complement of black outer wear before the bull charged into the room. I expected the worse, a serious illness or accident that would not be fatal. I speculated on a thousand and one adverse possibilities but never once did I suspect, even remotely, impotence. But three days after the dream I became impotent, I had no libido.

White generally symbolizes life and black symbolizes death so beneath the symbol of death was life. On the basis of that interpretation of the symbols I was certain the impotence would be temporary but I had no idea how long I shall be impotent. I did not know what to do beyond prayers and meditation for a cure or healing and that was what I decided to do. I did not consult any doctor because I was certain the problem was beyond conventional medicine not could not help me. My problem was persuading my wife to bear with me until such time that my cock kicked up again. I could give no assurance or estimate of time frame in which I expected to become a man again. I made no attempt to seek conventional medical treatment because I was convinced the condition was not physical but spiritual. I had not been in Kumasi for more than six months and yet I was facing my second spiritual trial. I wondered what the future held for me in Kumasi. I was willing to endure the condition for as long as it would take but Obenewa convinced me to seek spiritual help from some of faith healers in the city. I had not been in Kumasi for long so I did not know any spiritual church or pastor.

I was therefore compelled to consult one of my colleagues at the office who was more familiar with the city for advice on reputable spiritual churches and pastors in Kumasi. The colleague, Abotsi referred me to Prophet Asare, one of the most popular faith healers in Kumasi at the time. He was the pastor of a large church located near the Kumasi Sports Stadium area. I consulted the Prophet at his church one afternoon but somehow I did not feel the spirit of God or the Holy Spirit in the church; I saw things that made me skeptical whether he was a genuine man of faith or follower of Christ. He was almost like a cult hero to his followers but what put me off were the herbs and frogs around his altar or pulpit. He invited me to return to worship with him at the church later that evening but that was the last time I saw him, I never went back.

The faith healing I practiced while in Australia relied on nothing but prayers thus when I saw herbs and frogs I thought they were incompatible with faith. I did not understand how a man who was reputed to be a wonder miracle worker could have herbs and frogs in his church. There is a place for herbal remedies but I was expecting spiritual help not herbal remedy; I was not convinced he could help me spiritually. It appears that my apprehension might have saved me from a bigger catastrophe. Less than a year after I consulted the prophet he and his church were destroyed by irate soldiers after the military coupe that brought Rawlings to power for the second time. The Church was razed to the ground, the prophet killed and his body dragged through the streets of Kumasi by the soldiers. It was rumored in Kumasi that the pastor and some of his followers had a spat with some soldiers. The disaffected soldiers took advantage of the confusion that followed in the immediate aftermath of the coupe to terrorize the pastor and his church, killed him and some of his assistants.

I did not go back to the pastor and I did not know any other spiritual church or pastor so I continued with my regular meditation and prayers for healing. My wife appeared to be more concerned with my erectile dysfunction than me. One day she came home with information about a church she had heard about at Santasi, a suburb of Kumasi. The church was known as the Musama Disco Christo Church, MDCC. The Santasi church was a branch of the main church located at Musama in the central region of Ghana. The branch was led by a young and beautiful female pastor. They were gentle faith healers without the delirium and swooning of most healers or apostolic churches in Ghana. I followed the pastor's instructions and washing rituals. I used to go for early morning prayers and ritual baths once or twice a week followed by Sunday services. We used to go for the church service as a family affair because my wife introduced me to the church and she also had a stake in my recovery. For more than six months I was impotent, and during those months I did not get even a tepid erection such as rigidity from of a full bladder before urination. I had the first inkling that all was not lost when I went on a business trip to Accra in the sixth month of the impotency. During the trip I gave a ride to a woman and at the sight of a strange woman in the back seat of my car I got an erection. But when I went back to my wife I was still not there. I was aroused at the sight of a woman who was not my wife but impotent before my wife. But that was the beginning of my healing. I started getting tepid erections and was back to full strength after about eight months. My libido was restored and I went on to father three more children with my wife.

In the end I think the recovery from the erectile dysfunction occurred as I had expected, the prayers and ritual baths at MDCC did not hasten the recovery. I cannot however vouch that without the prayers and ritual baths the impotence would not have lasted longer than it did. However throughout the ordeal I never lost my faith against full recovery. I do not think impotence at that age would have been the worse thing that would have happened to me. It would have given me the opportunity to take the vow of celibacy in service of the gospel knowing that I had already fulfilled my promise to my mother. I had three children at the time of the incident. I have fathered six more children since the impotency, three more with Obenewa and three after my second marriage. The dream and its aftermath influenced my sartorial choices; as much as possible I avoid black monochromatic clothes; I prefer bright colors over white underwear.

Home Business Venture At Kumasi

I started life afresh at Kumasi from a position of strength. I did not start from the scratch as when I graduated from college with nothing, this time I had most of the material things that are the hallmarks of the middle class. Going forward, my aim was to maintain my lifestyle without slipping back into the kind of poverty and deprivation that plagued me before I went to Melbourne. I began my new work life at Kumasi in the first or second week of December and quickly established good personal and working relations with the junior staff at the office. I took over the office from Abotsi who was in charge before my arrival. I relied on his knowledge and experience to run the office and work with landlords and the business community at large. We established a rapport that made it possible for us to do private real estate appraisals on the side. As a longtime resident of the city he was familiar with the business community and was instrumental in generating the appraisal assignments that kept us afloat. We inspected and wrote the reports together and shared the fees equitably to our mutual benefit. This symbiotic relationship helped both of us to maintain a modicum of middle class life.

For the next six months I made several futile attempts to acquire a suitable apartment before my personal effects arrived from Australia. I considered it fortunate that Grace Brothers did not ship the items as expeditiously as they had promised and the delay while uncomfortable at least saved me from renting a house or apartment I did not need immediately. I continued searching for an apartment half heartedly without any great enthusiasm until the day the ship with our personal effects docked at the port. Until then I did not care very much whether I had an apartment or not, the apartment I shared with my sister was adequate for my immediate needs. .The situation changed and became urgent when I received notice that the ship with our personal effects had finally docked at the port of Tema. It took another four to six weeks to clear customs and for the goods to get to Kumasi. From the day I received notice that the ship had docked at the port, I made several frantic efforts for an apartment but all my attempts were unsuccessful. This time I was really concerned, I feared I would have no place to store my household items and furniture when I took delivery of them from the port. I decided that if by the time the luggage arrived in Kumasi and I still had not secured an apartment or house then I would store them in my office until I got a suitable apartment or flat. But miraculously, my frantic efforts bore fruits on the day the truck set off from the port for Kumasi with our luggage. And by the time it landed in Kumasi I had keys to a three bedroom apartment at Suame. I unloaded our personal effects into my new apartment and was spared the inconvenience of converting my office into a storage warehouse.

As soon as we finished unpacking the luggage and settled down in our new apartment we started to put into effect our plan for a dressmaking business. Word spread even before we had unpacked all our things that an overseas trained dressmaker was setting up shop in the neighborhood. Obenewa hired a local dressmaker to assist her with the cutting and sewing. Initially we had a lot of clients but the honeymoon was short lived when the young women realized that Obenewa was not any better than the local dressmakers; the orders dried up. It appeared that our business endeavors failed before it took off. We let the local girl go because there was nothing for her to do. I then suggested to Obenewa that we hire another dressmaker to help her polish her dressmaking skills. Obenewa turned down the suggestion and as far as I was concerned that should have been the end of the dressmaking business. I understood her reluctance; it was not easy to climb down after having been hailed, for a few weeks, as an expert overseas trained dressmaker. The sewing machines would have been mothballed but for the timely arrival of my nephew Abu with Kofi from Wa. Abu, it turned out, was a good trained tailor and breathed life into the moribund business. He picked up from where the local girl left off but with a different emphasis, we changed from making women's wear to boys and men's wear. Finally we found some good use for our four industrial sewing machines, edger and about three domestic sewing machines. We would not have known what to do with the machines without Abu. Had Obenewa accepted training under a private tutor she would have improved her skill and competency at her own pace to have made a difference in our endeavors and investments and perhaps the dressmaking business would have been successful after Abu refused to move with us to Accra. She would have started over as a skillful dressmaker with the halo of an overseas trained moniker.

The direction of the business was changed to suit the skills of Abu. Thus we made men's and boys wear and a few simple ladies wear on request or made to order. Abu did not like working under the supervision of my wife because of her incompetence and did not hide his feelings. He was good and competent enough to provide us a supplementary income from tailoring until we packed and left for Accra. The business became a nightmare when we moved to Accra.

LONG ROAD TO ACCRA

September 1981 marked the second coming of Flt. Lt. J.J. Rawlings to power in another successful military coupe and with that began my slow and long march back to Accra. I was transferred out of Accra at my own request but the return of Rawlings after another successful coupe-de-tat began my slow march back to Accra. In 1979 Rawlings headed a mutinous government of junior and non commissioned officers who overthrew the existing military government on the eve of elections for return to civilian rule. The Armed Forces Revolutionary Council literally supervised those elections and returned power to the elected civilian government under Dr. Hilla Liman. The government that Rawlings and his henchmen helped to install in 1979 was the very government they overthrew a little over two years after the inauguration. And the witch hunt for corrupt government ministers and officials began. It is almost a ritual that after every military coup, the architects and leaders of the coup start a witch hunt for corrupt ministers and officials of the previous regime. I call the process a witch hunt because unless a military government is forced from power by another coupe they always indemnify themselves before handing over power to the next government. The accusations and innuendos of bribery and corruption against the members and officials of the deposed regime are followed by the establishment of a committee or commission of inquiry to investigate the incomes and assets of members of the deposed government. The proceedings of the committee are given wide publicity in the state controlled media to provide justification for the violent overthrow of the government. I had a temporary assignment with one such commission, after the coupe, that sent me back to Accra.

I was summoned to Accra by my boss to provide valuation services to a commission of enquiry into the assets of some ministers of the deposed government and their collaborators and enablers in the financial sector. This was the second time I found myself in this position. When the Busia government was overthrown in 1972 I was assigned to provide valuation services to a committee to investigate the assets of the ministers and other officials of the Busia government. At the time I was given the assignment with the committee I was an inexperienced appraiser barely a year out of college. But I was given the assignment more as a payback or retribution for my contemptible and impetuous attitude towards my boss. The assignment was however a welcome relief from my financial woes at the office. The committee gave me a chauffeur driven car, I slept at some of the best hotels and rest houses in the country and flew by plane for the first time from Accra to Tamale. By the end of the assignment I was ten pounds heavier and that was the only time I gained so much weight within a year. I was very happy with the extra weight as that was an indication that I was well fed or lived well and had the body to prove it. I reveled in my new heavier bodyweight while it lasted. Unfortunately I could not keep on the weight once the work was over; I lost the weight quicker than I gained it. I reprised my previous experience into the new assignment. My duties were basically the same but the actors were both former government officials and bank bosses.

I lived and worked in Accra for about one to two years and during that time I visited my family once or twice a month. The freedom of living away from my family paved the way for sensuous temptations and the sexual proclivities that began my spiritual downfall or fall from grace before the Lord. I had the means and the opportunity and though I never actively sought to be a skirt chaser but the skirts often found me and I took advantage of the skirts that fell into my laps. The deference and respect I commanded for driving an expensive car brought undeserved attention from the opposite sex though I did not have the resources to live up to the expectations. But I was able to keep mistresses at no cost beyond the false status symbol and cost of fuel for rides in a Mercedes Benz car. I guess most of my mistress's must have endured hunger but were too shy to ask because I rarely eat outside the house. My propensity to give rides to women was my spiritual undoing; I could not help giving rides to women I saw on the side of the road though I was reluctant to extend the same courtesy to men for fear of robbery or violence.

I was an enigmatic Mercedes Benz car owner. My personality did not match the profile of the typical expensive or luxury car owner in Ghana. The typical expensive and luxury car owner had rounded cheeks, pot belly and rather plump. I was the picture of hunger or poverty, lean and lanky with prominent cheek or collar bones otherwise called poverty bones. Those features in the immediate aftermath of the second Rawlings coupe protected and prevented me from being roughed up at security check points at a time when the military and police were gunning for luxury car owners as villains of the economic woes of the country. Most luxury car owners locked away their cars and a few sold them at fire sale prices. But I had only one car and it was very essential for my livelihood I therefore could not afford to hide it.

I was a mid level civil servant who drove an expensive car but I did not have the personality or the profile of a senior corrupt public official. I was often viewed suspiciously as I drove around the country going through one check point after another. I had to explain time and again how a civil servant like me came by an expensive car. The officers often approached my car aggressively sometimes with guns drawn and ordered me out of the car. But the moment I stepped out of the car they mellowed. Next they asked for the owner of the car and my claim of ownership was often met with incredulity and skepticism until I showed evidence of ownership to prove that I was not a front man for some hidden fat cat. My lean and gangly personality at the steering wheel of a Benz car puzzled the general public and security officers alike. On many occasions women frowned on me when they thought I was a chauffeur. But they instantly lit up and become affable and charming the moment they realized I was the owner of the car. The only reason women and other people glanced at me was because of the car not because of my personality, by Ghana standards I did not have the personality befitting the owner of a luxury car.

For the duration of the assignment I was offered a free apartment in the boys quarters of a college course mate. I lived independently of his family; I had a piece of mind and privacy that I did not have at Kumasi. I had no family distractions except when my younger brother of same name accompanied me back to Accra after visit to my family.

YEARNED FOR EXTRA BODY WEIGHT

Until I was about thirty years old or thereabout, I did not appreciate or like my lean and gangly personality, I longed for extra bodyweight or pounds of flesh. Being overweight or carrying extra pounds of bodyweight in Ghana symbolized prosperity and wellbeing. The overweight man or woman commanded respect because they were perceived as prosperous and were well fed people. I therefore did not like my personality as that portrayed me as being hungry and underfed or malnourished. I was anxious to portray myself as a successful college graduate, though in truth I was starving, but I did not want that to be the face I portrayed to the world. I was not malnourished during infancy but I never had more than enough to put on extra weight. I carried that eating habit into adulthood and while I yearned for extra bodyweight I ate sparingly.

I yearned to have extra pounds of flesh though I hardly had more than one or two meals a day throughout the period that I longed for fat and extra pounds of flesh. I returned from Australia with a different worldview. My attitudes for fat and extra pounds of bodyweight had changed and I came back from a country, where I could eat to my heart's content, with the same spare frame and proud of it. Cat calls were often made after me when I drove through the streets of North Suntresu where I lived with my sister. Children shouted Benz-hunu when I passed bye in my car. The cat call in the Akan language meant empty Benz or say empty suit. The catcalls made after me implied that I was a poor and hungry man who drove a Mercedes Benz. The implications were true, I was relatively poor compared to the typical Mercedes Benz car owner and my personality was not much to look at but I was proud and not the least not embarrassed or offended by the catcalls.

I was raised on one or two meals a day and I never had more than two meals until I completed middle school and went to boarding colleges, but I was never as healthy on campus as when I was on vacation. When on vacations I could hardly afford one meal a day on my own but I did not associate my good health while on vacation with hunger. I made that association or discovery during my first or second year at the university.

I discovered that I never had even a headache while on vacation as compared to the frequent visits to the college infirmary. And the only difference between my life on campus and my life on vacation was the amount of food I had. On vacation I was lucky if I had more than one meal a day but on campus I was served three meals with deserts and snacks. So I decided to skip one meal and snacks to test my hypothesis and the results were overwhelming and I continued with two meals till I graduated. After graduation, I wallowed in poverty and could barely afford one good meal a day and yet I wanted to put on pounds of extra flesh. It never crossed my mind that food and weight go together. So when my personal finances improved it still never occurred to me that to gain weigh I ought to change my eating habits. I never once thought that to change my personality I had to eat more than once or twice a day to gain weight; that realization came much later when I was in far away Australia. Our education was more concerned with adequate nutrition, the concept of going on diet or eating less to prevent overweight was not part of our problems.

During the three month long vacation in 1968 I never came down with any sickness throughout the vacation. But shortly after I went back to campus I started going to the college infirmary. I reflected on my life on campus and on vacation. The only difference I found was that during the vacation I could hardly afford one meal a day but on the campus I was provided three meals with deserts and snacks. I therefore decided to skip one meal and the results were astounding, The tummy aches and other minor illnesses that used to bother me on campus disappeared and my visits to the college infirmary were reduced by more than half. The change made tremendous improvements in my health on campus. And I have subsisted on one or two meals a day since 1968.

My world of what constituted good living, prosperity and the good life was turned upside down when I went to Australia. I used to imagine before I left for Australia that by the time I returned to Ghana I would be chubby with rounded cheeks and all my 'poverty bones' nicely covered up. It did not take long before I realized how wrong or misguided I was about chubbiness or extra pounds of fat. My secrete love affair with with extra fat or bodyweight came to an end; carrying extra fat or pounds of flesh had a different connotation in Australia than in Ghana. .In one, extra bodyweight, connoted glutton or overeating and in the other a sign one was well fed. I could not believe all the commercials on radio, television and newspapers that extolled the virtues of lean bodies or the sales of diet programs. Suddenly I felt good about myself and for once I appreciated my spare personality and was happy with my weight. By Australian standards I had the ideal bodyweight and I did not have to be on a diet program to maintain my weight.

CORNERED WITH A MAN'S WIFE

My fall from spiritual grace was because of my weakness to resist the flirtatious charms and attention of admirers of the opposite sex. I guess I was a womanizer at heart but was more comfortable with casual sex without commitments or perhaps I was too bashful to take initiatives on courtships until the opportunities literally fell into my laps. Thus I had an affair with a married woman because the opportunity presented itself or fell into my laps. When I began going out with the woman I suspected that she was married but she assured me to the contrary and allayed my suspicions. The relations could have ended in a disaster but for the grace of God. I am generally a shy person but the bashfulness was not enough to prevent me from having an affair with Mamle, a married woman, who egged me on and dispelled my suspicions that she was either a married woman or engaged. Our affair began casually and innocently when she used to stop by me while I cleaned my car in the morning before I readied for work. I fell for her attentions and charms when she engaged me in casual conversations. The casual conversations led from one thing to another and before long she was riding with me to the office in the mornings. The rest as they say is history. We became an item for about three months until her husband caught us together in my office and that brought the affair to an end.

My office was our rendezvous where we met in the afternoons and hung together until late at night when I sent her home. I suspected that she was either married or in a serious relationship when I could not drop her at the door of her home on three consecutive occasions. That roused my suspicions but she denied being married when I asked her. Then why do get off in the middle of nowhere? Are you a ghost? I enquired. I therefore threatened to breakup with her unless I could take her to her door; that would assure me that she was not married. She allayed my fears and suspicions the next time we met. I drove her home and was introduced to her parents. Her parents welcomed me warmly and my fears were put to rest. And from that night I picked and dropped her at the home whenever necessary. We never spent a single night together but we were often together from lunch time till late at night. She had a two or three year old child and I guessed that was the reason she went home every night.

One afternoon we were together at the office with my younger brother during lunch hour when a young man walked into my office. The man proceeded to accost my girl friend Mamle, asking what she was doing at the office. He then turned to me and introduced himself as the husband of my date and ordered her to pack up and leave for home. But instead of following her man meekly home she feigned anger at her husband for impugning her character and leveling false accusation against her. She pretended to be so aggrieved she threatened to walk out of their home that night. The threat mellowed the belligerence of her husband who did not expect that kind of response or outcome from her. He was as confused and bewildered as I was watching the melodrama unfold before me. When I saw the anguish and confusion on his face I broke my silence and intervened to calm the situation for reason to prevail.

My worse fears unfolded before me, I was inadvertently sleeping with another man's wife. And the marriage was in danger of unraveling before me added to my sense of shame and disgrace. The guilt I would have felt from their breakup as a result of my indiscretion led me to intervene to try to reconcile them and save their marriage. I do not remember what I said but Mamle calmed down and the couple walked out of my office hand in hand in perfect harmony. I was happy with the turn of events, the worse was over and I guess I was let off the hook. I counted myself lucky that the man did not turn his wrath on me when his marriage appeared to be heading for the rocks. But my brother was mad and angry at the woman for egging me into an affair and misleading me about her marital status. Apparently the husband was informed about our movements and rendezvous. He came to my office and found us together at lunch time as he was informed.

The following day the man surprised me by coming back to my office at about the same hour. This time he adopted an aggressive stance towards me. His purpose according to him was to find out whether I had slept his wife. To show me that he meant business or was not joking he threatened to invoke the wrath of the gods against me if I did not tell him the truth. And then he asked me 'do you know my wife?' To me it was so obvious that it did not merit an answer or affirmation as such I said nothing. After a long pause he repeated the question as if I did not hear him the first time, 'do you know my wife?' Again I said nothing, but after he asked me the third time whether I knew his wife I looked him in the eye and all but confirmed that I did without being so explicit. I also asked him whether he really wanted to know the truth. Yes! He replied. And then I proceeded to draw a scenario by a series of rhetoric statements. "I have known your wife for about three months. I spent hours with her alone in my room, she is not my sister or relative we do not even speak the same language and we are not from the same tribe. You are a man; if you were in my shoes with a woman on your bed behind closed doors, what would you do? When I finished with the statement he bowed down his head and said nothing for about fifteen minutes, fifteen minutes that seemed like an eternity. And when he spoke, he asked me to compensate him for defiling his wife. I told him I was sympathetic with him but I slept with his wife inadvertently with the connivance of his in-laws. "Your wife told me she was single and her parents all but confirmed her assertion that she was not married. I was misled by your wife and your in-laws and if you deserve any compensation then your in-laws should compensate you but not me. He sat pensively for anther twenty minutes or so before he finally left the office and I never saw either him or his wife again. Apparently Mamle used her parents' home as her staging ground and rendezvous with me. I used to pick or drop her at the parents' home. And after I dropped her she would then take a taxi home with her baby who was left in the care of his grandparents.

I did not consider myself a womanizer as such I felt a sense of guilt with every affair and I had the opinion that every sensual affair estranged me from the Lord. Mamle was the first woman I slept with since I got married and when it ended I was relieved and hoped to pick up the pieces of my spiritual life without any further distractions for the rest of my stay on the temporary assignment. But it did not take long before I started an affair with the younger sister of my benefactor in whose house I lived. I was contrite after the affair with Mamle and I resolved to turn over a new leaf. But I could not keep my resolution when the young woman started coming into my room late at night. I began obliging her late night visits despite my best intentions. I used to observe a quiet hour of meditation and prayers between ten o'clock and midnight. My young suitor came to my room between those hours when her brother and wife were in bed. I could not pray or meditate while she was with me and by the time she left I was tired and so sleepy I could not keep my eyes open. I could not help groping her each time she stepped into my room and as a result my prayer and spiritual life took a back seat and suffered. I kept on praying for forgiveness while indulging in the same sensual pleasures night after night. Her intrusions became so routine I looked forward to her though guilt would not let me go out of my way to find her when she was late. I stopped making any attempts at meditation or prayers and lay like a possum waiting for her to come. I could not concentrate on anything while I waited for her nightly intrusion. And by the time she sneaked back into her brother's quarters I had nothing left in my tank but to retire for the night. The above stories are not meant to show that I was a woman killer but that sometimes despite our best intentions we are still powerless in the face of some temptations. The affairs were antithetical to my being and I think Satan used the opposite sex to estrange me from God before it pounced on me when I was spiritually weakened and vulnerable. And if God were to judge man by his purity very few of us would qualify to be His followers. My nightly trysts with the young woman ended only after she left for her hometown to get married. My spirituality was not the same in spite of my attempts to redeem myself before God.

HELP FOR AN ADDICT

This is a story of help for an alcoholic addict but the help came through sexual proclivities. I came across a former coworker, Tosh, whom I used to admire on the streets of Accra. During the time we were coworkers I did not have the wherewithal to court her and was also too timid to be seen casting amorous glances at her by her boss. I was glad and flattered that Tosh recognized and acknowledged me by name on the streets of Accra after so many years. She was the secretary to the cabinet minister of the department so we did not cross paths at the workplace unless I went to her office on an errand. Thus we did not have much in common hence I was surprised and flattered when she called me by name though I did not know her name. The chance meeting on the street began an affair and by the time the affair ended she was a sober woman, freed from alcohol addiction. During the affair I was warned in a dream while she lay by my side of the consequences of my sexual proclivities. My material and spiritual woes began a few months after we drifted apart and went our separate ways without any acrimony or misunderstanding. I did not know much about Tosh before I came across her on the streets of Accra. I did not even know her name at the time but she was still as beautiful as when I used to steal glances at her whenever I went into her office. I was very happy when I stumbled into her and was ecstatic that despite the scant contact we had in the office she recognized and knew me by name, something I could not say about her. I went out of my way to invite her for dinner. Normally I do not eat outside my home so it usually never occurs to me to chat with friends and acquaintances at the dinner table. But I guess that was the only way I could get to sit down with her and get to know her. I ordered her choice of food and drinks from the menu and watched her eat and drink. As I watched her eat and drink I concluded that all was not well with her. The rate at which she drank the bottles of beer surprised me and I could not help wondering whether she liked the beer more than the food. When I prodded her a little about the way she drank she literally confessed to being a virtual alcoholic. From the moment I knew she had an alcohol problem my interest in her went beyond the sensual to helping her deal with the alcohol problem. That made me interested in her as a person of more than sexual interest. Thus far I knew nothing about her than her beautiful face.

I discovered after a few days of prodding that Tosh's addiction to alcohol was caused by heartbreak. She was duped by a brave double crosser into a polygamous marriage. She married under the pretext of an only wife not knowing that her husband was already married with a wife and children at Kumasi. Her husband kept his marriage secrete from her by maintaining two households, one in Kumasi with his first wife and another in Accra with Tosh. And through three children Tosh was under the impression that she was an only wife or in monogamous marriage. She was therefore devastated when she found that she was the second one in the marriage, the shock drove her to alcohol.

Unfortunately there is no such thing as bigamy in Ghana so Tosh had no remedy, polygamy is legal and tolerated. A man can marry one woman under customary law and another under ordinance both marriages existing side by side. Her marital status turned her into an alcoholic. The extent of her addiction was worse than mine ever was; I was addicted for approximately four months while she had been addicted for years. She was so addicted that she went to bed drunk almost every night and she said that sometimes when she could not get alcohol she brewed tobacco as substitute. She was separated when we started dating so I did not have the guilt complex of an affair with a married woman but I was bothered by my own conscience that I was violating my marriage or taking advantage of a troubled and helpless woman.

I did not have the guilt that I was sleeping with another man's wife but saw her as someone vulnerable to manipulation because of her insoluble personal problems. That guilt made me made me determined to help her with her problem with counseling and prayers. While I counseled and pray with her I could not help jumping into bed with her at every opportunity. We therefore had the dichotomy of combining illicit sex with prayers. Whenever we met we prayed before ending up in each other's arms and I guess the prayers worked. I tried to impress upon her while I held her in my arms that she had to overcome her ruinous habit for the sake of her children, in her absence her children would end up in the custody of her hated rival. I therefore encouraged her to sober up for her children. Gradually my lifestyle and sobriety began to rob on her. She became uncomfortable to drink in my presence and the third or fourth month into our relationship she began sobering up. Her road to sobriety was hastened unexpectedly by an unusual event that gave her the final push into sobriety for good. We visited a friend at Winneba Training College who welcomed us with two bottles of beer. The cold sweat on the bottles of beer, on a hot and muggy afternoon, was too much for Tosh to resist. She therefore drank one bottle in spite of my protestations. And that bottle of beer did for her what three or four months of counseling and prayers could not do. But I think the unexpected drunkenness was the answer to our prayers. For some inexplicable reason she got so drunk that she threw up in the bathroom of our host and again on our way back to Accra. She woke up the next morning with hangover and a splitting headache. She could find no reason to explain how she got so drunk on a bottle of beer as to have a hangover and headache. She concluded that I might have jinxed her because she could find no explanation for being so drunk on just one bottle of beer but from that day she never drank another bottle until we drifted apart. The last time I came across her on the streets of Accra she hugged and mopped me with gratitude.

Tosh was the last of three or four women with whom I had affairs over a three to four year period while I was shuttling between Accra and Kumasi and lived apart from my family. My yoga exercise and meditation practice began eroding over the three year period. I guess by the time Tosh and I drifted apart I was in the back pocket of Satan and the devil was not about to let me go back to a life of prayer and meditation without a fight. This was the period when my attempts at prayers and meditation were thwarted by invisible cobwebs, itching and scratching my body.

On my last night with Tosh I dreamt that I was attacked by satanic forces that were bent on killing or ending my life by preventing me from calling the name of the Lord, the source of my power and strength. The dream impressed upon me that my salvation lay in the cross and I started drifting back to my Christian roots. When I started practicing yoga meditation I said to myself that God is one and so I turned myself into a free thinker with no religious affiliation. But that dream taught me to redirect my steps back to the Christian religion that nurtured me during infancy. After that night I began drifting back to the cross, the drift was gradual and began when I came under attacks by invisible cobwebs and a Pentecostal or spiritual church pastor helped me with prayers and ritual holy baths to overcome them. Even though I overcame the invisible cobwebs and itch attacks my meditation practice was never the same again.

Loss of Spirituality Vitality

I found material and physical balance in my life after I became an earnest practitioner of yoga in Melbourne. Maintaining this balance was the principal reason I requested for transfer out of Accra. But my family life was thrown into disarray when I started shuttling between Kumasi and Accra. My life was in perfect balance at Kumasi; I faithfully followed my yoga practices and never succumbed sensual temptations. I depended on regular meditation and prayers to maintain my center of gravity and when that was disrupted I began to drift and became vulnerable to the temptations that eventually led me to fall from grace.

The temporary assignment that sent me to Accra morphed into a permanent job offer as head of the valuation division of Architectural and Engineering Services Corporation, AESC. I lost the room that had hitherto been my home in Accra while I was on the temporary assignment. Thus when I started my new job in Accra I moved back with Elisha and shared his roomy house with him until I had a suitable place. My new job included provision of housing depending on availability and because of the dearth of housing in Accra there was no guarantee of when I could have a suitable apartment. Sharing one room between two adults deprived us of privacy. We did not have enough room to do the things that mattered most to us, prayers. I did not have room for either exercises or meditation.

I was sorry for the inconvenience I brought on Elisha and hoped that within that my employer would obtain suitable housing for me so that I could end the inconvenience. I also prayed for suitable housing so that I could bring my family to Accra and have some order in my life or at least have room for quiet time. Sometimes I tried to lessen the inconvenience on Elisha by staying late in the office to observe quiet time.

I did not know how much I had fallen from grace or the extent satanic forces would go to prevent me from reconnecting with God to find favor with Him until I got a temporary room where I had room and privacy for exercise and meditation. I was offered a room in a house at Teshie-Nungua residential estate by a cousin of Elisha. He intended to rent the house to me after he relocated to Takoradi for another job. He therefore gave me a room in his boy's quarters until he gave me possession of the house. I was happy with the offer, because for the first time in many months, I had a room where I could do the things that mattered to me; exercises, meditation and prayers. But when I moved into the room I found it almost impossible to meditate or pray. When I sat down to meditate or pray I felt cobwebs crawling on my face and arms with the result that I could not concentrate to meditate or pray. Apparently Satan liked it when I did not have room or privacy to observe quiet time and now that I had room satanic forces were bent on thwarting my attempts at meditation and prayers. I did not realize it at the time but the dream or nightmare I had on my last night with Tosh was unfolding before me. My tongue was not swollen and I was not choking or suffocating with my tongue but I was just as helpless in the face of cobwebs I could not see or touch and an itch that had no cause. The cobwebs and itch stopped as soon as I stopped any attempt at meditation or prayers in frustration. I did not have the peace of mind to pray for salvation and while that went on I was at the mercy of the devil. The incidents marked the beginning of a series of bad luck that in the end reduced me to a state of financial despair.

BROKEN CAR ENGINE

Thus far I had weathered the attacks by the invisible cobwebs and body itch, thanks to a pastor who helped me with prayers and ritual baths. The next attack was aimed at the heart of my means of support, my car. In a country with poor public transport

I could not work effectively without a car. My car was my lifeline and indispensable tool of my work as a real estate appraiser. Without a car I would have been reduced to administrative work unable to do the extra field inspections and jobs that made it possible for me to support my family. Until my family moved to Accra, I shuttled regularly between Accra and Kumasi every fortnight. I used to leave for Kumasi after work on Friday and returned to Accra on Sunday evening. One Sunday, while on my way back to Accra, I was blindsided by a potential financial disaster. I was halfway between Kumasi and Accra when I heard a loud rattling noise from the car. I pulled to the side of the road and opened the trunk, what I found shocked me.

I saw a large hole the size of a tennis ball on the side of the engine block and oil splattered all over the trunk. I turned off the motor which was still running and left the car on the spot. I went back to Kumasi and arranged for a tow truck to take the car back to the workshop of the local Mercedes Benz dealership. And while waiting for assessment of the damage or problem I fired a telegram to Daimler Benz. The workshop informed me a couple of days later that a connecting rod broke and the force tore a hole through the engine block. It appeared I was done for, my pride and means of support was almost over. But somehow I felt all was not lost though I could not think of an immediate solution if the car was out of warranty. In the meantime I held my breath and prayed for the best outcome from Daimler Benz. I was on pins and needles while waiting to hear from Daimler Benz. I reflected on my investment in the car and the alternative things I could have done with the money. I even regretted for not selling the car for a house when I had the opportunity.

I did not know the terms of the warranty on the car but it appeared it was different from the current three year- thirty six thousand mile standard warranties. I do not remember the mileage on the car at the time of the mishap but I used to travel extensively before the mishap. Daimler Benz sent a factory engineer to Ghana to examine the car when they received my telegram. The engineer asked for my service records and when he was done he promised a new engine to replace the broken motor. A new motor was subsequently flown in from Germany and installed at no cost to me. I was back in business after about four months. I have forever been grateful to Daimler Benz for the humane way they handled my particular problem. A short time after this latest incident AESC, my employers finally found me an apartment.

HOME BUSINESS IN ACCRA

The assault on my prospects and means of support was unrelenting, everything that could go wrong in my life went wrong. I used to blame my fall from grace on sensual temptations or illicit sex but through all the sensual temptations I never ceased meditating or praying though the prayers might have been perfunctory and ineffective due to my difficulties and distractions. My employer obtained a three bedroom apartment at *Kokomlemle,* a neighborhood of Accra for me. Finally I had a home where I could live together with my family in peace without shuttling back and forth between Accra and Kumasi. I wasted no time in moving my family to Accra as soon as I had the keys to the flat. Abu who had sustained our dressmaking business at Kumasi did not come along with us. But we decided to continue the same line of business that was made possible by Abu's tailoring skills. One of our bedrooms was converted into a cutting and sewing room and we hired a local tailor by name Santana to take over from where Abu left off. We then registered a business name, Obza Fashions, made business cards and stationery before we started making the first samples to canvass the market. And last but not the least we applied for a manufacturer's license from the Ministry of Trade and Industries. A manufacturer's license would have recognized Obza Fashions as manufacturers with privileges to buy fabrics and accessories at wholesale from textile factories and textile wholesalers. The initial capital outlay for Obza Fashions came from my rainy day funds in Australia.

The business seemed to have an auspicious beginning. Santana made samples of boys' wear that we hoped to use for canvassing the local retail market for potential customers. The samples were barely finished when Obenewa ran into an old workmate and friend from Akan Press, her last place of employment by name Edith. She was an itinerary trader that plied the Ghana-Nigeria route smuggling merchandise between the two countries.

Our problems with the set up of Obza Fashions made me to realize that Satan is one of us and not an alien entity out of this world. Satan or the devil comes to us in the form of our family members, friends, relatives or people we know and even trust. Edith was the Satan or devil that Obenewa knew as a friend and former coworker. She offered to buy all the samples that were being made for sale in Nigeria and pay us in full on return from Nigeria. She lived under our roof with us in our apartment for about three to four days while Santana worked hard at completing the samples. I did not know Edith but she sold me after four days under my roof and she seemed so genuine I had no reason to doubt her sincerity as long as Obenewa trusted her. After four nights with us we packed all the manufactured samples into two large suitcases. I drove and saw her off at the Accra-Lagos lorry park and that was the last time I saw Edith.

Edith disappeared from the face of the earth. We did not hear from her again for over two months, all our working capital was tied up in the samples, Edith held our business fortunes and prospects in her hands. My rainy day funds were depleted; I did not have any extra funds to keep the business afloat. In our desperation Obenewa decided to go after Edith at her last known address at Kumasi. Obenewa tracked her down in Kumasi and dragged her to the police station before she received partial payment and retrieved our suitcases.

THE SATANIC MIRACLE

While Obenewa was away in Kumasi pursuing Edith through the streets and byways of Kumasi, I scrapped together just enough money to make babies underwear following in the footsteps of Grace, our family friend and Elisha's wife. Grace supported herself and children by making and selling babies' underwear with hand cranked sewing machine. With the little money I had I decided to make similar underwear until Obenewa came back. The underwear's were cheap and fast moving items but with very little profit margins. It was the only viable alternative I could think of with the little of money I had on hand to breathe some life back into the faltering business. The quick turnover would compensate for the low margins. I bought some yards of suitable fabrics and Santana made a few samples, finished each of them with edger machine and Obza Fashion label attached. They looked as attractive as any ready made baby wear item from any garment factory in Ghana or import. The samples were well received when I showed them to potential customers at the Makola market. The market women liked the quality of the samples and ordered a few dozen items from me. The women even selected the colors and type of fabric they preferred to be used in fulfilling their orders. At the end of my rounds at the market I was pleased with myself and I bought the preferred color and fabrics of the traders to complete the orders as soon as possible. I left the market beaming with smiles full of confidence and hope about our business prospects.

The very next day I put Santana to work making the underwear to fill the orders. I was pleased with the quality of the finished products. I surmised that by the time Obenewa returned from Kumasi I would have laid the ground work for a new line of business with new customers for her to follow. A day before the delivery of the finished underwear to the market women I invited Grace to give me the benefit of her experience and expertise by helping me to package the items for delivery to the traders. Grace sent her oldest daughter to help me pack the underwear. She packed them into bundles of a dozen per package. Each package was bundled or wrapped with one of the finished underwear.

I got up early the next morning and went through my exercise and prayer routine. I intended to deliver the orders before going to office. After my prayers I went into the sewing room with a bag to pick up the packages for the market.

As soon as I stretched my hand to pick the packages from the table a light flashed before me. I glanced through the window and about me looking for the source of the light. I found nothing but by the time I turned my attention back to the packages on the table they were not the same. It appeared that in the few seconds that I took my eyes from the table an invisible magician switched the new bundles of underwear on the table for old ones. The bright and vibrant colored underwear suddenly lost their luster and appeared to be old, used or worn underwear. I robbed my eyes in disbelief; It is not only God that performs miracles. I saw a miracle performed by Satan! It was every bit a miracle as a miracle can be but it was nothing to celebrate, it confused and confounded me. Within a blink of an eye the underwear that were bright and colorful and pleasing to look at only moments ago were now my source of grief. I did not believe my eyes and desperately wanted another opinion to prove me wrong, that I was seeing things. I was crest fallen, beaten and defeated even before I picked up a single bundle for the market.

I was a crestfallen and discouraged man but I hoped against hope that somehow the transformation was only in my eyes and the potential customers would see them differently. My enthusiasm and optimism just before I entered the sewing room was gone, I was suddenly reluctant to take the merchandise to the market. But it was the only way to find out whether I had a daydream. So reluctantly I bundled the packages into a bag and headed for the market. I was not the least surprised at the reaction of the first potential customer as she proclaimed "*Aw, se eyi ye broni wawu*" or Aw but these are secondhand items. I received orders of two to four dozen from four market women and they all had the same expression and reaction, that the items were *broni wawu* or secondhand. By the time I left the market, almost in tears, I knew that some inexplicable and wonderful transformation had indeed changed the luster and appearance of the underwear. And none of the potential customers on whose orders I made the underwear would accept or touch them. I went back home later that day with a trunk full of unwanted underwear.

I was saddled with over ten dozen baby underwear, I did the next best thing, try and sell them by ourselves. I pressed Yaa Boatemaa my house helper to hawk them around the local markets and *trotro* or passenger lorry stations. All our attempts and efforts to sell them at the local market or lorry parks by ourselves were futile. Nobody would touch them at any price or with a ten foot pole. We could not give them away even for free. The endeavor was a flop, the ten dozen underwear were a total bust. We never sold a single one out of the ten dozen, we ended up using them as cleaning cloths around the house otherwise we had no use for them. All the money I had in the world was invested in the underwear and when that also failed I was brought to my knees financially. I had nowhere to turn. All my other sources of extra income dried up. I was dependent more on side jobs to support my family than on my salary. My monthly pay was barely enough to fill my tank for a month let alone put food on the table. I was in dire straits.

The bottom fell out from under me. Within a period of three months since we set up our home sewing business my savings, both domestic and foreign, were all exhausted and I had nothing to show for it. Poverty, deprivation and starvation stared at me in the face. My financial condition was so dire and hopeless that I could not afford the equivalent of a nickel worth of doughnut for my baby girl. I wept as I watched Lamissi in tantrums screaming for one lousy doughnut and I could not afford it. I cast my mind over the adversities and misfortunes that have befallen me since I returned from Australia and finally concluded that satanic forces were out for my financial destruction as they did before I went to Melbourne. I went through the list of problems that have affected me in the recent past beginning with the difficult childbirth of my wife, the convulsion of Lamissi, my impotency, my broken car engine, attack by invisible cobwebs and now the total failure of our business with a product that nobody wants to touch. These were not accidental co incidents but a coordinated effort by satanic forces to bring me to my knees just when I thought the hunger and deprivation of the past was behind me. I could not deny that satanic powers were behind every inexplicable adversity and misfortune that has befallen me in the recent past. This was one time when I felt that the problem was bigger than me and I needed help. It was the one time I voluntarily sought for spiritual help and not persuaded or talked into seeking help. I faced imminent poverty and starvation unless I got help.

Once again I remembered the dream about the gold cross that saved me from iniquitous entities; I needed the power of the cross again to save me from the latest catastrophe. The impact of recent events convinced me that my prayers were no longer effective or enough to protect me or prevent satanic influences in my life. I needed the power and strength of the cross to take me out of the unfathomable financial abyss into which I had fallen. I did not know where to turn to for the help I so desperately needed. I asked acquaintances and friends for references to a reputable spiritual church.

HEALING CHURCH OF SALVATION

My enquiries for a good spiritual church led me to *Dzorwulu,* a developing residential neighborhood of Accra where a new church was taking shape. The new church was squatting in an uncompleted house. The Healing Church of Salvation was the branch of an established church in the Ashanti region that was being introduced into Accra by the founder prophet Ebenezer Tweneboah himself. I went to the church on Sunday and stayed through over four hours of service. These spiritual churches tend to have very lengthy services but I did not have the luxury to complain of the lengthy service or leave without talking to the prophet. At the end of the service I had a private audience with the prophet and I should say he met or exceeded my expectations and made the wait worthwhile. I did not tell him what brought me to his church; he told me about the personal problems that took me to his church.

Prophet Tweneboah diagnosed my problem and like a good doctor gave me a prescription for cure. His prescription was fasting and prayers, he had no magic wand that he could wave for my problems to go away. He told me that he would come to my house to observe three days of fasting and prayers from the next Thursday. Accordingly I picked him up to my apartment early on Thursday morning. He asked me not to eat anything that morning and by the time he set foot in my apartment I had already started fasting. Fasting was not new to me; I used to observe a twenty-four hour fast every week for therapy and not for spiritual purposes. The prophet set up a small altar in my bedroom and we prayed at hourly intervals around the clock. We had the first of the hourly prayers together before I left for the office and he continued praying with my family while I was away. At sundown I expected to break fast after twenty four hours but he told me to hold on till the third day. From that moment hunger deflated me like a balloon; I could hardly stand on my feet for prayers during the night. The next day I was so weak I did not go to the office and continued praying every hour with the prophet while I sprawled on the floor. I lay on the floor from Thursday evening till Saturday morning; I did not have enough strength to stand up for showers. On the other hand the prophet was full of energy; left to me alone I would have slept through the three days of fasting, but he would not let me. He kept vigil and roused me every hour on the dot for prayers.

Prophet Ebenezer introduced me to the Old Testament style of fasting without food or water for three days. During the hourly prayers, Ebenezer gave me optimistic prophetic messages. Among the messages was that within a short period of time I shall get a rewarding assignment. We called that kind of fasting dry fasting because you did not eat or drink for three days, I had many more such fasting rituals after the first one. Until I actually fasted and survived the fast I had never thought that the Old Testament stories in the books of Esther and Daniel were real or humanly possible. I used to think that the Old Testament characters were mysterious beings out of this world that did super human things, going for three days without food and water. After my experience I appreciated that the characters were ordinary humans who had intractable problems and called upon God for help through self sacrifice and God heard their cries. Over time I developed enough stamina to fast and pray for up to five days while going about my normal chores.

After we broke fast Ebenezer went back to his church where he also lived. From the first initial fasting and prayers in my apartment, I spent many weekends fasting and praying on the dusty grounds of the Healing Church of Salvation. I used to fast from Friday to Sunday morning because after the first day I did not have enough reserve energy to combine fasting with other chores. I used to prostrate myself on the dusty outdoor prayer grounds from Friday night till Sunday morning when I broke fast, went home for breakfast and returned later for service. God answered my prayers after about four to six weeks of prostrating myself before Him; the big rewarding assignment prophesied by the prophet during our first fasting and prayer sessions was fulfilled and I recovered from the financial doldrums.

About four or five weeks into my weekend fasting and prayers I had an assignment from some American missionaries. I do not remember exactly how I came across the missionaries who were linguists working to translate the New Testament into some of the dialects of Northern Ghana. The missionaries were negotiating to purchase a house at Tamale to use as their base of operations in northern Ghana. I was engaged to appraise the house. I went to Tamale on the assignment and at the end of it I earned a professional fee of about GH¢120,000 or the equivalent of about $3,000 at the time. That amount is the largest professional fee I ever earned in my professional career for any one assignment or job.

Ghana was mostly a cash economy and up to that date I had never seen or handled such a large amount of cash in my hands. I was therefore afraid to carry a large amount of cash on my person back to Accra. I transferred ¢100,000 through an old savings account at the Tamale branch of Standard Bank to my account in Accra while I took GH¢20,000 with me. I passed through my hometown and shared the GH¢20,000 between my father and mother at Wa. It was the first time I gave any money to my father and his reaction at the sight of GH¢10,000 convinced me that the impression I had about my father was wrong. I was given the impression during infancy that my father was wealthy but miserly. His body shook or shivered like a leaf in the breeze when I handed GH¢10,000 to him. I guess that perhaps like me, it was the largest amount he had ever handled at any one time. He was a small scale itinerary trader and it was likely he had never received or handled up to ¢10,000 at any one time in his life. I formed a different opinion about my father after that day and forgave him in my heart for his tardiness in paying my school fees during the primary and middle school.

Despite my father's reputation as a miser, he came through for me when I completed middle school and needed money and supplies to go to college. I could not have gotten a start in an academic career after middle school if he had not provided me the school supplies that made it possible for me to go to St. John Bosco's College in 1960. My father's wealth, if any, was perhaps held in the number of cows he was reputed to own. In our traditional society, a man's wealth was measured in the number of cows he owned. When he passed away, his wealth died with him because none of his children ever got an accounting of that wealth from the extended family members who were the caretakers of his cows. What became of the cows I may never know.

SATAN EXPOSED IN BROAD DAYLIGHT

The evil and satanic forces that cut me down to size and brought me to my knees were finally exposed before me by the power of Jesus Christ. Tweneboah introduced us to the concept of family prayers, he began praying with us as a group and we continued with the practice after he left. We continued praying together as a family in the morning and evening. The turmoil that roiled my world taught me that the devil does not give up or relent and thus I could not relax or relent in my prayers if I hoped to prevail against my adversaries. I made fasting three days every week part of my lifestyle. Fasting every week and praying morning and night became a routine part of my life and I incorporated the practice into the fabric of my life. After about six months of continuous fasting and prayers, God revealed and exposed the satanic forces behind my recent financial meltdown in a dream. The dream manifested into reality in my living room three days after the dream. The devil walked into a trap set by God and exposed her like a deer caught in the glare of bright lights.

The genteel concentration and meditation that I used to practice on my own yielded to ruckus songs of praise and prayers with my family. When I retired to my room I resorted to genteel concentration and meditation followed by prayers. My prayer routine when alone always followed the calming after effect of meditation when I was spiritually receptive. The night in which I had the dream was one of the ruckus nights in which we sang a lot of songs of praise with loud prayers. That night we felt spiritually uplifted by the Holy Spirit during our family song and prayer period. And that night I had a dream in which the Lord told me he would show me the people behind my recent problems. And as He spoke I saw a woman walking ahead of children in order of height emerge from fog or smoke and then the Lord said to me, 'see, these are those responsible for your troubles'. I did not know the identities of the people in the dream, they were in silhouettes identities hidden by the smoke and fog. I did not know or see the faces of the woman and the children in the dream but it confirmed my suspicion that Satan was behind my recent financial downfall. The dream confirmed that there were other unknown forces behind the miracle that took place in my apartment. It also showed that I was on my way back into the good graces of the Lord. My sins were forgiven and my relation with God was on the mend. I was dreaming again, having hunches and intuitive impulses, hearing the voice of God, qualities that deserted me when I was in spiritual darkness. I was gradually coming out of the spiritual wilderness but I had to remain steadfast with fasting and prayers.

The identity and face of the woman and the children were exposed and unmasked on the third day after the dream in my living room during broad daylight. They were exposed and unmasked exactly as I saw in the dream. They emerged from my smoke filled kitchen walking in the same order as in the dream. There were two entrances into my apartment, the main entrance was used by family and general public and second entrance was reserved for family and very close friends. The second entrance went through the kitchen to the dining room. My housekeeper, *Yaa Boatema,* was deep frying fish to prepare dinner. The burning oil created a cloud of smoke in the kitchen that billowed through the window and into the dining room. I was sitting around the dining table at the time with a few friends and when I lifted my head I saw Grace emerging from the smoke filled kitchen followed by her children into the dining room. They walked in the same order that I saw in the dream, she was followed by the youngest with the oldest at the back of the pack. As I saw the emerging picture it hit me; this was what the Lord reveled to me. 'This was the scene I saw in the dream a few days ago' I told myself. At that very instant our minds clicked or met telepathically; Grace recognized the significance of their march from the smoke filled kitchen into my dining room and she knew that her game was up, her innermost dark secrets were laid bare by the Lord at the scene of her satanic deeds. She was shocked by the exposure and I was still processing the picture and had not opened my mouth except gape in surprise but she was so uncomfortable that she and her children unceremoniously left the apartment in virtual panic without another word.

Her quick and unceremonious exit from the apartment surprised my family and friends who knew how close we were to ask what had come over Grace. I explained the dream and how she and her children fit the profile in the dream exactly as seen in the dream. The devil like God comes to us in human form but I was surprised at the unexpected revelation. We were close family friends, her children used to visit and play with my children for hours. We were almost like family, her husband gave up his room to me for about two months when we returned from Australia. And it was through her that I met Obenewa. But on reflecting on the recent events I realized that she was present at all our transactions that went sour. She was in our apartment with Edith as she was negotiating to take our samples for sale in Nigeria. Edith, Grace and Obenewa were all friends and former workmates at Akan Printing Press. And Grace's daughter. After they rushed out of the apartment we sang and praised the Lord for exposing and unmasking the faces of the satanic forces that brought me down financially in my living room.

It was unlike Grace to rush out of my house while the evening meal was still on fire, at worse she would have left her youngest child behind until after dinner since our houses were only a few blocks apart. Elisha was the third 'husband' of Grace and the misfortunes that hit her previous husbands after the marriages unraveled always gave Elisha a pause. The successful businesses of her previous two husbands foundered after the marriages ended. We were such good friends that I used to discuss the stories and inferences that she was a witch who jinxed the fortunes of her two previous husbands with her. She denied ever being the cause of their downfall but always added that they had it coming to them by the way they mistreated her before throwing her out to pasture. I believed her when she said that the events were unrelated and were mere coincidences. Elisha was the poorest of her two previous husbands and though they were not formal husband and wife, the incidents haunted Elisha anytime his relations with Grace came up in conversations. Grace was in effect his concubine or mistress, they were not formally married as such but I referred to them as man and wife because they had been together for a long time.

The face of Grace became for me the human face of the devil or Satan and everything that Satan stands for. Because of the revelation I questioned some of the basic assumptions and knowledge about sorcery and witchcraft. Grace was not my family member and under normal circumstances could not have attacked me without a betrayer from my family. In other words somebody from my family should have met and betrayed me or sold me to Grace before she could have exercised any spiritual dominion over me. I was therefore anxious to find the kindred spirits from my family or my wife's family that aided her to cause such havoc to our financial fortunes. I therefore decided to talk to Grace before Elisha through whom I got to know her. But for Elisha I might never have met or known Grace and for that matter Obenewa. It was only prudent to talk to her before the man that brought us together. This was a delicate matter built principally on dreams and circumstantial evidence. I could not prove in a court of law that she was demonic and responsible for our recent financial setbacks. But the recent events that linked her with my business fortunes were enough to bolster my accusations that she was the human face of Satan.

I threw a lot of hints at Elisha that I had found the face of evil, Satan or witchcraft and the face was unmasked in my apartment. In the Akan dialect I told him I had unmasked a witch in my living room. He was aware of the history of his wife and his suspicions at once fell on his wife. I was not in a hurry to confront or accuse Grace openly because of the delicate nature of the subject matter. When I was ready, I asked Elisha to arrange for a meeting with Grace before him. When the day finally came I was restrained in what I had to say. I could not accuse Grace of being a sorcerer or witch but I began by recounting the recent events that had adversely impacted my life. May be the events were mere coincidence but Grace was present at every transaction that went bust. When I asked for help as a good friend she sent her daughter to help me. She was the last person who handled the underwear before I sent them to the market. Last but not the least she escaped or scurried out of my apartment when she realized that I had discovered her nefarious deeds. And since that afternoon neither she nor any of her children has set foot in my apartment again.

Naturally Grace denied having anything to do with our financial setbacks but she could not deny or explain the circumstantial evidence tying her to the setbacks particularly the baby underwear debacle. She had no reasonable explanation for scurrying out of my apartment and had since not set foot in the apartment though we have never had any spat. She could not contradict my inferences but said that only time would tell, that if she jinxed our business she was not alone. In other words she had evil collaborators and time would reveal her collaborators. That assertion restored some of my faith in the ethical boundaries of demonic spirits and witchcraft. That was also the last time I saw Grace though we lived in the same neighborhood. I never saw her again until I moved out of the neighborhood and eventually out of the country altogether. I did not remain long enough for any of her collaborators to be revealed. But Obenewa was almost gleeful when her mother, whom she blamed for her setbacks, passed away. There was no hint of regret or sorrow when she gave me the news of her mother's passing. By then it was too late her business and marriage had collapsed and could be resuscitated.

I may never know her spiritual accomplices but Obenewa believed that her mother was complicit with Grace in our business and financial setbacks. She believed that her mother was the cause of the miserable conditions of her father and siblings. The only sibling who seemed to be doing well was the one in faraway Ivory Coast who scarcely ever came home on vacation or visit. Our belief systems hold that evil entities cannot cross boundaries to commit nefarious deeds in other communities under different spiritual jurisdictions hence the need for collaborators and proxies. It is believed that the guardian spirits of one community or town do not allow sorcerers and witches from another community to enter their area of spiritual jurisdiction to commit spiritual crimes.

Elisha and I remained fast friends until the day I left the shores of Ghana though I stopped going to his house for fear of encountering Grace and putting him in an awkward position. But Grace and Obenewa were forever estranged and they have not spoken or crossed paths for over thirty years.

THE FINAL DOWNFALL OF OBENEWA

Thanks to fasting and prayer I found my financial footing again and Ebenezer became both a father figure and friend to me. I was grateful to him for introducing me to a form of fasting that I had hitherto not considered as humanly possible. Apart from solving my financial and personal problems, the fasting enlightened me on the practical meaning of the passage in *Matthew 17:21 'However, this kind does not go out except by prayer and fasting.* Fasting and prayers helped me to overcome the series of bad luck that led to my financial downfall and exposed or unmasked the faces of the satanic forces behind the setbacks.

The home based business limped along and hung by a thread. No amount of money I put into the business ever yielded any returns but I continued sinking money into it because I wanted Obenewa to succeed and become self supporting. At the back of my mind I harbored thoughts of migration in the not too distant future and if I was not around Obenewa should be able to support herself and the children when that day came. Whatever we produced we were able to sell but we scarcely ever broke even. I gave her financial and moral support but was reluctant to insert myself into the business as that would have defeated the purpose of supporting her. I was content to support her with the fees I made from my appraisal practice. Gradually I came to the conclusion that Obenewa would never succeed at business. But I continued to support her for the sake of her self esteem that she was engaged in productive economic activity. I provided her financial and moral support until the day I left for the United States.

A few years after I left the country our application for a manufacturer's license was finally approved. The license was a big deal; it was an unexpected big break that breathed new life into Obenewa's business prospects. Since manufacturing had never paid off she decided to buy the fabrics and accessories at wholesale for distribution to retailers at Makola market. She was fairly successful at this aspect of the business; her only limitation was the size of her capital.

I was a car service operator when she asked me for financial capital for her new business. The request was my priority and I scrimped to provide her with working capital of $4,000 within a period of two years. I managed to send her $2,500 in the first year and $1,500 the following year. It appeared that she was finally on the road to financial independence.

The manufacturer's license we applied for at the outset of our business was approved after more than four years. And the license was the basis of Obenewa's new business for which she required capital. Obenewa had finally found her niche in business and I could now live my life and seek my own level in New York without worrying about the needs of my family. My optimism was short lived; she operated her business satisfactorily for about two years and the bottom fell from under her. She built a good customer base at Makola market that she supplied with fabrics and accessories on credit. The customers paid her gradually as they disposed or sold the merchandise. The peace of mind I expected lasted only a few months after I sent her the last remittance of $1,500. A few weeks after she received $1,500 I received an emergency request for more money. She had fallen victim to the same scam that was perpetrated on us by Edith. She gave her entire stock of merchandise valued at about $7,000 to $10,000 to a single market woman on the promise of full payment. The woman vanished from the market. But she knew next to nothing about this woman beyond her place at the market. Unlike Edith she knew next to nothing about this trader; she did not know her full name, address or hometown. She did not know enough about this trader to report the scam to the police or find her whereabouts. Makola is a very large market, the woman could be hiding in another part of the market under another name. She made a desperate request to me for another infusion of capital after the disappearance of the woman. I scrapped the bottom of the barrel when I sent her $1,500; I had not worked long enough to accumulate any money to help her with new capital infusion. The year of her great promise became the year of her final financial downfall. She fell flat on her face and never rose up again. This latest scam was also my proverbial last straw; I cut financial ties with her to the barest minimum.

I was angry that she had fallen victim to the same scam twice. It appeared she never learned anything from the first scam perpetrated against us by Edith on the promise payment in full. I gave up on her, I stopped trying to prop her up; I reached the end of my patience and financial tether. She made several fruitless attempts scouting the market for the mysterious woman without ever getting a whiff of her. For all I know the woman could have been a ghost, nobody at the market knew enough about her. This latest scam sealed her business and financial fate. She never recovered from this scam. She sold off all the sewing machines but she was paid in dribs and drabs never enough to provide new working capital. She then tried to sell the home she lived with our children but thanks to my foresight she was unsuccessful. When I was leaving Ghana I gave power of attorney on the house to her and a friend, the friend did not consent to the sale of the house. Had she succeeded she would have become homeless eventually. The Cross of Jesus was my tower of strength when I was down and out on my knees. She turned to Jesus and became a pastor or a servant of God.

BREAKUP WITH MY SPIRITUAL BENEFACTOR

I became a faithful follower of Prophet Ebenezer and his church, The Healing Church of Salvation. I spent my weekends at the church fasting and praying unless I was away on business. One Saturday while I was observing a fast at the church Ebenezer prophesied that in the not too distant future I shall breakup with him and call him a good for nothing man. This prophesy came out of the blue and at the height of our camaraderie when I thought he could do no wrong. In my mind I separated his pastoral and spiritual work from his personal life. Those who are called to the service of God by the power of the Holy Spirit have no formal training and are called to the service with all their faults and shortcomings. Thus in my mind's eye I could not foresee any event that could be so grievous as to tear us apart. I had a high regard and respect for the quality of his pastoral work, Ebenezer in his pastoral work could do me no wrong. I did not have much in common with him outside the church. Honestly, I loved and respected him for the self-sacrifice he made on my behalf by fasting and praying with me in my home. I did not know of another pastor or prophet who would have done that for me, a potential church member.

The fulfillment or manifestation of the prophesy began inauspiciously when an itinerant prophet I knew at Kumasi paid an unexpected visit to me one Friday afternoon. The prophet, Evans Arthur a/k/a Sofo Atta spent the weekend with me. We went to church together that weekend and he distinguished and endeared himself to members of the church by his prophetic gifts. Sofo Atta was introduced to us by our next door neighbor at Kumasi. Shortly after we became acquainted we discovered that he and my wife were from the same Akyem tribal clan. That discovery made him family instead of just a casual acquaintance or friend. Thus when he called on me at the office it was tantamount to a visit from a family member, I sent him home as a member of my wife's family.

Sofo Atta came to me with nothing but the clothes on his back I therefore did not expect him to spend more than a few days with us. But he became a fixture in my house and our pastor and prophet in residence. He led my family in our morning and evening prayers and we went to church together on Sundays where he continued to give prophetic messages to members of the Healing Church of Salvation. He was liked by members of the church and some of those members began coming to my apartment to take part in our prayers and consult him for their fortunes. Sofo Atta became a popular seer or fortune teller for some members of the church who started a quiet campaign to bring him into the fold of the Healing Church of Salvation as one of the assistant pastors. Sofo Atta liked the idea of being associated with the church but Ebenezer, my benefactor, opposed it. For unknown reason he did not want to have anything to do with him particularly as a pastor in his church. I thought that Ebenezer's reluctance was due to the financial burden of an extra pastor. Sofo Atta was already dependent on me for his livelihood including the clothes he wore to church on Sundays. I therefore offered to be responsible for the pay and upkeep of Sofo Atta so that he would not be a burden on the church. Ebenezer declined my offer; maybe he saw something in Sofo Atta that those of us with mere mortal eyes did not see or was it professional jealousy?

I had reason to doubt the honesty and sincerity of Sofo Atta after he took advantage of his affiliation with my wife to defraud us of money and foodstuffs we gave him for delivery to my mother-in-law in her village. The fraud came to light when Sofo Atta and my mother in-law met in my house by chance and it became apparent that the two had never met contrary to his assertion that he personally delivered the money and foodstuffs to my mother in law in the village. He apologized and the apology was accepted, thus I could not hold it against him. In spite of Sofo Atta's willingness to be drafted into the service of the Healing Church of Salvation I still held out hope that he would return to Kumasi. I could not imagine that a man in his fifties could just uproot himself without even a tooth brush but the clothes on his back. I never bothered to ask him as I did not want to create the impression that I was eager to get rid of him. Little did I know that while I expected Sofo Atta to go back to his family he had found life so comfortable he had no intention of returning to Kumasi. Sofo Atta then became my headache and affected my relations with Ebenezer. But I continued going to the Healing Church of Salvation on Sundays until unforeseen circumstances transformed my family prayer group into a virtual church.

Our morning and evening prayers became an informal prayer group or church in the sense that other people not associated with Ebenezer's church began taking part in our prayers. The prophetic skills of Sofo Atta continued to draw people to my apartment after he stopped going to The Healing Church of Salvation. I do not know how word about a seer or prophet in my apartment got around but we began having visitors from morning till night by fortune seekers. I did not have any intention to have a prayer group with public participation let alone a church that would cause breach with my spiritual benefactor. I never stopped going to his church until we became a virtual church. The need for space to accommodate members of the public who wanted to pray and worship with us compelled us to move the prayer group out of my apartment.

I lived on a second floor apartment and whenever I was on my balcony I used to see a beautiful young woman pass by on the street below my flat. I stopped seeing the woman pass bye on the street below and forgot about her. I did not know who she was beyond seeing an attractive woman pass on the street while I was standing on my balcony. She was beautiful and I admired her beauty but I never exchanged a polite word with her while she went up and down the street. The next time I saw her pass on the street she was not the same person. She was a sickly and emaciated old woman who could barely walk with the help of a walking stick. I was shocked by her gaunt appearance, she was but a shadow of her former self. I felt very sorry for her and felt an urge to invite her to take part in our morning prayers. I had no idea what was wrong with her but as I looked at her from my balcony God asked me to invite her to take part in our prayers. I have not had that urge from God since I returned from Australia so I prevailed upon Sofo Atta to invite her to our prayers as I was not a minister. When she began coming for prayers with us I did for her what Ebenezer did for me when I was down on my luck. I encouraged Sofo Atta to fast with me for three days while we prayed for her. I learned from her that during the months I did not see her walk by on the street she was on admission at the hospital. Whatever ailed her was declared incurable and she was discharged and advised to go home for hospice care from her family. She was preparing to go to her hometown when I had her invited to our prayers.

We did not think we could make a significant difference in her condition but we decided to continue praying with her until she left for her hometown. And it appears that God accepted and heard our prayers for intercession, she never left for her village and she became part of my family.

I knew the young woman only as Davi which in her local Ewe dialect meant sister. Davi showed signs of improvement after a few days of prayers. In the weeks that followed she discarded her walking stick and regained some of her luster and cheerful personality. By the fourth week her 'poverty bones', sunken eye sockets, cheek and collar bones began to fill up with flesh. She blossomed again and looked every bit the young woman I used to admire from afar. Davi gave us publicity that no radio or television commercial could have given us. She was testament of the power of the cross to heal and renew. Once again the passage in Mark 16:17 that occurred to me in my sleep when my wife was sick and was the catalyst that made me a spiritual healer in Melbourne came to the rescue of Davi. We laid hands on her in the name of Jesus

Christ and by the grace of God she recovered. Her recovery was not instantaneous but it was still miraculous considering the emaciated and weak condition in which we found her, her physical improvements was noticeable particularly by those who were close to her before she came into our ambit. Her cotenants and neighbors as a result of her physical improvements came for prayers with us in the apartment in the mornings and evenings. The apartment was too small and used to be overcrowded during our prayer time. As a result we lost our privacy as a family due to the constant stream of visitors coming in and out of the apartment from morning till night. We thus began contemplating moving the prayer group out of the apartment.

By the grace of God we had permission to use a classroom at Kotobabi Primary School for our evening and weekend prayer meetings. The moment we started having prayer meetings outside my apartment we became a church with no name. I tried to persuade Ebenezer Tweneboah to adopt our nascent church with no name as a branch of the Healing Church of Salvation. I do not know what was in Sofo Atta's head but I had no intention of founding or starting a church; we were just responding to the circumstances and events that were overtaking us. I resisted cutting ties with Ebenezer but Sofo Atta was the stumbling block between us. His uncompromising attitude towards Sofo Atta eventually led to breach in our relations after we formed the church.

My pastoral relations with Ebenezer Tweneboah came to end when we became a virtual church without a name. Sofo Atta and I considered a number of names but eventually settled on The Three Holy Names Church on the recommendation of Sofo Atta. After we formally became a church I tried to have some sort of association with him and his church; but he declined our invitation for the formal inauguration of our church. I would have loved to associate with him but he refused to compromise with us on a loose affiliation or association. His prophesy was fulfilled largely because he did not like Sofo Atta and I could not force Sofo Atta out of my life.

I never saw Ebenezer after he declined my last invitation to our church inauguration up to the day I left Ghana. I tried to reconcile with him years later when I returned to Ghana after almost two decades away. Unfortunately by the time I went back he was no more in Accra, he had gone back to the head quarters at Kumasi as such I never saw him. Ironically the branch of his church was located about two hundred yards from Sofo Atta's church. The two who never saw eye to eye with another have their churches only a few hundred yards apart. I bought some clerical vestments for him but since he was not in Accra I gave them to the pastor of his branch church to be forwarded to him. I will never get the opportunity to reconcile with him in this life because he passed away in 2011.

THREE HOLY NAMES CHURCH

The Three Holy Names Church was formally born at Kotobabi Primary School with Sofo Atta as pastor with me as the church elder. I modeled the church after the Healing Church of Salvation whose teachings on fasting saved me and exposed the devil in my life. in running *The Three Holy Names Church*. As a direct beneficiary of fasting and prayers I made that the centerpiece of our healing and prophetic ministry.

By any measure, the Three Holy Names Church prospered financially and spiritually. The fledgling church became popular with the youth; it was more or less a youth ministry. We bought musical instruments within six months of moving to the primary school. Fasting and Prayer was also the distinguishing character of the church. We fasted routinely every week. Sofo Atta and I never spent a night in any member's home fasting and praying with him as Ebenezer did with me in my home. But I made my house available to any member who was fasting to hang around during the fasting period. Although I was not a minister or preacher I was the de facto head of the church, I encouraged Sofo Atta to fast and pray with our members as I observed of Ebenezer. He boasted that he could fast for seven days without food and water but during our initial fasting for Davi he briefly passed before recovering. We fasted and prayed at regular intervals until we broke bread at sun down together. I believe that fasting with prayers is the ultimate tool or weapon when assailed by

367

satanic forces. My belief in the power of fasting and prayers is not academic but from real life experience. The experience confirmed for me the veracity in the truths of certain passages of scripture on fasting and prayers.

I lost the lease to my apartment largely because of our church activities. The apartment was leased initially for three years, it was not renewed at the end of the three years ostensibly because of the inconvenience caused by our church activities on the tenant below my apartment and the landlord who also lived on the premises. I was moved into a larger house at *Ablemkpe*, another part of the city. The new house was roomier, larger and situated on a large leafy lot. The configuration of the new house made it possible to keep the church separate from my family. My family enjoyed privacy while coexisting with the church in the house. There was ample room to accommodate the pastors and church members on one side of the house and my family in another part. The large leafy backyard was ideal for quiet reflection during fasting and prayers.

The problems and setbacks that led me to The Healing Church of Salvation are similar to the problems and setbacks that lead many to make spiritual churches their places of worship. Spiritual churches are practical problem solvers, I learned from the experience that sometimes our problems are not mere coincidences or mistakes but deliberate sabotage by evil and satanic forces beyond our control. The churches through fasting and prayer rituals are the bulwark against witchcraft, sorcery, voodoo and the like. It is easy to ridicule these forces as delusional or gullible but I know from experience that they are as real as the God I serve. If there is no evil then there is no God, God and Satan are two sides of the same coin. The solution of personal material and spiritual problems differentiates the spiritual churches from the old established and orthodox churches. The churches make it possible for us to live to our potential without being stymied at every turn by devilish and satanic powers. The Three Holy Names church used fasting and prayers as our spiritual tool or weapon to communicate with God and plead for His mercy and salvation. The spiritual church is not a gentle place of worship; it is thus the church or place of last resort where bible promises come alive. While there are charlatans who parade as spirit filled Christians there are genuine pastors and prophets called to the service of God warts and all and who have no training. I met a blind illiterate pastor with a mastery of the bible from cover to cover; his wife read his bible passages and quotations in Twi. And I had the privilege to work with an illiterate pastor who when he was called to the service of God was able to read the bible in his native tongue, Twi. The pastors of spiritual churches therefore tend to have messy personal lives.

We had a predominant youthful membership whose problems were typical of the aspirations of the youth, good jobs and travel opportunities for Europe and North America. Most would have given anything or paid any price for a ticket out of Ghana for any country in Europe. For these members fasting and prayers was a small price to pay for God to bless them with a ticket and visa out of Ghana. This was the number one wish list of every young man's prayer quest. A ticket and visa was the ultimate symbol of future of success or progress in life that we yearned for. I introduced the fasting and prayer rituals that I learned from Ebenezer's Healing Church of Salvation. We encouraged the members to fast and pray at all times and not wait until confronted with a problem or sickness. Thus as a church our members fasted and prayed routinely every week. The combination of fasting and prayers affected our mental and physical outlook on life. Fasting by itself is therapeutic and the combination of fasting and prayers healed us of most common ailments without formal treatments and gave us great optimism about our endeavors. Some of our youthful members eventually realized their aspirations and dreams; I saw a few of them off at the airport on their way to Europe or Britain long before I left Ghana. During my first decade in New York a number of these ex-church members contacted me from Britain, Germany, Netherlands and Denmark to commiserate about our past.

The location of the church in a classroom made us a magnet or a place of call for itinerant preachers and prophets. We welcomed a number of these roaming preachers and prophets into our church from time to time.

Some of these itinerary preachers and prophets were walking bible tracts. They came carrying tracts for free distribution or peddling other church books and literature. One visiting preacher peddled invitation letters from a USA based church at $20 per invitation. In Ghana we had the impression that the church was a powerful and influential institution in the USA and an invitation from a US based church was sure to win one a visitors visa from the US consulate. Unfortunate the asking price of $20 was more than most of us could afford on the spur of the moment. Another roaming or itinerant prophet came to our church and I found his story so compelling that I went home with him after service and he became part of my expanding household. He was the illiterate prophet who read the Twi bible when God called him to His service.

KWAKU APPIAH: A MODERN DAY JONAH

That pastor or prophet was Kwaku Appiah. The story of how Kwaku Appiah was called to the service of God was like modern day story of Jonah. He was an illiterate young man who like most of our youthful church members went to a spiritual church to pray for job opportunities. But during the service he was swept up by the power of the Holy Spirit and he made several revelatory prophesies to the astonishment of the people in attendance at the church that Sunday. His prophesies were uncannily accurate and so revelatory that the pastor of the church tried to make him a prophet or pastor in the church. In my experience nothing fills a church more than healing and prophetic services. The churches that emphasize healing and prophesy as part of their services always overflow with expectant visitors hoping for prophetic messages or healing. Mr. Appiah declined the invitation to serve God as a prophet in the church. He instead went to Nigeria which, in the early eighties, was the popular destination for Ghanaian migrants seeking for greener pastures. He was eking out an existence in Nigeria when all foreigners without valid residence permits or visas were ordered out of the country by a date certain. During the rush to leave Nigeria he lost most of the little material possession he had accumulated and returned to Ghana almost empty handed.

When Appiah was deported along with many of his countrymen from Nigeria he again went to a spiritual church on returning to Ghana. And this time he had a prophesy that God was calling him to His service. In spite of his uncanny gift of prophesies he could not see him himself as a minister or pastor. He had no skill for anything except the gift of the Holy Spirit; whenever he went to a church he was mopped because of his uncanny prophetic gifts. One day when he was down on his luck with no where else to turn he knelt before God and asked Him how he could serve "You when I cannot read or write". Three days later, on a hunch, he picked up a copy of the Twi bible and to his surprise he found he could read the Twi bible without basic knowledge of letters of the alphabets. When he visited us at Kotobabi Primary School he had no church home, we gave him a home; he became an assistant pastor to Sofo Atta. He could only read the Twi bible and nothing else. I was present when he took the first baby steps in my house teaching himself how to write a sermon in Twi. His sermons were extemporaneously from the heart because he could not write.

I was the de facto head of the church by default. The church took shape in my apartment and my house was the virtual parsonage. We worked together as a team to advance the interest of the church and our members.

I was the glue that held the church together and the one member of the team who did not have the gift of prophesy. I was the dreamer among the three and I did not begrudge or envy their gifts. *Joel 2:28 (emphasis mine), "And it shall come to pass afterward that I shall pour out my spirit on all flesh; Your sons and daughters shall prophesy, Your old men shall dream dreams and Your young men shall see visions."* I was content with my role as a church elder guided by my dreams and intuitions.

I brought Christ or the cross of Christ into my home as a solution for my struggles against satanic forces. The prayer group or church in my house was my insurance policy against demonic and satanic forces. The founding of the church was accidental; it progressed from my family praying together as a unit to praying with outsiders. Thanks to Prophet Ebenezer the groundwork for group prayers was already in place before Sofo Atta became a fixture in my house. As a result of seeing a church rise from my living room I appreciate the business side of churches. The many splinter churches and groups are mostly the result of greed and avarice. Perhaps the greedy and untrustworthy nature of Sofo Atta was foreseen by Ebenezer. Churches are profitable business enterprises, the pastors under my roof made enough money from fortune telling or prophetic consulting. They did not charge for telling fortunes or prophesying but they received donations which were quite substantial over the course of a week. When Sofo Atta began living with me my personal finances were still shaky, I was just beginning to come out of the hole that Satan dug for me. My financial position improved over time, I made enough to care for my expanding household and church family without asking for contributions. I never turned down any voluntary contribution but as a matter of personal policy I never asked for contributions. By the grace of God I was able to care for my family and expanding church family.

Church members used to sleep overnight in my house throughout the week. The number of church members who slept over and those who made my home their home expanded or grew larger as time went bye. After morning prayers we sat around the pastors and discussed our dreams, hunches and nightmares we had during the night. The pastors helped us to interpret our dreams with their prophetic insights. All who slept in the 'church house' overnight were encouraged to participate without fear of ridicule because a dream or hunch seemed wacky. I harbored ambitions of migrating for greener pastures someday but I did not have a set time frame. I put my plans in the hands of the Lord and waited for as it is said "God's time is the best time." Meanwhile about a year or two before I set out of my country I had a dream that foretold of the difficulties I shall face when I went to a foreign country. The dream was interpreted by Sofo Atta at one of our morning discussions and the dream manifested into reality about two years later. When I landed in New York my diet consisted mostly of fish and vegetables. But within a few months of arrival I began eating poultry as a result of financial difficulties. My host, who was a temp employee, did not have the financial resources to provide meals with fish for me and poultry for herself. I had no choice but to eat the same food as my host since I had no job.

Jesus And His People

When I was down on my luck and long before I went to Australia I had a dream that I have never forgot though it faded in and out of my consciousness until the day the dream manifested before me. This was a dream in which I met Jesus Christ but he did not look like any of the representations or paintings that adorn every church or Christian home until I came to Brooklyn and saw Orthodox Jews. Until I came to Brooklyn I had not met or seen any Jew on the streets of Accra or over the high fence of Israeli embassy who was not dressed like me. In my ignorance I thought that Jews lived in heaven or in the pages of the bible and the stories about Jews of the modern era are different from the Jews of the bible. Every Catholic school student of my era knew the hymn *Jerusalem My Happy Home*. As a school boy I never thought that Jerusalem was a city or town on earth, I thought that Jerusalem was a home or city in the high heavens. Imagine my surprise and excitement when during my first week in Brooklyn I took a stroll around Kensington neighborhood and came across a group of people on a Saturday morning who seemed to have walked out of my dream. They were dressed like the people I saw in my dream long ago walking up and down the street. The man who introduced himself to me as Jesus Christ was dressed like one of the men I saw that Saturday morning in Brooklyn.

In this particular dream I was walking along a street with other people going up and down. The houses in the city had flat roofs similar to the mud roofs of my home village in north-west Ghana. The people in my dream wore similar type clothing, smocks or capes with twines or ropes hanging underneath the smocks and capes. I passed by a lightly bearded man along the street and he turned around, stopped me and looked me in the eye and asked 'do you know me?' I looked him in the eye and shook my head. He appeared surprised that I did not know him, so he asked me again "do you know me?" and again I looked him over, up and down, furrowed my brows as if trying to recollect whether I had ever met him somewhere and again shook my head, no. The stranger asked me the same question the third time 'do you know me?' and for the third time I answered no! After that he then introduced himself saying "I am Jesus Christ whether you know me or not I am going and I'll be back". I shrugged my shoulders like who cares and woke up. The dream has haunted me ever since that night; and I have never forgotten the environment or scene I saw in the dream that night.

I cannot find the right words to express the feeling of surprise and excitement at the sight of men dressed as if my dream had come alive; it was as if I was dreaming the same dream again. In time, I got to know that the men I saw that morning were Orthodox Jews. I lived in the Jewish world for over ten years until I moved from Brooklyn. I had an inner joy that I could not explain and was drawn to Jews and Jewish institutions during most of my first decade in America. Whether it was sheer coincidence or divine plan I do not know but my fortunes were tied to Jews. My first landlord in a roomy house was Jewish; I bought my first car, a Pontiac station wagon from a Jew of Crown Heights and he took care of me when I had a problem with the car. Professionally the appraiser who gave me the first appraisal assignment was Jewish. The doctors and specialists for me, my wife and child were all Jewish. Our pediatrician was located in Borough Park; I used to be the only one of my kind whenever we visited him. I contemplated worshipping in a Jewish temple but I did not know how to go about it. I did not know whether I had to conform to a dress code similar to them. I was interested in everything Jewish but was limited by language and income. If I had the means I would have studied Hebrew so that I could read the bible or torah and other Jewish literature in Hebrew. I hope I may have the opportunity to walk the streets of Jerusalem someday before I die.

DEATH OF THREE HOLY NAMES CHURCH

I was the glue that held the Three Holy Names Church and the pastors together and kept their propensity for greed and avarice in check because I did not demand anything from them. But once I left the country it became free for all, the pastors bickered openly over money and the semblance of camaraderie and unity that existed between them quickly evaporated. Churches are human-institutions as such they are run out of the glare like any other for profit business despite the high sounding and selfless rhetoric. But behind the high sounding and selfless rhetoric lurks greed and avarice typical of most human institutions. At the heart of most new age churches is the mad rush for riches in the name of God. Not all pastors and founders of new churches can be painted with the same broad brush; there are countless number of them who toil selflessly for members of their churches. I had no financial interest in the Three Holy Names Church other than spreading the efficacy of fasting and prayers for the solution of personal and spiritual problems the way I learned it from Ebenezer when I was down on my luck. The Three Holy Names Church was not any different from any competing business partners particularly after I left the scene. The church that was started in my apartment was subjected to the greed and avarice of the competing partners-the pastors.

I noticed shortly after Sofo Atta started spiritual consulting in my house that he had the propensity to be greedy and avaricious. He came to live with me at the time when I was still struggling to recover from the spate of bad luck that for sometime made me penniless. We placed a donation plate in front of the bedroom where he did his consulting for donations from his clients or visitors. By the time I left home for work in the mornings the plate would be full with currency notes of every denomination. I used to take some money out of the plate with the full consent of Sofo Atta to help meet my household expenses including taking care of him. Then suddenly I noticed that only dirty and small denominated currency notes and coins were left in the plate by the time I was ready to leave for the office. I became suspicious, thinking that perhaps some of our visitors were stealing or pilfering from the plate. I decided to keep an eye on the plate for the culprit.

I noticed a short time later that it was none other than Sofo Atta who surreptitiously removed any large value currency note from the donation plate as soon as it was put into it. I confronted him for literally stealing from himself; the money was his to do as he pleased with it instead of giving me the wrong impression that the money was being pilfered or stolen by some of our visitors. He apologized and I let bygones be bygones but I stopped taking an active interest in the donations from his prophetic works. After the apology he never gave me cause to doubt his sincerity until the day I left Ghana. The events after my departure was an indication that the propensity for greed was hidden from view while I was present but was unleashed as soon as I left.

That episode was the precursor of what doomed The Three Holy Names Church only a few months after I left Ghana.

The church had an account at the Agricultural Development Bank with Sofo Atta and me as the signatories. I expected that after my departure my family and the church would be evicted from the house provided by my employer. The church had enough funds in the bank account to rent a comparable house for the church family including the pastors and my family. But the account was the first bone of contention between the two pastors; Appiah and Atta. They could not agree between themselves about the control and division of collections and donations. This was the eventual death knell of the Three Holy Names Church. I left my family in the care of my church family just as I had taken care of them while I was present with them. The two pastors openly squabbled over money long before they were notified to surrender the house. The elders and most of the original members found the financial squabbles distasteful and began going their separate ways from them. As a result of their financial squabbles they eventually split up and killed the Three Holy Names Church. The day they surrendered the keys to the house was the day the Three Holy Names church died, each pastor went his own way to start a new church where he could retain every penny for himself.

Each pastor went his own way and formed a separate church independent of the other. Sofo Atta and I founded the Three Holy Names Church and as a founder he should perhaps have retained the same name after he parted company with Appiah. But both he and Appiah chose different names for their respective churches. Sofo Atta called his new church Center for Christ Meetings, Inc. It is understood that he adopted a different name ostensibly to preclude me from ever making any demands on him for a share of the profits or spoils of the church. I do not know the name Appiah adopted for his church. I never saw him again after I left Ghana up to the day he passed away in 2009 at a relatively young age.

I have no idea how the money in the bank was divvied up between the pastors but I know that my family got nothing when they parted company. My family was left in the lurch though to be fair to pastors each of them took one of my children with him to his new destination for a brief period. The children were all returned to their mother after less than six months. Whether by coincidence or plan the children were returned to their mother about the same time. Once the children were returned the break between my family and the pastors was complete. They have not seen one another or had any contact with any of them for all these years. I was apprised by my family and close associates in the church of the financial squabbles that eventually doomed the church but I did not take to heart the hearsays. But the rumors and hearsay were virtually confirmed when I met Sofo Atta and was treated like a total stranger. I did not take to heart the hearsay stories because I had no financial interest in the church, my interest was spiritual, I was content with the prayer culture in my house. We prayed virtually around the clock. I broke up with the pastor who made some sacrifices for me out of deference for my wife's distant relative but I had no material goals in mind when I opened my doors to the pastors, their families and the larger church family.

Although I had no financial interest in the church yet I felt betrayed by the reasons or causes that led to the demise of the church. When Sofo Atta came to me at the office the first day he had no more than the clothes on his back. I therefore did not expect him to stay longer than one week since he did not even have a change of underwear. I did not only feed him I also clothed him for more than three years. We shared my bedroom which also served as his consulting room and in course of time he practically became a member of my family and household. I returned to Ghana after more than twenty years and paid a courtesy call on him at his church and home. On the day I left for the USA the Three Holy Names Church was conducted in a classroom and my house served virtually as the church house. His new church and home were located on the same lot; I was thus disappointed when he did not receive me in his house but in the church like a casual visitor who dropped in from the street to see him. I lived with him under my roof for over five years and I expected nothing more than a glass of water in his living room so that we could exchange pleasantries and reminiscence over the past. My reception all but confirmed the rumors and greediness that led to the demise of the Three Holy Names church. He was like a big brother when we were together even when I had reason to kick him out of my house. We did not part in acrimony, but his avarice and greed overshadowed the cordial relations we had before I left the country. A cup of water in the privacy of his home would not have cost him a penny and it was the least he could have done to establish goodwill between us.

THE MOTH AND THE FLAME

I gave Satan an opening into my life by my sins and transgressions against God and Satan took advantage and turned my life upside down. After my life turned around I resolved to keep the devil and Satan out of my life by changing my way of life. My greatest sin or weakness was extra marital affairs thus sinning against the sin of adultery; "Thou shall not commit adultery". Generally I do not engage in extra marital affairs when I live with my family under the same roof or in the same place. I play what in sports parlance is called away games, I had extra marital affairs only when I lived apart from my family over extended periods of time. I therefore assumed that living with my family was my best assurance against extra marital affairs, the temptations to do so would be minimized. Thus as soon as my employer obtained an apartment for me I brought my family down to Accra from Kumasi. I tried to be as good a father and husband as I could be. My life had a lift when I began praying with my family.

As time went on my family group prayer grew to attract outsiders and eventually the prayer group became a church. I could not have a better insurance against keeping devil or Satan out of my life than having a church in my house. I never took account of the cunning and resourcefulness of Satan; he planted a possum of a beautiful woman in the middle of our fledgling prayer group who worshipped with us until the time was ripe when she woke and struck like a possum. The woman came into our house just as my family group prayers began attracting outside participants. Satan wormed its way into my house in the form of an attractive young woman who came seeking a place of worship. She lay low and was with my family as we progressed from a small family praying together until the group became a church.

The seeds of my temptation started innocuously with an unexpected visit from two sisters about the time outsiders began trickling into my apartment to participate in our morning prayers. At this time only members of the Healing Church of Salvation were aware of Sofo Atta and used to drop in on our morning prayers. One morning two young women, walked into my apartment during our morning prayers. The young women, Mary and *Ojaah*, lived more than three miles from my home; I do not know how they heard about our nascent prayer group because Davi had not yet come into our group, we were still basically a small family prayer group with a few participants from the church where we worshipped on Sundays. The two young women were the first outsiders with no connection with our church that came to pray or worship with us. As soon as I set eyes on the sisters I felt that the taller of the two sisters, Mary was my temptress that would lead me up the garden path into extra marital affairs. I determined to keep her at arms length as much as possible.

Mary was the older of the two sisters, the younger sister stopped coming after two weeks but Mary continued coming week-in-week-out. The prayer group became a church with her participation. She was around when Davi became part of the prayer group and the prayer group grew to become a church. For more than two years Mary came to the prayer group at least once or twice a week. She hung around with us until the no name prayer group became The Three Holy Names Church. Mary was therefore one of the founding members of the new church and as such an automatic church elder. She became almost like a member of my household, she spent long hours in the house and slept overnight from time to time. After more than two years during which she did not make any attempt to ask me for any favor I let down my guard and concluded that my first impression about her must have been wrong. But it was not long after I let down my guard that Mary began asking me for small favors such as rides when I was leaving for the office. I had let down my guard and did not suspect that she had any eye for me. After rendering her small favors and an occasional ride she started calling on me at the office sometimes just around closing time. Calling on me at the office was the trap that finally caught me like a deer in the glare of headlights. I found myself succumbing to her flirtations and within a short time began an affair with her in my office usually after hours. I fell into Satan's trap and I did not know how to get out of it, I wonder whether I was willing to get out of the trap.

I rued the day she entered my home but I was helpless once the affair started. Reason deserted me and any resolution crumbled as soon as I saw her. We had the perfect set up for deception and subterfuge; Mary had been coming in and out of my house for more than two years before she asked me for an innocent favor. When she asked me for the first favor it did not occur to me that what I had feared for more than two years was finally beginning to take shape. I did not know that I was treading slippery slope when I acceded to her first request for favor. The fact was that I formed an impression about her before I knew anything about her and after more than two years of seeing her almost every week I concluded that she was not who I thought she was. Thus when the affair started nobody in my household suspected any hanky-panky affair between Mary and me. She was virtually a fixture in my house and had woven herself into the fabric of my family and came and went as she pleased without arousing any suspicions. When the affair broke into the open it was difficult for those who knew me to believe that I could stoop that low particularly among the women. When women slept overnight in the 'church house' they slept in my quarter of the house they therefore could not comprehend that I could have an affair if I never took advantage of any of the women who slept in my house. For these women they could not believe that I was having an affair with a church elder until the affair finally burst into the open after Mary was betrayed by some of her friends to my wife.

My wife was heartbroken when she learned of my extra marital affair and I promised to end the affair but like a beast of burden I did not have the willpower to breakup with her. She became estranged from my house but not from the church or my office where we had our trysts. I felt very guilty and wanted to end the relations but reason deserted me whenever I set eyes on her, I became like an animal on heat. I was impervious to reason though I knew I was hurting my family and the church. My wife should have kicked me or the church, which she blamed for facilitating the affair, out of the house. I would have been relieved if my pastors had attempted to impose some discipline on me. But they were impotent because the church and her pastors were housed under my roof. I would have welcomed such a discipline as it would have given me a peg to hang my hat on and perhaps ended the affair. I was a bad example and role model but instead of being treated with the contempt that I deserved some of the misguided young men treated me like some folk hero and impugned bad motives against those who condemned or criticized me in private. About the only thing that I still had going for me was constant fasting and prayers for the forgiveness of my sins. So while I fasted and prayed for forgiveness I carried on the extra marital affair sometimes while I was fasting.

I was driving myself to oblivion both physically and spiritually through sex. My intimacy with her became worse than a dog on heat during mating season when Mary moved to *Ablempke* and lived only a few blocks from my house. From the time I began having intimacy with her I fasted routinely for about three days and three to five days a week when I became embroiled in litigation. I could be on the fifth day of a fast but as soon as I set eyes on her I lost my senses and my animal instincts took over. Satan found the ultimate weapon to destroy me physically and spiritually, the effects of my fasting and prayers were fritted away with adulterous sex. *Matt 10:28 And do not fear those who kill the body but cannot kill the soul. But rather fear Him who is able to destroy both soul and body in hell.* She was the proxy that tempted me with sex that could have destroyed my body and my soul. For instance one day while engaged in intimacy with her I had a brief heart attack. For a brief second my whole body went limp but I could not tear myself away from the intimacy after the scary moment passed. Had I died I would have died while having illicit sex and I guess I would have lost my body and soul, I would have died while actively committing sin. I did not know where the energy for the sex orgies came from when I had not eaten or drank for three or more days at a time. Could it be that fasting by itself bestowed energy? I was slowly committing suicide by sex. God eventually saved me from myself when He made it possible for me to migrate from my country. Getting out of my country at the time I did was the only factor that finally prevented and saved me from suicide by sex with Mary. She was leading me to oblivion but I was too blind to see it and not even a brief heart attack was enough to wake me from the hypnotic influence and let me see the errors of my ways. I was like a moth attracted to a flame that could kill me.

God's intervention in my life through the granting of an unexpected visa was my salvation. God removed all the impediments in my way and spirited me out of Ghana perhaps just in the nick of time. The next heart attack would probably have been fatal since I never learned from the first warning about adverse effects of incessant sexual orgies on me. I was so mentally ashamed of myself that my departure from the country could not have come soon enough.

The Divine Father intervened in my life when He asked me out of the blue to apply for a travel visa to the USA one morning at work. I went to the consular office to educate and familiarize myself with the visa application process but came away at the end of the day with an approved visitor's visa. My travel plans could have been derailed by lack of funds. I lent funds, I had set aside to buy a ticket in case of any unexpected travel opportunity, to Mary for trading between Ghana and Nigeria. She planned to buy scarce goods from Nigeria for sale in Ghana. Her very first trip tied up my funds, the items she brought from Nigeria did not sell as she expected. I did not have any extra money to procure a plane ticket. I overcame the setback by selling my Peugeot 504 car to pay for the plane fare. I obtained enough funds from the sale to cover the fare and a little extra left over funds to cover about three months of household expenses by my family. I asked and was given three months leave of absence with pay by my employer. Thus I provided for my family for approximately six months on the day I left Ghana. But it appeared that I had unrealistic expectations about my prospects in the new country; I thought that by the time my family ran out of money I would be in good financial position to help them. It took much longer than six months before I was able to be of any help for my family.

Sold Mercedes Benz For A House

I came close to losing my car when the motor broke down. I could not have replaced the broken engine if Daimler Benz had left me in the lurch. The mishap brought me to my senses; I thought about the absurdity of driving around in a car that was as valuable as a house when I had no place to call a home of my own. Homeownership then entered my psyche and became part of my thinking after the car was repaired. I waited for the right opportunity to sell it and use the proceeds to buy a house whether I had another car or not. I was flirting with the idea of migrating for greener pastures to a western country. But I could not leave until I had a place to settle my family. The opportunity to sell the car presented itself unexpectedly and I jumped at it. A retired high court judge, Justice Lassey offered his rental house for sale through a friend. The friend helped me to sell the car to one of his high value clients and I used the proceeds to pay for the house. Thus I sold my Mercedes 200D and bought a house and a used Peugeot 504 car, I killed two birds with one stone. After the conclusion of the transactions I waited to obtain possession of the house to settle my family and clear the path for me to travel.

The easy part of the transaction was paying for the house. Obtaining possession of the house would not come easy. In the process to obtain possession I became embroiled in a cantankerous and protracted landlord tenant litigation for more than one year.

Nothing in my life ever came easy or smoothly without unexpected twists and turns. I completed and duly signed and registered the deed at the lands department. When we were done with the signage the Justice informed me that his tenants were a difficult bunch and that I should give him time to evict them so that he could give me vacant possession of the house. In effect I had legal possession but the Justice still retained physical possession pending the eviction of the tenants. He was in the eviction process when he died suddenly from heart attack. The Justice lived at the Airport Residential area and I used to visit him about once a fortnight or month for progress reports on the eviction. Then one weekend I went to his house in the afternoon and saw people with long and somber faces; Justice Lassey was dead. His untimely death threatened to derail my travel plans; the death thwarted or made it impossible to have an easy and quick resolution of the tenancy problem. I had no alternative than to start the eviction process from the scratch. The tenants initially were quite cooperative with me but asked me to allow them to continue with occupation. That would have negated my whole purpose of buying the house so I rejected their demand and with the rejection they stopped cooperating with me and went further to deny my legal ownership of the house. They found upon investigation from the family of the late Justice that my title to the property was unimpeachable. They turned around and colluded with a next door extended family member of the late Justice who shared a common boundary with the house. They colluded with that relative to assert an interest in the property under Ghana customary land law in order to frustrate my ownership and delay eviction for as long as the case was in the courts system. And land cases in Ghana courts were notorious for the length of time it took to decide or settle even the simplest cases.

I served written notice of eviction on the tenants as required by law and followed up the notice with legal action in the courts. The relative joined the tenants to assert that I had an invalid title on account of customary law and procedure. It was asserted that the property was family property, and therefore under customary land law the late Justice could not alienate the property without the consent and concurrence of principal members of the family.

Ghana has a confusing land tenure system, and though I had a duly executed deed, it did not matter, the customary law challenged the legitimacy of the deed. The tenants pooled their rents together to fund the litigation. Thus began twelve months to twenty-four months of frustrating litigation. The litigation became my obsession and a battle of wills between the tenants and me. I was outnumbered by eight to one and outspent by them. I depended on my regular income to fund the litigation; while they pooled their rents together for the litigation. In practical terms, I was funding their litigation against me. They had the services of a crafty old lawyer whose sole aim was to delay the case from ever coming to trial. On this they succeeded in frustrating me time and time again, the case was postponed time after time without a hearing on procedural grounds. I was beginning to lose confidence and patience with my counsel; I blamed him for not trying hard enough and allowing himself to be steam rolled by the other counsel. Without a hearing, there could not be a verdict either way. There is strength in numbers, and the tenants appeared to be one step ahead of me when it came to buying influence.

The lawyers had an indirect financial interest in an indefinite litigation; the longer the case went on, the more fees they made at my expense. The landlord-tenant litigation was only one of the many problems I faced at the time. The battle between us was both

381

metaphysical and physical. I was pitted against the collective will of eight families. The house contained eight single occupancy rooms in two one-story buildings on the same lot. I knew deep down that the struggle for the house had both physical and spiritual dimension and no amount of education or literature could convince me otherwise. I have experienced both the good and the ugly side of the metaphysical world. I believed that evil and satanic forces were arrayed against me and that turned a simple landlord tenant case into complex land tenure litigation. *Ephesians 6:12 states thus: "For we do not wrestle against flesh and blood, but against principalities, against powers, against the rulers of the darkness of this age, against spiritual hosts of wickedness in the heavenly places."* I was informed as much from dreams and prophesies at church that they were consulting oracles and mystics together with other powers of darkness just as I fasted and prayed for a just and expedited end or solution to the contentious litigation.

I did not know what I could do to expedite or have a just solution than fasting and prayers. And over a six month period I fasted about three to five days a week. It was during this period that I faced my greatest challenges and temptations. I could not resist my animal instincts whenever Mary stepped into my office while I was observing a fast. I fasted and prayed for forgiveness yet continued to indulge in the same sinful ways. But despite the temptations I never broke any fast prematurely. I guess it was the fasting and prayers that probably saved me from a fatal heart attack. During the fourth month of fasting and prayers, I began getting positive and encouraging messages from the seers and prophets at church. The messages were that the leader of the tenants would die and his death would scare his cotenants to flee from the house. I did not believe the messages; I was under the impression that the seers or prophets knew my problem and were merely consoling me with optimistic and positive messages.

I continued with my fasting and prayer routine while I waited anxiously for the next scheduled hearing date. At the next hearing, the physical appearance of the lead tenant shocked me. My heart melted when I saw his emaciated and gaunt appearance. His physical condition was as shocking as the condition in which I saw Davi. He was almost a walking skeleton who could hardly walk on his own. He had a walking stick but he could not walk without the support of his cotenants. They supported him on both sides and dragged him slowly up the steps of the courthouse. His condition persuaded me that there was a kernel of truth in the prophetic messages about his death. Right at the court house I decided that I could not have his death on my conscience. I had been warned repeatedly about his death and while I could not say that my fasting and prayers was responsible for his sickly physical condition I had been fasting and praying for six months for a solution. But in my mind death was not a part of the solution I sought from God. I did not think a piece of earth was worth the loss of life. We were legal antagonists but I did not consider any of them a mortal enemy to wish him harm let alone death. Death is too final to ever wish on my worst enemy.

I could not metaphysically accept his blood on my head no matter how much I desired the property for my family. I hurried home from the courthouse and as soon as I reached home, I broke my fast and began praying actively for him. I continued praying for him until our next court date when I found that his condition was on the mend. I breathed easier and stopped praying actively for him. During my prayers I told God that he could resolve the litigation without taking the life of another person. I said "Surely the almighty, omnipresent, and omniscient God can end this lawsuit without loss of life. Nothing is impossible before God".

I could not claim any credit or responsibility for the recovery of my adversary; but I freed my conscience from any guilt by ending and praying for his recovery. After the turnaround in his condition I was then inspired to try a different tack that I had never considered. I wrote a petition to the chief justice and the attorney general complaining about the abuse of court procedures to frustrate or prevent the case from ever coming before a judge for hearing. I accused the counsel of the tenants for obstruction of justice. That a member of the bar whose judicial oath required him to help in the administration of justice had chosen obstruction and subterfuge as his modus operandi to sabotage and thwart the cause of justice. The strategy of the counsel was sabotage the case from ever being heard by whatever means possible. This member, I contended, was flouting and sabotaging his judicial oath by sabotaging fair hearing before a member of the bench.

I presumed that the petition must have had the intended effect. The counsel of the tenants, the subject of my petition, casted hostile glances at me the next time we met in the court. And for whatever reason he did not use or was not allowed to continue sabotaging the hearing, I had my day finally in the court. That was all I ever asked for, the opportunity to tell my side of the story in an open court of law and let the chips fall where they may. If the court found in favor of the tenants and the conniving relative so be it, heart wrenching as that might have been. But I could not be left in limbo twisting in the wind without a decision one way or the other. I had the opportunity to present my case with supporting documentation before the court, after that I was done. The onus fell on the tenants and their colluding and conniving partner to prove that the house was indeed family property. The case at the end was decided in my favor and the tenants were given notice by the court to vacate the premises by a date certain. After that date the remaining tenants who had not yet found alternative accommodation were forcibly evicted by court bailiffs and police from the nearby police station. The house has been my family's home ever since we gained possession.

SEARCH FOR BETTER OPPORTUNITIES

I think that there was a hand of destiny in the direction of my eventual travel destination. Although I flirted with the idea of migration no firm destination was on my mind not even a wish list of countries and destinations. But as my court case wound down I turned my attention to the purpose of buying the house, migrate for a better tomorrow. And for the first time I began thinking of travel destinations. I was moved more by fear to migrate than reality. My monthly pay was barely enough to buy gas or petrol for my car for a month. I survived more on income from side jobs than on my regular monthly pay. While I was not starving I wondered the consequences if these jobs dried up. I experienced that condition when my family came from Kumasi and we put together our home based sewing enterprise. I could not adequately survive and take care of my responsibilities without the benefits of the appraisal jobs I did on the side to supplement my income. I was not confident that I could survive in private practice without my income from public service because I did not have any influential friends or family members in the corridors of power who could help me win jobs and assignments that would have made any practice worthwhile. The eighties was also a time of great turmoil in the country, many of the brightest minds migrated to wherever they could find better opportunities for survival than prevailed in Ghana. The most popular destination then was Nigeria. But I had a foreboding that Nigeria would do to Ghanaians what Ghana did to Nigerians in the late sixties, it was only a matter of time. In 1968-69 Ghana deported en-mass all so called aliens in the country without valid residence permits or visas. The people most affected by the mass deportations were Nigerians. Less than twenty years later the tables were turned and Ghanaians flocked to Nigeria without visas or resident permits. It is said that what is good for the goose is good for the gander. Nigerians eventually implemented their own version of Aliens Compliance Order and those most affected were Ghanaians.

The mass deportations were carried out by the government of the second republic under Prime Minister Dr. K.A Busia. The government faced continuing economic decline and high unemployment in the country. They took the myopic view that if they deported the Nigerians who dominated the small scale retailing business then those businesses would be taken over by Ghanaians. The Aliens Compliance Order was therefore an economic and not a security tool. The law did not make any exception for children born in Ghana by Nigerians and who knew no other country but Ghana. When I decided to make my move I narrowed my preferences to Australia and Canada because they are English speaking countries.

By the 1980's Ghana's lofty place in international affairs had plummeted and she had become so irrelevant that Australia relocated her diplomatic mission in Accra to Nigeria. That effectively removed Australia from my list of desirable destinations. I could not afford the cost of an expensive trip to Nigeria for an Australian visa with an uncertain outcome. I therefore settled on the one country left on my list, Canada whose diplomatic mission was still open in spite of Ghana's diminished role in international affairs. I wrote to a nephew, Francis a citizen of Canada, to provide me with a letter of invitation for Canada. I was still waiting for the invitation when a fluke application to the US consulate earned me a traveler's visa for the country.

My application for a traveler's visa to USA was by accident or happenstance and not due to any prior plan or decision. One early morning as soon as I got to the office a subordinate colleague asked me for a reference letter for an application for traveler's visa to the USA. I wrote and signed the reference letter for the colleague without more. And a few minutes later I had a strong urge to apply for a US visa myself. Accordingly I asked the personnel manager of the corporation to provide me a similar letter of reference since I could not write one for myself. Things happened so quickly that by ten o'clock that morning I was in a queue at the consular offices at Osu, Accra. That was the first time that USA as a destination crossed my mind largely because a colleague asked me for a reference letter. I was much too cowardly and timid during the period I flirted with leaving my country to have considered USA as a point of destination.

A long line was already forming by the time I arrived at the consular offices and I took my place in the line and waited. At about ten-thirty or thereabout, a consular official came down and ushered the first thirty or more people in the line into the office. I was one of the lucky ones in line that morning who was invited into the consular offices; those who did not make the cut were asked to try again the next day. By the time I emerged from the office about an hour or so later I was approved for a six month visitor's visa. I was delighted and surprised at the ease with which I obtained the visa. USA visa was said to be one of the most difficult to obtain. Most of my fellow applicants were probably better prepared for the application than me; I had no idea of the requirements for a visa. I did not know that a fee and a passport picture were required for a visa. I was thus unprepared when my application was approved; I neither had the required $30 fee nor the passport photo. I had limited resources so my first impulse was to go home to rummage through my things for any old photo and luckily I found an extra copy of an old passport photo that I used for my driver's license. And for the $30 fee I went to the downtown area to buy dollars on the black market.

I picked up my passport with the visa stamp a few days later. The irony about the visa was that the colleague whose request for a reference letter prompted me to apply for the visa had not yet applied for one by the time I left the country. I was overwhelmed at the sudden turn of events; I was not yet quite prepared to make the final move. My court case was winding down towards final decision but not yet made. Thus my family did not have a permanent place to call home but I had taken the steps that would guarantee them a home of their own in the near future. I did not know how lucky or miraculous my visa was until I heard horror stories of people who had sought visa for more than three years and were not any closer to getting one. I was the toast of my friends and acquaintances when rumor spread that I had a visa for USA. I had some concerns for my family but in the end I concluded that the best time to make my move was when I had the opportunity, there might never be a perfect opportunity and time than now. I was afraid and ambivalent about the country I was going to make my new home.

I had no illusions that things would get worse before they got better at my new destination, but the difficulties came sooner than I ever anticipated. I was warned of the difficulties that lay ahead of me in a dream long before I was prompted to seek a travel visa for US. At the time of the dream US was not on my radar screen as a travel destination. And I never associated the dream with life in the USA until the day the dream was fulfilled about three months after my arrival. I dreamt that I was slogging through darkness, fog and slush until about daybreak. When the sun came up I was famished so I bought fried chicken from a fast food restaurant. At the time I had the dream I was a semi vegetarian and was not familiar with KFC or the like. The interpretation of the dream by Sofo Atta was largely accurate. I ate chicken less than three months after my arrival due to financial difficulties. My first chicken meal was provided by my host though I ate KFC fried chicken later. One of my favorite aphorisms in Ghana was that "circumstances alter cases as noses alter faces"; my financial condition forced me to alter my diet to include poultry. As a new arrival in USA I was surprised at the high cost of fresh unprocessed food items versus processed foods. That was the exact opposite of where I came from. The poor in the Ghana I left behind hankered for processed foods while the rich treated processed foods as status symbols or civilized life. A can of corned beef for instance was more expensive than a pound of beef and a can of say tuna was more expensive than a pound of fresh or smoked fish. The vast majority of us was content to subsist on fresh products and once in a while treated ourselves to canned fish or corned beef. It was a feast in my family whenever my mother prepared rice with canned fish sauce for us. Generally I ate cheap in Ghana subsisting on fresh products but eating cheap in America meant substituting fresh unprocessed food items with processed ones.

I expected that when I landed in the USA I would have been able to weave myself into the fabric of the American society as a black man by pretending to be a black American, but I soon found my accent generally was stronger than color barriers. In some communities my accent was welcome and considered none threatening while in others my accent was threatening to their very livelihood as a competitor for scarce jobs. I landed in a Jewish and white community and my accent was not threatening but when I moved a few blocks away I was viewed skeptically as a competitor. My personal theory of the inconsistency was that my accent assured prejudiced whites that I was not who they thought I was and considered a competitor among my own for scarce low wage jobs. The two situations became consistent after I broke into the real estate appraisal profession and later a public servant with the city of New York. My accent was a reassuring voice when I knocked at any door whether black or white. This was one of the most violent periods in New York City and the face of every black man was suspect, it was the period when black men could be shot for hold innocuous objects by jittery policemen. The initial inconsistency might be illustrated by two events that occurred minutes apart. I was giddy with excitement when I came across orthodox Jews who seemed to have come alive from my dream but on the same day I came across the first black American on the streets of Kensington, smiled broadly at him and greeted him 'good morning brother'. He just turned around, glared at me in stony silence and walked away without a word. I learned later that Americans were not used to formal greetings like the way I greeted the first black American but he could have returned my smile if he felt awkward to answer formal greetings. That reaction was contrary to the friendly image I formed about black Americans I came across in Ghana. It appeared that the black Americans I met in Ghana and the black Americans I met on arrival were different breeds.

I got my first job about six months after I landed in Brooklyn as a night security guard at a small Brooklyn hospital along Kings Highway. My hourly wage was about a nickel above minimum wage. The wages were enough to meet my immediate needs of keeping body and soul together. Shortly after I got the job I parted company with Regina, who gave me board and lodge until I was in position to care for myself after I got the job. I obtained a room in a roomy house within the same neighborhood only about three to four blocks away.

The monthly rent for the closet size room cost me more than half my monthly wages. We were three tenants on the second floor apartment above a store front at 307 Ditmas Avenue. One was a retired gentleman and the other was a fellow countryman, Sam. Moving into the roomy house was the best thing that happened to me since I came to the USA. Sam, my countryman was a public servant with the city of New York and I benefited from his years of experience that shortened my learning curve about life and survival in New York. I learned how to navigate the job market including stint as car service operator for years until I found my way into the real estate profession and eventually as a public servant with the city of New York.

CAR SERVICE OPERATOR

The end of my life as a minimum wage security guard came after I managed to save about eight hundred dollars from my paltry wages and ventured into self employment. I bought a car for $600 and joined a stable of car service operators. The first car I bought in this country was a Pontiac Station Wagon with more than 137,000 miles on the odometer though it was less than four years old. I bought the car from a Lubavich Jew of Crown Heights section of Brooklyn. Most often when one bought a car from an individual he was on his own if he had any problem. But the man paid to fix the car when I had a problem within the first month of the purchase. I quit my job as a security guard after I bought the car and joined a car service company, *Your Car Service* with its base in the Bay Ridge section of Brooklyn. Car service operators who cruised and picked up street passengers were fodder for criminals in the eighties and nineties. I was afraid to become a statistic and chose to become part of an operation. I reckoned that operating the service as part of a group offered security more than cruising the streets and picking up passengers at random on my own in a city I barely knew. And for more than two years I was part of the stable of cars operating under the aegis of *Your Car Service*. The income from the car service financed my education first as a real estate sales person and later as a real estate appraiser and also enabled me to take care of my responsibilities back home in Ghana. I took the real estate sales person course in New York City and travelled to various college campuses in the south for the appraisal courses conducted by the American Institute of Real Estate Appraisers. I travelled around the south by Grey Hound buses and Amtrak trains to Athens, Oklahoma and Chapel Hill for the appraisal courses. Successful completion of the courses opened the path of the real estate appraisal profession to me. Until completion of the courses I could not attract the attention of any employer even when I offered my services free so as to get a peek into the profession. The imprimatur of the Appraisal Institute made all the difference.

I was a qualified and experienced real estate appraiser in my own right when I came to this country. One of my lecturers in Australia was a designated appraiser of the Appraisal Institute. I traced the lecturer, Bob Reichert and obtained a reference letter from him. But the testimonial was irrelevant until I actually passed the examinations.

I landed in America as an elder of the Three Holy Names Church. I continued with the fasting and prayer culture I cultivated from my association with the church in New York. And I guess the fasting and prayers strengthened me in the face of every adversity. I drew my strength and continued with regular practice of yoga with weekly fasting and prayers as I used to do in Ghana. Throughout all the challenges and problems that faced me as a new migrant my guide and strength was always in the Lord. I continued to be guided by the mental roadmap I discerned for walking with Lord during my life in Melbourne. I followed the voice of God or my guardian angel and as long as I followed Him all went well except when I thought I knew better. As long as I walked with the Lord he took care of all my problems and sustained me. The words of the hymnist: *"When we walk with the Lord, In the light of his word, What a glory he sheds on our way! While we do his good will He abides with us still and with all who will trust and obey."* I virtually lost my way after my feet were firmly planted on American soil. My spiritual life was derailed or sidetracked as my responsibilities increased and I was steeped in the pursuit of the American dream. Realizing the American dream had a cost, I lost my spiritual life. I went astray from the strict ascetic observation of fasting and prayers, concentration and meditation.

INDEX